Principles and Practice Informal Education

Informal educators work with individuals and groups in the community to promote their learning. They work in ordinary places, rather than formal classrooms, and use informal methods of teaching and learning such as conversation and shared activity. Focusing on ways of working with people, this book builds on the essentially human abilities to query, adapt, rethink, understand and problem-solve. The book argues that people learn from each other, in social exchanges which rarely involve a professional educator; so any community can be a setting for learning.

Principles and Practice of Informal Education provides a much-needed, and accessible, exploration of learning beyond the classroom. Written by practitioners across a wide range of professional fields, this book will be topical and valuable to those working in youth and community work, as well as those in health education, careers guidance and social work.

Linda Deer Richardson is a freelance educator for the Open University and YMCA George Williams College in London.

Mary Wolfe is a tutor in informal and community education at the YMCA George Williams College.

Principles and Practice of Informal Education

Learning through life

Edited by
Linda Deer Richardson
and Mary Wolfe

London and New York

First published 2001 by RoutledgeFalmer
11 New Fetter Lane, London EC4P 4EE

Simultaneously published in the USA and Canada
by RoutledgeFalmer
29 West 35th Street, New York, NY 10001

RoutledgeFalmer is an imprint of the Taylor & Francis Group

Typeset in Baskerville by Wearset, Boldon, Tyne and Wear
Printed and bound in Great Britain by University Press, Cambridge

British Library Cataloguing in Publication Data
A catalogue record for this book is available from the British Library

Library of Congress Cataloging in Publication Data

Principles and practice of informal education : learning through life/
edited by Linda Deer Richardson and Mary Wolfe.
    p. cm.
Includes bibliographical references and index.
    1. Non-formal education–Great Britain. 2. Community
education–Great Britain. 3. Experiential learning–Great Britain.
I. Richardson, Linda Deer, 1945– II. Wolfe, Mary, 1952–

LC45.8.G7 P75 2001
370'.941–dc21

                                              2001019457

ISBN 0-415-21689-3 (hbk)
ISBN 0-415-21690-7 (pbk)

Contents

vi   *Contents*

Notes on contributors

Sarah Banks lectures in Community and Youth Studies at the University of Durham. Her books include: *Ethics and Values in Social Work* (1995). She recently edited *Ethical Issues in Youth Work* (1999) London: Routledge.

Huw Blacker is a youth worker and researcher, based at Romford YMCA. He is a graduate of YMCA George Williams College and a part-time lecturer there.

Mary Crosby is the Principal of the YMCA George Williams College. She has a background in youth and community work practice, tutoring, counselling and management within the voluntary sector. She has a particular interest in supervision.

Michele Erina Doyle has worked as a youth and community educator (supported by the Rank Charities). She is currently editing a history of a Christian Settlement in Bermondsey and co-writing a book on Christian youth work. She can be contacted at the informal education homepage – infed@globalnet.co.uk

Alan France is a Research Fellow in the Department of Law at Sheffield University. He is presently evaluating the Joseph Rowntree Trust Communities That Care Initiative. Prior to this, he was the principal researcher on the national evaluation of the DfEE GEST funded Youth Action Initiative. His publications include: *The Youth Action Scheme and the Future of Youth Work* (1997); *Dangerous Futures: Social Exclusion in Late Modernity and a Role for Youth Work* (1997); *The National Evaluation of Youth Action Projects* (1996) (all joint authored with Wiles, P.). He also writes on youth issues and has published a number of articles on youth and citizenship. These include: 'Youth and Citizenship in the 1990s' (1996) and ' "Why should we care?" Youth, citizenship and questions of social responsibility' (1998).

Alison Gilchrist has worked for many years as a community worker, mainly in inner-city neighbourhoods, and is an active member of the Standing Conference for Community Development. Having taught on the Community and Youth Work course at the University of the West of England, Bristol, she now works for the Community Development Foundation as their Regional Links Manager. Her research interests include the use of informal networking for community empowerment.

Tony Jeffs is a member of the Community and Youth Work Studies Unit, Department of Sociology and Social Policy, University of Durham. He is a joint editor of the journal *Youth and Policy*.

John Mahoney is a youth worker based in North London and a graduate of the YMCA George Williams College.

Ted Milburn is Professor of Community Education and Director of the Centre for Youth Work Studies, University of Strathclyde, Glasgow. Formerly a youth worker, adult educator, training officer and assistant director of education, he is currently researching street youth work in South Lanarkshire and youth worker ideologies.

Malcolm Payne is senior lecturer in youth and community development at De Montfort University, Leicester and Director of the University's Youth Affairs Unit.

Pauline Riley is Senior Worker, Cheshire and Wirral Federation of Youth Clubs.

Alan Smith worked mostly with young offenders before being appointed as Senior Lecturer in Youth and Community Work at Havering College of Further and Higher Education, London, in 1994. Since then he has completed his MEd in the Practice of Community Education, based on research into the creation of a National Training Organisation for the sector.

Alan is currently Secretary of the Community and Youth Work Training Agencies Group (TAG), the professional association for youth and community work lecturers in the UK and Ireland. In this role he has served on several Government advisory bodies on training and occupational standards. He is a member of the DfEE Youth Service/Connexions Transition Working Group.

Mark K. Smith is the Rank Research Fellow and Tutor at the YMCA George Williams College, London. Among his other publications are *Developing Youth Work* (1988), *Local Education* (1994) and *Informal Education* (1999) (with Tony Jeffs).

Jean Spence works at the Community and Youth Work Studies Unit of Durham University. She is an editor of the journal *Youth and Policy* and has particular interests in gender and in the history of community and youth work.

Graeme Tiffany has a background in youth, community and adult education. He has worked in environmental and adventure education, detached and centre-based youth projects, regeneration schemes and initiatives to deliver community action training. Graeme is currently working as a freelance consultant in several areas including disaffection from school and voluntary sector development.

Alison Tomlin is a researcher in the Leverhulme Numeracy Research Programme at King's College, University of London. This chapter is based on research undertaken as a PhD student at King's College London, with a student grant from the Economic and Social Research Council.

Annmarie Turnbull is Director of Policy Development for the National Centre for Volunteering. Prior to this, she was senior tutor in community work at Turning Point, a voluntary organisation based at Goldsmiths College, University of London, that trains youth and community workers and provides training and consultancy to statutory and non-statutory agencies working with local communities.

Mary Tyler is Principal Lecturer and Division Leader of the Youth and Community Division at De Montfort University, Leicester. She has worked in many roles with young people and in the community including adventure playground worker, social worker, group worker and youth and community worker. While employed by Cambridgeshire Community Education she worked in schools and became involved in managing and training part-time youth and community workers. She worked for the National Youth Bureau (now National Youth Agency), and the Open University before taking up her present post, which involves teaching youth and community work students at undergraduate and postgraduate level, and undertaking research and consultancy with the Youth Affairs Unit.

Mary Wolfe is a full-time tutor on the Informal and Community Education Programme at YMCA George Williams College, London. She is Bulletin Co-ordinator for RaPAL: Research and Practice in Adult Literacy.

Janet Woods is a tutor for Supervision on the Informal and Community Education Programme at the YMCA George Williams College, London.

Acknowledgements

The editors are grateful to these publishers for permission to reproduce the following figures:

Tony Old for permission to reproduce the photo of a young climber, from page 9 of Burke, T., Hand, J. and McFall, L. (1999) *Moving on up: how youth work raises achievement and promotes social inclusion*, in Chapter 13, 'Activities';

Open University Press for permission to reproduce the diagram of the shift between formal and informal education from page 94, Ellis, J. 'Informal Education – a Christian Perspective' in Jeffs, T. and Smith, M. (eds) (1990) *Using Informal Education*, in Chapter 2, 'What is informal education?';

Introduction

Mary Wolfe and Linda Deer Richardson

Origins

All books have a history, a reason for being written. This book arises out of the YMCA George Williams College's distance learning BA in informal and community education, which incorporates a professional qualification in youth and community work. When revising the study materials for the early stages of the qualifying course, we decided to build them around a text outlining key elements of theory and practice at Level One (Certificate of Higher Education). The publication of this book means that we have the chance to share this work with a wider audience. As well as serving our own students, we hope that it will interest, and benefit, a wide range of colleagues in the field: new workers in voluntary and local authority schemes, their trainers and managers; students and lecturers on other qualifying programmes; professional practitioners at all levels of experience.

The book is an edited collection of chapters exploring the principles and practice of informal education in areas including youth work and community and adult education. Its authors argue for an approach which is relevant to a number of professional fields and which takes its identity from a way of working, rather than from a specific target group. We describe such work as essentially educational and as based upon working with people, rather than working for them or on them.

We emphasise this idea of working *with* learners because we want to highlight a specific quality of the learning relationship: mutuality, or give and take.

Learning relationships

Perhaps surprisingly, it seems to us that the relationship between a professional and a client is not often seen as mutual; rather it is assumed that the professional gives while the client takes. The teacher gives information, the student takes notes; the advice worker gives advice, the client takes it. But as informal educators, whether working with young children, adolescents or adults, we believe that the relationships which we foster need to be based upon the understanding that learners, as well as educators, bring experiences, motivation and abilities to the exchange. We work therefore with people's potential for learning – with what Paulo Freire calls 'the human orientation toward being more' (1996: 159).

Informal education is thus based on relationships in which both educators and learners recognise their own, and each other's, potential to 'be more' within their respective roles.

The authors of this book seek to better understand the learning brought to, and gained from, such interactions. We focus on ways of working with people which build upon the essentially human abilities to query, to adapt, to rethink, to understand or to be confused. We see these abilities as the basis for learning, whether formal or informal. Our interest happens to be the informal, an area of study which at times seems to suffer from being so ordinary, so everyday, indeed so downright obvious, that we may forget its importance. For us, there is no special value in moments of great upheaval or achievement. On the contrary, our writers show how everyday exchanges can and do enhance and even transform the understanding of those involved.

But how does this happen? Where are these opportunities for everyday learners to flourish and to demonstrate their potential?

One of us lives down the road from a Premier League football team's stadium. The rumours of the club moving out, which have been circulating in the neighbourhood over the last few years, seem to be coming true. The local authority has circulated leaflets to residents outlining possible plans for the large space which would be created by the club's move. Details of public meetings to be held locally are posted through each door. Residents are invited to read the planning application in the local library, neighbourhood office or Town Hall and to register their views. Coincidentally, perhaps, the same neighbourhood is part of a government-funded regeneration scheme. More leaflets, more public meetings, more invitations to become involved. And people do become involved to varying degrees. There is discussion of the latest proposals between neighbours, in shops or at the bus stop; people may read the leaflets and the papers; some will also attend the meetings.

There is a complex and unpredictable interplay between the formal aims set out in the meetings and leaflets and the informal exchanges on the streets and in the shops. For example, in a nice example of persuasive liter-ature, the council suggested that the newly-vacant site could be used for housing, open space and community amenities such as a doctor's surgery. The next day at the shops, the much-expressed view is that this means they are planning to put a needle exchange there.

Here, in this community, is a setting for learning, facilitated both by those who may see themselves as professional educators and those, such as the rep-resentatives of the local council or the stadium owners, who probably do not. The planners, councillors, community workers and owners interact with local people at a moment of change: change in the built environment, but also people's changing knowledge of, and involvement in, local government and the local economy; changing social resources and expectations.

As this example shows, people learn from each other, in social exchanges which only rarely involve a professional educator. What is important for us, if we are to promote or nurture learning, is to base our practice upon an acknowledgement of clients' existing and effective experiences and abilities as learners, in a wide range of everyday encounters like these.

As with all education, the outcomes are unpredictable: the reassuring leaflet is read as a threat; support for the move waxes and wanes with each rumoured development plan.

This approach to education requires us to deal with uncertainty and with apparently undesirable outcomes. The planners may not meet local hopes (certainly not everybody's!). That young girl may become pregnant; this man may not attend his court hearing; Kris may not enrol for college and Pat might not leave an apparently abusive relationship. As practitioners, we could remain stuck within a discourse of moral panic, struggling to achieve, or impose, the desirable outcome. Alternatively, we could risk responding as learners ourselves and appealing to the learner in others. This second course of action invites us to approach new situations with curiosity and openness, seeking to recognise potential rather than to confirm stereotypes. As we strive to work with people, so we focus upon our and their strengths, rather than upon apparent deficits.

This approach to learning is one which we seek to follow in our own College's programmes in informal and community education. Through it, we hope to acknowledge the contribution made by clients within working relationships.

The field

It seems that whenever an institution decides to stop and take stock of its current practices – as our College did with its course materials in 1998 – it becomes freshly aware of the climate of change within which it operates. Whether driven by Albermarle or Kennedy, the agenda of social exclusion or widening participation, MSC or SRB funding mechanisms, we are constantly required to review and relocate our practice within different organisational contexts.

Today we face changes within the Youth Service, Health Service, in adult and further education, in the Careers Service and elsewhere. In this book, we seek to examine how learning relationships work in a range of nominally different fields of professional practice: in particular, but not exclusively, youth work, community work, community and adult education. Because these fields are currently subject to change and redefinition, it seems timely to focus attention on the similarities of practice and approach which draw us together, rather than to allow ourselves to be overwhelmed by the definitions which separate professionals from each other, professionals from clients and clients from each other.

This broadening of the professional field was very much behind our College's thinking in developing our BA programmes as 'informal and community education' (not youth and community work) over five years ago.

This means that the book will focus on exploring how people achieve their potential as learners within a range of social and professional contexts. Its main attention is upon the principles and practice associated with fostering learning, whatever the age of the learner.

Our contributors

We have invited contributors to join this project because of their experience as workers and as educators, as well as, often, a reputation as published authors. Some of them have worked with us before on distance learning course materials.

The book has given us the opportunity to work with practitioners across a wide range of professional fields, all of whom identify learning as a key concern within their practice. We have become involved in numerous conversations with contributors, both written and spoken, some quite brief and others far lengthier and extending over time. There is another whole book in these conversations, and they have in turn shaped the book you hold. Our own ideas for the collection have developed and been revised in the light of these conversations, as have our approaches to, and understanding of, practice. It has always been a highly rewarding piece of work and often a challenging and unpredictable one. As editors, our practice has been to read each contribution separately and then to meet and discuss it. We hope that this has given us a chance to respond initially as readers, and only subsequently as editors. The accounts of practice recounted here are not presented as solutions or as quick-fixes. They are intended to encourage and to provoke further curiosity and questioning; they are based upon, and here offered as, discussions and debates among educators.

For us, this book has been an opportunity to develop our thinking in response to change: to reassess key principles and respond to organisational pressures. We have aimed throughout to hold onto those aspects of practice which we consider it right to maintain, while recognising new opportunities for professional flexibility and exchange.

The book is divided into four unequal parts, dealing with definitions, core values, elements of professional practice and aids to professional development. It is up to you as a worker to make sense of these chapters by connecting these ideas with your practice. Questions in the text ask you to think about specific examples from your own work. Beyond that, we hope that you will make the conscious effort required to draw together your principles and your practice. As Carl Rogers (1983: 136) reminds us, we are none of us empty vessels waiting to be filled with information. As readers, you too have a wealth of experience and skills to work with as you approach these chapters. As educators, you are seeking to establish a helpful meeting place between your clients' experience and skills and the educational opportunities you offer. The challenge we all face as educators is to develop our own abilities as learners: as professionals who recognise and work with our own and other people's abilities.

Informal learning recognises the importance of the quality of the relationships that exist between youth workers and young people, advice workers and consumers, health education workers and the general public, teachers and students, careers counsellors and school-leavers. We hope that a learning relationship may also flourish between our writers and you as readers.

Finally, both of us wish to note the unfailing support and energy of Chris Ball, the administrator for this project. It is no exaggeration to say that this book would not have been possible without her hard work – and our achievement would have been the poorer without her input. Our warmest thanks go to her.

References

Freire, P. (1996) *Letters to Cristina*. London: Routledge.
Rogers, C. (1983) *Freedom to Learn for the 80s*. London: Charles E. Merrill.

Part I
Exploring education

Introduction

Linda Deer Richardson

Part I begins our exploration of the methods and values of informal education with an attempt to define what we mean by the term, and with some basic questions. What does it mean to say that you are an educator? What are the characteristics, in general, of informal education? What are the origins of informal education theory and practice?

In 'On being an educator', Michele Erina Doyle seeks to identify the attitudes and values, rather than simply the activities, that make someone an educator. The task of educators is to work so that people learn; to foster learning. To do this effectively, they first need an understanding of what learning is and an ability to relate theory to practice in order to choose the best ways of working. They need other qualities as well, Doyle argues: qualities which together make up the 'heart' of the educator. These qualities include spirit or passion; a moral sense; and a way of being and acting that reflects educational values. Put these qualities together with the intent to foster learning, and you have a true educator.

John Mahoney's 'What is informal education?' offers an introduction to some of the characteristics of informal education practice, together with examples of current key areas of work with young people. Rather than seeking to define informal education by what it is not – not schooling, not social work – he explores what it is, using case studies to reveal an approach based upon informal learning relationships. However, informal and formal education are not opposites. Just as education in the classroom has informal elements, so informal education may use formal methods and styles. This means that informal educators need to be aware of, and able to evaluate, both product and process elements of their work.

'First lessons: historical perspectives on informal education' is an attempt to set current education practice in an historical context. Tony Jeffs introduces today's informal educators to the tradition which they have inherited, helping them to see the similarities and differences between earlier practice and their own and to identify important consistencies running through the work. The chapter encourages a critical reading of history in order to help readers develop a questioning approach to contemporary practice. Jeffs is highly critical of current policies for formal education, but rejects heroic accounts that see informal education as inherently radical and liberatory. However, informal education has the capacity to act as a counterbalance to schooling, especially when formal education is centralised and controlled as it is today.

Taken together, these three chapters provide a theoretical, practical and historical overview on which the rest of the book will build. Discussion of the values introduced here will be expanded in Part II, while the varied methods which informal educators may use are highlighted in Part III. Part IV explores ways in which educators can reflect on and improve their practice: a theme which brings us back to the beginning and our definition of the true educator.

1   On being an educator

Michele Erina Doyle

Less and less is it presumed that [schoolteachers] should know anything beyond what the students are tested upon. Indeed knowing 'too much' can make them a less efficient delivery person. It can tempt them to stray from the curriculum. Also, as others select the methods, it becomes unnecessary for schoolteachers to understand theories of learning or education.

(Jeffs and Smith 1999: 109)

Many of those we may label as informal educators such as youth workers and community workers do not fully understand themselves as educators. Few professional training programmes pay proper attention to educational theory and practice, and there is only a rudimentary understanding of it in the field.

(Doyle and Smith 1999: 79)

It may seem odd to entertain the idea that educators are not expected, nor required, to know much about learning and education. But it is a natural result of the way in which education, formal and informal, is managed in the UK today.

Schoolteachers in state schools in the UK must abide by the national curriculum, which tells them what, when and increasingly how to teach. They implement pre-designed tests to measure the performance of their pupils against pre-determined standards. This, along with the introduction of league tables for schools, encourages a focus on the outcomes of education. It is not surprising that much of the literature of the field is taking on the look of the cookbook, with recipes for success and 'how to' approaches. The serious and sustained study of the philosophy and sociology of education has all but disappeared from teacher training courses. There is increasing pressure for schools, teachers and pupils to perform well, and less time for them to work out for themselves how this might happen.

Informal education tells a similar story. Although informal educators, for instance youth workers and community educators, are not yet required to follow a national curriculum, the pressure for curricula is building. Both youth work and adult education are moving toward a focus on outcomes and accreditation of learning. Many practitioners do not have enough understanding of their role or the nature of their work to critically analyse such approaches or argue against them. Some practitioners tend to reject formal education, defining themselves as 'not teachers'. This undervalues the educative qualities of their own work and dismisses the extent to which their aims and their practice are similar to those of teachers working in formal settings (Doyle and Smith 1999: 79–80). Programmes of qualification in the UK are inclined to focus on training rather than education, and tend to have an anti-academic quality as a result. They seem designed to produce doers rather than thinkers. This is reflected in the lack of recent practice-based texts. For club work we have to go back to the 1970s, for example Leighton (1972), and for detached work to the early 1980s, for example Rogers (1981), Masterson (1982) and Wild (1982). Much of the responsibility for generating ideas and theories of informal education in the UK in recent years has been left to a handful of writers, in particular Jeffs and Smith (e.g. 1999).

Educators do need to understand and work with theories of learning and education if they are to do a decent job. Yet governments, employers, colleges and universities are sending schoolteachers, youth and community workers, and the like into the field without the means to practice their craft properly. If such guardians of education are not encouraging the understanding and development of theories of education, it is little wonder that educators themselves do not see this as central to their practice. The purpose of this chapter is to bring ideas about learning and education to the forefront of our discussions about being educators. But what do we mean by these terms?

Thinking about learning

> **Q1:** What do you mean by 'learning'? Before you read on, jot down your own definition (or definitions) of learning. Keep your notes handy to compare with the ideas about learning you will meet in this section.

People think and talk about learning often during their daily lives. Phrases that use the idea pepper our conversations. We may hear people say, 'You learn something new every day' or 'A little learning is a dangerous thing'. We talk of the 'University of life'. Often these sayings are contradictory: 'You're never too old to learn' and 'You can't teach an old dog new tricks'.

However, not only do people know of and talk about learning, we encounter it on a daily basis. It is part and parcel of our lives (Tight 1996: 21). We might not plan our day so that we will learn, but things happen and we do. We learn simply by being around each other. For example, suppose you have a disagreement with a colleague at work and end up shouting at her. At home later that night, you replay the events of the day and think about what happened. You might come to the conclusion that you acted unfairly. On meeting your colleague the next day, you discuss what happened with her and apologise for your bad behaviour. As a result, you might decide to act differently if faced with similar situations in the future. What is described here involves learning: the processes of experiencing something, thinking about it, coming to new understandings and moving on, or changing. At times we may be more, or less conscious, of this happening, but the same processes occur. We 'live and learn'.

Learning can also be seen as a product or outcome. For example, we might say we have learnt something new. Psychologists, particularly during the 1950s and 1960s, looked for changes in behaviour as evidence that learning had happened. Learning was thus seen as the outcome of the process rather than the process itself (Merriam and Caffarella 1991: 124). As argued above, current formal education relies heavily on this product approach to learning. It is concerned with specifying what is to be learnt, via the curriculum, and what is actually learnt, via performance indicators. The way in which learning happens – the process – is given less emphasis. Traditionally, informal education has focused on relationships and thus on the process by which learning happens, rather than on what is learnt. The current drive for a 'youth work curriculum' can be seen as a backlash against the uncertainty, or ignorance, of informal educators faced with questions about what the aims and purposes of their work are. The split between formal and informal education is part of the problem. We would all do better if we concentrated on being in the same field – education – rather than trying to convince ourselves and others of our differences. Learning involves process *and* product, not process *or* product.

Understanding learning as process and product is developed in the work of Erich Fromm (1978: 8). He talks of 'having' and 'being' as contrasting ways of living. People who view learning in a 'having' way are interested in owning and keeping knowledge, in product. Those who see it in a 'being' way are interested in experiencing and developing knowledge, or in process. Fromm describes them like this:

> Students in the having mode must have but one aim: to hold onto what they have learned, either by entrusting it firmly to their memories or by carefully guarding their notes. They do not have to produce or create something new ... The process of learning has an entirely different quality for students in the being mode ... Instead of being passive receptacles of words and ideas, they listen, they hear, and most important, they receive and respond in an active, productive way.
>
> (1978: 37–8)

There are other ways of thinking about learning which extend these opposites into a continuum. In an interview-based study, students were asked what they understood by learning. Saljo (1979), who conducted the study, grouped their responses into five categories:

1   Knowing a lot – a quantitative increase of knowledge; getting information.
2   Memorising – storing information that can be reproduced.
3   Gaining facts, skills and methods – these can be registered and used when needed.
4   Making sense or finding meaning – relating bits of knowledge with one another and to the real world.
5   Understanding the world in a different way – comprehending reality by reinterpreting knowledge.

(Quoted in Ramsden 1992: 26)

Here we are introduced to five ways of thinking about learning. Saljo said that not all people would understand learning as all these things. Some might recognise one or more, others might recognise all. He argued that the first three categories put forward a simpler understanding of learning than the last two. Those that view it as knowing a lot (1) or memorisation (2), see knowledge as something that exists outside of its relationship with the learner. It is a commodity that we can get, keep and own. Learning here can become something that is done to people by teachers or that happens by chance, with learners as the passive receivers (Ramsden 1992: 26–7). Following our previous explorations, we can see this as 'having' learning, with a focus on product.

Saljo holds that seeing learning as the latter two categories displays a more complex understanding. Here, people undertake learning activities in order to understand the world. Learning is not something that happens to them or that is imposed by others. Learners are active participants (Ramsden 1992: 26–7). We can understand this as people 'being' learners, with a focus on process.

He also argues that taken as a group, this list of five categories is hierarchical and in ascending order of complexity. If we conceive learning as understanding the world in a different way (5), we would also understand it as the previous four categories. However, if we understand it as knowing a lot (1) we may not understand it as the following four categories. So our understanding of learning builds.

Q2: Compare your definitions of learning with the ones in this study. Can you fit your ideas into one or more of Saljo's categories?

Thankfully, the world cannot be divided up into people that think of learning in either one way or another. Human understanding is a lot more complex than that. There are people that think learning can be described in all the ways explored so far and many more besides. Though there are many ways of viewing learning, each involves gaining knowledge of some kind and in some way.

The ideas we have about learning influence the way we think it comes about. Thinking of learning as something that we can 'have' means that we are more likely to want to be told things, to be given facts and information by others. We will also be more inclined to try to give knowledge to others, by making statements and telling them what we think they should know, or need to know. Seeing ourselves and others as 'being' learners means we are more likely to want to share and develop knowledge, to ask questions and encourage critical enquiry.

What does all this mean for us as educators? Our job is to work so that people learn. We need to know about learning and how it comes about if we are to be able to work so that it happens. It is fairly obvious that if someone has no knowledge of learning, they cannot be an educator. But all people know something of learning – we experience it daily. What special knowledge would we expect from an educator? An example may be useful. Each day we may wash or take a bath. We might make ourselves a cup of tea. These activities involve getting water from taps. So we experience plumbing in our daily lives. Are we plumbers? No. Why not? Because we do not have the special knowledge required to do that job. We might know that water runs to earth rather than skyward or that radiators in a central heating system need to be 'bled' if they are to get hot. But this is not enough to call ourselves plumbers. Educators, like plumbers, need a thorough understanding of their subject. We should expect them to understand simple and complex theories of learning and education and be able to relate them to practice. Educators also need to make some judgements about how they will work so that learning happens. This involves weighing up alternatives and critically analysing their worth, which in turn means developing a knowledge of learning theories through study. Being educators also involves developing knowledge in practice – for themselves and with others. People that educators work with will have their own understandings of learning. Educators need to take this into consideration when they are with people and work to further the understanding of each and all. Despite recent government action and trends in the field, it stands to reason that educators need sophisticated understandings of learning and education if they are to do a good job.

An intent to foster learning

What else is involved in being an educator? Learning can be either incidental or undertaken with intent. Much of our everyday learning, such as the earlier example about a disagreement at work, takes place by chance; it is incidental. But at one time or another, all people undertake activities with the object of fostering learning for themselves or with others. This learning is intentional. It may involve us working with someone else with the intent of helping him or her to learn: for instance, a father teaching his child to cross the road safely. It can also be something we do for ourselves, like searching out information on the Internet or in a local library. Both these activities involve us setting out and doing things so that learning happens. Activities like these are often called education or self-education. An educator, then, can be seen as someone who works with the intention of fostering learning.

Educators differ, however, in their definitions of the purpose and process of education. Here, I am going to briefly consider three broad theories:

- education as transmission, or what Rogers (1983, 1990) calls 'traditional education' and Freire (1972) 'banking education';
- education as 'drawing out' learning that exists already inside the learner: a theory that goes back to Plato (1956);
- education as 'drawing out' learning that comes from the experiences and situations we encounter; in particular the thinking of Dewey (1933) and Boud *et al.* (1993).

Education as transmission

Speaking on *Newsnight* (October 23, 1999) Chris Woodhead, then Chief Inspector of Schools for England, described the purpose of education as transmitting those valued aspects of our culture worth preserving.

Transmission can, of course, be two-way. And messages sent can be heard or remain unheeded. But Chris Woodhead's statement suggests an assumption that the older members of society, especially teachers, are transmitting the values and the younger ones, pupils or students, are receiving them. This reminds me of what Carl Rogers (1990) calls traditional education, which is sometimes called the 'jug and mug' theory. Here, the teacher is a jug full of knowledge and the student is an empty mug. The teacher (or jug) pours knowledge into the learner (or mug) and the learner accepts it.

Returning to our earlier explorations, we can see that this view of what education means has more to do with 'having' than 'being' in Fromm's terms. It involves the teacher 'having' knowledge that can be given or put into the learner. Also we can see that this approach would tend to favour Saljo's first three aspects of learning and neglect the last two. Seeing the purpose and process of education simply as transmission might seem a rather unsophisticated approach, and one rarely championed. However, Rogers saw traditional education as dominant in the American schools of his own day; he calls it the 'inevitable system' rather than the best one (Rogers 1990: 326). The Chief Inspector's comments, coming as they do from someone in a position of influence in shaping education policy and practice, suggest that what Rogers calls traditional education is still dominant in British schools today.

Rogers, in somewhat similar terms to arguments used by Freire (1972), is critical of this definition of what education means. He identifies a number of problems with 'traditional' education, which I shall summarise briefly here. The student is seen as having little or nothing to add to the educational encounter. The teacher is conversely seen as all-knowing, with little or nothing to learn. Their roles are fixed: the teacher cannot learn from the student, and the student cannot teach. The student has little say in what, when and how things are learnt. The teacher (or, in the current climate, central government) takes control of these aspects. Students are not trusted to be active in the education process. They have no democratic voice or choice in educational policies or procedures. Instead, the teacher is central to the process and is a figure of authority. The students are expected simply to conform. Traditional education also uses a narrow range of methods. Teachers 'tell' students what they need to know. Conversation has little importance. Traditional education is largely an intellectual activity, with little room for emotion. The student is expected to learn facts and absorb information, but not to explore feelings. So the uniqueness of each individual is ignored (Rogers 1990: 323–6). Last, the role of the group and the fostering of community and democracy are undervalued in traditional education. Relationships between people are not celebrated or encouraged.

Freire and Rogers both put forward their own ideas of what education should be like, which Freire calls 'problem-posing' (1972: 45–59) and Rogers 'person-centred' (1983: 185–94). You may be familiar with these theories, but if not, the Further Reading suggests some sources that you can follow up.

Drawing out learning

The verb 'to educate', in Latin *educare*, is linked to *educere*, which means 'to draw out'. Some people believe that knowledge lives within people and is drawn from them with the help of the educator, others think it comes about through experience and is drawn from situations. Plato described the former theory in the dialogue called *Meno*. He thought that we have knowledge inside us from the moment we are born, in the form of memories from our previous lives, and that under the right conditions it can come out. Plato attempted to prove his theory that all learning is really remembering in a famous experiment in which Socrates shows that a slave boy can prove Pythagoras' theorem although he has never been taught it (1956: 130–9). This is described in Peterson *et al.* (1998: 317):

Despite having no knowledge of geometry, the boy, in conversation with Plato [Socrates], displays a sophisticated understanding. Plato argues the boy was born with dormant knowledge that, in response to questioning, was brought to life.

This may be. However, working solely on the assumption that knowledge comes from within the individual poses some problems for the educator.

Q3: Assume for a moment that Plato was right. What would the implications be for your practice as an educator?

If all knowledge lies inside us, the process of education would have to be concentrated on the self. We would not need to experience much to learn – just the process that allowed our existing knowledge to be drawn out. Perhaps the most efficient way for this to happen would be in pairs or even alone, since any focus on other people might get in the way of drawing out learning from our self. As a consequence, education would not involve group activities. We would have nothing to learn from others. Their ideas, theories and feelings would be of little consequence to us. History and the present context would play little part. The accumulated wisdom of humankind would have little significance. We would need no books and reading would become a redundant activity. The educator's role would largely be reduced to asking questions, as Socrates does in the dialogue. The educator would become more like an interrogator trying to drag out bits of knowledge from the other person. Education would become an isolated, isolating experience. As we work through the consequences of such an assumption, we can see it becomes less and less recognisable as education. Working all this through in the context of a classroom or youth club would be nigh on impossible.

However, there may be an alternative explanation for the slave boy's understanding of geometry. For example, we might try to build and fly a kite. Trial and error may lead us to working out the best materials and shapes for flying. At the finish, we might have learnt something about aerodynamics and geometry. We are not likely to see it like that. We are more likely to conclude that we know how to make and fly kites. Suppose we then meet a mathematician and an engineer who engage us in conversation. In talking to them, we might draw on our experiences of kite-making and flying. They would be able to relate what we were saying to their theories of aerodynamics and geometry. They could ask pertinent questions that enabled us to express and explore our practical experience. Perhaps their contributions would open up new worlds for us. We might learn to describe what we have done in other ways, naming things differently. We would then have alternative and perhaps better understandings of our kite-making. This does not mean that we always knew about these things. It means that we have come to understand our experiences better. Learning has been drawn out from our experience, the situation, and our conversation with wise and knowledgeable people.

Drawing out learning from our experiences

Drawing learning from our experiences is something that John Dewey, a key twentieth-century educational thinker, was interested in. He said that the 'business of education might be defined as an emancipation and enlargement of experience' (1933: 340).

We often see experience as a one-off. It just happens to us and then it is over. But because we have thoughts and memories, experience is much more than this. It lives. Thinking about our past, incidents surface. They might be times of great joy or sadness. More often than not they are significant or special to us in some way. Perhaps they had some lasting effect or helped us define who we are. We may only think of these things occasionally, but they are there, ready to be called upon. When thinking back, we recall events and feelings. We try to make sense of what happened in the light of our present position. Our recollections, feelings and understandings may change over time.

Experience is not always striking and can seem mundane. Taking my dog Maisie for a walk four times a day, every day, can be a chore. We leave the flat, go down in the lift and off to the park. We walk around for a bit, she goes to the toilet, we play and then go home. Daily experiences and routines like these seem to have little to do with learning, but these activities have more to them than meets the eye. Dog lovers and their canine friends experience a special kind of relationship. They bond in some way, and experience something of what love means. Part of that bond involves chores, like walking and feeding. There are, however, other things that may spring from dog-loving. Walking Maisie also roots me as part of the local neighbourhood. People often smile, wave or strike up a conversation. I have come to know many of my neighbours in this way. It opens all sorts of opportunities. If I think about it, I realise that this kind of socialising adds to my happiness. It is nice to experience friendliness. I also feel safer, because I know and recognise others and vice versa. By thinking about my experiences, I can see that my relationship with Maisie, and in particular the daily experience of walking her, has enabled all this to happen. So even everyday, seemingly mundane experiences, when thought about carefully, bring about learning. They help us understand ourselves and our lives better.

Through this process of reflection on our experiences, we may learn. This is something that can happen as a matter of course, but if we are in the business of education we have a responsibility to work for it. We can try to do this by enhancing the processes of reflection.

According to Boud *et al.* (1993: 26–31) reflection involves three linked, overlapping actions:

- Returning to experience – 'going back' over events and recalling important details.
- Attending to (or connecting with) feelings – being in touch with feelings, past and present. Identifying if they are a help or hindrance and trying to move on positively.
- Evaluating experience – making links and judgements. Re-examining situations in the light of new knowledge. Fitting new learning into our existing understandings.

Working on the assumption that learning is drawn from experience and/or situations poses fewer problems for the educator than assuming that it is drawn from within the individual. It focuses the process on events and how people experience them, rather than on the self. It enables sharing, so that learning can happen in groups as well as being an individual endeavour. The educator may use a range of approaches to enable learning to be drawn out.

So if educators are to be true to the process of education, they need to be concerned with drawing out learning. This leads us to the fundamental problem with the traditional model of education we discussed earlier: learning is seen as being put into people and situations, rather than being drawn out. School teachers, youth and community workers and others need to move beyond the processes of traditional education if they are to truly educate. Given the current state of affairs, with the focus on outcome and performance, this is becoming increasingly difficult, but not impossible.

So far we have seen that being an educator involves drawing out learning with intent. But there is more to it than this. What else does it involve?

Heart

In my earlier work with Mark K. Smith (Doyle and Smith 1999) we argued that education concerns drawing out learning not only with intent, but also with heart. What do we mean by heart? We all know that our heart is an internal organ that pushes blood around our bodies. But our use of the term 'heart' suggests that this organ is more than just a pump; it has special qualities. As we wrote, the heart 'is central to the body; it is at the core of things. It supports life; it is vital' (Doyle and Smith 1999: 32).

In a similar way, we have argued that as social beings there are three linked dimensions of ourselves that are central, supportive and vital to our relations with others. As described in *Born and Bred – leadership, heart and informal education* (1999) these are:

- spirit – the passions that animate or move us;
- moral sense or conscience – the values, ideals and attitudes that guide us;
- being – the kind of person we are, or wish to be, in the world.

We would argue that these three qualities are central to being an educator. What do we mean by them?

Spirit

Spirit is a word that has a multiplicity of meanings. Plato described the human mind or soul as divided into three parts, controlling reason, the emotions or passions, and appetite; and housed in the head, chest and belly respectively. He defined the second of these, the 'spirited soul' as:

> That element in the person from which comes the dynamism for living. A person with 'spirit', a 'spirited person', is one who is 'alive': a person who is 'spiritless' is lacking in vital qualities and not fully alive.
>
> (Rodger 1996: 48)

Spirit, then, involves passions. These are the things that animate or move us – our passions. They are the feelings, ideas and commitments we hold dear. Looking closely at our actions gives us and others some clues about what these might be. Often what speaks loudest is not what we say and do but how we say and do it: the spirit, as we might say, in which the action is taken. The simple act of saying 'thank you', for example, can be motivated by a number of passions. We may say it sincerely in recognition of another person's kindness. Moving us might be the belief that the good actions of others should be appreciated, and that saying 'thank you' is one way of honouring that. Or it could be said with sarcasm. Perhaps we think the other person has not helped us in the way we would have liked. What moves us in this case might be feelings of anger, frustration or hurt. Behind these emotions might be the belief that people should help those in need.

We shape our dealings with others by our spirit or manner, which reflects in our actions. Sometimes this is done consciously. At other times we might be less aware. By exploring such actions and their roots, we can identify patterns of behaviour and find out about the kind of person we may be. We can ask ourselves, am I rude, appreciative, polite and so on? This questioning allows us to learn and to change our commitments and behaviour where appropriate.

What we are exploring here is the spirit (in the sense of tone or character) of our words and actions as individuals, but this sense of spirit can also be applied to situations and groups. Walking into a room where people are congregated, we may be able to pick up on the atmosphere. We might sense good or bad vibes. The spirit of the situation or group is something that lives around us and can be felt. It can also be created and fostered. For example, telling a distasteful joke at an otherwise jovial gathering could have a dampening affect. People may accuse us of ruining the atmosphere, or may complain that we have spoiled their enjoyment. On the other hand, the entrance of a lively group may uplift proceedings and introduce a new spirit of fun. Whatever we say and do, we all play our part in creating, encouraging and maintaining the spirit of situations and groups.

Education works well when undertaken in the spirit of conversation. At its best, conversation can be a place of inspiration and enjoyment; connecting us with others. It can also uplift; connecting us with God or truth. Educators are committed to cultivating not only conversation, but a conversational spirit: a group spirit in which conversation can take place and flourish. This means that qualities like openness, hope, critical enquiry, humour and curiosity will need to be encouraged.

As we saw earlier, spirit is about the character of our actions. It is also about our character as people or at least about some valued, 'vital' aspects. Educators themselves, as well as their work, need to be hopeful, curious, open, etc. The way they are with people should encourage talk and the seeking of knowledge.

Being spirited or moved by our passions does not mean letting our desires take over or doing what is best for ourselves. It involves working out what is important to us and aiming to act for goodness for each and all. In this way, it connects with the second of our core qualities.

Moral sense or conscience

When something happens that rouses our conscience, there are a number of ways we may respond. Our choice often depends on feelings, ideas and relationships that we are passionate about. As we have seen, our passions are motivators; they affect what we say and do. Responding in situations is a complex process and there is usually more than one of these passions present. Sometimes they sit well together. Other times they clash.

For example, we may notice that one of our colleagues is often rude and snappy with another, particularly in meetings where all the staff gather. We feel uncomfortable and sense that others are also ill at ease with the situation. We dislike bullying and believe that people should be treated with respect. Our commitment to good association and group life is strong. We feel upset about the situation. So the next time we witness our colleague's rudeness, we ask her to be more respectful. Here the ways in which we think and feel come together and animate us to act in a particular way.

Add in a belief that people should be able to deal with their own issues and problems, and the mix becomes more complicated. Swooping in to 'rescue' our colleague under attack, however well-meaning, might undermine his autonomy. But what about our commitment to group life? Here our different moral thoughts and feelings are at odds. So what do we do?

What if we are also fearful? Perhaps confronting our overbearing colleague might lead to her picking on us. This fear, of being subjected to bullying ourselves, might be so powerful that it overshadows all our other thoughts and feelings. The next time we witness our colleague's rudeness, we say nothing. Here, one passion reigns.

Though we may seek to satisfy all our passions, this is often not possible. We must choose to follow some, while leaving others unfulfilled. Whatever our actions, we have to live with the consequences. This means being honest about what has happened and what we think and feel about it. If our fear is influencing our actions, we need to admit it. This can be painful, but if we try to bury things they may come back to haunt us in some way. Besides, we can learn from looking at our actions and the reasons behind them.

Living with the truth of situations involves thinking: working out where our passions converge and conflict and making some judgement between them. Within this process, we appeal to a moral sense, trying to determine what is good for each and all. Our ideas about 'the good' can be seen as the clusters of passions that have stood the test of time and thought. Such ideas have been called upon and worked out in our daily lives. They might include, for example, a sense of justice or respect for people. These groups of passions are sometimes called values or core values. They come about through our experiences and are subject to change and development. They guide our actions and we encourage them to flourish.

Some groups of people are able to come to some agreement about the values they share. Families may decide together how they are going to live and the kind of family they want to be. They will have some idea about what is right and wrong or good and bad. They will cherish particular ways of being over and above others. Professional groupings can also agree on codes of ethics stating their values. These are often teamed with guidelines on how to behave, or codes of practice. Whether these codes enhance good practice is questionable, but nonetheless they exist. Educators can certainly do without such external guidelines. Part of their job is to work with, and work out, their values as they go along.

Some of the values held by educators involved in these processes are:

- respect for persons;
- the promotion of well-being;
- truth;
- democracy;
- justice.

(Based on Jeffs and Smith 1999: 80–1)

These values are difficult to define and will be the subject of debate. Not all educators will agree that these are the core values of the field; and individuals may interpret each of them differently. However, most educators would see these values, among others, as integral to their practice. Committing to such values involves working so that they can flourish in the situations in which we work.

Being

The third core quality which makes up the heart of the educator is being. Being is about the kind of person we are. This is shown by our actions and inactions – what we do and don't do. It has to do with how we are as well as what we are. For example, I could say that I am a mother. In simple terms (of *what* we are) this means that I have given birth to a child. However, some people might say there is more to being a mother than giving birth. So along with the title goes the expectation of particular qualities of motherhood, like patience or love (*how* we are). If these expectations are met, we might say that someone is a 'good' mother. On the other hand, our own experience or that of others might tell us that some mothers are not 'good'. The qualities needed to be a good mother will always be up for debate, but there may be some that we can agree on.

In the same way, being an educator is not only about what educators do, but also about the special qualities they bring to their work. We argued earlier that educators work with and for particular values. If they are to be true to these, their behaviour should reflect them. So educators need, for example, to be just and democratic in their dealings with people. If they do not bring these qualities to their work, they are undermining the values they claim to hold dear.

Conclusion

What we mean by heart is perhaps easiest to see in action. Here is a Quaker lawyer's account of an encounter with his neighbour, almost two-and-a-half centuries ago.

> A neighbour ... desired me to write his will: I took notes, and, amongst other things, he told me which of his children he gave his young negro: I considered the pain and distress he was in, and knew not how it would end, so I wrote his will, save only that part concerning his slave, and carrying it to his bedside, read it to him, and then told him in a friendly way, that I could not write any instruction by which my fellow-creatures were made slaves, without bringing trouble on my own mind. I let him know that I charged him nothing for what I had done, and desired to be excused from doing the other part in the way he proposed. Then we had a serious conference on the subject, and at length, he agreeing to set her free, I finished his will.
>
> (J. Woolman 1756)

Among other things, a passion for justice is present in this account. John Woolman chose not to act in a fashion that would oppress, not only the slave, but also his neighbour and himself. He was moved to act with compassion, performing his duties diligently, but without compromising his own beliefs and those shared with other Quakers. His approach was conversational and he was animated by, and showed, a concern for each and all. Add the intention to draw out learning – and we have an educator.

Further reading

Fromm, E. (1978) *To Have and To Be*. London: Abacus. For those who want to explore the nature of having and being, this is a key text.

The informal education homepage – www.infed.org – page upon page of resources and articles for all educators, but a must for youth and community educators.

Jeffs, T. and Smith, M.K. (1999) *Informal Education – Conversation, Democracy and Learning*, 2nd edn. Ticknall: Education Now. An easy-to-read, yet thorough, introduction to informal education.

Palmer, P.J. (1998) *The Courage to Teach. Exploring the Inner Landscape of a Teacher's Life*. San Francisco: Jossey-Bass. For anyone who feels called to the field this is an inspiring and informative read.

Ramsden, P. (1992) *Learning to Teach in Higher Education*. London: Routledge. A sturdy and systematic review of educating and learning.

References

Boud, D., Cohen, R. and Walker, D. (1993) *Using Experience for Learning*. Buckingham: Open University Press.

Dewey, J. (1933) *How We Think*. New York: D.C. Heath.

Doyle, M.E. and Smith, M.K. (1999) *Born and Bred – Leadership, Heart and Informal Education*. London: YMCA George Williams College.

Freire, P. (1972) *Pedagogy of the Oppressed*. Harmondsworth: Penguin.

Fromm, E. (1978) *To Have and To Be*. London: Abacus.

The informal education homepage (1999) Learning. www.infed.org/biblio/b-learn.htm

Jeffs, T. and Smith, M.K. (1999) *Informal Education – Conversation, Democracy and Learning*, 2nd edn. Ticknall: Education Now.

Leighton, J.P. (1972) *The Principles and Practice of Youth and Community Work*. London: Chester House.

Masterson, A. (1982) *A Place of My Own*. Manchester: Greater Manchester Youth Association.

Merriam, S.B. and Caffarella, R.S. (1991) *Learning in Adulthood*. San Francisco: Jossey-Bass.

Peterson, W. *et al.* (1998) *Reason and Religious Belief*, 2nd edn. New York: Oxford University Press.

Plato (1956) *Protagoras and Meno*, translated by W.K.C. Guthrie. Harmondsworth: Penguin.

Ramsden, P. (1992) *Learning to Teach in Higher Education*. London: Routledge.

Rodger, A. (1996) 'Human spirituality: toward an educational rationale', in R. Best (ed.) *Education, Spirituality and the Whole Child*. London: Cassell.

Rogers, A. (1981) *Starting Out in Detached Work*. Leicester: National Association of Youth Clubs.

Rogers, C. (1983) *Freedom to Learn for the 80s*. London: Charles Merrill.

Rogers, C. (1990) 'The interpersonal relationship in the facilitation of learning', in H. Kirschenbaum and V.L. Henderson (eds) *The Carl Rogers Reader*. London: Constable.

Tight, M. (1996) *Key Concepts in Adult Education and Training*. London: Routledge.

Wild, J. (1982) *Street Mates*. Liverpool: Merseyside Youth Association.

Woolman, J. (1756) 'Honesty and integrity', in *Quaker Faith and Practice*. London: British Yearly Meeting.

2 What is informal education?

John Mahoney

As informal educators we can find ourselves involved in various projects and activities.

Our job title may be youth and community worker, project worker, detached worker or drugs/alcohol worker, the list goes on. As for activities, these may include residentials, music groups, art, sport, discussion groups or one-to-one work.

Although our job titles and our tasks within the organisation we choose to work in may look different, our overall aim stays the same: *education*. All these projects and activities not only provide opportunities for us, and children, young people, or adults, to learn, but also an opportunity for us to reflect on and develop our practice. In this chapter we look at this central aim and at the different opportunities which our work as informal educators provides.

Firstly though, what is informal education? It seems far easier to define our work as informal educators by saying what it is not, rather than what it is. If we were a sculptor working on a block of stone, we would chip away the pieces we did not want, in order to make the statue that we have in our mind. As informal educators, we can often be seen doing something similar when we try to define our work: we choose the pieces that we think are important to our work, and chip away the others which for us are not so important. This creates difficulties when trying to define our work to others, because what is important for one worker may not be for another. Some of the pieces that get chipped away may include working as schoolteachers, social workers, probation officers, sports instructors or counsellors. We could go on defining our work by what we are not, but what we need to do is to look more directly at what informal education is and can be.

In this chapter, we will try to do just that. We will explore some of the characteristics of informal education and draw out some of the main themes that relate to our work, using examples of work with young people. This will hopefully create some discussion, and encourage us to think about ourselves as informal educators.

To start us off, we will explore what it means to be informal and work informally with young people.

What makes our work informal?

What is it that we do as workers that allows us to say we are 'informal educators'? A good starting point for us is to think about how we engage with and relate to the people that use our centre or project. For the most part we will be meeting and talking with people from the local area. If we think about how we do this, and how local people relate to us as workers, we can start to uncover what it means to work informally.

> **Q1:** Think about how you meet and talk to people when at work. What makes this informal?
>   Here you might like to think both about your approach and the environment you are in. Jot down some words that bring to mind some of the qualities of being informal.

When we think about how we engage with young people at work we can start to see that the daily life of individuals and groups is a main focus for us as workers. It is this daily life that interests us, because this is where we begin to understand the young people we are working with. In order for us to do this we need to be approachable, friendly, open to talk, have a sense of humour and so on. So the words commonly used by various workers when thinking about how they go about 'being informal' seem to have a relaxed atmosphere and everyday feel about them. By associating our role with words like these and the ones you may have come up with, we can start to get to grips with what it means to be informal. These characteristics, and the ones you have probably named, also enable us to work better with young people.

For example, informally talking to someone about the lack of facilities in the area while playing pool is a way of getting to know both the person and the local area. For us as informal educators, finding out the interests of those we work with allows us to develop our work of fostering learning. We use a wide variety of tools in order to do this, and what we mean by learning can include becoming more confident, organised, expressive, or more skilled in practical subjects. As we shall see, working informally creates many possibilities for us as educators.

We all have some sense of what it means to be informal in our everyday life. If we think about how we interact with others outside work and how we act in different social settings, this gives us good examples of being informal: casual dress, ordinary locations, using first names and so on. Our experience tells us what being informal means to us, and this can also begin to suggest what aspects of 'being informal' it is appropriate to use in the work place. No doubt we all transfer what we perceive to be informal ways of behaving into our practice, but how do we choose between what is appropriate and what is not?

If you look back at Question 1, you can see that I asked you to connect being informal with being at work. In doing this, you were looking at being informal in a different way than if you were outside work. As informal educators, we are not just being informal without care or reflection; we enter our work place with an aim of working, or rather of educating, in an informal way.

One way of approaching this is to consider what 'being informal' means to those we work with. Most young people will enter the youth project in order to meet with friends, socialise and have fun. If we were to try and work with these young people formally, as though we were teachers in a classroom, we could imagine the outcome. In order for us to engage with these young people productively, we need to bear in mind why they come to the youth project in the first place. This means we need to be aware of our actions as workers, and how the particular environments we find ourselves in affect our work.

If we link the notion of the informal with education we can see more clearly what our aim is. Putting these two parts of the equation together gives us a better position from which to think about our work.

As workers our primary task is education. But how do we do this informally? How do we manage the task of working with young people educationally? We will now explore this theme a little further, starting with the ways in which we use the environment to further learning.

Educating by using the environment

> **Q2:** If you go back to the words you used to describe meeting and talking to young people in Question 1, you may find that you were describing the environment around you as well as your interactions. Look back at your notes from Question 1 and see if any of the words you used are about the environment, or the setting, in which your work takes place.

If you go back to some of the words you used to describe meeting and talking to young people, you will probably find that it was hard to ignore the environment around you. You might have thought about aspects of the physical environment, such as the building, the furniture within it, the pool table, TV, posters on the walls. These help form the physical world around us.

Other environments you described could have been social, emotional or political. These have to do with the people who are in that physical setting: how they interact, their backgrounds, beliefs and states of mind, for example. These also form part of our world, in similar ways to the physical environment.

If we observe the everyday situations we find ourselves in at work, we can start to identify these different environments. For instance, if we look around our youth project when it is full of young people who are engaged in different activities, we will be able to observe a particular social environment. Although at times what is going on around us may seem chaotic and without any structure, we know as informal educators that this is not the case: people are behaving in predictable and familiar ways. The social environment is often more complex than we imagine, however, and there are new social and cultural norms that need to be learnt when entering into a new setting. As workers we need to understand these various processes, because they enable us to learn about other people's view of the world.

If we look at the example overleaf we can see how a worker is trying to develop a piece of work, using a given environment.

Example 1: coffee and *EastEnders*

Being friendly and talking about what is on television while having a coffee with a young person is a clear example of being informal. I am sure we have probably all done this, whether we have been at work or not. The difference though is that when we are at work our aims as workers enable us to decide how to develop this opportunity for learning. Depending on the television programme, we could be talking about all sorts of topics. If we take watching *EastEnders*, for example, we could be talking about how the programme presents stereotypes of people from different cultures. This would be a good question for us to take further. Here we could learn from each other about what we both think about this issue.

If we now place this example in a busy youth club where other young people are playing pool, table tennis, football, talking to other workers and within their own peer groups, we can see how this piece of work fits into a particular environment and relates to what the rest of the youth club is doing. Although this piece of work may seem relatively small when compared to other activities within the club, the important question for us as educators is, has some learning occurred? Young people may be involved in all sorts of activities, but have they learnt or experienced something new? These are questions we should ask ourselves when we are engaged in or have finished an activity or session.

Q3: I am sure you have experienced being in a similar situation to the example above. Can you think of a similar recent activity you were involved in as a worker where a person or group of people may have learnt something new?

Here are my thoughts on the kinds of questions we might ask to decide whether an informal activity is educational, using the coffee and *EastEnders* example.

1.   How did we get there?

If we look again at the example we can explore what was happening. Firstly, how did we get into the situation? As workers we do not just 'happen' to be around, as if we bumped into someone we know in the street. We aim to place ourselves in situations and intervene as appropriate. For example, as the worker, you may have seen a particular young person you wanted to get to know. One way of doing this could have been to make coffee and offer the young person a cup. Alternatively the worker and young person may already know each other. The worker might know that this particular young person likes watching *EastEnders*, and so this provides a good way in to starting a conversation.

2. Intervening: what did we do?

If we move on, we can see that in this example both people found something that they could engage with. Here it was talking about *EastEnders*, but it could be anything. Finding common ground is an important part of informal education, because here we begin to learn about, and work with, what people bring. The fact that the conversation moved on to stereotypes in *EastEnders* helps us to identify a clear topic for exploration, but these topics are not always so easily identified. In particular, conversation can often switch from one subject to another. Talking about *EastEnders* could have been a 'way in' to a discussion about stereotyping, but the conversation might have led on to very different topics. For example, if the young person was sitting alone, there may have been a reason for this, which we as workers might want to explore. The point is that all these different approaches and observations that informal educators use are not just coincidental – we choose how to work with young people so that we can foster learning.

3. What tools did we use?

Where the conversation took place had an effect on what was discussed. Here, the TV was used as a tool to engage with a young person. The pool table, posters on the wall or even the weather are all tools or ways of using the environment around us to get to know people.

The topic itself is also a tool. Stereotyping is an interesting subject and will probably evoke different responses from different people. As informal educators we need to be aware of the many different processes that are involved when exploring such issues. Being aware allows us to introduce different angles to the debate. For example, if a debate on stereotypes is causing an emotional response, it might be useful to explore the social and political aspects of the topic: who decides how particular individuals or groups are portrayed, for instance? This might bring out different ideas and thoughts that young people have. Again, by doing this we are fostering an environment for learning.

Relationships: developing different approaches

Thinking about how and what we say when meeting and talking to people is important for us as informal educators. Reflecting on how well we relate to others enables us to develop our practice. The first interventions we make when building a relationship with another person can be difficult. Even when we have developed relationships, it takes a lot of work to sustain and develop them further. Being aware of what works best for us personally, and being sensitive towards other people and their different personalities, culture, or present situation, can make a great difference to our interventions. Weighing up the pros and cons of what we might say or do when at work may seem like something we do anyway, but how often do we think about our interactions until they appear unsuccessful?

Thinking about different approaches that we might use means that we are thinking about our practice as educators, and how we can work better with people. In doing this we are also developing our own body of knowledge for the future. This knowledge can either be used again 'as is' or adapted to suit a particular situation; either way we are developing our practice.

For instance, if you were approaching a young person, as in our *EastEnders* example above, would you:

- go straight over and sit down nearby?
- take a cup of coffee over and sit nearby?
- take the young person over a cup of coffee as well?
- ask 'Would you like a cup of coffee/a game of pool?'
- suggest other games or forthcoming trips that are on offer?

Depending on your 'style' and 'taste', these are all possible approaches when thinking about intervening. Whether you know the young person, and the stage you have reached in your relationship, will also play a part when deciding which way to go. Only by making judgements and trying them out will you know or find out what will work well and what will not. Even if the response is negative, you have still found a way to engage with someone. For example, suppose you ask a young person for a game of pool and get the reply, 'I don't like pool.' This still opens up an opportunity for you as a worker to build upon.

Q4: If you were in this situation what response might you think of?

One response that comes to mind is, 'What *do* you like doing?' Changing our approach and thinking on our feet enables us to learn about young people's interests and what they might like to do. This example is very simple and it will probably need a lot of work to take the relationship forward, but it is from these relatively small interventions that we begin to develop areas of work and find out what people think and are interested in. Opening doors to new possibilities is something informal educators do quite often, but that is only the beginning. If we are to develop these opportunities we need to encourage both young people and other workers to get involved and take part in achieving goals.

If we think about our work and how we create opportunities and achieve some of our goals within the work place, building relationships and 'getting to know' young people are essential characteristics of informal education.

From our examples above we can see that beginning a relationship may need a push start (usually from the worker). We can also see that it is important for us to think about interventions and how the environment can be used as a tool for working. If we look at how we might do this, we will probably need to think about our approach, and what we will say, before making contact. The environment we are in will also probably have some effect on what direction we will take. We can then go on to talk and find some common ground from which to develop a piece of work. Finding something in common to talk about, or an activity in which a young person or young people are interested, enables us to get to know them better. We only have to think about how we build relationships with our friends or colleagues in order to understand the value of this way of working.

So far we have looked at being informal, developing work, and how we might do this, but what makes a *good* approach or a *good* piece of work? How do we evaluate what we do as workers? This is something we will now begin to explore.

Being 'OK' and beyond

Our initial interactions will have consequences for us to consider, as I have outlined already. These interactions also have an effect on how other people perceive us and relate to us. As informal educators we can reflect on our work and discuss issues with our colleagues in order to develop our practice, but what do the people we work with think?

When I think about how the young people my colleagues and I work with see us as workers, there is one phrase that springs to mind – 'They're alright.'

Being described as 'alright' or 'OK' as a worker by young people has been a good indication for many informal educators that they have developed good relationships with the young people they are working with. There is certainly value in this as a guide to evaluating our work. Encouraging young people to get involved with various activities has an effect on how our relationships with them develop. The more involved we are with young people, the more contact we will have with them. Their response to us as workers therefore enables us to evaluate our work with more insight.

Some of the qualities which have been used to describe workers as 'OK' have been being able to take time to talk and listen to people, getting involved in what is going on, making things happen, being friendly and supportive, genuine and trustworthy. There are many others but these are some of the common things you will probably hear. No doubt you can add to this list, as different people will give you different answers. Because being 'OK' can mean different things to different people, it is important for us to find out what other people think.

But is this really enough to go on? The problem here is whether young people are choosing to describe us as 'OK' because of our personalities or because of our approach to the work we do. As we all have different personalities, it is probably more useful to focus on our work and ask what makes a good piece of informal education.

Q5: From your experience, think about what makes a good piece of work. What qualities would you associate with this? Thinking about what doesn't make a good piece of work may help. Try to focus on a particular piece of work as it was taking place and try to identify what you think was good (or bad) about it.

Instead of trying to guess what you might have put down as good qualities of informal education, we will explore another example. If we take a group of young people who want to go on a trip to the cinema, we can begin to look at what makes for good informal education. The cinema could quite easily be something else, but it is how we work together to organise the trip that is important.

Example 2: the cinema trip

If we split this example into two roads or ways of working, and take each of them in turn, we can see what might happen.

Way 1: So young people want to go to the cinema, what do we do?

If, for example, we have a group of four young people we might want to get others involved. We could do this by asking young people ourselves. This would give us definite numbers, so when we flick through the Yellow Pages to find a suitable cinema we can ring up and book the seats. While we are on the telephone we can also choose the film we are going to watch. Once we have this information, we can draw a poster and advertise it in the project.

Way 2: So young people want to go to the cinema, what do we do?

If we have a group of four young people we could divide up the various tasks between us. One of us could find out if there are others that want to go. We could flick through the Yellow Pages and choose together which cinema we want to go to. Someone could telephone for availability and book the tickets, but what film do we want to watch?
   As Robert Frost said, 'Two roads diverged in a wood, and I took the one less travelled by, and that has made all the difference'.

As we can see from these two options, the second one stimulates more thinking. Involving the young people in the process of organising the trip will create more opportunities for learning. Decision making, choice, organising and responsibility can all be identified within this second example. It also holds more meaning, as young people can 'own' what is happening and can shape it to their needs.
   The first option leaves all the work up to the worker, and takes away the opportunities for learning. Although the first one may take up less time and be more efficient, it does not foster learning within the group and therefore it is not informal education. Being aware of these differences is important because every so often we need to pull ourselves up, and say 'Is what I am doing informal education?'

Q6: If you now reflect on your answers to Question 5, can you see anything you might have done differently? Do you think the piece of work you thought about was informal education?

Reflecting on a piece of work we have done is probably one of the best ways of learning about ourselves as workers. Our past experiences of working with people are very valuable, because they allow us to see how little or how much change is needed in our approach.

What makes a good piece of work? I suspect that being able to identify clear learning, as I asked you to try to do in Question 3, is a good source from which to draw when evaluating our work. If we think about the last session we were involved in at our projects we should be able to identify some learning. Even if we cannot be one hundred per cent certain that learning has occurred, we can make informed judgements on how a particular activity developed and whether it was likely to foster learning or hinder it.

The difficulty with informal education is that the learning can be hard to identify. Practical activities like learning how to paint, play music, canoe or play football do not necessarily capture the spirit of informal education. What these activities mean, what young people feel and think, and how young people organise, work together and achieve goals, capture our attention. Exploring how young people see the world, and what they think, arouses the interest of the informal educator. This process may take the shape of an hour-long session or a five-minute conversation, but if we have consciously fostered that environment for learning we are doing our jobs as informal educators.

Learning from each other

Learning from our colleagues and other workers in the field is another way to learn the craft of informal education. But what may be a useful approach for one worker might not be useful for another. Like our sculptor, we all have different pieces that will be left on the floor. Being aware of how we approach our work and talking about how and why we favour different ways of working enables us to understand other workers, while also learning about ourselves.

We have probably all witnessed a situation or intervention that we would have approached differently from another worker, but this is not to say our style or taste is the right one.

By observing work in this way, we are developing our own reference points to draw from when next faced with a similar opportunity.

As informal educators it is important to understand our role. Thinking is the only way in which to do this. We might work in different ways from each other, but education is our common focus. This is what connects us to other informal educators. Thinking and reflecting on our work gives us opportunities to question and develop our practice.

So far we have looked at how we approach our work and begin to develop it. We will now explore this further by looking at the potential opportunities for learning we are faced with in our projects.

Being aware of opportunities

As educators we are faced with dilemmas and difficult decisions all the time, so it is especially important for us to understand our role, and why we are there. For example, letting young people smoke cigarettes in the youth project when it is a no-smoking building may make you 'OK' with the young people, but is it 'OK'? Of course we shouldn't allow smoking in a no-smoking building, but the issue does not have to end here.

Issues such as this can be a common occurrence within the youth project, but for the informal educator they should not simply be viewed as headaches. Instead, they are an opportunity to reach some understanding with young people. Having no smoking in the building is a policy that may not change, but unless it is discussed it will surely never change. This raises an important aspect of informal education, that we foster environments for learning so that young people have an opportunity to express themselves. Taking part in debates like this raises awareness, and can activate the power young people have when deciding their needs.

As informal educators, then, we find ourselves working in various environments. Within these environments we work with young people in an attempt to identify and develop areas of work. Because we enter our project or centre with this in mind, we no longer take the situations we find ourselves in, like the young people who want to smoke in the building, for granted. Talking and interacting with the people we work with provides us with opportunities for learning.

If we take two examples of opportunities that can be presented to us when at work, we can start to explore the processes involved.

Example 3: a discussion about alcohol use

Imagine a worker who is playing pool with young people, and socially interacting with them. What the worker will probably find is that various topics for conversation will emerge. If, for example, alcohol consumption is one of those topics, and has been raised by the young people, then the worker will have an educational opportunity which comes about quite by chance. By encouraging people to talk and become involved with this topic, the worker is then fostering learning. Sharing experiences and knowledge enables us to learn from one another. Although the physical environment such as the pool table, chairs, and the four walls around this group will not have changed, the social and emotional environments will.

If we compare this example with some features of informal education that Tony Jeffs and Mark Smith have highlighted, we can see how this process works. The worker as informal educator:

* joins in with an activity;
* uses an everyday setting where people have chosen to be;
* engages people in conversation; and
* seeks to foster learning.

(Jeffs and Smith 1996:6)

We can see from the example and the four points above that the worker is thinking about being an educator and how best to engage with the young people. Here the worker joined in with a topic of conversation that was raised by the young people, and encouraged others to participate.

Although we sometimes bring our own ideas and issues to talk about when talking with young people, engaging with what young people bring to us has great significance for us as educators. Within our work we can often identify certain topics or issues to explore, but we have to be aware of why we are choosing them. 'Going with the flow', and working with what young people bring to us, enables us to learn about what is important to them and holds meaning for the people we work with.

Opportunities like this may arise from various aspects of our work. Observing what is going on in the work place, talking to young people and other local people, talking to other workers, both internally and from other centres, and global issues all may influence our work, but these all need to be thought about critically. It is important as informal educators that we consider how our work fits in with the everyday living of the people we work with.

If we go back to our alcohol discussion example, we can identify two different ways of moving forward from this point, and evaluate them critically.

Firstly, the worker has already engaged with this topic successfully over a game of pool, which means that there is potential for developing this topic in the future. This was done informally, without any formal structure such as a discussion group. Young people chose to engage with the issue around the pool table.

As workers we have a choice. We can either use this same setting for future conversation on this issue, or try to create a new one.

In our haste to develop areas of work we can often structure and formalise issues in ways that discourage participation. If the pool table setting is suitable for young people to engage with the issue of alcohol use, then why would we want to change it? But we could try and set up a new environment and structure a formal session around alcohol use if we wanted to. The difficulty here is that by gently exploring alcohol issues around the pool table, we are engaging with young people on their terms. If the topic of conversation changes to something else then so would we. By moving the issue to a structured session we could kill the interest and prevent any further work. This would also prevent other topics coming up, as the focus and content of a structured session would already be determined.

As informal educators we also have to consider who is defining this need for formal sessions. Who really wants these sessions, the worker or the young people? If we were to decide to plan and develop future sessions on alcohol awareness, who would do it, we or the young people? Also, what would young people learn from this? Would they learn about alcohol, or would they learn to keep quiet when we were around in case we tried to set up another session on another issue? The possibilities for all types of learning need to be considered.

Thinking critically about our approach and how we can successfully engage with the opportunities that are presented to us is an important and skilled aspect of our roles as educators. Rather than paying attention to the actual product of alcohol awareness, as a 'thing' that participants might 'hold' after a session, informal educators need to explore and think about the process of learning as a journey. For example, if the worker set up a session on alcohol awareness that took three hours, what would happen after the three hours were up? If the same worker kept the issue around the pool table, it could probably be raised and explored many times.

Education as process and product

At this point we can introduce two new concepts. We have mentioned them above, but have not explored them. These are *process* and *product.*

We can see these two concepts in action in Example 3 (p. 126). Working with young people around the pool table pays attention to the process of education. The worker is not trying to determine the topic for discussion, and does not try to predict the outcomes. By 'going with the flow' we can create a wider choice of topics. This we would call a process way of working, as there is no specific end in sight.

If the worker set up a session to explore alcohol use, then this would pay more attention to product. Here we would determine the topic for discussion, and try and predict the outcomes.

This limits the scope for other issues to be explored, as the session is specific. By predicting the outcomes we are making choices about what experiences and learning will be recognised.

This we would call a product way of working, as there are specific expected outcomes and a possible end in sight.

We will now move on to another example while keeping these two concepts in mind. What we will find is that we move *between* process and product when developing work, and that they are very closely linked. The next example develops the question of opportunity further and explores how we can move our work on over a longer period of time.

Example 4: the music session

As workers we have probably highlighted various needs to be met at our places of work. From a simple chat about music and what young people like to listen to, we may find that some would like to learn to play instruments. It is doubtful at this point that we would rush out and buy guitars and keyboards in order to meet this need, as this may not be what they want after all. What we might do is try to find out a little more, and ask other young people what they think of this idea.

Here we are starting to foster the idea and use it to create environments for other young people to express their thoughts. These first steps are the beginning of a process. As in the last example, young people have engaged in a topic and expressed an interest. This means we have more scope for development. The shape of this piece of work will now begin to change from something that was quite unpredictable to something that is beginning to take a particular form.

By this we mean that a conversation, such as the one around the pool table, can twist and turn and change from one topic to another quite quickly. But having a focus brings us back to a particular task, and therefore structures the content of what we are engaged in.

Already we can see that process and product have become linked. Young people are becoming involved in the process of learning how to meet their needs, but are also learning how to work towards specific goals.

Once we have explored the idea further and decided with the young people that a music session could be developed, we can start to explore other areas. Together with the young people, we could think about:

- the environment: where and when will the sessions take place?
- what musical instruments do the young people want?
- the cost, and whether we should raise funds.
- how will the young people learn the instruments?
- what else apart from the instruments will they be learning?
- group dynamics: different roles people might play.
- how can we encourage participation, and learning from each other?

All these areas offer an opportunity to us as workers to encourage young people to get involved and participate. This will not only develop our relationships, but will also enable both young people and workers to learn.

So far we know that it is possible to set up a session, but we now need to know specifically what instruments are needed. We would probably already have an idea by now, as young people would have expressed some preference, but involving young people as much as possible encourages ownership. The music session becomes part of something that the young people are creating, and so holds stronger meaning for them and the youth project.

If we think about the various parts of planning the session, there are many roles that young people could get involved with. For example, young people could:

- organise when the session would take place. This would involve negotiation, working out times, adding the times to the centre's programme, advertising the sessions and so forth.
- work out the budget. Here young people would need to work out what money was available and ring round to find the prices of the musical instruments they wanted. This could involve visits to music shops and so on.
- choose learning materials. Young people would need to decide together what books or tuition guides might be useful.

These are just a few of the learning opportunities that we might identify from this example. As informal educators we need to pay attention to the learning processes involved. Here, these include decision making, democracy, conversation, and thinking. What we can see here is that when we refer to learning opportunities we are also referring to the educational process. When we develop work we are concerned with what people think, therefore the process of learning, experiencing, and thinking new thoughts are important characteristics of our work.

> **Q7:** Think about a previous session at work. Using the music group example as a guide, what balance of process and product can you identify within what was going on? Were there activities where you could (or could not) distinguish the two?
>
> If you look back over some of the other examples in this chapter you will also be able to identify process and product. Take another look at our *EastEnders* and cinema trip examples, and see what you come up with.

If we briefly look at a familiar activity we can more easily identify process and product. For example, the rules of football are a product. We can hold them and use them to determine the game, but it is how we reach that point that interests us. Learning the rules has an end in sight, but it is up to us how creative we are before we reach it. In between learning the rules and knowing the rules we go through a process.

Also, we cannot determine how a team will play together. Organising, team work, group dynamics, all provide us with opportunities to continue this learning process. Although the rules may not change, the relationships and the development of the team will.

If we take our music session example, we can see that the worker could purchase instruments, set up the environment, and instruct young people how to play. This will 'do the job' in product terms, but it pays little attention to process, and to learning opportunities.

Approaching the work in this way does not invite young people to create the contents of the music session, and actively become part of and develop it. Rather, it invites young people to consume the contents of the session without much input.

Paying little attention to what people think does not stimulate thinking. The thoughts of others and how they feel are important aspects of our work. Our aim is centred around education, so unless we stimulate thinking, and this includes ourselves as well as young people, we cannot say that we are educators.

For instance, if as workers we look for learning opportunities, we will be interested in both young people learning instruments, and the various conversations that are going on in the room at the same time. Our difficulty here is what we choose to get involved with, as there can be many different things going on at once. Let us take it one step at a time, by looking at learning a musical instrument.

Learning an instrument has a clear aim, and involves learning certain skills and knowledge in order to continue. We can set goals and work towards achieving them. By doing this we are working with product in mind.

What is more difficult is working with the feelings, thoughts and attitudes that are woven into this process. This involves working with how young people see the world. Dealing with frustration when learning a new instrument and learning how to cope with new information means we sometimes need to support and encourage young people to stick with it. Once the learning process has begun, it will become easier to learn new information and deal with the experiences of playing an instrument.

This is one aspect of the session, but there are other questions to consider, such as how are young people engaging with the session, are certain young people dominating the group, do some young people need a little more support and encouragement to join in, and what does music mean to these young people? These topics give us more scope to work with.

Once the session is up and running, what next? Like our alcohol session, what do we do next to develop it? So far we have the music session as part of the programme in the youth project, and although the content is determined, it is open to change. This change allows us the freedom to explore new ground and develop the session further. Asking young people to reflect on the session so far and think about its future will enable us to work towards new goals, but there is a difficulty when we come to evaluate our work so far.

Evaluating how well young people have learnt to play musical instruments is relatively simple. We can look at where they started and measure their progress. This will give us a good indication of the skills and knowledge that have been learnt. This is the product from the session, and we can identify this learning quite easily and record it.

The difficulty comes when we try to evaluate the process of learning. How one particular young person dealt with frustration, and how participants experienced the music session are more difficult to measure. What young people have learnt apart from the instruments are areas that the informal educator develops an eye for. One way of developing this skill is through recording.

By keeping recordings we can start to build up a picture, and identify areas of work that we think are interesting and worth developing. For example, we can record how a session went and possibly identify new areas to explore. If at the end of a session we record that particular young people are working together on particular songs, then this could be developed. We might also note that one of the young people has become more interested in the session and spends more time learning to play. When the music sessions began, this same young person would walk in for five minutes, pick up a guitar, say it was too difficult to play, and walk out again. Here we can see a change, but we may not necessarily be able to evaluate it in terms of product, but more as a process.

These 'other things' that are going on within the music session are what we look for as informal educators. For this is just as important as learning the musical instrument itself.

Informal and formal education

What then is informal education, and how does it differ from formal education? Having got this far in the chapter, we can now explore this topic more clearly. As the music example shows, within a given session we may move between product and process ways of working, and we need to be able to evaluate both sorts of learning. We may associate formal education with particular settings, such as schools or colleges, and with a way of learning that emphasises product – learning an instrument, or the multiplication table – rather than process, the way in which that learning takes place. But John Ellis (1990) suggests that, even in the settings we work in, our working styles can move from formal to informal within a session or in different sorts of work. He represents this as a diagram, on which our work may be closer to the informal end, at A, or the formal end at B, or somewhere in the middle:

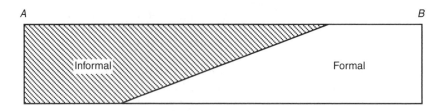

Figure 2.1

If we use our music session example and compare two different situations, we can see how the diagram works. Firstly, if young people are engaged in learning how to play the various instruments, then this would mean our session has moved towards B. Although we would probably not call ourselves teachers when showing young people how to play music, we are undoubtedly instructing in some way or another. While young people are engaged with learning chords, notes, rhythms and songs the session is more formal than informal.

But if the young people stop playing and begin to talk about the music they like, or any other topic, then the session will become more informal than formal. This move from B to A and back again can either happen quite quickly or quite slowly, depending on what we are engaged in at the time. So for us as educators, this learning process is best seen as a continuum. At times we are both informal and formal educators, and need to pay attention to both process and product.

> **Q8:** Think about a piece of work you are involved in at the moment. If you think about where this work is taking place and what type of work it is, where would you position it on the diagram above? When you have done this, can you explain why you have placed it there?
>
> Do you agree with Ellis that your work involves a mixture of product and process, formal and informal?

To end this chapter we can conclude that the artist will be left with pieces on the floor, but there will also be a sculpture. Within this sculpture there are the characteristics of the informal educator. As workers, we engage with people and foster learning. We aim to work with people and what they bring to the project. Our emphasis on relationships enables us to learn about the people we work with. We favour process over product, and move between informal and formal settings. We are concerned with the conversations that are going on just as much as we are with the activities: indeed at times we are more interested in the conversation. The use of conversation and talking is important if we are to work successfully with people.

So our reply next time young people want to go on a cinema trip might be, 'OK, what do we need to think about doing first?' While the young people are working out their response, we will be thinking about ours, and developing the conversation. This is informal education.

Further reading

Jeffs, T. and Smith, M. (1996) *Informal Education – Conversation, Democracy and Learning*. Derby: Education Now. This is a good introduction to informal education, and takes some of the ideas in this chapter further.

Rogers, C. and Freiberg, H.J. (1994) *Freedom to Learn*, 3rd edn. New York: Macmillan College Publishing Company. I think that this book offers a good framework for exploring person-centred learning in formal settings. These ideas can also be transferred to informal settings, giving the reader a good perspective on the process over product debate.

Smith, M. (1980) *Creators Not Consumers*. Leicester: NAYA Publications. This booklet also highlights the importance of thinking about our work, using the example of an ice-skating trip to explore ideas.

Those of you that want a break from reading might like to watch:

Dead Poets' Society (1989) Touchstone Pictures. Directed by Peter Weir; written by Tom Schulman. This follows a group of students through their time at college, with Robin Williams as their inspirational teacher.

References

Ellis, J. (1990) 'Informal Education – a Christian perspective' in T. Jeffs and M. Smith (eds) *Using Informal Education*. Buckingham: Open University Press.

Frost, R. (1930, 1950) 'The Road Not Taken' from *Complete Poems of Robert Frost*, reprinted with permission in F.O. Matthiessen (ed.) *The Oxford Book of American Verse*. New York: Oxford University Press.

Jeffs, T. and Smith, M. (1996) *Informal Education – Conversation, Democracy and Learning*. Derby: Education Now.

3 First lessons

Historical perspectives on informal education

Tony Jeffs

> Education at its best is always informal, largely unstructured and even an unsystematic process, characterised by spontaneity and closely related to the living experience and interests of both teacher and taught ... Education, set aside in formal classrooms and too exclusively directed to examination success, loses its vital connection with life and degenerates into a dull spiritless routine.
>
> (Howie 1988: 9)

Prologue

No adequate history of informal education exists. This means that, if I am to introduce you to your heritage as informal educators, we will need to build on the histories of the adjacent areas of practice that make up informal education: notably youth work, adult education and play work. The progressive school movement, from Pestalozzi and Fourier onwards (Zeldin 1969), has also experimented with informal alternatives to the classroom-bound approaches of the formal sector. This short chapter obviously cannot provide a comprehensive history of informal education. Rather, it seeks to offer some insight into early developments and how, throughout a long history, the balance between formal and informal approaches has shifted.

Why consider informal education from a historical perspective? First, I hope that this account, brief as it is, will help you to see the similarities and differences between earlier work and your own. (I have included questions to encourage you to make some links.) Second, if you are able to take a critical approach to the history of your discipline, it will, I hope, encourage you to develop an equally critical approach to contemporary practice. Informal education, then and now, is not all heroic and wonderful, as I hope this chapter will demonstrate.

Finding a starting point

Practitioners often answer the question 'what is informal education?' by saying how it differs from formal education. They compare their way of working with those of schoolteachers and lecturers; contrast the settings where they operate with schools, colleges and classrooms; and highlight differences such as the absence of exams, testing and curriculum. This response is understandable, for, whereas many people claim to be unfamiliar with informal education, everyone knows about schooling, which has been compulsory for five generations. Is it not logical to begin a dialogue on the nature of informal education from a shared point of understanding?

It is a seductive approach, and in this chapter I too will sometimes be contrasting formal and informal approaches. But this encourages us to focus attention on what are often superficial differences, rather than on a shared responsibility to promote learning. Educators, whatever sector they work in, have overlapping roles, both in their own eyes and those of the wider society. These include preparing people for employment; making good citizens and responsible adults; transmitting the dominant ethics and morality; and introducing cultural, spiritual and aesthetic values (see for example Hirst 1973, 1974; Carr 1995; White 1997).

This list of educational aims may appear unproblematic until we seek to formulate policy and discover that these words mean different things to different people. For example, research found that 86 per cent of Americans want schools to teach courses on values and morality. However, consensus quickly evaporated when the sample was asked to say what values and what morality. Predictably, the 'popular' decision of the government to encourage schools to teach morality produced a maelstrom of conflict in school districts across the United States (Melville 1995).

What about the expectation that educators should prepare young people for employment? Who would possibly disagree with that as an aim? However, a moment's reflection tells us that even employers lack a collective notion of what they want. A few seek bright, well-educated applicants capable of thinking for themselves. Far more, although too cowardly to admit it, want half-educated servile candidates for the 'McJobs' defined by Coupland as 'a low-pay, low-prestige, low-dignity, low-benefit, no-future job in the service sector. Frequently considered a satisfying career choice by people who have never held one' (1991: 6). This circle cannot be squared.

Q1: Should educators, including yourself, collude with an education system that prepares young people for work that you would be unwilling to perform?

Corporations are also now aggressively moving to colonise education: to get 'corporate-sponsored teaching materials into the classroom…and indoctrinate young minds in their beliefs and values' (Korten 1995: 155; see also Apple 1993). For example, sponsorship and marketing strategies use young people to pressurise their parents into buying certain products. Companies such as News International and Tesco are already exploiting British schools for commercial ends, getting educators to collect tokens and promote products in return for 'free' books or equipment (Hoggart 1995; Jeffs 1999a, 2001).

As might be expected, the situation is worse in America, but not for long, one suspects. There, the National Education Association has already condemned Nike, which has flooded schools with a 'faux teaching aid, the "Air to Earth lesson kit"', for its 'despicable use of classroom time'; while the American Consumer Association accused the company of 'the warping of education' (Klein 2001: 93). Students have been suspended for wearing a Pepsi T-shirt in a school where Coca-Cola was sponsoring events, and for refusing to watch the adverts shown on Channel One, which is beamed daily into thousands of classrooms during compulsory lessons (*Ibid.*). Basically these and other companies are subverting the educational process, seeking to turn education into indoctrination, citizens into tame consumers. Such ends are clearly irreconcilable with what committed educationalists or informed, enlightened parents desire.

Informal educators are not immune from these pressures (Jeffs and Smith 1999a). Undoubtedly, they will have to learn to resist sponsorship that curtails conversation or obliges them to prioritise their sponsor's interests above those of their clients. Informal educators also have an implicit duty to challenge and question what Klein (2001) dubs the 'branding of education': to offer those they work with the opportunity to discuss and question the commercialisation of education and the dubious practices by sponsors that young people and their parents encounter in schools and universities. Monbiot (2000) argues that the great struggle that will come to dominate the 21st century will be between the people and the corporations. Indeed, he and others have come to believe that the very survival of democracy may depend on our ability as citizens to wrest control from multi-national corporations and trade organisations. It will not be a conflict that informal educators will be able to ignore. Nor should they, for their capacity to practise requires a democratic environment and ethos; once that is surrendered, they will become actors without an audience. Some informal educators have always recognised this reality.

As these examples indicate, even in an imperfect democracy, education inevitably creates friction regarding aims, priorities and control. We should not deplore this, but rather welcome this debate, because it confirms that some educators are thinking about their roles, not simply doing what they are told. As an educator, you, in the informal sector, have the same responsibility as colleagues in formal institutions to reflect on the purpose of your work. You must also expect that in asking such questions you will annoy employers and associates.

Such confrontations over aims, objectives and methods have been a constant feature of our work and will hopefully remain so. The history of informal education is littered with examples of rows, splits and conflict over aims and purpose. Organisations such as the Boy Scouts have spawned numerous breakaway groups since their formation. Similarly, histories of community groups and projects tell us of growth, and sometimes decline, following disputes over matters of principle (Robins 1992).

The early history of informal education

Informal education probably pre-dates the formal variety. Philosophers, teachers and clerics have traditionally gone to places where people gathered in order to engage them in dialogue and conversation. It is a matter of conjecture as to the importance and frequency of such encounters. However, we know that those who hoped to bring about change or secure influence sought an audience on the street or in the square. This was often the only way to reach adults, especially those denied a school education. It was a hit and miss approach. Practitioners not only had to cope with the vagaries of the climate; they had to be entertaining, at the risk of being superficial, and handle a fickle crowd uninterested in their message.

Given the difficulties inherent in delivering informal education, it is easy to see why the formal variety has been around for so long. Schools existed in

Ancient Greece and Imperial Rome. Although Athenians left education to private enterprise, by the fourth century BC the state had formulated regulations regarding hours of opening, proper moral supervision and the age of pupils, requiring 'the exclusion of adults from the schools' (Castle 1961: 44). But even in this early phase, the shortcomings of schools were evident to sagacious observers. As a youthful, but disgruntled, Seneca complained, they tended to offer 'learning for school not life' (quoted in Howie 1988: 9).

Formal schooling in Britain, until the late nineteenth century, was a minority experience, just as it was in Ancient Greece or Rome. Mega-rich parents usually opted for private tutors or governesses until, in the case of young men, their progeny were deemed ready for university. Merely prosperous families sent male, and sometimes female, offspring to boarding or day schools. But few parents could afford the fees, or the loss of income from child labour, that schooling entailed. Those who valued education either instructed their children at home or entrusted the responsibility to others by sending them away to become apprentices or servants. In their master's house, young people acquired domestic skills or a trade, along with a wider perspective, through instruction and observation. Within this system of education – which by the sixteenth and seventeenth centuries generally lasted a decade or more – boundaries between the formal and informal were hard to distinguish. For example, apprentices might learn their catechism or letters in class from a priest, deportment and proper behaviour within their master's home, and their craft in the workshop. Depending on the time or task, their 'teacher' could be their master, mistress or co-worker. As Ben-Amos notes, the 'informal nature of such learning makes it difficult to gauge its precise dimensions' (1994: 147). Guilds exercised some control over who was judged qualified to practice a trade or profession, but overall the system was unregulated, suited to small communities where word of mouth and personal relationships protected consumers from charlatans.

By the mid seventeenth century, the first modern examples of centres established to cater for informal education had emerged. Coffee-houses, of which over 2,000 existed in London and the provinces by 1700, operated according to strict rules which ensured orderly and democratic behaviour. Irrespective of rank or wealth, all paying their penny were admitted and entitled to the first vacant seat on condition that they engaged in civil conversation and participated in any discussion already underway. Different coffee-houses quickly acquired a reputation for specialising in topics such as politics, religion, science or literature (Kelly 1970). Clearly there is a direct line between these informal meeting places and contemporary cyber- and youth cafés. Simultaneously, an assortment of other informal education agencies – debating societies, museums, music clubs and circulating libraries – all emerged. Besides offering all ages instruction in literacy and religion, Sunday schools, founded in 1780 by Robert Raikes, provided social activities, shelter and welfare support. Their success can be measured by the fact that a decade later the inter-denominational Sunday School Society claimed 250,000 members.

Initially Sunday schools and similar bodies catered for all ages. However, in 1811 Thomas Charles of Bala in Merionethshire established what was possibly the first purely adult education centre, because of the 'aversion I found in the adults to associate with the children' (quoted in Pole 1814: 3). This began the convention that alongside adult provision resides something designated youth work. Differences between them in relation to practice are often difficult to discern. For example, Glasby's account (1999) of the Temperance Pub established by Birmingham Settlement prior to 1912, and of the men's clubs founded by churches, settlements and missions in the nineteenth century, indicates that in terms of activities, purpose and content little distinguished the two. Nevertheless, the division opened up by Charles nearly two centuries ago remains to bedevil debates regarding informal education. We still talk of youth work and adult education as distinct activities, even though youth workers often work with those over 25 and adult educators cater for many under that age. This would perhaps not matter so much if it did not encourage us to think in terms of different ways of working, labelling the youth work process and andragogy, even when our activities are in no way age specific.

> **Q2:** In what ways do adults learn differently from young people, or require different methods, in your experience? Is the historic division between youth work and adult education still worth preserving?

The rise of mass schooling

As British trade, population and urban centres expanded in the nineteenth century, so pressures for regulation and homogeneity grew. Literacy changed from an optional extra to an essential requirement for those wishing to escape the most menial employment. But how could mass literacy be delivered? The solution to most observers was self-evident. You adapted the highly successful factory system, that used mass production techniques to manufacture an increasing volume of goods at ever lower cost. So the 'factory school' emerged, to 'manufacture' workers and replace the 'workshop' variant of teachers instructing small groups in their own homes. Factory schools possessed another great advantage. They enabled small numbers of adults to supervise large numbers of young people at minimal cost, releasing parents for employment while preventing children from 'running wild'.

By the 1840s, experts in Britain and elsewhere had seemingly solved the core problems of containing, controlling and processing enormous numbers of working-class pupils at minimal unit cost. During the first half of the nineteenth century, schools acquired most of the attributes that continue to distinguish them: the gap in status between adult teacher and child pupil, classrooms, desks, terms, punishment rituals, uniforms, bells, whole class teaching, externally imposed curricula, blackboards, prefects, timetables, prizegivings and reports. Architecturally too they developed familiar features: classroom doors with windows to enable headteachers to monitor pupil (and teacher) behaviour; playgrounds with railings; and headteachers' offices placed next to the entrance. It is a salutary experience to visit one of the 'living museum' heritage schools with a school party: first, because after adjusting to changes in decor and dress, the impression is of familiarity. Second, it is alarming to observe how easily contemporary pupils take on the roles of their Victorian counterparts. Instinctively they know what is required to play a part which differs little from their daily experience.

Although the modern formal system was established in embryonic form by

1800, it took time to move from provision for the few to mass schooling. Apart from the issue of funding, which was a consistent political disincentive, apprehension regarding the rise of mass formal education was widespread. Poor parents often resented the loss of their children's labour, which could mean the difference between survival and 'going under'. Indeed, so unpopular were schools in poor districts that it was often essential to protect them from damage during construction and afterwards (Robson 1874). Wealthy reactionaries also resented the cost and feared the social repercussions of mass education. As one argued:

> However specious in theory the project might be of giving education to the labouring classes of the poor, it would, in effect, be found prejudicial to their morals and happiness, it would teach them to despise their lot in life, instead of making them good servants in agriculture, and other laborious employments to which their rank in society had destined them; instead of teaching them subordination, it would render them factious and refractory,... it would enable them to read seditious pamphlets, vicious books, and publications against Christianity; it would render them insolent to their superiors; and in a few years ... legislators would find it necessary to direct the strong arm of power against them.
>
> (Giddy, quoted in Donald 1992: 20)

Such views obliged those advocating public education to prove that it would lead not to disaffection but good order, efficiency and social harmony. They did this by accepting a narrow minimalist curriculum and brutal discipline. State funding was provided on condition that schools accepted an oppressive system of inspection and management, designed to break the spirit of the teaching profession, who, as much as the pupils, were to be taught their place. By 1900 it was generally accepted that schools had met these aims. As Helen Bosanquet, a community worker and liberal advocate of welfare reform, reported,

> the greatest influence in our parish outside the home is beyond doubt the school ... For good or for evil the rising generation is there receiving instruction and discipline ... in our schools the children are being firmly and gently brought into line.
>
> (Bosanquet 1908: 50)

Not everybody was happy with a system that granted the state and Church of England a virtual monopoly of education. So although mass schooling achieved a growing dominance over informal education during the nineteenth century, this was never complete or unchallenged.

Informal education in an age of mass schooling and welfare

Informal education survived alongside the growing formal and welfare sectors for a number of reasons. Political and religious dissenters, excluded from the state schools, had few alternatives open to them. From the beginning, political libertarians, like Godwin, profoundly distrusted the motives of those advocating a national system of education – or perhaps any education system:

All education is despotism. It is perhaps impossible for the young to be conducted without introducing in many cases the tyranny of implicit obedience. Go there; do that; read; write; rise; lie down; will perhaps for ever be the language addressed to youth by age.

(1783: 23–4)

Political radicals and libertarian liberals such as John Stuart Mill (1968) feared that state control would impose a deadening conformity, while religious dissenters suspected an Anglican plot to enforce dominance. Both groups fought to keep and extend the informal educational provision that was available. Secular and religious Sunday schools, meeting halls, circulating libraries and clubs were viewed as essential if democracy was to be extended and religious pluralism preserved. Chartist reading rooms, Clarion Cycling Clubs, Socialist Sunday schools, Kibbo Kift (a 1920s scouting-type organisation linked to the Social Credit Movement), the Plebs League (an autonomous working-class adult-education group) and the Woodcraft Folk are all examples of attempts to promote alternative ideas, using informal education activities, that emerged during the late nineteenth and early twentieth centuries. The government, although willing from the 1890s on to allow local authorities to support religious and non-denominational adult education and youth and community work, steadfastly refused to fund even the most mildly radical groups. Indeed it even encouraged the development of the Workers' Educational Association (WEA) and LEA adult education in order to undermine these efforts.

> **Q3:** State funding is, of course, paid by the taxpayer. Should taxpayers be obliged to fund educational programmes that they find unacceptable?

Religious groups similarly established organisations designed to reach out and secure new recruits. Radicals and dissenters, like Felix Holt, the protagonist of George Eliot's novel of the same name, went into the streets and taverns to engage in conversation in order to secure converts (Jeffs and Smith 1999). Clubs for men and women were widespread, as well as Sunday schools and, from the 1880s, uniformed organisations for young people. Apart from the cadet forces established by schools and community groups, these were almost always linked to a specific religious group and viewed as an effective way of securing the allegiance of young people to a particular faith. Therefore the non-conformist Boys' Brigade (founded by William Smith in 1883) was rapidly copied, with the establishment, for example, of the Church Lads' Brigade, the Girls' Brigade and the Jewish Lads' Brigade. The membership of these organisations declined between the wars and fell rapidly after 1945. Some have vanished, but a few have managed to recover lost ground, usually by recruiting younger members (Jeffs 1979). Arguably they have been replaced by far more interventionist evangelical approaches, designed to convert young people (Pugh 1999).

As well as providing support for marginalised groups and ideas, informal education in the nineteenth and early twentieth centuries sought to meet identified needs. Initially, in a period of minimal welfare and educational provision, it was viewed as an efficient and cheap way of delivering certain services. Reformers argued that home visiting, street work and clubs could raise educational standards; encourage attention to health-related matters such as cleanliness, exercise and diet; help young people transfer successfully from school to work; and neutralise the negative influences of slum homes and neighbourhoods. Alongside friendship, support and informal education, practitioners often distributed essentials such as clothing, vocational training, shelter and food. They perceived themselves as having a dual responsibility: to respond to needs and to highlight the plight of those they served. To achieve the second aim, they often tried to involve the wealthy and privileged in their work, hoping that these men and women would, like Emmeline Pethick, come to see those they worked with 'as individuals' (1898: 101) deserving social justice and respect, rather than as actual or potential enemies.

Gradually working-class pressure and liberal sensibilities produced a growing commitment to state welfare. The volume of state funding grew slowly from the end of the nineteenth century, but as the value of informal education with certain groups was increasingly recognised, state subsidies multiplied, along with inspection and monitoring (Jeffs and Smith 1999a).

However, as such provision expanded, so informal education often became regarded as mere 'icing on the cake', a means of reaching those elements within society whose attitudes and behaviour made them difficult to work with. By the 1950s, many social democrats and reforming Tories were questioning the continuing need for even this minimalist role. The requirement for such providers as the youth service, settlements and non-vocational adult education was seriously scrutinised during this period (Jeffs 1979; Davies 1999; Gilchrist and Jeffs 2000). However, informal education survived and within a decade was expanding. This was largely because many – not least those who recently had argued that poverty, inequality and class were no longer substantive issues – became convinced that prosperity and escalating leisure now threatened good order and social progress. Teenagers with too much money in their pockets seemed as big a threat as those with too little had been (see HMSO 1960: Jeffs 1979).

This brings us to a third, closely linked, factor influencing the investment of resources in informal education – social control (Jeffs and Smith 1994, 1996; Jeffs and Banks 1999). Competing and complementary pressures, aims and dogmas have always fashioned and sustained informal education. These contradictions are echoed in contemporary conflicts between practitioners and sponsors. Frequently these tensions can be seen in individual workers. Hannah More, often depicted as the first modern youth worker, is one example. An innovative informal educator, she developed, ran and funded clubs, welfare programmes and outreach work despite deep-seated opposition from landowners, employers and churchmen: men who viewed such work as at best a waste of effort and at worst a support for insurrection. Yet More, who, like her opponents, unequivocally denounced the rights of men and women, nevertheless saw her work as essential if the old order was to be preserved. For, in a return to the doctrine of original sin, she viewed children and young people as a threat and danger which had to be countered, arguing:

> Is it not a fundamental error to consider children as innocent beings, whose little weaknesses may, perhaps, want some correction, rather than as beings who bring into the world a corrupt nature and evil dispositions, which it should be the great end of education to rectify?
>
> (More, quoted in Hendrick 1994: 24)

Fear of crime and the underclass, once personified by hooligans, then by Teddy Boys and today by single teenage mothers, has always provided a reason for intervention and given workers the opportunity to portray themselves in heroic terms. A century ago, a club worker complained that wherever he went, colleagues seemed to lay claim to working in the toughest and most destitute of neighbourhoods (Pilkington 1896). They may have been engaged in what Richard Wright more recently described as 'lying for justice' (quoted in Jencks 1994: 2): a dangerous practice which may secure resources, but does so at the expense of further stigmatising the already stigmatised. More often, however, this technique is cynically employed to enhance their own status as workers and wheedle funds from nervous politicians by exaggerating the danger posed by their clients (Jeffs and Smith 1999a).

The ebb and flow of social control agendas and moral panics always profoundly influences funding for informal education, along with the priorities and actions of workers. There is, it must be stressed, nothing inherently progressive or 'empowering' about a great deal of practice: much of which unthinkingly accepts 'problems' as defined by those in power and responds accordingly. This was true of Hannah More; shows in Maude Stanley's (1890) horror of over-population and early marriage; and appears in the vapid acceptance by contemporary workers of teenage parenthood and truancy as serious social problems, rather than, in many instances, as rational responses to an irrational world.

However, clients are always partially protected from the worst excesses of the social control agenda by the voluntary nature of the informal education relationship. If clients are not treated with respect, workers risk losing them; for this reason, they must listen to them and seek to respond to their needs.

The shifting balance

Since 1800, the informal sector has largely retreated before the formal. Sometimes ground has been surrendered willingly. After 1920, youth clubs abandoned most welfare work, because the social security system was providing a superior safety net for the destitute (Spence 2001). At other times, the retreat has occurred only after a struggle: for example, the lengthy rearguard action fought by autonomous adult education providers since 1945 to resist the dominance of government-funded agencies (McIlroy 1990).

In part, this shift is because informal education, as Stanley explained, often moves 'with the pace of the tortoise' (1890: 55). Rarely does it offer the illusion of instantaneous learning provided by tests and essays. In the two examples below, we see how the balance has shifted and why practitioners should be prepared to respond accordingly.

Prayer in schools

The first example relates to the inculcation of religious beliefs. In some countries, like the United States, the teaching of religion in state-funded schools is prohibited. Consequently those wishing to educate or indoctrinate young people regarding such matters must operate outside the state classroom. Some remove their children from the state system to ensure that they receive an 'education' which reduces their likelihood of encountering ideas that challenge parental prejudices. Many religious organisations recoil from such separatism, while others are ill-equipped to establish independent schools. Either way, all religious groups face two linked predicaments: how to provide young people with a spiritual education; and how to recruit members from the wider community. Often their solution is to provide social services and engage in informal education. Therefore in some countries, churches provide welfare services ranging from hospitals, residential homes and day centres to home visiting, outreach work and soup kitchens. Alongside this welfarist approach, informal education initiatives, especially for young people, are developed by religious groups. The hope is that, through clubs, community centres and street work, individuals unaware of their existence, or resistant to their message, can be converted through dialogue, example and imagery. Whatever the aim, informal education is usually viewed as a second-best alternative, undermined by its voluntary basis and open-ended nature. Hence the millions of dollars spent by the American Religious Right to get the Constitution amended to allow Christian worship and instruction onto the school timetable (Provenzo 1990; Alley 1994). If they succeed, the equilibrium between formal and informal provision in the United States will shift, much as it did in Ireland once persecution of Catholics eased in the nineteenth century and adherents could operate their own schools and colleges. This made redundant such informal educational initiatives as the 'hedge schools', which operated in fields and barns, providing rudimentary education for those unable or unwilling to attend schools run by a Protestant state (Dowling 1968).

> **Q4:** Should we teach Christianity (or other religions) in our schools? Should programmes seeking to convert people to a particular religion be funded from our taxes?

The legacy of New Lanark

The second example illustrates how a constantly shifting balance can tip in either direction. Robert Owen, when founding his New Lanark school in 1814, introduced parity between the arts of industry and humanity. Pupils were taught the 'three Rs' but also music, dance, painting, handicrafts, games and, through outdoor activities, a love of nature. Over 20,000 visitors came to admire the school, yet within a decade Owen was driven out. His refusal to allow religious indoctrination or corporal punishment was too radical for powerful opponents within the press, churches and industry, who persuaded his partners to oust him. With Owen and his colleagues ejected, the school came under the influence of one of the two religious bodies then managing the bulk of British schools. Corporal punishment and a minimalist curriculum, approximating to the Government's Code or national curriculum, imposed in 1870, were introduced.

Owen's defeat was significant because it obliterated the alternative model, allowing the Gradgrinds controlling British education to exclude the arts of humanity from state schools for almost a century. This obliged those who believed that everyone should have an opportunity to acquire an appreciation of culture, literature and the arts to work outside the mainstream. By the 1880s, a vibrant movement fostered an appreciation of the arts by informal means. Thousands, including figures such as Ruskin, Wilde and Morris, voluntarily taught classes; sponsored reading circles; supported cultural activities in clubs and centres; encouraged the establishment of libraries, theatre groups and galleries. Boys' and girls' clubs responded by providing cultural activities. Young people, starved of a richer diet than the thin gruel of the Board schools, attended clubs to paint, act or simply read in the quiet of the club library, just as they did to play games, go on holiday and visit the countryside, activities which Board schools were also forbidden to undertake.

Successful campaigning by community activists and reformers such as Samuel Barnett eventually led to reform of the school curriculum (Gilchrist 2000). Games and sports were introduced; trips and visits allowed; drama, art and music assigned timetable slots and new specialist staff often developed clubs and events to promote interest in their subjects. Final abandonment of the repellent Code in 1926 allowed schools to slowly transform themselves, until some became, as Henry Morris, founder of the Village Colleges, hoped they would, 'microcosms of life and places of liberal culture' (1924: 37). As this happened, so again informal education retreated. Youth clubs overwhelmingly became cultural deserts: purveyors of entertainment, cheap leisure activities and sport, with those workers not reduced to Redcoating becoming advice workers, counsellors and Agony Aunts. The Working Men's Clubs, their libraries sold, were reduced to misogynist drinking dens offering cheap and often nasty 'entertainment'. Education, in the fullest sense of the word, became something left to school and college-based 'professionals'.

This process was halted, then reversed, in the 1980s. First, industrial action and rigid adherence to contractual obligations by teachers led to schools offering fewer out-of-school activities. Second, growing cultural diversity meant that formal institutions felt unable to cater for the diverse needs of students. Third, an authoritarian conservative agenda forced feminists and radicals to turn to informal education as a space they could partially colonise for their own ends. Finally, the re-introduction of a narrow National Curriculum, linked to league tables ranking schools according to pupil performance, forced them to focus on what is measured.

Schools became once again essentially intellectually and culturally barren, dominated by the narrowest of economistic and productionist models of education. Any pretence that formal education is shaped by a philosophy of life became exposed as a sham, as schools became divorced 'from creation of all kinds, from play and love and tragedy, from religion and art and discourse' (Morris 1924: 38; see also Jeffs 1999). This re-drew the boundaries between the formal and informal, allowing the latter to reclaim what Brew (1956) termed 'avenues of approach' long abandoned. Suddenly arts programmes, as well as other domains overlooked by the schools such as sport and spirituality, flourished again in the informal sector. However, things rarely remain static for long and there are already indications that this relocation may be in the process of being reversed. As formal education units are driven to compete for students and encounter difficulty in motivating them, some have employed informal educators to work their corridors and canteens, to offer advice and support (Hazler 1998), run leisure activities, and co-ordinate out-of-school sporting and cultural activities.

The future, perhaps

Predicting the future equilibrium between the sectors is risky and probably foolish. As informal educators, you must constantly monitor changing patterns of need and be prepared to re-align your focus and priorities accordingly. For example, when a teacher admits (as one recently did to the author) that the Literacy Hour and SATs meant his pupils are no longer encouraged or given classtime to read 'whole books', it is clear that an opportunity for informal educators has opened up. We might create, for example, reading circles for young people similar to the growing number formed by adults, re-introduce libraries into clubs and community centres and look to creative writing as an alternative to outdoor activities for residentials.

As Personal Social Services and Probation become more directive and supervisory in their approaches and abandon those elements of their work which involved befriending and education, so once again informal educators must be prepared to engage with groups they long ago abandoned to these 'professionals'. Informal educators will need to show a willingness to collaborate with other welfare agencies, in particular potential allies who, like themselves, find their work and values threatened by a narrow funding-driven agenda and who are increasingly denied the opportunity to work creatively with individuals and groups.

Q5: What social, political and economic changes do you think will significantly alter the shape of informal education during the next decade?

It may seem as if informal educators are doomed to work on the fringes, obliged to fill the gaps and pick up the pieces, and in a sense this is true. We live in a highly centralised society in which democracy is narrowly circumscribed. The virtual destruction of local democracy and the dominance of a managerial ethos grants little space for individuals and groups to control their own destiny or shape policy. Whether in prisons, schools or communities, informal educators work largely with the powerless – either to manage and control them or to educate them. This has always tended to be the case and will remain so unless we fundamentally change the way in which institutions are run and decisions are made. In societies where participatory democracy is far more widespread, the opportunities for informal education to thrive and for informal educators to come in from the margins are far more substantial. This should not depress you, but rather strengthen your determination to extend democracy and oppose all attempts to curtail and restrict it, both in the micro context of your working environment and the macro world of civil society.

Conclusion

Within education, a tiny minority wield enormous power, not because they hold the purse-strings or manage staff, but through control of the curriculum. A handful of politicians and civil servants, supplemented by educators selected because they are 'biddable', define knowledge as either 'essential' or 'optional'. They cull the subjects, then place those spared in a hierarchy of importance, with English and maths always at the top. This ranking determines the timetable space allocated to each. The chosen subjects are then gutted to isolate what is 'worthwhile', 'testable' and 'important'. The rest, comprising the overwhelming bulk of human knowledge, is judged 'inessential', even trivial. Satraps such as these also decree, for example, which adult education programmes receive funding. Are they vocational (worthwhile) or non-vocational (unimportant)? An inevitable consequence of this process is that powerful institutions train us to view what is taught, tested and examined in schools as synonymous with worthwhile knowledge. This is why informal education networks have always been vital, because they can offer a route to really useful and liberatory knowledge. This potential means that when they acquire most influence, they run the greatest risk of being reined in and standardised by selective funding, centralised control, imposed curricula, assessments and inspection.

William Maclure, who, with Owen, was expelled from New Lanark and forced to emigrate to America, warned us that because 'knowledge is power in political societies' (1831: 5) it will always be unequally distributed. This, he argued, meant that 'Until the many are educated, they must continue to labour for the few' (ibid.: 561). Little has changed. The explosion in knowledge since Maclure reached that conclusion would, I imagine, not lead him to change his fundamental analysis. The formal sector still seeks to suppress the spontaneity of teacher and taught, to narrow the field of vision and focus on the manufacture of workers rather than the creation of rounded, autonomous, creative human beings. For that reason, if no other, we need a strong informal sector, able to offer an alternative experience: to expand, rather than narrow, the gaze. This applies as much today as it did two centuries ago when individuals like Raikes, More and Owen initially launched their programmes. Today, educators are still being pressured to produce compliant consumers and tame workers. We must still focus our attention on the educational needs of those we work with, not the outcomes desired by those we work for. Perhaps, if the history of informal education teaches us anything, it is that to achieve that goal is rarely easy.

There is a great deal of sanctimonious humbug about the inherently liberatory and radical nature of informal education. It is not, and never has been, axiomatically either. It can be, and sadly often is, as narrow, controlling and devoid of serious intellectual challenge as the worst examples of formal schooling. However, because it engages with learners through dialogue, it does have the capacity to allow individuals and groups to engage in a democratic discourse: to offer all the opportunity to identify the knowledge they value and to negotiate their own learning pathway. Therefore it always has the potential to serve as an alternative to a formal system which, as Carr notes, short-changes its students, skipping their education to ensure their market value (1995: 58). This means that it has always attracted to its ranks many of the most creative and challenging educators of each generation.

Our responsibility is to ensure that, in a period of growing professionalisation, centralisation, managerialism and corporate control over education, this tradition is sustained; that space is created for transformative intellectuals, not just managers and technicians. Such a goal may prove more onerous than we imagine, more difficult for us than for earlier generations. Let us hope such fears are misplaced.

Further reading

Among the books listed in the bibliography that follows are many texts which you will find helpful in following up an interest in the historical development of informal education. Here is a selection to get you started.

Davies, B. (1999) *From Voluntaryism to Welfare State: A History of the Youth Service in England 1939–1979.* Leicester: Youth Work Press.

Davies, B. (1999) *From Thatcherism to New Labour: A History of the Youth Service in England 1979–1999.* Leicester: Youth Work Press. These two volumes are a history of the post-war development of the Youth Service in Britain. Both are scholarly and accessible and provide a detailed insight into how the Youth Service, which has always had close connections with informal education, adapted to changes in the policy agenda.

Gilchrist, R., Jeffs, T. and Spence, J. (2001) *Essays on the History of Youth and Community Work.* Leicester: Youth Work Press. A collection of essays on individuals and projects who have influenced informal education practice during the last two centuries. In particular it contains a biographical essay on the life and work of Josephine Macalister Brew by Mark K. Smith.

Glasby, J. (1999) *Poverty and Opportunity: 100 years of the Birmingham Settlement.* Studley: Brewin Books. We do not have many histories as detailed as this of a community project engaged in informal education for over a century, so we should be grateful for one. It is an added bonus that it is well written and enjoyable to read.

Jeffs, T. (1999) *Henry Morris: Village Colleges, Community Education and the Ideal Order.* Nottingham: Education Now Books. I'm somewhat embarrassed to recommend a book of my own, but Henry Morris is a crucial figure whose contribution to both the theory and practice of informal education needs to be acknowledged and appreciated.

References

Alley, R.S. (1994) *School Prayer: The Court, the Congress, and the First Amendment.* Buffalo, New York: Prometheus Books.

Apple, M. (1993) *Official Knowledge: Democratic education in a conservative age.* London: Routledge.

Ben-Amos, I.K. (1994) *Adolescence and Youth in Early Modern England.* New Haven: Yale.

Bosanquet, H. (1908) *Rich and Poor.* London: Macmillan.

Brew, J.M. (1956) *Informal Education: Adventures and Reflections.* London: Faber.

Carr, W. (1995) *For Education: Towards Critical Educational Inquiry.* Buckingham: Open University Press.

Castle, E.B. (1961) *Ancient Education and Today.* Harmondsworth: Pelican.

Coupland, D. (1991) *Generation X: Tales for an Accelerated Culture.* New York: St Martin's Press.

Cullen, J. *et al.* (1999) *Informal Learning and Widening Participation.* London: Evaluation Development and Review Unit, Tavistock Institute.

Davies, B. (1999) *From Voluntaryism to Welfare State: A History of the Youth Service in England 1939–1979.* Leicester: Youth Work Press.

Donald, J. (1992) *Sentimental Education.* London: Verso.

Dowling, P.J. (1968) *The Hedge Schools of Ireland.* Cork: Mercier Press.

Gilchrist, R. (2000) 'Place of the arts in the settlement movement', in R. Gilchrist and T. Jeffs (eds) *Settlements, Social Change and Community Action: Making Good Neighbours.* London: Jessica Kingsley.

Gilchrist, R. and Jeffs, T. (2000) *Settlements, Social Change and Community Action: Making Good Neighbours.* London: Jessica Kingsley.

Glasby, J. (1999) *Poverty and Opportunity: 100 years of the Birmingham Settlement.* Studley: Brewin Books.

Godwin, W. (1783) *An Account of the Seminary That Will Be Opened on Monday the Fourth Day of August at Epsom in Surrey.* (Reprinted London: Gainsville 1966).

Hazler, R.J. (1998) *Helping in the Hallways: Advanced Strategies for Enhancing School Relationships.* Thousand Oaks, California: Corwin Press.

Hendrick, H. (1994) *Child Welfare: England 1872–1989.* London: Routledge.

HMSO (1960) *The Youth Service in England and Wales* (Albemarle Report). London: Stationary Office.

Hirst, P.H. (1973) 'Liberal education and the nature of knowledge', in R.S. Peters (ed.) *The Philosophy of Education.* London: OUP.

Hirst, P.H. (1974) *Knowledge and the Curriculum.* London: Routledge and Kegan Paul.

Hoggart, R. (1995) *The Way We Live Now.* London: Chatto and Windus.

Howie, G. (1988) *Aristotle On Education.* London: Collier Macmillan.

Jeffs, T. (1979) *Young People and the Youth Service.* London: Routledge and Kegan Paul.

Jeffs, T. (1999) *Henry Morris: Village Colleges, Community Education and the Ideal Order.* Nottingham: Education Now Books.

Jeffs, T. (1999a) 'Are you paying attention? Education and the media' in B. Franklin (ed.) *The Media and Social Policy.* London: Routledge.

Jeffs, T. (2001) 'Children's Rights and Education' in B. Franklin (ed.) *Children's Rights.* London: Routledge.

Jeffs, T. and Banks, S. (1999) 'Youth workers as controllers: issues of method and purpose', in S. Banks (ed.) *Ethical Issues in Youth Work.* London: Routledge.

Jeffs, T. and Smith, M.K. (1994) 'Young people, youth work and a new authoritarianism', *Youth and Policy* 46: 17–32.

Jeffs, T. and Smith, M.K. (1996) ' "Getting the dirtbags off the streets": Curfews and other solutions to juvenile crime', *Youth and Policy* 53: 1–14.

Jeffs, T. and Smith, M.K. (1999) *Informal Education: Conversation, Democracy and Learning.* Derby: Education Now.

Jeffs, T. and Smith, M.K. (1999a) 'Resourcing youth work: dirty hands and tainted money', in S. Banks (ed.) *Ethical Issues in Youth Work.* London: Routledge.

Jencks, C. (1994) *The Homeless.* Cambridge, MA: Harvard University Press.

Kelly, T. (1970) *A History of Adult Education in Great Britain.* Liverpool: Liverpool University Press.

Klein, N. (2001) *No Logo.* London: Flamingo.

Korten, D.C. (1995) *When Corporations Rule the World.* San Francisco: Berrett-Koehler.

McIlroy, J. (1990) 'The demise of the National Council of Labour Colleges', in B. Simon (ed.) *The Search for Enlightenment: The Working Class and Adult Education in the Twentieth Century.* London: Lawrence and Wishart.

Maclure, W. (1831) *Opinions on Various Subjects.* New Harmony: New Harmony Press.

Melville, K. (1995) *Contested Values: Tug-of-War in the School Yard.* New York: McGraw Hill.

Mill, J.S. (1968) *Auguste Comte and Positivism.* Ann Arbor: University of Michigan Press.

Monbiot, G. (2000) Captive State: The corporate takeover of Britain. London: Macmillan.

Morris, H. (1924) *The Village College.* Cambridge: Cambridge University Press.

Pethick, E. (1898) 'Working Girls' Clubs', in W. Reason (ed.) *University and Social Settlements.* London: Methuen.

Pilkington, E.M.S. (1896) 'An Eton playing field', in F. Booton (ed.) *Studies in Social Education.* Hove: Benfield Press.

Pole, T. (1814) *A History of the Origins and Progress of Adult Schools.* (Reprinted London: Woburn Press 1968).

Provenzo, E. (1990) *Religious Fundamentalism and American Education: The Battle for the Public Schools.* Albany: State University of New York Press.

Pugh, C. (1999) 'Christian youth work: evangelism or social action?' *Youth and Policy* 65.

Robins, D. (1992) *Tarnished Vision: Crime and Conflict in the Inner City.* London: OUP.

Robson, E.R. (1874) *School Architecture.* (Reprinted Victorian Library Leicester: Leicester University Press 1972).

Spence, J. (2001) 'The impact of the First World War on the development of youth work: the case of the Sunderland Waifs Rescue Agency and Street Vendors' Club', in R. Gilchrist, T. Jeffs and J. Spence (eds) *Essays on the History of Community and Youth Work.* Leicester: Youth Work Press.

Stanley, M. (1890) *Working Girls' Clubs.* London: Macmillan.

White, J. (1997) *Education and the End of Work.* London: Cassell.

Zeldin, D. (1969) *The Educational Ideas of Charles Fourier.* London: Frank Cass.

Part II
Working with

Introduction

Linda Deer Richardson

In Part II we consider the core values and key elements which underlie informal education as defined in the last section. One of these core values, as we said in the main introduction, is the idea that educators work *with* people, not *for* them or *on* them. What do we mean when we speak of 'working with'?

In 'Working with people as an informal educator', Mary Crosby defines what she sees as 'working with' and identifies the kinds of relationships that develop as a result and the capacities which informal educators need to develop in order to work with others effectively. Her emphasis is not on what educators do but on the thinking, values and attitudes from which those actions grow.

This 'internal work' is also the focus of Sarah Banks' 'Professional values in informal education work'. Building on earlier writing which considered ethics and values in social work and youth work, Banks identifies some significant values in relation to educational practice and considers areas where personal and professional values may conflict. The values of informal educators are not as easy to determine as those of established occupations such as social work or nursing, where professional bodies define the nature of the work, its requirements and underlying principles. Rather than depending on others to determine the standards of their practice, informal educators need to pay individual attention to the values which determine their work.

Confidentiality is a key value for many helping professions. In 'Developing professional practice' Mary Tyler uses 'what if' scenarios to explore the meaning of confidentiality and enable workers to apply the principles to their own practice. As her examples reveal, the important value of confidentiality can often conflict with other principles, such as the welfare of a client or legal obligations. There are no easy answers here.

Huw Blacker uses examples from youth work to draw out our understanding of a central feature of informal education: the process of 'Learning from experience'. As educators, we need to be aware of how we learn, or fail to learn, from the experiences we have, in order to help others learn in turn. This process has been described by theorists such as Dewey, Kolb and Boud; what is important is that educators should develop their own theories by reflecting on the experiences they themselves have. Once again, the process of informal education requires workers to think about and evaluate their own learning.

'Relationships and learning' are concepts which are fundamental to the question of 'working with'. Graeme Tiffany attempts to distinguish learning relationships from everyday uses of the word and to identify the qualities in such relationships which make them educative. He uses the idea of exchange to describe working relationships in a more analytical and objective way. Tiffany argues strongly for the importance of the relationship between learner and educator, including its affective aspects, in promoting learning. Conversely, negative relationships can weaken learning opportunities.

Alison Gilchrist uses her experience as a community educator and researcher to extend this discussion of relationships. 'Working with networks and organisations in the community' seeks to place work with individuals in a social, cultural and political context. She argues that informal education has a particular emphasis on working with those in society who are disadvantaged and marginalised, and on fostering participation and local democracy. The social context within which learning takes place, combined with particular values, give informal education a political dimension. Individual educators will differ in the extent to which they see their work as political or indeed share Gilchrist's collectivist values. But her argument that, in order to foster individual development, we need to be aware of the political and cultural pressures which influence our lives, is one which it is difficult to deny.

These six chapters approach the question of 'working with' from different angles and bring out different aspects of the relationship between learner and educator. Part I is concerned with *what* informal education is, and Part III with *how* it works in practice. Taken together, the chapters in this linking section describe what we might call the *why* of informal education: the attitudes and values that make it what it is.

4 Working with people as an informal educator

Mary Crosby

Informal educators* work in many different kinds of settings with individuals and groups who choose to engage with them. Their purpose is to work in ways which encourage people to use their experiences of everyday living as opportunities for learning about themselves and others (YMCA George Williams College *Handbook* 1998: 4).

But what precisely do we mean when we talk about 'working with' people? In this chapter I want to look at what I believe to be the nature of 'working with', the kind of relationships within which it can flourish, and what capacities informal educators need to develop within themselves in order to work with others effectively.

Often when we think about working with someone we focus on the external actions which the worker performs. Of course this is important. However, it is impossible to separate the actions of a worker from the thinking, attitudes and values which generate those actions (Carter, Jeffs and Smith 1995: 4). They are part of the same whole. It is the values, attitudes and thinking involved in 'working with' which I want to focus on; the processes in which workers need to engage within themselves, which we might call their 'internal work' (Whitaker 1989: 193).

Working with people means extending ourselves

Dewey regarded education as a way of 'emancipating and enlarging experience' (1933: 240). But how can experience be emancipated or 'set free'? How can it be enlarged? Surely experiences are something which simply happen *to* us? However, they can be thought about and understood. We can act *upon* our experiences rather than simply 'have them'. It is this process of drawing out meaning from experience, often through reflection and discussion with others, which extends and deepens that experience, freeing us to learn from it: 'meanings arise in the process of interaction between people...' (Bullough, Knowles and Crow 1991: 3).

If informal educators aim to encourage this process through their interactions, then clearly they must spend time learning about the experiences of those they work with and seeking to understanding the meaning these have for them. Informal educators will be unable to do this unless they can 'make room', as it were, in their minds to think about the world as it appears to those they work with. Making room for this kind of thinking entails workers

*(Note: the terms 'worker' and 'informal educator' are used interchangeably in this chapter)

recognising and managing their own opinions and feelings so that they do not get in the way.

Each person with whom they work has a unique set of perceptions and experiences but, too often, informal educators do not take the time to learn about these. It is important that they do so because: 'while ... others may attempt to impose their meanings on us, we ultimately define our own experience...' (Boud, Cohen and Walker 1993: 10).

Of course, we can never view other people in ways which are value free, objective or neutral because our perceptions will always be filtered through the many layers of our own experience. So a vital part of informal educators' 'internal work' is in seeking to recognise and reduce the effects of distortions in their perceptions of the other person. This entails submitting their perceptions to a continuous process of reflection, checking and analysis:

P was an outreach youth worker on a large, inner city local authority housing estate. He had identified some young men who tended to hang around a row of shops on the estate and was attracted to working with them, feeling he could understand them because of his own experience of growing up on a similar housing estate. In thinking further about this, P reminded himself that he was in danger of making assumptions about the young men because of his own experiences. 'I had to be aware of this – that even if my experiences might be similar to those of the young men, they were not the same. I needed to spend time finding out from them how they thought and felt about their lives rather than assuming I already knew.'

Peck (1990) has called this process of working to appreciate the experiences of others 'extending ourselves' because it entails pushing out the limits of our thinking and feeling, assumptions and prejudices so that we can take in the perceptions and experiences of the other person. It involves deliberately setting out to do so out of a commitment to those we work with.

This means that working with others also means working with *ourselves* in this process of self-extension. Without this we will not be 'big enough' to work with others in any meaningful way because our own desires, beliefs, prejudices, assumptions and needs will cloud our view of them and limit our capacity to appreciate their world.

Implicit in this approach to working with people is an attitude of respect which does not depend upon how the worker feels about them or whether she or he agrees with the way they see things. Developing this attitude of respect requires workers to become increasingly self-aware, open to change, willing to question and challenge themselves: in other words to engage in 'a constant process of self-education' (Schön 1983: 299).

J was working with S, a young woman who attended the 'drop in' project with a group of her friends. S and some of her friends were involved in prostitution and the workers at the project had tried to persuade them to join in various programmes aimed at changing their lifestyle. The behaviour of S and her friends was at odds with J's own beliefs and values. However J realised that she had little understanding or appreciation of how they saw and felt about themselves and their situation and that it was important for her to learn about this from S and her friends. So instead of approaching the work with a pre-set agenda for the young women, as other staff had done, J spent time with them: 'I engaged in their conversations about their views and concerns.' This enabled J both to build a working relationship with the young women and begin to understand how they saw themselves and their lives. 'I found that my personal values were challenged and I had to work really hard to keep my mind open and to prevent my feelings from taking over. But, despite this, I continued to work with them on the issues they raised and the feelings they expressed.' Through these conversations J began to appreciate how the young women's common experiences enabled them to understand and accept each other. The friendship group functioned as a kind of extended family through which they supported, advised and set their own moral guidelines for each other. This was valued by the young women who did not receive this kind of acceptance and support elsewhere. A change of lifestyle for any of them carried with it the risk of isolation from this important resource. 'The young women were aware that I was concerned for their health, safety and well-being; we discussed this at length in the group. I may not like what they do, but I have grown to respect them, and I can now understand their situation and what is important to them. Hopefully, my continuing work with them can grow out of this.'

We can see from this example how J's commitment to 'extending herself' made it possible for her to work *with* these young women as opposed to working *on* them as some of her colleagues had done. J's internal work of managing her own values and feelings meant that she was not so much looking *at* the young women 'but looking *with* them at what they are seeking to communicate' (Jeffs and Smith 1996: 19).

The work of attention

Fundamental to this process of extending ourselves in order to work with others is what Peck calls 'the work of attention'. He regards attention as work because it is an act of will, of 'work against the inertia of our own minds' (1990: 128). It may be much easier and more comfortable for us not to really attend to those we work with; to stay with our own preconceptions and agendas; to imagine that we already know what they need.

The work of attention demands self–discipline and constant practice but it underpins all other aspects of working with people. It includes, as demonstrated in the example of J, observing, thinking, listening, exploring, in an effort to appreciate the other person's perceptions and experiences: what Erikson has called 'their universe of one' (Erikson, in Lerner 1958: 72).

All this is hard work so it is not surprising that many of us tend to avoid it. We may, for example, regard ourselves as good listeners, but in reality we often listen selectively with a pre-set agenda in mind, wondering as we listen how we can re-direct the conversation in ways more satisfactory to us.

This is not to say that workers should never express a view of their own, disagree or challenge the other person's perceptions or behaviour. But it does mean that, when they do so, it grows out of an appreciation of the other person's world.

Of course, informal educators engage in all kinds of activities with people and this may not always involve sitting down having long conversations with them. Often their contact with people may be quite fragmented. Nevertheless it is always important that they engage in the work of attention; noticing what people say about themselves and how they say it; how they interact with the worker and with others; how others (including the worker) respond to them. At the same time workers need also to be paying attention to themselves, working 'internally' to recognise the impact of their own feelings, attitudes and agendas.

M was in contact with a group of young men who attended the youth project in which she worked. She was trying to get them interested in some activities at the project which she felt would be useful to them. She was frustrated that the group did not take up her suggestions and she felt 'they are just not interested in anything'. Their main interest was in playing football together but M had not thought about this in her efforts to work with them. Thinking this through in supervision, M realised how little she knew about the young men or appreciated what their experiences, interests and priorities were. 'I realised that I was always coming up with my own agenda for them and not actually taking time to find our theirs. I need to spend more time doing their normal activities with them, trying to understand them better.'

In order to reach this conclusion and begin to act differently toward the young men, M first had to understand something about herself. She understood that she had been acting as though she already knew what the young men needed. She realised that perhaps this was more about what *she* needed in order to feel that she was achieving something. Instead of seeking to accompany (Green and Christian 1998) the young men on their 'road' she had been making working with them conditional upon their joining hers.

So the basis of attending to someone is spending time with or around them, and using this time to engage in the work of learning about them and about your own response to them. It involves staying in touch with your own feelings and attitudes and how these may be influencing the work. As I said earlier, workers are not neutral, and your feeling response to someone may be telling you something about them, about yourself, and about the relationship. As a worker your task is to discern whether these feelings are connected to your own issues (as seen in the example of M) rather than those of the other person.

Often, however, this task is far from easy, especially when workers identify closely with the feelings and experiences of the people they are working with. Workers will only be able to disentangle the emotions if they are constantly working to 'know themselves' and are able to acknowledge their own issues and feelings. If not, then they will remain unaware of how they may be affecting the quality of their work with people. They may even attribute any difficulties in the work to the other person, as M did in our example when she saw the young men as 'just not interested in anything'. Here is another example of this process:

H was working in a youth project which was coming to the end of its funding. She had worked particularly closely with a group of young women throughout the life of the project and she felt very concerned about what would happen to them when it ended, because they had become so used to being a part of the project. As the time for the closure drew near she felt that the young women were not willing to face up to it and avoided talking about it.

On reflection H began to consider her own feelings about the closure and realised that she had been avoiding these by focusing on what she imagined the young women were feeling. She realised then that she was part of the problem, that she had been placing her own feelings on to the group instead of owning them. Because she could not face up to the ending she was unable to work with whatever the young women felt about it.

As H faced up to her own concerns, talking them through with her line manager, she found she could open up conversations with the young women and pay attention to their experience instead of only to her own.

Delivery or discovery?

Compare the examples of work done by M, J, P and H with the approach of those who work to an externally–set curriculum or agenda. This often involves them in 'delivering' programmes to people where the desired 'learning outcomes' are already set.

Many informal educators, perhaps due to the demands of funders, appear to be increasingly pre-occupied with this kind of approach rather than working with people's experiences and concerns, with what is important to *them*, in order to 'foster learning in life as it is lived' (YMCA George Williams College 1998: 4). An emphasis on delivery of programmes can imply a ready-packaged approach to education where the workers assume they already know what people need to learn.

Any programmes or techniques used need to be thought about carefully. An over–reliance on techniques can be a way of workers avoiding their anxiety about dealing with new and uncertain situations, by trying to somehow standardise them or make them 'the same' as those already encountered. Schön (1983) sees this as workers trying to '… preserve the constancy of their knowledge', turning practice into an application of techniques rather than an evolving process of discovery.

Informal educators often have to work in practice situations which are complex, uncertain and full of conflicting values and demands. They therefore need to avoid what Mills called 'the fetishism of method and technique...' (1959: 245) and instead engage creatively with the people and situations before them.

But workers may find it difficult to give up their sense of knowing what to do; it can be difficult to remain in uncertainty and to think things through without reaching prematurely for an answer. Knowing can give a feeling of control and security, however illusory. But to work with what people bring, with their experiences and perceptions, requires workers to develop an ability to tolerate uncertainty, their 'negative capability' as the poet Keats described it, because this is a pre-requisite for learning and discovery:

> If we ... do not allow ourselves ... to experience newness we also shut ourselves off from the perception of something different, discovering new things ... producing something fresh ... however, if we do not thus rigidify our thinking we pay the price of the agony of helplessness, confusion, dread of the unknown, of being in a state of beginning once more.
>
> (Salzberger-Wittenberg, Henry and Osborne 1983: 9)

Small wonder that many workers prefer the less painful, well-trodden pathway of 'delivery' and techniques! But unless workers can bear the anxiety of uncertainty, how will they take time to learn about their clients and work with *their* experiences and concerns, so that they may become 'creators' of their own learning rather than simply 'consumers' of programmes (Smith 1980)?

Of course, the traditional view of professional workers is that they *do* have answers and know what is best for their clients. But the approach to working with people discussed in this chapter demands that workers develop a different kind of relationship where the client is 'an active participant in a process of shared inquiry' with the worker (Schön 1983: 302), and where the worker's chief concern is to discover and work with the client's meanings. In this kind of working relationship, worker and client are engaged together in a process of discovery.

Bruno Bettelheim (1990) gives a lovely illustration of this kind of working relationship when he describes his first meeting with his psychoanalyst. Bettelheim was feeling anxious about entering analysis so he asked the analyst, 'Do you think this will help me?' The analyst replied that he did not know, but that they could do some work together and Bettelheim would probably know the answer to this question before he did. At first Bettelheim felt disconcerted and rather alarmed at this unexpected reply. Surely this professional must *know*! But then he realised that the analyst's reply had placed their working relationship in a more realistic and humane context:

> [analysis] was not something he would unilaterally do *to* or *for* me, but rather a joint undertaking in which the participation of both of us was critical ... we were equal in our efforts to learn significant things about me.

The development of this kind of working relationship depends upon the worker being willing to let go of their certainties and extend their capacity to:

reveal [their] uncertainties . . . make [themselves] confrontable . . . give up the comfort of relative invulnerability, the gratifications of deference. The new satisfactions open to [them] are largely those of discovery. . .

(Schön 1983: 299)

Conclusion

Working with people is often a confusing, complex and demanding experience, both mentally and emotionally. I have tried to show how workers may retreat from these demands in a variety of ways, though perhaps not deliberately or consciously. Their retreat may be concealed, even from themselves, by all kinds of activities which may look like 'working with' people but are, perhaps, more a means of managing their own anxieties.

I have argued for an approach to practice which respects the uniqueness of people and the validity of their experiences; which is committed to working with people rather than on them; and which requires workers to engage in the constant discipline of their 'internal work'.

Further reading

Boud, D. and Miller, N. (eds) (1996) *Working with Experience.* London: Routledge. The authors argue that learning from experience can enable us to face new circumstances with fresh insights. They examine the roles that workers in a variety of professional settings have played in animating other people's learning.

Green, M. and Christian, C. (1998) *Accompanying Young People on their Spiritual Quest.* London: The National Society/Church House Publishing. This short book explores the values, attitudes and skills that enable us to 'be with' young people in a way which regards them 'as complete people who have as many answers to their condition as they do questions . . .'. The authors argue that 'explicit in the process of accompanying is the idea that the best solutions and thoughts are not provided by an expert but are arrived at by the individual himself or herself'. Draws useful distinctions between this process and those of mentoring, befriending and counselling. Equally useful for those working with adults.

Schön, D.A. (1983) *The Reflective Practitioner: How Professionals Think in Action.* New York: Basic Books. Donald Schön makes the case that, in order to work effectively within ever-changing practice situations, it is essential that professionals develop the ability to reflect critically on their actions as they work. He explores this process in detail through case studies of workers from a range of professions.

References

Bettelheim, B. (1990) *Recollections and Reflections.* London: Thames and Hudson.

Boud, D., Cohen, R. and Walker, D. (eds) (1993) *Using Experience for Learning.* Buckingham: SRHE and Open University Press.

Bullough, R.V. Jr., Knowles, J.G. and Crow, N.A. (1991) *Emerging as a Teacher.* London and New York: Routledge.

Carter, P., Jeffs, T. and Smith, M.K. (eds) (1995) *Social Working.* Basingstoke and London: Macmillan.

Dewey, J. (1933) *How we Think.* Massachusetts: D.C. Heath & Co.

Green, M. and Christian, C. (1998) *Accompanying young people on their spiritual quest.* London: The National Society/Church House Publishing.

Jeffs, T. and Smith, M.K. (1996) *Informal Education – conversation, democracy and learning.* Derby: Education Now Publishing Co-operative Ltd.

Lerner, D. (ed.) (1958) *Evidence and Inference.* Glencoe 111: The Free Press of Glencoe.

Mills, C. Wright (1959) *The Sociological Imagination.* Harmondsworth: Penguin.

Peck, M. Scott (1990) *The Road Less Travelled.* London: Arrow Books Ltd.

Salzberger-Wittenberg, I., Henry, G. and Osborne, E. (1983) *The Emotional Experience of Learning and Teaching.* London: RKP.

Schön, D.A. (1983) *The Reflective Practitioner: how professionals think in action.* New York: Basic Books.

Smith, M. (1980) *Creators not Consumers: rediscovering social education.* N.A.Y.C.

Whitaker, D.S. (1989) *Using Groups to Help People.* London: Routledge.

YMCA George Williams College, London (1998) *Programme Handbook.* 1998–2000.

5 Professional values in informal education work

Sarah Banks

This chapter explores the values that influence the work of informal educators. It focuses particularly on professional values, that is the values that are said to underpin or define the work. Other values are also influential, for example the personal values of the people who work as informal educators, and the values of employing organisations. Often these overlap, or are complementary, but sometimes they are different and potentially contradictory. This chapter first discusses the nature of professional values, before examining the values that underpin informal education work and the potential for conflict between personal, professional and agency values.

Professional values

'Values' is a broad term encompassing many different meanings. Indeed, Timms (1983: 107) quotes a literature review which found 180 different definitions. For the purpose of this chapter, a value will be taken as a particular type of belief concerning what is regarded as worthy or valuable. Values have also been defined as opinions, attitudes or preferences. However, in the context of professional practice, the use of the term 'belief' reflects the status that values have as stronger than mere opinions or preferences.

> **Q1:** Before you read on, spend a few minutes jotting down the personal, professional and organisational values that you can identify for your own work situation.

Clearly there are many different types of things that can be regarded as valuable. Seedhouse (1998: 78) lists: physical objects (for example, furniture); aesthetic qualities (for example, beauty); intangibles (for example, creativity); principles (for example, truth telling); or ideologies (for example, communism). In the literature on professional values, it is generally principles, and particularly ethical principles, relating to how people should be treated, what ideas or actions are worthy or unworthy, good or bad, right or wrong that are regarded as values (for example, respect for the individual; a commitment to democracy). Some of the literature also includes what Seedhouse calls 'intangibles' as professional values (such as creativity or integrity), although these characteristics might be better distinguished as 'virtues' or character traits of workers and will not be the subject of this chapter.

I will use the term 'professional values', therefore, to refer to a set of ethical or moral principles that means something to people doing a particular type of job, usually as members of an occupation or professional group. Indeed, values are often said to define the nature of an occupation or profession and the literature may refer to 'the value base' as if values are the very foundation on which professional practice is built. Professional values can be distinguished from personal values, in that personal values may not be shared by all members of an occupational group. For example, a person who works as a youth worker may have a personal belief that abortion is wrong, but this is not one of the underlying principles of youth work.

Insofar as professional values are located within and influenced by broader societal values, then they may reflect particular ideological or political positions (for example, liberalism). But lists of professional values do not usually include direct statements of ideological or political beliefs. Employing agencies' values are usually similar to those of the profession as a whole, although some specialist organisations may include explicit religious or ideological beliefs. A worker's personal values, however, will encompass all of Seedhouse's range of categories, and may include religious as well as aesthetic and ideological beliefs.

The values of informal education work

Most of the established occupational groups in the welfare and caring field have developed a literature on the theme of professional values. This is true particularly in the social work and the health care professions (see Timms 1983; Horne 1987; Banks 1995; Pearce 1996; Dracopoulou 1998; Tadd 1998). This is not the case, however, in the informal educational field. Indeed, informal education is not a defined occupational group in the same way as is, for example, social work, nursing, architecture or accountancy. These groups all have professional bodies of some sort, which define the nature of the work, the qualifications required to undertake it and the underlying principles and values. Informal education is a type of work undertaken by members of several different occupational groups – most commonly, youth workers, community workers and adult educators. Some would argue that it may also be undertaken by other professionals whose core business is something else, but who may on occasions use informal education techniques (such as nurses, police officers or town planners). While this is doubtless true, the main concern of this chapter is with those people for whom informal education is the core of their work, and in particular the focus will be on youth workers and community workers.

Q2: What are the values that, for you, underlie your work as an informal educator and the work of your agency? Try to think of as many as you can and note them down to compare with the ones discussed below.

Jeffs and Smith (1996: 10), in the context of discussing what it is to be an informal educator, focus on education as the core and suggest that:

for something to be called 'education', whether it takes place in the classroom or the canteen, it must be informed by certain values.

They identify these values as:

- a respect for persons;
- a belief in democracy;
- a commitment to fairness and equality.

They suggest that these values distinguish education from indoctrination or training. However, the values do not distinguish formal from informal education. Indeed, Jeffs and Smith are at pains to stress that educators in formal and informal settings have far more in common than they often admit. Being an informal educator means 'first and foremost, being an educator' (op. cit.: 14). However, because these values are very general, they not only fail to distinguish a youth worker from a schoolteacher, but could equally apply to a social worker, a nurse, or even a police officer. In fact, they could be said to be the fundamental values of any liberal democracy. This is not to say they should not be shared by informal educators. They should. Most statements of professional values reflect the underlying values prevalent in society. However, in order for a set of values to be recognisable as a set of professional values, they should be more specific to professional practice.

A working party (NYA 1993: 14), set up to explore the core of youth and community work, identified informal education as the core process of the work and listed the following as elements critical to the educational purpose or outcome:

- collective action;
- autonomy of individuals and groups;
- change and development;
- justice and equality.

Although these elements are not called 'values', they are discussed in a way that suggests they form a set of principles underlying the work. While some of these values are common to many professions, others are not. The belief in the value of collective action is particularly significant for youth and community work, and does not feature in the value statements of professions such as social work, nursing or policing. Similarly the stress on change and development is more characteristic of youth and community work (and to some extent social work). Studying this list of values and comparing it with similar lists for other professions leads to the conclusion that, although the values are very general and probably no professional group would regard any of them as dis-values, or unworthy, the fact that some values are included rather than others tells us something about this particular occupational group.

The guidelines to professional endorsement produced by the National Youth Agency for qualifying training in youth and community work (NYA 1997: 6–7) contain a slightly longer and more specific list of values:

- respect for basic human rights – for example, justice, freedom;
- respect for the individual and rights to self-determination;
- respect for the different cultures and religions in society;
- the principle of equality and a commitment to anti-discriminatory practice;

- a commitment to empowerment and participatory democracy;
- collaborative working relationships and collective action; and
- an acknowledgement that all relationships and activities with young people and adults are based on their consent.

The first three principles are very general and reflect basic liberal democratic values. However, the inclusion of 'respect for different cultures and religions' is significant in that it reflects a preoccupation in youth and community work with multi-cultural and anti-oppressive work and leads on to the fourth principle of equality and commitment to anti-discriminatory practice. It is the last three principles that relate more to professional practice and begin to distinguish youth and community work from, say, social work or nursing.

Interpreting the values

For these values to be useful, they need to be discussed in more depth. Unfortunately the NYA document does not do this, which leaves the list of values open to interpretation. In trying to unpack the possible meanings of some of these statements, I will draw on the literature on values relating to other professions (particularly social work and health care) and the literature on the role and function of youth, community and adult education work.

Respect for the individual and basic human rights

The first two statements focus on respect for the individual and the rights of the individual. Respect for the individual entails valuing the uniqueness and dignity of each person, which means treating each individual as a person in her or his own right, not, for example, as on object to be acted upon. 'Respect' is a commonly used term in statements of values and has been defined by Downie and Telfer (1969) as an active sympathy towards another person. It involves seeing the other person as a fellow human being, as someone who has hopes, fears, desires and the ability to make choices and decisions. Statements of values often elaborate that, in respecting other people, the worker should not treat them unfavourably on account of ability, gender, religion, 'race', class, sexual orientation or other irrelevant qualities. In this sense, everyone has certain basic rights, which are the kinds of rights enshrined in the United Nations Universal Declaration of Human Rights (1948). These include not just the right to justice (for example, a fair trial) and freedom (for example, freedom of speech), but also the right to an adequate standard of living, security in the event of unemployment and to education. The worker must respect these rights, although clearly it cannot be the role of the worker alone to ensure that each individual's rights are realised.

The right to self-determination

The 'right to self-determination' is another very commonly expressed professional value for those working in the welfare professions. 'Self-determination', or 'autonomy' refers to the ability of individuals to make their own choices and decisions, and to act on them, 'without let or hindrance' as Gillon (1985: 112) puts it. Clearly people may be able to make decisions (autonomy of will) without having the ability to act on them (autonomy of action). In simply talking about 'respecting' people's rights to self-determination, rather than promoting or developing them, this implies that workers should leave people alone to make their own decisions and to act on them if they can. However, other professions sometimes formulate this principle differently, with the worker having a role in actualising service users' rights to self-determination by encouraging them to see that they have a choice, helping them to look at a broader range of options and enabling them to develop the means to act on their choices. This has sometimes been called 'positive self-determination' (Banks 1995: 43) and it is clear from the youth and community work and adult education literature that this is the kind of role often expected from informal educators (see Jeffs and Smith 1996; Smith 1988; Jarvis 1997).

One difficulty with this formulation of the principle of self-determination is that it does not take into account the fact that one individual's right to self-determination may conflict with that of another, or may be contrary to the interests or well-being of that particular individual or other people. For example, a member of a local community group may devise a careful plan to defraud a local business of money in order to purchase equipment for a community centre. She knows the risks, she is in a sound state of mind and she has freely made the decision to take this action. However, should the community centre worker respect her decision? Surely there are other people's rights involved (such as the right of the business owner to keep the money earned) and there may be dis-benefits for the broader community if this activity is discovered. This example suggests that the principle of respecting the individual's rights to self-determination should be modified to include a proviso along the lines of 'providing this is not damaging to the rights or interests of others'. Indeed, particularly when workers are responsible for young people or vulnerable adults, we might add: 'providing this does not seriously damage the well-being of the person concerned'. This, of course, opens the door to all sorts of interference by workers. However, this is part of their job, which entails protecting the interests and well-being of the people they work with and balancing this against promoting their self-determination.

Respect for different cultures and religions in society

This value can be regarded as a development of the principle of respect for persons in that it implies that people who belong to different religious and cultural groups should not be ridiculed, judged or treated unfavourably. But the fact that the statement is worded in terms of respecting cultures and religions, rather than the people who are part of them, suggests that the worker should respect a culture or religion as whole, as well as the people who subscribe to it. This raises the issue of whether a culture or religion that appears to oppress its members and disregards their rights to self-determination (for example, through female circumcision) or that persecutes members of other cultures or religions (for example a religious minority) should still be respected. Such a case raises the possibility of a conflict between two principles in the list of values. Such conflicts are often experienced by workers, although usually in a less extreme form. Imam (1999) gives an example of a practitioner working with a young woman of South Asian origin whose choice to have a white boyfriend caused problems with her family and the wider community, and whose mother asked the worker to intervene.

Equality and a commitment to anti-discriminatory practice

When we talk about 'equality' it is important to realise that this term is ambiguous and that we need to be clear what form of equality we are committed to (see Spicker 1988: 125; Banks 1995: 44). Equality of treatment (preventing disadvantage in access to services) and equality of opportunity (removal of disadvantage in competition with others) are more achievable in practice, although in social work and youth and community work there is a lot of rhetoric about equality of result (removal of disadvantages altogether). The linking of 'equality' with anti-discrimination emphasises the active and quite radical role required of professional workers in this sphere. 'Anti-discrimination' has developed a particular meaning in the literature of the welfare professions (see Thompson 1993) and is about more than just not discriminating against people. It is about challenging negative stereotypes, about confronting service users and colleagues who are racist, sexist and in other ways discriminatory, and working towards setting up structures and systems that do not embody in-built and unnecessary discrimination.

Commitment to empowerment and participatory democracy

This value also suggests a more active role for the worker than simply respecting the individual's rights to self-determination. It hints at the idea of transferring power in society, although 'empowerment' is another over-used and much contested concept. It refers to the commitment of youth and community workers to challenging existing power structures both in local communities and in society generally, and working with people who are traditionally regarded as oppressed or powerless to take more power and control over their lives, not just at an individual level, but also in collectives. The reference to 'participatory democracy' emphasises a crucial concept in youth and community work, that of 'participation'. This entails a commitment to encouraging and enabling people to take part in decision-making, both in the context of a youth and community project, and local and national policy decisions. What counts as participation (ranging from the involvement of service users in activities to total control over decision-making) is an important issue for workers to consider and has been much discussed in youth and community work.

Collaborative working relationships and collective action

This statement can be interpreted in several different ways. 'Collaborative working relationships' may refer to the relationships the workers have with the young people and adults they are working with – implying that the work should be a shared process and involve workers and participants working together (this fits in with the idea of empowerment and participation). However it probably largely refers to the way that youth and community workers work with other professionals in an open and sharing fashion. Adding 'collective action' to this statement takes the idea of working together further, since to act collectively is about more than just sharing ideas and information; it is about acting with one voice, with one aim, or for a common cause. The collective action referred to here probably relates to youth and community workers encouraging and supporting those they work with to see certain issues as common and to act together for change. So, for example, a worker may support a group of residents in a locality to work together to campaign against a school closure; or a worker may be involved with a number of young people living in the local authority looked-after system to form a group to provide mutual support and to make demands on the local authority to change some of its practices and procedures.

Acknowledgement that all relationships and activities with young people and adults are based on their consent

The use of the term 'acknowledgement' in this statement is odd, but presumably it refers to the fact that the relationship of youth and community workers to those they work with is a voluntary one, and that this is a valuable and defining feature of the work. The use of the term 'consent' relates back to the principle of respecting an individual's right to self-determination and suggests that the people worked with should consciously agree to the relationship and the activities undertaken with the worker. Often in a professional context (especially in the field of health care) this principle is phrased as 'informed consent' and puts an onus on the worker to give out sufficient and comprehensible information for people to make up their minds about whether to participate (Taplin 1994).

There may, however, be exceptions to this principle. For example, what if the worker is working with a group of very young children or with people with severe learning difficulties? It may not be possible for these people to give 'consent' to participating in an activity or becoming members of a group. In such cases, parents or guardians may be the ones who consent. Often, however, in youth and community work the kind of work being undertaken is not like having an operation in hospital; it is not something for which the workers will seek people's active consent. Rather, it is assumed that the relationship is, as we said earlier, a 'voluntary' one and therefore consent may be implied. There is also a difference between a relationship being voluntary and an activity being voluntary. There may be a situation where a worker judges that she must compel a young man, against his will, to complete an activity he is unwilling to do. For example, if in the middle of a rock climbing exercise in pairs, one of the partners refuses to help the other up the rock face with the rope, the youth worker may have to order the young person to do this because the life of the other young person is at risk if he does not.

An additional value: safeguarding and promoting the welfare of young people and adults

This last point highlights a conflict between the value of respecting the individual self-determination of one young person and the value of safeguarding the welfare of another. Yet safeguarding or promoting people's welfare is not one of the core values identified by the NYA as underlying youth and community work. Arguably it should be. It is certainly a fundamental principle underlying some of the other professions we have spoken about, ranging from nursing ('promote and safeguard the interests and well-being of patients and clients' (UKCC 1992)) to policing ('to safeguard lives and property' (IACP 1991)). Like the other principles, its meaning is complex and what counts as 'welfare' will depend on views about the nature of the good society and what are regarded as the basic human needs. Welfare may include happiness, pleasure, material goods, safety or health. A worker may have a particular view of what someone's welfare is, yet that person may disagree. Promoting or safeguarding the welfare of one person may reduce or put at risk the welfare of others. The classic example in youth work is whether to exclude from a group a very needy individual who is breaking the rules (say, drinking alcohol or disrupting the group) in the interests of the majority of participants.

This discussion has highlighted several problems with the NYA's list of values, which suggest some modifications and expansion would be beneficial. Firstly, it omits a fundamental value relating to the promotion and safeguarding of people's welfare. Secondly, it does not acknowledge the complexity of certain values, and the potential for conflict within them – for example, the fact that respecting self-determination for one person may conflict with the right of another to determine their own choices and actions. Thirdly, it does not take account of the potential for conflict between different values, such as respecting different religions and respecting the rights of individuals. Indeed, having a list of values tells us what a profession or occupational group values, but it does not tell us how those values are prioritised in cases of conflict. This leaves plenty of room for ethical dilemmas in the work, which arise when workers are caught between two conflicting and equally important principles. Fourthly, it does not acknowledge the potential for conflict between professional values and the personal values of practitioners or the values of employing agencies.

> **Q3:** Can you identify any conflicting values which have emerged from your own practice?

Value conflicts

Since conflicts between the values in the list (for example, between respecting a young person's rights to self-determination and valuing another culture; or between the rights of two individuals) have been covered quite extensively elsewhere (Banks 1997, 1999; Imam 1999), I will focus here on conflicts between personal, professional and agency values.

When workers talk about the conflict between personal and professional values, they are often highlighting the difference between how they would have acted in a situation if it had arisen in their private lives and how they felt they should act in the role of a professional worker. For example, a 16-year-old voluntary youth worker, who was an Irish Catholic, working in a youth centre in Eire, described how a 14-year-old woman came to him for advice regarding her pregnancy:

> I had a young woman, pregnant, and undecided what to do. She wanted me to tell her, but I felt that I had to try to will an answer from her, as she was the one who would hold the consequences. Although I tried this, she wanted my advice, as a friend and a worker. I was concerned about this, but gave a personal opinion as a desperate friend.

There are many issues here for this worker, including the importance of his own religious beliefs in relation to abortion and how these should influence his professional work. As a worker in a professional role he felt he should encourage the young woman to make her own choices and he attempted to discuss with her the pros and cons of each option and what this would mean for her. He felt strongly that he must not only respect her right to self-determination, but positively encourage her to exercise this right. Yet she wanted his advice not just as worker, but also as a friend. Although many of us might be wary of advising our friends in such difficult matters, it is nevertheless regarded as acceptable for a friend to say, 'If I was you I would keep the baby.' This worker did not say what he actually advised the young woman, although he is clear that he thought he gave the advice in the role of a friend, not as a worker. It is also clear that he regarded the situation as a difficult dilemma and he described himself as being in a 'precarious position'.

Another poignant example was given to me by a Dutch colleague and relates to a worker in a residential children's home who was on duty over Christmas, looking after a 10-year-old boy. This boy was the only one from his group of seven who had not been able to go home for Christmas. This is the situation from the worker's perspective:

> It was Christmas Eve and John [the boy] and I were alone sitting next to the Christmas tree. The tree looked rather bedraggled and was already losing its needles. We had some music on and had been eating cake and chocolate, but the atmosphere seemed dull and silent. I thought of my own Christmas tree which my kids had just decorated, and of what it would be like to be at home with my wife and kids having a good time. John looked so down and I began to think about what it would be like to take him to my house for Christmas.

The problem for the worker is that the institution does not approve of workers taking the children to their own homes. This is thought to be an unacceptable mixing of personal and professional roles, and could lead to all sorts of problems relating to insurance if the children were abused or hurt. All outside visits have to be approved first anyway, and the worker knows he would get into trouble if it was discovered he and John had gone to his home for a night. The values of the agency stress the responsibility and accountability of the workers and the welfare of the young people. However, the worker wants to be able to offer John some love and warmth and do for him what he might do for a lonely friend of his son's who had nowhere else to go at Christmas. His personal values of care and friendship conflict with both agency and professional values which require some distance between workers and service users and emphasise more impartial and impersonal values like justice, fairness and accountability.

Particular issues may often arise for workers employed by explicitly religious organisations. Ward (1996: 2–3) gives an example of a youth worker working for a church who was so successful at outreach work with the 'unchurched' that a large group of 'tough working-class' young people living on a nearby estate began to meet in the church and also swelled the numbers attending the weekly youth club. However, the adults in the church regarded these young people as troublesome and began to put pressure on the youth worker to do more work with their young people who were already involved with the church fellowship. This sort of situation would raise a dilemma for a professional worker, who might see the greatest need for youth work activities lying with the 'unchurched' young people. The church might only prioritise the outreach work on the assumption that these young people would be brought into the church. This also raises the question of how persuasive or coercive the worker should be in encouraging the young people into the Christian faith. The youth and community work values of individual self-determination and consent suggest that the workers should not put undue pressure on the young people to join in the church activities (Green 1999).

Ward (1997: 2–4) speaks of the difficulties for Christian workers trained in a secular setting and taking on secular values such as those put forward by the NYA. Many of the early youth work organisations had as one of their prime aims the spreading of the Christian faith and influencing the people they worked with to adopt Christian values (Ward 1996: 23–44; Green 1999). For a long time youth work had a concern with the moral and spiritual development of young people. This terminology has largely disappeared in the mainstream statutory and voluntary sector, although this does not mean that youth and community work is not concerned to transmit certain values to the people being worked with (see Robb 1996; Young 1999). The values include, for example, encouraging people to value participation in activities and in society generally, and challenging discrimination. So if an adult or young person expresses a racist view or harasses someone, then the worker has a duty to intervene and would be expected to work towards changing these attitudes. This is, of course, part of the educational role, which includes the transmission of certain values as well as encouraging people to become aware of and develop their own sets of values.

Yet the values of youth and community work, with the strong stress on respect for the individual and rights to self-determination, also reflect a very Western view of what is regarded as good for human beings. Imam points out the difficulties this may create for workers coming from non-Western cultural and religious origins, where the group or family may be more important than the individual. The stress in informal education work on the value of collective action is an important counter-balance to the tendency towards individualism, but the predominance of values stressing the rights of the individual is still apparent and presents dilemmas for practitioners working with people from different cultures.

Conclusion

We examined three lists of values relevant to informal education work and noticed their tendency to include very general principles. This leads to the conclusion that the main function of professional values is to affirm what kind of society workers in this field value and believe in. It is the kind of society where individuals have rights; where these rights are respected as far as possible; where individuals have the freedom to make their own decisions and choices and are encouraged and enabled by workers to do so; where being part of a collective – a group, movement and society – is important and where participating in that collective is also important; and where people are treated equally (with due regard for their differences and needs) and justly (without unfairness or unwarranted prejudice).

Since these are broadly accepted values in society, we may ask why it is important for members of an occupational group to affirm these values. The answer is partly in order to prevent their practice being used for purposes which may exploit, undermine, use or control the people they are working with. Professional values are a counter-balance to the values of an employing agency which may have a different emphasis (such as control, conversion or surveillance) and to a worker's personal values (which may include beliefs about God, abortion or vegetarianism). Finally, professional values help to clarify the purpose of the work and to create a sense of professional identity (Banks 1996). However, there is a need to do much more than just list a set of general principles. The varieties of meanings and interpretations need to be explored in the context of professional practice in the informal educational field. Much more work needs to be done to develop, interpret and refine these values.

Further reading

Banks, S. (ed.) (1999) *Ethical Issues in Youth Work.* London: Routledge. This book has chapters by different authors covering a range of value conflicts and dilemmas for youth workers, including issues relating to confidentiality, religious conversion, social control, sources of funding and participative research.

Chadwick, R. (1994) *Ethics and the Professions.* Aldershot: Avebury. An edited collection with several useful chapters exploring the nature and role of professional codes of ethics, accountability and professional behaviour in an organisational context. Some of the chapters are about professions in general, others focus on medicine, nursing, social work and law.

Norman, R. (1998) *The Moral Philosophers: An Introduction to Ethics,* 2nd edn. Oxford: Oxford University Press. A clear overview of moral philosophy from Plato to the present day, which would be useful for anyone wishing to develop their understanding of ethics. It comprises chapters on key thinkers such as Aristotle, Kant, Mill and on contemporary themes such as facts and values, and the ethical world.

Young, K. (1999) *The Art of Youth Work.* Lyme Regis: Russell House. This book develops a view of youth work as 'an exercise in moral philosophy' and is an account of the nature of the work, drawing heavily on youth workers' and young people's own accounts of youth work practice. Almost half of the book comprises a section entitled 'Philosophy' and there is a lot of discussion of youth work in relation to values – those of the workers and the young people themselves.

References

Banks, S. (1995) *Ethics and Values in Social Work.* Basingstoke: Macmillan.
Banks, S. (1996) 'Youth work, informal education and professionalisation', *Youth and Policy* 54: 13–25.
Banks, S. (1997) 'The dilemmas of intervention', in J. Roche and S. Tucker (eds) *Youth in Society: Contemporary Theory, Policy and Practice.* London: Open University Press/Sage.

Banks, S. (ed.) (1999) *Ethical Issues in Youth Work*. London: Routledge.

Downie, R. and Telfer, E. (1969) *Respect for Persons*. London: Routledge and Kegan Paul.

Dracopoulou, S. (ed.) (1998) *Ethics and Values in Health Care Management*. London: Routledge.

Gillon, R. (1985) 'Autonomy and consent', in M. Lockwood (ed.) *Moral Dilemmas in Modern Medicine*. Oxford: Oxford University Press.

Green, M. (1999) 'The youth worker as converter: ethical issues in religious youth work', in S. Banks (ed.) *Ethical Issues in Youth Work*. London: Routledge.

Horne, M. (1987) *Values in Social Work*. Aldershot: Wildwood House.

Imam, U. (1999) 'Youth workers as mediators and interpreters: ethical issues in work with black young people', in S. Banks (ed.) *Ethical Issues in Youth Work*. London: Routledge.

International Association of Chiefs of Police (1991) *Law Enforcement Code of Ethics*, reprinted in J. Kleinig (1996) *The Ethics of Policing*. Cambridge: Cambridge University Press: 236–7.

Jarvis, P. (1997) *Ethics and Education for Adults*. Leicester: National Institute of Adult Continuing Education.

Jeffs, T. and Smith, M. (1996) *Informal Education – Conversation, Democracy, Learning*. Derby: Education Now.

National Youth Agency (1993) *Report of the Working Group to Define the Distinctive Elements Which Form the Core of All Youth and Community Work Training*. Leicester: National Youth Agency.

National Youth Agency (1997) *Professional Endorsement of Qualifying Training in Youth and Community Work Training*. Leicester: National Youth Agency.

Pearce, J. (1996) 'The values of social work', in A. Vass (ed.) *Social Work Competences: Core Knowledge, Values and Skills*. London: Sage.

Robb, W. (1996) 'Values education and voluntary youth organisations in the United Kingdom', in W. Robb (ed.) *Values Education: The Contribution of Some Voluntary Youth Organisations*. Aberdeen: Centre for Alleviating Social Problems through Values Education.

Seedhouse, D. (1998) *Ethics: The Heart of Health Care*. Chichester: Wiley.

Smith, M. (1988) *Developing Youth Work. Informal Education, Mutual Aid and Popular Practice*. Milton Keynes: Open University Press.

Spicker, P. (1988) *Principles of Social Welfare*. London: Routledge.

Tadd, W. (1998) *Ethics and Values for Care Workers*. Oxford: Blackwell.

Taplin, D. (1994) 'Nursing and informed consent: an empirical study', in G. Hunt (ed.) *Ethical Issues in Nursing*. London: Routledge.

Thompson, N. (1993) *Anti-Discriminatory Practice*. Basingstoke: Macmillan.

Timms, N. (1983) *Social Work Values: An Inquiry*. London: Routledge and Kegan Paul.

United Kingdom Central Council for Nursing, Midwifery and Health Visiting (1992) *Code of Professional Conduct for the Nurse, Midwife and Health Visitor*. London: UKCCC.

United Nations (1948) *Universal Declaration of Human Rights*. Geneva: UN General Assembly.

Ward, P. (1996) *Growing Up Evangelical: Youthwork and the Making of a Subculture*. London: SPCK.

Ward, P. (1997) *Youthwork and the Mission of God*. London: SPCK.

Young, K. (1999) 'The youth worker as guide, philosopher and friend: the realities of participation and empowerment', in S. Banks (ed.) *Ethical Issues in Youth Work*. London: Routledge.

6 Developing professional practice

Mary Tyler

Introduction

This chapter is designed to help you clarify your understanding of the concept of confidentiality and use that understanding in your practice as an informal education worker. 'What if' scenarios are used to explore the meaning of confidentiality and enable you to apply this to your professional practice, recognising that this practice is not only a personal responsibility but is set in the context of the organisation you work for (paid or voluntary) and its role in society.

What first comes to mind when you think about the concept of confidentiality? Perhaps locked filing cabinets, computer data, and quiet one-to-one sessions with counsellors? What does it mean in your everyday work as a practitioner? What kinds of confidences have people shared with you? What were some of your feelings and concerns about this? Maybe holding confidences has made you feel good about yourself and the positive role you could play, but have you sometimes felt uncomfortable or anxious about whether it was right to 'hold' certain information and take no action? Alternatively maybe you have had to break a confidence. Were you able to voice your concerns somewhere and get advice and support if you needed it?

Meaning and significance of confidentiality

Dictionary definitions of 'confidential' include words like 'trust', 'faith', 'reliance', 'assurance', 'private' and 'secrets'. Generally it is information of some sort which is to be treated as confidential, and there is an assumption that this information will be kept private. Words like 'trust', 'faith' and 'reliance' name complex values that are key to our role as informal educators, alongside principles like respect for person, and commitment to social justice. Confidentiality is about the way we conduct ourselves in relation to confidences so it is all about how we apply such values in our work, how they guide our behaviour. It could be argued to be a principle in itself which determines that information shared with us by others is secret.

But is something confidential automatically a secret between you and the person you are working with? Is it so straightforward? Banks argues that 'User's rights are not absolute and may be limited by a higher duty to self, by rights of other individuals, the social worker, agency or community' (1995: 26–7). This chapter will enable us to explore some of the complexity of confidentiality.

We know that doctors hold confidential information about their patients and that there will be necessary occasions when this information will be shared with professional colleagues. These colleagues will need to know this confidential information for the benefit of the patient in order, for instance, to contribute to their treatment. Patients understand this and would not usually describe the information they have told their doctor as a secret but as confidential. There is a kind of contract associated with this confidentiality of the doctor–patient relationship and the confidential information contained within it. A similar contract can be identified, for example, between a youth worker and young person about confidential information. However, unlike patients, young people may assume that a confidence is a secret not to be shared and would not necessarily check this explicitly with a worker they have been talking to.

Integral to the notion of confidentiality is a trust in the person or persons with which the confidential information is shared. The contract could include trusting the confidante not to disclose the information to anyone, or it may be agreed that they will be trusted to share it with certain other people. The person's trust is linked to their belief in the judgement to be made by the worker about who the information should be shared with.

Information about individuals that might be shared could be seen to be on a private–public path or continuum. At one end is the completely confidential or private where something is only shared with one other person and goes no further. Somewhere in the middle is confidential information which is shared when necessary with certain people in specified roles, and at the other end that information which may be shared with the express intention of making it public with the help of those with whom it is shared.

There is a general principle in law about confidentiality although there is nothing spelt out in legislation. This principle recognises the concept of a confidential relationship and that the 'person receiving the confidence is under a duty not to pass on the information to a third party. Disclosure of confidential information can give rise to an action for breach of confidence in which an injunction or compensation may be claimed' (Hamilton 1998: 29). As your defence, were anyone to prosecute, you would have to show that the disclosure could be justified as in the public interest if you did break a confidence. Consider Sarah Banks's earlier quotation and the notion of 'public interest' as you read through this chapter.

What makes some information or knowledge confidential? Think of some information you have kept confidential in your private life rather than your work life. What factors influenced you to keep it confidential? It might be because of the legal principle and notions of a contract of confidentiality already mentioned. The person who shares it identifies the information explicitly as confidential, or there is an implicit understanding by the person who shares it that it is confidential to themselves and their confidante. So information we overhear might not be included as there is no contract of confidentiality. However the nature of the information in itself would also generally secure its confidentiality, and morally it would usually be wrong to share it. We would expect, for instance, to keep confidential information about a young man being beaten up regularly by his father, whatever its source. If we could identify serious implications of revealing some information, such as emotional hurt or physical harm this could also signal that the information should be treated as confidential whatever the circumstances in which we came to know it.

What if in your own social life an acquaintance tells you something about someone's personal circumstances without realising s/he is a member of a group you work with? Morgan and Banks argue that information you find out by chance or unintentionally as a private citizen you may decide not to reveal (for instance to your co-worker) because you respect that person's 'right to privacy, not confidentiality' (1999: 148). There was no contract, or opportunity for you to discuss your potential obligation to reveal certain information to others in your work role. You know this information only in your capacity as a private citizen.

Confidentiality and your role as an informal educator

Why is dealing with confidentiality different in your work role as an informal educator from your role as friend and private citizen? Why is it different in your informal educator role than if you played a different caring or educational role such as a social worker or teacher? If you can be clear about the answers to these questions your understanding should provide the framework for you to make judgements and decisions about how you deal with confidentiality in a variety of circumstances at work.

So, why is dealing with confidentiality different in your work role as an informal educator from your role as friend and private citizen? What extra and different responsibilities do you have in this work role? Although friendly, you are not a friend in the usual meaning of the word but a person working with people in a sympathetic, professional and responsible way as a member of an organisation, agency or project.

As a worker who and what are you accountable to? Make a list.

There is accountability in professional practice to not only the service user who shares a confidence but also to yourself and to your values and professionalism, to your colleagues, to the agency you belong to, sometimes to colleagues in other agencies, as well as to other agency users, one or more communities, and society in general. That accountability may mean a need in some circumstances to disclose or act upon someone's confidence. People you work with need to understand who employs you and for what purpose if they are to understand any notion of contract, rather than the kind of secrecy they may expect of a friend. There is often no clear contract unless you as worker negotiate it.

All community and youth workers undertake their work for an agency and, whether paid for their work or not, they will be expected to comply with that agency's policies. In the introduction you were asked to identify the kinds of issues people have shared with you in confidence. Which of those issues shared with you in your practitioner role may be affected by agency policy? Where are the limitations on you as an employee in relation to confidentiality?

If you are not sure, find your agency's policies or speak to your manager or management committee. It is their responsibility to provide such documented principles and procedures. Policies will be influenced where appropriate by the law, and by the nature of the agency concerned, such as whether it is a voluntary organisation or part of the local authority.

The agency you work for may have a policy on confidentiality spelling out when the agency considers you must disclose confidential information and who in the agency you need to discuss the issue with. For instance your agency's policy might state that you must undertake to 'make it plain to young people that confidence is maintained within the team, and not on an individual worker basis' (Devon: 7). Or it might state that 'workers should contact the police immediately and report to their line manager preferably within 12 hours – where adults over the age of 18 are involved in the supply of illegal substances on youth work premises' (Rodger 1997: 11).

How do you feel about your organisation having policies that set out the ground rules about some of these issues? Does it cramp your style and autonomy or enable you to work effectively? Does it depend on the circumstances?

In what ways is dealing with confidentiality different in your informal educator role than if you played a different caring or educational role such as social worker or teacher?

Unlike many other professional workers such as social workers or doctors, youth workers and community workers do not normally need to ask those they work with for confidential information as we have no legal powers. Instead people choose to share confidences with workers, especially where we have established good quality safe and trusting relationships. In fact you might describe being told something in confidence as a measure of success in achieving such meaningful relationships, those in which real learning can take place. The power and control of the information in these circumstances is with the person concerned and, based on our values about empowerment, needs to remain that way if possible. This is especially important bearing in mind that, for some young people and adults, you may be one of the few people in their lives at the time who does listen and treat them with respect. As the informal education worker hopefully you do not discriminate against them on the basis of their age, race, gender, sexuality or other aspect of their identity, although this may be their experience of many other people.

'Confidentiality is much more difficult for informal educators. Information is gained in many different settings' (Jeffs and Smith 1996: 58). Unlike most teachers, informal education workers spend their work time alongside people in their leisure time, working informally. We do not only work one-to-one (as doctors and social workers often do) but with groups too, and often in very public places. You may hear confidences unexpectedly on a residential late at night, or as you clamber the hills, on a street corner or while cooking together at the centre. We often have no previous knowledge of people, so when we first meet we engage with them as we find them, rather than with labels attached by other agencies. So because of our work style, lack of legal powers, and the amount of time we have available to get to know people we work with, we are more likely to be party to voluntarily shared confidential information from them and important to them, than our colleagues are with their more formal roles. As an informal education worker you tend to have more autonomy than other similar professionals and also less formal obligation to disclose confidences.

However, compared with other professions, youth work, community work and much of informal education also have what Morgan and Banks describe as a 'much more radical educational focus, with a greater emphasis on working for societal change, as well as personal development' (1999: 151). This can mean a commitment to confidentiality is overridden by our commitment to promoting equality and tackling oppressive behaviour and structures (Jordan 1991, in Banks 1995).

What are the implications of the principle of empowerment in your work in relation to confidences? As we have already said, people ideally need to retain control of the information they share, and need to be able to make informed decisions about whether to share information with you. So it is very important that you are honest and explain clearly to people before you are likely to hear confidences, when and why you cannot always keep these just to yourself. Hopefully by doing this you can avoid breaking confidences and potentially destroying the trust that has been built up. Is it right to listen to confidential information and then tell a young person that you have to tell someone else? Is it right to listen and not tell them you will have to disclose this information, so they only find out at a later stage from you or someone else that you have broken the confidence? A young person may have experienced many adults as people who mistreat them and breaking a confidence would be another form of mistreatment and removing of personal control.

With reference to this, Hamilton writes:

> unlike adults who are allowed to take grave risks to their health, well being or even life, the need to protect children from significant harm means that no confidential service for children or young people, nor any individual, should guarantee a child absolute confidentiality. The boundaries of confidentiality, should be made clear to young people before they make use of a service.
>
> (Hamilton 1998: 26)

If there is trust will the person still share with you the confidential information? The motivation to do so is still there. If you have explained your role successfully they hopefully understand that, although you may need to disclose what they said, it will remain within certain clear boundaries and be disclosed ultimately for their benefit. (It is crucial that they know what you are going to tell, to whom and why so they know the bounds of this sharing of confidences.) There is a contract. It will be very important that you keep them involved and/or informed during whatever process then follows.

What if . . . ?

In order to apply some of the principles discussed so far, and to identify other factors which you need to take account of, we will use some 'What if . . . ?' scenarios and introduce some necessary legal and policy information. What would you do about confidentiality in each case? Try to do this thinking with someone else.

All the case studies involve some form of offending. What offences have you been informed about in confidence or become aware of in your work? Which of these caused you any dilemma about telling anyone else?

> What if . . . you have built a relationship over time with a local unemployed man who uses the computer classes for himself and the play scheme for his children at the community centre where you work? Eventually due to your encouragement he has joined your centre's management committee and is gaining confidence steadily. One day you admire his daughter's new outfit and she tells you confidentially that her father has shoplifted the clothes. You know this parent is living on a low income.

What would you do about this confidence? Why? Would you tell the father about the child's confidence? Which is more important, maintaining the trust of the family in the context of the long-term development work you are doing, or taking action on this common form of law breaking?

There is no general duty in criminal law to report criminal offences (Hamilton 1998: 26), or to provide information to the police if questioned by them. However you need to avoid providing false or misleading information as you could then be prosecuted. Not reporting shoplifting does not mean you have to agree with this man's actions or lead him to believe you agree. You may understand and be in sympathy with the need to have new fashionable clothes for your children like their friends, and how difficult that can be on a low income but is condonement of crime appropriate in your role as an informal education worker? What are the implications for his role on the management committee and its responsibilities? What issues could you explore as a source of learning with him in relation to his role in the centre?

> What if ... you work in a young people's sexual health drop-in centre. You arrive one evening to find a timid young woman you do not know hanging around outside looking uncomfortable. You approach her as you walk in to ask if you can help and she asks if the doctor is available. You explain that the doctor is available the following night but invite her to come in and have a cup of tea and see what else the place may have to offer. You show her round and spend some time with her. She tells you she has her first boyfriend with whom she is having sex and wants to get some contraception. She is very scared her father will find out and beat her up and send the boyfriend packing. She is 14. Her boyfriend is 17. She then cries and reveals that she has been brought up by her father on his own who has been sexually abusing her for the last two years. She asks you not to tell anyone.

What would you do about this confidence? Why? What issues do you identify in this situation? What agency policies might there be in such a centre about some of the issues? What policies are you aware of in your work place that would apply? What criminal offences are being committed?

The young woman's father and her boyfriend are both committing an offence. How do you feel about the father's offence? This is a child protection issue. How will you weigh up this young woman's situation and needs? Whose interests are you serving in the long run by not disclosing and acting in these circumstances? Do you feel differently about her situation in relation to her father and her 17-year-old lover? Why? Can you judge whether she is sufficiently mature to cope with the situation with the boyfriend or is she being exploited by someone with far more power? How will the age issue affect your approach to confidentiality? 'The younger the girl, and the greater the 'exploitative' nature of the relationship, the more serious the penalty is likely to be' (Hamilton 1998: 38) for the offender.

Why do people sometimes choose to tell you very difficult and painful things? Is it a first step, conscious or otherwise, towards changing or resolving the issue? If so, what is your role? Perhaps to enable that person to talk, offload and reflect, hopefully gaining a greater understanding of their situation, which could later lead to them taking control and making changes themselves. The issue may be so serious, as in the case of the father's incest, you may need to take action with them or on their behalf and hopefully with their agreement. As informal educators we are not only engaging in conversation, but with individual and social change as our long-term aims in doing so. Our values in informal education work mean we have a responsibility to work towards a better, safer and more just world. Do we achieve that by being a sympathetic ear? Will that be enough if it means allowing someone to continue to be exploited or abused indefinitely? You may feel needed in this listening role but whose needs are more important if serious harm continues? Whose interests are you serving in the long run?

One of the reasons the problem of child abuse (sexual or physical), particularly in families, continues so extensively is the secrecy surrounding it and the way abusers establish control. Therefore there are strong moral arguments on the basis of tackling oppression and inequality, for workers to be reporting this behaviour eventually, but there are also many risks associated with this. The young person may, for instance, deny the abuse, and they could be dealt with badly by the police or social services.

Daniel (1997) points out that a key 1988 Department of Education and Science Circular (now DfEE) acknowledged the importance of confidentiality in relationships between youth workers and young people but argued that eventually statutory authorities will need to know. This circular recommends that local education authorities should spell out the 'procedures and circumstances' (Daniel 1997: 19) when youth workers should talk to other professionals and agencies. Local authority youth and community work employees are expected to provide information about abuse to Social Services colleagues as this department has a duty under the Children Act 1989 Section 47 to 'investigate situations where the child could be suffering significant harm' (Mabey and Sorensen 1995: 96). Health-funded agencies also have such legal obligations.

If you work for an organisation which is not part of the statutory sector, such as a voluntary counselling agency, then there is no legal obligation under the Children Act for you to inform social services unless they request you to (Mabey and Sorensen 1995). However, Rayment (1995) points out in her writing about policies on confidentiality that the spirit of the Act is about partnership between agencies like youth counselling services and social services in the protection of children, and ultimately the work of such agencies is about protecting young people. Therefore, ideally, such agencies will work with children and young people to get them to report abusive behaviour. Hopefully your voluntary agency also has a policy which spells out who you should discuss such an issue with in the agency, even if there is no legal obligation involved.

Why does the nature of the agency make a difference here? Local authorities and other public welfare bodies, funded by our taxes, are expected to provide services for the public good, and to prevent harm to individuals. They are accountable to the public. Voluntary organisations may well have the same intentions but are not necessarily obliged to prioritise the public good in the same way and may make their own rules as their legitimisation does not originate in law or through the ballot box.

If you are obliged to disclose such a confidence about sexual abuse or under age sex, what about the timing? Do you need to react immediately? Would you dial 999? If someone has been the victim of abuse for months or years are their lives any worse tomorrow? Presumably the person has developed strategies to survive physically and emotionally. Can you offer a little time and space to talk the situation through, and support them to take action for themselves?

> What if . . . a woman who you do not know well but who is a regular, quiet member of the local action group is the only person who stays behind on this occasion to help to clear up after the meeting? As you stack chairs she sighs and in response to your question about her sighs she confides in you about the bullying and racism she is experiencing at work which is wearing her down. She does not want to do anything about it as she has a good job and feels the racism is an inevitable part of working life for black workers in the town which she can do little about.

What would you do about this confidence? Your values that inform your work tell you that racism is totally unacceptable. This woman wants you to keep her situation confidential.

How could you work with her to ensure she has a clear understanding of what is going on and can believe that the racism is the responsibility of the organisation concerned, its managers and the perpetrators of the racism, and not her as the person experiencing the racism? What information, support and contacts could you provide to enable her to make an informed decision about taking action, formally or not? Could you promise to work alongside her all the way through the organisation process or legal action?

How might this situation be different for you as the informal education worker depending on whether you are black or white? If you are white, do you feel you or the woman might benefit from discussing this with a black colleague? If you are black would you benefit from involving a white colleague? Is it important in such circumstances for a representative of the majority white community to play a part with her in taking action against this racism? All this presumes a need to negotiate with her to reach a point where either she takes action or agrees to you sharing the confidence to ensure action is taken against the perpetrators. Is it right in the long run for you to hold this confidence and no action to be taken so the perpetrators continue to bully this woman or others? Whose interests are being served?

> What if . . . you and your detached work colleague have been working in the area for sometime and know most of the young people who hang around the public spaces? You have been concerned for a while about the poor physical and mental state of one young man called Derek but have been unable to get him to acknowledge any difficulties. You come across him with one of his mates at the back of the park. His mate Jason explains that Derek has been talking of suicide which Derek denies. Jason is known to be a regular user and small-time drug dealer and explains confidentially that he has been supplying Derek with cocaine cheaply to try to make him feel better. You persuade the two of them to go back to your project office for some warmth and a cup of tea. Your colleague and Jason have to go but you stay on with Derek who does eventually disclose that he is very low and has been contemplating suicide, but states adamantly that he does not want anyone else to know. He also discloses that he is gay and is very scared about how any of his friends or family would react if they found out.

What would you do about this confidence? Why? What issues do you identify in this situation? What agency policies might there be about some of the issues?

How seriously should you take such disclosure? Suicide is the extreme form of self-harm. Young men in particular feature in high proportions in suicide statistics and often no-one knew there was a problem, so it is wise to take such disclosures extremely seriously. Is it more important to prevent death and get help for that person, or is it more important not to break confidence and respect someone's wish to die? No worker should have to carry that responsibility without at least discussing this suicidal person and their role anonymously with someone else. If any young person has attempted suicide before, they are at particular risk. Homophobia and heterosexism mean that gays and lesbians can have a very isolating and miserable time especially as young people.

What would you do about Jason and his drug dealing? What factors might affect your decision?

What do you know of his level of involvement and the nature of the drugs? How much harm is he causing himself and others? Are you clear about your legal position and your agency's policies on drugs? If you keep this information confidential you need to take care to avoid being seen as aiding and abetting. You should not knowingly allow illegal drugs to be used or sold in your project, or hold onto illegal drugs handed over to you (pass them onto the police immediately – you do not have to identify who handed them over). Would you discuss with this person, for instance, how they live with the risk they run of having their freedom curtailed if caught dealing? Do they think they, their family, or anyone else is harmed by their drug use? Bear in mind that illegal drug use and dealing is part of everyday life for some people in some neighbourhoods in the same way that the legal use of alcohol and tobacco is part of everyday life for the majority of people of all ages. To what extent could your reporting the drug dealing affect your ability to work with people in the neighbourhood who you feel are your priority? Is it worth the risk to lose the trust of them all?

How will you weigh up the difficult balance between the interests of the individual concerned (and the confidentiality of their information) and the public interest? When does the public or common good override that of the individual?

Support, supervision and teamwork

As the 'What if . . . ?' scenarios illustrate, dealing with confidentiality is complex and personally demanding. How have you and are you going to cope? It would be irresponsible to take on more than your present experience, time and competence can cope with. Depending on the nature of the confidence, you may well need support, advice and possibly an agency decision about what to do. Would it be helpful to share anonymously the confidence you are holding to get support and a sounding board to think it through, especially where you are managing serious risk? How would you go about doing this?

As discussed, in some cases you will be obliged by your organisation's policy and procedures to discuss a confidence with your line manager, particularly about child abuse. In some cases would non-line management supervision be appropriate so you get regular support outside the agency while handling something really difficult? Is such an option available in your agency?

Do you keep records for yourself of difficult situations? Does your agency expect you to do so? In gaining useful supervision it can help to share records that you have made about the situation, your feelings and perhaps some of the facts. These can be anonymous to retain confidentiality, or may need to be specific and kept in a locked file depending on the situation and your agency's policy. These kind of personal records cannot normally be accessed by the police except in rare cases via a judge's order (Hamilton 1998: 28).

When might it be necessary to share with the team, and why? What are your experiences of confidential information being shared in your team, and what did this achieve or prevent? It could ensure everyone is working in the same helpful direction with a particular person. What if someone's mother is dying and they have shared this with you? You may feel that colleagues should know at least that something major is happening in their life so they can be sensitive to their mood and behaviour, or it may even be appropriate to explain the precise nature of the troubles. The person may need the project very much but perhaps their erratic behaviour or drink and drug use could lead to them being excluded if others are not aware. Due to the part-time nature of much of our work you may not always be working when the person concerned is visiting your project but colleagues will be. How can you negotiate with the person concerned so they agree to this team knowledge?

What about sharing beyond the team? Decisions to break confidence to another agency or within an interagency team should be made with others – a decision made by the team or with your supervisor is generally going to be more sound than one made on your own. There can be shared responsibility for the repercussions and you then have support to see you through the next difficult stages.

Earlier distinctions were made between the role of the informal education worker and the social worker and doctor. These distinctions are significant for us in partnership work as the different professionals we liaise with, or work alongside in multi-disciplinary projects, will often have different understandings of what confidentiality means and may assume automatically that certain confidential information will be shared between professionals. What experience do you have of such differing approaches? How did this affect you? If you all work for different employers, their policies and legal positions could vary considerably, as already mentioned when considering sexual abuse.

Drug and alcohol agencies are generally funded from health authority money. In their booklet, SCODA/Alcohol Concern reflect the health perspective when arguing in relation to other agencies that 'it has always been good practice to have agreed policies on confidentiality which encourage the appropriate sharing of information within defined and clearly understood boundaries' (1994: 6).

Conclusion

So what factors can you identify from this chapter that need to be taken account of in negotiating and dealing with confidentiality? Is there a hierarchy of principles or values that you have been using in your reflections on the scenarios? Where does confidentiality line up in that collection of principles you use in your work like self determination, respect, and not colluding with but tackling oppressive behaviour? As a role model, what principles do you wish to be seen to be applying?

As you will realise there is not always a straightforward answer to whether something should remain confidential – it depends on:

- your role as an informal educator and the values you embed in that role;
- the nature and role of your employing agency;
- the nature of the 'confidential' subject matter;
- the needs of the people concerned at that time dictated by their age, maturity, gender, race and other factors;
- the implications of the information being shared and with whom it is shared;
- legal and policy implications.

Whose interests are you serving when keeping confidences? Those of the confidante, the wrongdoer, or the public? Whose interests come first and in what circumstances? You need to guide your decisions by aiming in the long run to be supporting the person to change their present situation for a safer and fairer one. Judgement and discretion will be needed about negotiating and dealing with confidentiality but if you are clear about your values, your role and that of the agency you work for, the law, and the roles other people play, and you respect others you will generally conduct yourself with integrity.

Further reading

Daniel, S. (1997) *Confidentiality and Young People: Working Together – Conflict, Contradictions, Chaos or the Best Interests of Young People?* Leicester: Centre for Social Action. This booklet explores the distinct legal position on confidentiality of street-based voluntary agencies as well as the independent roles they play in working with marginalised young people. A range of issues are identified, especially about partnership with statutory agencies, and detailed recommendations are made. It includes case study material and examples of confidentiality policies as well as information about the law.

Hamilton, C. (1998) *Working with Young People: Legal Responsibility and Liability*, 4th edn. Colchester: Children's Legal Centre. A regularly republished book covering the current legal framework. It is designed to deal with some of the legal problems faced by youth workers and others working with young people and includes a whole chapter specifically on confidentiality.

Hugman, R. (1991) *Power in Caring Professions.* Basingstoke: Macmillan. This book provides some background contextual reading on power in relationships between caring professionals and service users, and between different professional groups. It considers in particular the implications of race and gender.

Mabey, J. and Sorensen, B. (1995) *Counselling for Young People.* Buckingham: Open University Press. This book covers the context, theory and practice of youth counselling and includes various specific references to issues of confidentiality.

Morgan, S. and Banks, S. (1999) 'The youth worker as confidante', in Banks, S. (ed.) *Ethical Issues in Youth Work.* London: Routledge. A very useful chapter which explores meanings of confidentiality, and how it applies to youth work, using some example dilemmas. The final section recommends some principles to achieve ethical practice.

Rayment, B. (1995) *Confidential – Developing Confidentiality Policies in Youth Counselling and Advisory Services.* Loughborough: Youth Access. This booklet provides detailed guidelines for developing a policy on confidentiality in youth counselling agencies to ensure they behave responsibly and ethically. It includes an exploration of the meaning of confidentiality and of the law as well as example policies.

The National Youth Agency holds a number of examples of local authority and voluntary sector confidentiality policies that can be borrowed, and from the information service you can request a current list of policies, books and articles held on confidentiality.

References

Banks, S. (1995) *Ethics and Values in Social Work.* Basingstoke: Macmillan.

Daniel, S. (1997) *Confidentiality and Young People: Working Together – Conflict, Contradictions, Chaos or the Best Interests of Young People?* Leicester: Centre for Social Action.

Devon Community and Continuing Education Unit (date unknown) *Confidentiality Guidelines for Youth Workers.* Exeter: Devon County Council.

Hamilton, C. (1998) *Working with Young People: Legal Responsibility and Liability,* 4th edn. Colchester: Children's Legal Centre.

Hugman, R. (1991) *Power in Caring Professions.* Basingstoke: Macmillan.

Jeffs, T. and Smith, M. (1996) *Informal Education: Conversation, Democracy and Learning.* Derby: Education Now.

Mabey, J. and Sorensen, B. (1995) *Counselling for Young People,* Buckingham: Open University Press.

Morgan, S. and Banks, S. (1999) 'The youth worker as confidante', in Banks, S. (ed.) *Ethical Issues in Youth Work.* London: Routledge.

Rayment, B. (1995) *Confidential – Developing Confidentiality Policies in Youth Counselling and Advisory Services.* Loughborough: Youth Access.

Rodger, J. (1997) *Confidentiality: guidelines for youth workers.* Barnsley: Metropolitan Borough Council Community Resources.

SCODA/Alcohol Concern (1994) *Building Confidence: Advice for Alcohol and Drug Services on Confidentiality Policies.* London: SCODA.

Thompson, N. (1997) (2nd edn.) *Anti-Discriminatory Practice.* Basingstoke: Macmillan.

7 Learning from experience

Huw Blacker

As a student beginning a course of study it would not be unusual to hold the attitude – 'I'm going to learn a lot over the next few years.' However, I would like to explore the idea that we have been students all of our lives, and will continue to be so. The 'course' that we have been on, our 'area of study' has been provided by the experiences we have had in our everyday lives.

Our lives are surrounded by learning. The experiences we have from day to day help shape who we are, how we think and feel, how we act. It is from these experiences that we learn about the world and about ourselves. It is from these experiences that we have developed our knowledge, attitudes and skills.

If then we are learning from our everyday experiences, what is the importance of drawing attention to this process?

Firstly, as informal educators we are concerned with learning, especially the learning that takes place in everyday life. To have an understanding of the process taking place when people learn from their experiences can be helpful when thinking about the way we work.

It is also important to have an understanding about the way you learn from your experiences. We do not always learn from the experiences that we have. To have an experience alone, it would seem, is not enough. We have to engage in certain thought processes in order to learn effectively from these experiences. Sometimes we do this naturally, other times we do not and miss the opportunity of learning from an experience that may be of importance to our development. Here then we will look more closely at the process of learning from experience.

Experiential learning

We are aware then that we have experiences every day from which we may learn. What happens alongside this experience that enables us to learn from it? There are many theories that have been written about this subject. A term that is often used by theorists to describe this process is *experiential learning* – thus placing an importance on the role that experience plays in the process of learning. Here we are going to explore one of the more well-known theories on experiential learning by David Kolb.

Kolb (1976, 1984) presents us with a model that is comprised of four stages. Here I will briefly outline each stage, then move on to a practical example that demonstrates this process in action.

The pattern begins with an experience, this could be any event that takes place in daily life. Kolb calls this a *concrete experience*. This concrete experience may then lead to a period of reflection (*reflective observation* in Kolb's model), this is when we think about the experience itself. This then leads on to a process of theory making (which Kolb calls *abstract conceptualisation*). This is when we make connections to ideas or theories that we already have and, when necessary, change or develop them to fit in with the new experience. As such we are building our own theories based on our experiences. We then move into what Kolb calls *active experimentation*. This is when we test out our new theory or understanding in practice. From this we move into another concrete experience.

When the general principle is understood, the last step is its application through action in a new circumstance. In some representations of experiential learning these steps (or ones like them) are sometimes represented as a circular movement. In reality, if learning has taken place, the process could be seen as a spiral. The action is taking place in a different set of circumstances and the learner is now able to anticipate the possible effects of the action.

This process may be easier to understand if we use a practical example to explore the various stages. If, for example, I wanted to do a landscape painting and needed to mix the colour green for the first time, we can see how this model can be worked through.

The paints I have available are yellow, red and blue. I am aware from a previous experience that by mixing two colours together a new and different colour is produced. From this I decide to mix together the colours blue and red. The colour purple is produced. The *concrete experience* I have is that by mixing blue and red I produce the colour purple. This I know by my *reflective observation* of the colour mixing and its result. I then build a theory – blue and red do not produce green, so maybe the colours red and yellow do. I then engage in *active experimentation*, mixing red and yellow, to produce orange. This again is a concrete experience, with my reflective observation of the process enabling me to learn that red and yellow make orange. I then build a further theory – I have not yet mixed blue and yellow together, so maybe this is the formula that makes green. Again I move into active experimentation, mixing blue and yellow together and, at last, produce the colour green.

I have learnt several things from this process:

blue + red = purple; red + yellow = orange; blue + yellow = green.

The theories I now have may be transferable to other situations. For example, the above paints I used were watercolours, maybe the same theory applies to oil paint and acrylic.

This process can also take place in our work when we seek to understand certain general principles by reflecting on concrete events. Thus, an informal educator who has learnt in this way may well have various rules of thumb or generalisations about what to do in different situations. This also helps us to further develop our frame of reference as educators.

We can see then that to learn from an experience we need to engage our thinking upon it at some level. As such, all experiences have the potential to be learnt from, it is whether or not we engage with them at this level that seems to be the key to learning.

Kolb's theory on experiential learning has also been reflected upon, and further theories have been developed from it. For example, Kolb talks of four stages – when, in effect, everything can happen at once. We should not fall into the trap of thinking that such processes are this neat. However, theories like these do provide a good framework for reflecting on our processes.

Triggering reflection

If we were to think in depth about the experiences we have throughout the day it would be unlikely if we made it past breakfast time! Much of what we do we have already learnt about, or formed theories about, and these matters do not necessarily need a great deal of thought.

For example, I know how to get ready for work in the morning – how to turn the alarm off, dress myself, make my cornflakes, put toothpaste on my toothbrush and clean my teeth, wash etc. These experiences do not require a great deal of thought on my part. For much of the time then, we depend on tacit knowledge – we use ideas, images without necessarily being aware of them.

Why then do some experiences trigger the process of reflection and theory making? Thinking begins, according to Dewey (1933: 122) 'in what may be fairly enough called a forked road situation that is ambiguous, that presents a dilemma, that proposes alternatives.'

If then, I was to get up one morning, turn off my alarm, and then suddenly remember that I had an interview for a job that day, I could be faced with a dilemma – what to wear! There are alternatives – a suit, smart shirt and tie, casual clothes, shoes or smart trainers? I think back to the experience of reading about the advertised job, the job specification, questions asked on the application form and I build a theory about what the interviewers may expect from me. From this theory I make my choice of what to wear – then head off to my interview for some *active experimentation*. And so my early morning 'routine' reaches a *forked road*.

Q1: Think back over the last few sessions you have worked as an educator. What 'forked roads' did you encounter and how did you respond to them?

For myself I thought back to a recent streetwork session I was involved in. The 'forked road' came when a young person asked me for a lift to a health appointment she was having. From previous discussions I knew of the importance of this appointment and also realised she had no money to get there or any other means of transport. The policy of the service I was working for states we are not to give young people lifts in our own personal transport. Alongside this I realised the importance of attending this appointment for the person and that not to help in this situation would possibly affect the relationship we had been developing over recent weeks. With my car in sight this was a difficult situation to decide about. Reflecting on the various scenarios and possible ways of acting I made a decision that in this situation I would offer to cover the costs of the bus fare to and from the appointment explaining carefully the reasons for this decision. This situation also led me to reflect on other experiences of people asking to borrow money, and to decide to ask the service I was working for further, more detailed information on giving lifts to young people we work with.

There are many situations to which we have to respond instantly within our practice. Some of these situations we will have more time to think about than others. Thinking while we act (about what we are doing and the possible consequences of our actions) is a skill that we have to use regularly in our work. Donald Schön (1983) (see Further reading section) refers to this process as *reflecting in action*. From this we can see that experiential learning can take place relatively quickly. It is also important, however, to develop our learning opportunities when *reflecting on action* (as Schön calls thinking about our work after we have done it). We can then reflect in a more deliberate manner, and with more time to explore the possibilities that were available to us. This is using your experiences to learn and develop your practice further.

Using experience for learning

As a student practitioner, there are various processes you will need to engage in that encourage you to learn from your experiences. Supervision, self-assessment, recordings, assignments, even the questions in these chapters can be seen as activities that 'trigger reflection', much of it focused upon your work as an informal educator. To use the experiences you are having in your practice as a source for learning is crucial in order to develop your work and your understanding of what you are doing. As such, to work effectively with the above processes is to become an effective learner.

Q2: Here is a list of some of the activities you need to engage in as a student. Next to each one write a list of some of the experiences you have recently explored and learnt from.

Supervision:

Recordings/Journal:

Residential/study groups:

While I envisage that each of you had a very different and varied list, it is possible they all had something in common – the experiences explored were triggered by a 'forked road' situation, a dilemma of some kind, or a situation in which various alternatives were possible, or where you were unsure of your response.

It is interesting to consider why we choose some situations to explore and not others. There may be experiences in our work where we feel there is no dilemma, and hence choose not to reflect on it. However, there are also opportunities for learning from these sometimes taken-for-granted situations. By exploring them we can often uncover useful insights into ourselves and our work. This may be worth trying sometime, when recording or in supervision. Remember – all our experiences hold within them the potential for learning.

Reflection

We can see that to learn from our experiences it is crucial that we think about them, or *reflect* upon them. In the Kolb model we see this is an important step to take in the learning process, similarly, in supervision, recordings etc., this is an activity we engage in as part of the learning process.

Michael Eraut, in his book *Developing Professional Knowledge and Competence*, states that reflecting on our practice 'is a central part of a professional's responsibility for the continuing development and on-going evaluation of their personal knowledge base ... failure to engage in such reflection on a regular basis is irresponsible' (1994: 156).

When we reflect upon our experiences we must also recognise that our feelings or emotions are also involved in the process. Our emotions can, if unattended to, affect the way we perceive an experience we have had, or the judgements we make about it. As such, this can in turn affect what we may learn about and from that experience.

A useful approach to working with this has been presented by Boud *et al.* (1993). They see the process of reflection as involving three elements:

- Returning to experience – recalling, or playing through in your mind, the different aspects of the experience you remember.
- Attending to (or connecting with) feelings – this has two aspects: using helpful feelings and removing or containing obstructive ones.
- Evaluating experience – this involves re-examining experience in the light of one's intent and existing knowledge etc. It also involves integrating this new knowledge into one's conceptual framework. (26–31).

When referring to the aspect of 'returning to experience', Boud *et al.* comment:

> One of the most useful activities that can initiate a period of reflection is recollecting what has taken place and replaying the experience in the mind's eye, to observe the event as it has happened and to notice exactly what occurred and one's reactions to it in all its elements.
>
> (1985: 27)

From this it is important to recognise and work with the feelings and reactions you had at the time of the experience, and in thinking back on it. Our emotions and feelings are an important source for learning. However, they can also become a barrier to learning. By working with these emotions, acknowledging the negative, as well as positive, we can attempt to understand these responses in greater depth and explore the impact they may have had upon us and our work.

Q3: We can see that Boud *et al.* (1985) suggest that reflection involves returning to the experience and connecting with our feelings. This again is something we routinely do when recording. We also seek to make some judgements about the experience. I suspect it is also something that your supervisor encourages you to do.

Is this something you also seek to do when working with individuals and groups? Think back to some recent pieces of work.

For myself I thought back to a recent piece of work I was involved in with a group of residents from a hostel. The group had organised a day trip for other residents which only a few people attended. As a group we talked about the day itself and how we felt about not many people turning up. Some felt disappointed and angry that other residents hadn't supported the activity, while others felt a certain responsibility for the lack of numbers attending. From this we made judgements about the activity that we had offered other residents, how we'd publicised it and whether we could have improved these areas. We also discussed the success of the trip for those who did attend and that maybe the 'quality' of the day was more important than the 'quantity'.

This way of working, of encouraging people to reflect on their experiences and to build theories, is central to what we do, but I do wonder whether we place enough emphasis on returning to experiences and entertaining feelings. Often when people tell us about some experience or difficulty it is easy to slip into encouraging them to think about solutions before they have really connected with the events and the emotions they evoke. Yet before we can start to build theories about situations we do need to be in touch with our feelings and experiences. Otherwise, some of our anger about what another person has done, for example, may block our ability to see the situation for what it is.

By reflecting on our experiences we may find we need to add to, modify or change the knowledge, attitudes and skills we already hold. Essentially what we are doing is challenging our old ideas and attitudes where necessary, and through this process of learning, developing new ideas and attitudes and ways of working. We are using experience for learning in ways that help us to develop our practice.

Further reading

Boud, D., Cohen, R. and Walker, D. (eds) (1993) *Using Experience for Learning*. Buckingham: Open University Press. Here various authors explore some of the key ideas involved in learning from experience including: 'How do we learn from experience? How does context and purpose influence learning? How does experience impact on individual and group learning? How can we help others to learn from their experience?'

Boud, D. and Miller, N. (eds) (1996) *Working with Experience, Animating Learning*. London: Routledge. Various contributors working within professional practice explore what practitioners do to animate other people's learning and how they make sense of it.

Kolb, D. (1984) *Experiential Learning – Experience as the Source of Learning and*

Development. Englewood Cliffs, NJ: Prentice Hall. Looks at the theory of experiential learning, presenting various models including the model referred to in this chapter.

Schön, D. (1983) *The Reflective Practitioner. How Professionals Think in Action*. USA: Basic Books Inc. In this book Schön explores the idea of *reflecting in action*, and how this works in practice. He also explores the concept of 'artistry' or creativity in the work.

References

Boud, D., Cohen, R. and Walker, D. (eds) (1993) *Using Experience for Learning*. Buckingham: Open University Press.

Boud, D., Keogh, K. and Walker, D. (eds) (1985) *Reflection: Turning Experience Into Learning*. Kogan Page: London.

Boud, D. and Miller, N. (eds) (1996) *Working with Experience, Animating Learning*. London: Routledge.

Coleman, J.S. (1976) 'Differences between experiential and classroom learning', in M.T. Keeton (ed.) *Experiential Learning*. San Francisco: Josey-Bass.

Dewey, J. (1933) *How We Think*. Boston: D.C. Heath.

Dewey, J. (1938) *Experience and Education*. New York: Macmillan.

Eraut, M. (1994) *Developing Professional Knowledge and Competence*. London: The Falmer Press.

Jarvis, P. (1987) *Adult Education in the Social Context*. London: Routledge.

Jeffs, T. and Smith, M.K. (1987) *Youth Work*. London: Macmillan.

Kirkwood, G. (1991) 'Fallacy: the community educator should be a non-directive facilitator', in B. O'Hagan (ed.) *The Charnwood Papers. Fallacies in Community Education*. Ticknall: Education Now.

Kolb, D. (1976) *Learning Styles Inventory*. Boston, MA: McBer Co.

Kolb, D. (1984) *Experiential Learning*. Englewood Cliffs, NJ: Prentice Hall. A key chapter from this book is also included in M. Thorpe *et al.* (eds) (1993) *Culture and Processes of Adult Learning*. London: Routledge.

Rogers, C. (1993) 'The interpersonal relationship in the facilitation of learning', in M. Thorpe *et al.* (eds) (1993) *Culture and Processes of Adult Learning*. London: Routledge.

Schön, D.A. (1983) *The Reflective Practitioner. How Professionals Think in Action*. USA: Basic Books Inc.

Smith, M.K. (1987) *Creators Not Consumers*. Leicester: National Association of Youth Clubs.

Smith, M.K. (1994) *Local Education. Community, Conversation, Praxis*. Buckingham: Open University Press.

8 Relationships and learning

Graeme Tiffany

Introduction

This chapter argues for the importance of the relationship between learner and educator in promoting learning in both formal and informal settings. Such relationships are often defined as 'professional', but here I will call them 'learning relationships'.

We begin by seeking to define what we mean by a relationship in general. By considering relationships from a variety of perspectives, we hope to 'get inside' the concept. This analysis seems necessary, as our understandings about learning relationships have become entangled in our everyday uses of the word 'relationship'. We rarely think critically about what we are describing. Poets write about relationships with great power and impact because they take care to use words precisely, to express an exact meaning. When, to take a famous example, John Donne writes, 'No man is an Iland, intire of it selfe', he is using a vivid image to convey the interconnectedness of all humankind. As workers, we need to try to achieve that same clarity and precision in thinking and talking about relationships in our work.

Following a rapid survey of the many ways in which we speak of relationships, we consider the characteristics that make some relationships educative. The aim is to identify features that will help you, whose work is rooted in relationships, to facilitate learning through these relationships. Ultimately, you should be able to think about relationships in a more evaluative way, and make judgements about professional, working relationships based on a critical analysis and understanding of the relationships you are involved in.

What is a relationship?

Q1: Who, or what, do you 'connect with'? Note down quickly half a dozen examples. Can you identify what is the basis of these connections?

You may not have been quite sure what I meant by this question, but I hope it raised some feelings that allowed you to come up with some answers. For instance, you might have thought about somebody you 'get on with'. Probing a bit deeper, you might have asked why, and identified things that you and the other person have in common, shared experiences, or alternatively ways in which you differ and 'bounce off' one another. Let's now look at this question from a broader perspective.

> **Q2:** How many different meanings can you identify for the term 'rela-
> tionship'? Again, note down as many examples as you can and try to
> identify the different qualities and characteristics of the relationships
> that you have chosen.

This may be the first time you have considered what you mean by 'relationship' in any more than the briefest detail. Your efforts may have exposed the
complexity of the subject and resulted in some confusion. Let's begin by
looking at the origin of the word itself.

The origin of the word 'relationship' is from the Latin 'to carry back',
which comes across most clearly in a phrase like 'to relate something to
somebody'. This suggests communication, a relation between people and
ideas. We use the word to mean that, at least in some sense, a connection or
association exists, or is formed, between two or more things, people or ideas.
It might be the 'fit' between two bricks in a wall, the links among nations in
an association such as NATO, the logical connection between two ideas.
Other uses of the word have an inter-personal significance, signifying that
something tangible and meaningful exists between people. Characteristically,
this 'in-betweenness' has compassionate or sympathetic underpinnings.
Relationships include families, kinships, marriage and the relations – by
blood or law – that each of these bring. These ties are defined by law or tradition. Conversely, relationships may be based on something more personal.
You might have thought of friendships, or relationships based on sex and
love.

You may also have considered the concept of relationships in a wider
socio-political context. Social and political references can include personal
connections, feelings or dealings between or among individuals, groups,
businesses, peoples, nations, etc. Some examples of these might be professional or working relationships between, say, colleagues or business partners,
doctors and patients, and teachers and pupils.

These definitions are many and varied. For our purpose here, we need to
focus on those that reflect the human and communicative aspects of relationships which are, after all, the basis of informal education.

Working relationships

> **Q3:** Briefly describe three or four relationships that you have with indi-
> viduals or groups as part of your practice.

You may have described relationships with your employer or a young person
you work with. You may have made some reference to your feelings or made
a judgement about how bad or good the relationship is. You have probably
not said anything about the peculiarities or idiosyncrasies of these relationships – facets that would allow you to define that relationship (and your
experience of it) differently from others. Specific details, things that seem
unusual, give us evidence of the state of a relationship, especially if they are

written down. Scrutinising our relationships in these ways allows us to be more objective about what is going on.

Another way to define working relationships more specifically and objectively is to describe them in terms of the exchanges that take place between (or among) the parties. Goetschius and Tash, (1967: 137) for example, suggest: 'A relationship is a connection between two people in which some sort of exchange takes place'. To talk of a relationship as an exchange is to focus on what is given up, parted with, or transferred to the other person; and what is received in its place. Indeed, we might say that what gets exchanged is the central part of the relationship.

Let us look at these points more closely. That two people, at least, exist within a relationship implies two things. Firstly, at least two perspectives on the relationship exist. Secondly, two sets of interpretations and understandings are likely. This means that any kind of relationship is a two-way process. However, for Goetschius and Tash's connection to take place, something more is needed. The idea of exchange involves something moving between two people, an 'in-betweenness' to which both contribute and which affects both. A relationship in this sense involves a series of commitments and obligations over and above those typical of everyday contact.

Indeed, your descriptions of relationships might have included words like 'real' or 'meaningful'. They may also have mentioned the difference between establishing relationships and working to create an environment where learning can take place. Naturally, the former can help to foster the latter, and vice versa. Being in a certain place can help relationships to develop. But something more, or, indeed, something different is needed. We will come back to what that is later. In the meantime, we might conclude that what is important for a relationship is going beyond everyday contact and becoming more appreciative of and receptive to the other's perspective.

Q4: Think again about the relationships you described for Question 3. To what extent do your descriptions recognise more than one point of view? What is being exchanged?

The point here is to be precise about exactly what is being exchanged (and to what extent it is being received). Within an educational setting, this may involve the giving, receiving and interchange of specific information and ideas. At other times, it may be more to do with feelings and with non-verbal exchanges, such as giving and receiving attention or support or simply showing interest in the other person. In either case, we need to focus on the nuances of what is being said and done. Only then can we be clearer and more objective about the relationships we participate in.

Tash gives a useful summary of our findings as to 'What are relationships?':

> First, there are (at least) two persons in the relationship, each with thoughts and feelings about the other. Second, it can be seen (presumably by participants and/or onlookers) that the connection between the two people is of a particular kind, which results in people talking of a 'mother/child relationship', 'a sexual relationship', or a 'professional

relationship'. Third, the definitions imply that the two persons are in contact with each other, exchanging ideas, giving and taking, talking and listening. Fourth, they indicate movement, that a relationship is not static, but that changes as well as exchanges are taking place.

(1967: 19)

These four factors form a useful checklist for our thoughts when considering the working relationships we enter into. We cannot, however, claim that a relationship of this sort will necessarily lead to learning. It is what occurs within the context of these factors that gives it value as a learning relationship.

The potential of relationships for learning

So far, we have recognised that it is not enough to use simple statements like 'relating to' or 'being in a relationship with'. Using the idea of exchanges to be more specific lets us get in touch with what we really mean, and understand more fully what is happening between ourselves and those we work with. This is crucial if we are to appreciate the full potential of relationships to effect change and foster learning.

But it takes more than being specific about the terms of our relationships to realise this potential. For example, while we might readily associate youth and community work with the making and development of relationships, we might not necessarily make any connection between these relationships and learning. What is required is both the development of more significant relationships and an appreciation of the need to create an environment for learning.

What do we mean by 'significant relationships'? What is involved here requires almost a leap of faith, to reach an aim that transcends the sometimes mundane notion of what we are there to do. The idea that we are there to 'chat to young people' will no longer suffice. What is called for is a higher state of mental preparedness. Whenever we communicate, we need to be 'on the case': concentrating on identifying, and responding to, as many opportunities for promoting learning as possible. Failure to concentrate and be creative about our interventions undoubtedly means we will miss some of these opportunities.

My own understanding of my responsibilities as an educator did, indeed, go through such a process of transformation. In a way, it came almost as a revelation. It began with what at first felt like a personal attack, from a tutor angry at my sloppy preparation for a workshop presentation. It took me some time to realise that this challenge was a call for me to account, not so much for my own missed learning opportunity, but those of others. The revelation came from a sudden realisation that our relationships with others always have within them the capacity to facilitate learning. Not fulfilling this capacity was, in a sense, a failure to live up to professional ideals and values. Thereafter, I always tried to look for the minutiae of opportunities to facilitate learning and to foster a positive learning environment. It was a question of always seeing what could be squeezed out of any given situation, looking for learning opportunities as part and parcel of working relationships, rather than seeing the relationships as an end in themselves.

Of course, we must also recognise limiting factors. We cannot work with everyone, and there are those with whom we will always struggle to work. I can well remember trying 'every trick in the book' in an attempt to make some kind of connection with a particularly difficult young man who attended the youth project, albeit irregularly. Over time, I realised the difficulties I experienced in attempting to establish a productive rapport had as much to do with racial, ethnic and cultural issues as with my own relationship-building skills. Interestingly, this individual responded much more, and developed accordingly, when, on the basis of this analysis, I transferred my end of the relationship to a colleague. He had much more in common with the young man, and I was able to support his interventions rather than continue to be frustrated by my own.

It is worth stating that this particular young man would fit most criteria of being 'hard to reach'. He had been excluded from one school and received a series of temporary suspensions from others. He found it almost impossible to communicate with his parents, although he still lived at home. Criminal and anti-social behaviour had resulted in regular contact with the police and other criminal justice agencies. As a consequence, nearly all of his relationships with adults were based on authority. As youth workers, it was important for us to recognise the peculiarly important role we played in his life. We were the only adults with whom he had a personal relationship not based on authority roles. This is not an unusual situation for informal educators to find themselves in. As such, it is vital that we appreciate not only the responsibilities this brings, but also the potential these relationships offer for affecting the lives of similar young people.

We have seen that learning can and often does take place as a product of the relationships we have with young people. However, we need to do more than rely on the happy coincidence of learning taking place more by accident than design. Something more concerted and proactive is called for. What we do – and how – distinguishes a professional, or learning, relationship from any other. This will be our focus from now on.

Relationships and learning: theories, aims and implications

If we accept that the professional relationships we enter into have learning as their aim, certain questions arise. Can we be more explicit about the type of learning aimed at? What theories inform the process, and what are the central features of relationships that enable this learning?

Theories of learning

Most theories of learning tend to concentrate on cognitive rather than affective dimensions of the learning process. That is to say, they place greater emphasis on the mental act or process by which knowledge is acquired than on the kind of relationships within which learning takes place. This means that educational practice is more often informed by cognitive than by emotional and affective considerations.

This seems a shame for, as we have seen, relationships, and their affective aspects, do appear particularly important in all educational endeavours. In our early lives, the relationships we have with parents and carers sow the seeds for our future learning capacities. It is during this period that our minds begin to develop and we first learn to think. Our first thoughts are of ourselves as different from others. But equally, we come to understand the significance these others have in our own lives. Our early emotional attachments and interactions lay the foundation for all other learning experiences.

Indeed, Rustin (1998: 29) draws upon Shuttleworth's (1989) work to suggest:

> If emotional interaction is as fundamental an element as this in the development of the mind of the infant, it seems likely that emotions continue to be dynamic elements in the learning process throughout life, and certainly throughout childhood.

Implications for educators

Relationships appear all the more important when we consider those situations where we aim, purposefully and professionally, to enable others to learn. Indeed, it has been argued that 'the quality and kinds of learning that take place depend on the quality and type of relationship within which the learning process is embedded' (Rustin 1998: 22).

Differing views as to the importance of relationships are at the heart of many current debates about education and learning. Kelly, (1994) for example, fears that increased prescription – for instance, Government directives on what classroom teaching should contain and how it should be done – leads to teachers experiencing a loss of control and autonomy. This, he suggests, has implications for the way in which they interact with their pupils and for the possibility that genuine education can take place:

> Teaching can be conducted by remote control; education requires the interaction of individual pupil with individual teacher not only in an atmosphere of mutual trust and confidence but in a context which offers scope for such interaction to flourish and develop.
>
> (1994: 103)

High levels of prescription tend to go hand-in-hand with the belief that success and, indeed, fear of failure, are key motivators for learning. Conversely, more learner-centred, less prescriptive, approaches (such as those in informal and community education) see the experience of learning as motivational in its own right. Educators in this sense see themselves as charged with responsibilities over and above the transmission of knowledge. Their task is to liberate and bolster learners' motivation by engaging with their intrinsic curiosity and the context of their personal experiences.

The fact that Kelly considers schooling here does not, I suggest, matter for those of us who work in informal and non-formal traditions. What is important – and generally agreed by all educators – is the importance of the quality of the relationship and the contribution that feelings of trust and confidence make to the flourishing and development of the learner.

At this point, it seems important to emphasise again that the quality or value of the relationship does not imply that learning is taking place. Let us, therefore, consider how we might identify both a good learning relationship and one that is educationally profitable.

Virtues and vices: what makes a learning relationship 'good' or 'bad'?

So far, we have considered the diversity and complexity of relationships and their different qualities and characteristics. Now is the time to be a little more specific about what gives them value and, in particular, what makes for a good relationship. In themselves, relationships can be seen as neutral and, like many other things, can be employed both for good and bad.

Let us pose a question. What are the essential qualities of a good learning relationship?

> **Q5:** Identify several examples of learning relationships from your own experience as a learner. Try to work out why you perceived them to be good or bad, valuable or unproductive.

You have probably described what we might call typical learning relationships, such as those between pupil and teacher or student and tutor. Alternatively, you may have considered the learning contained within, for example, parent and child relationships.

Did your attempts to identify what made them good or bad for learning look at features of the relationship itself? In analysing these relationships, you may have mentioned your feelings towards the other person. You may have said that you felt confident in his or her company, or able to trust the educator to show respect for your opinion, or alternatively that negative comments about your abilities dented your confidence. You may have described ways in which you considered that both parties benefited and learnt from the experience.

I would guess that you struggled to describe these aspects in more than the briefest detail. This is understandable; they have a kind of intangibility because they deal with emotional as well as mental matters. These emotional qualities deserve exploring in greater depth.

I would suggest that relationships which are able to foster learning depend on three sets of qualities:

- trust and commitment;
- mutuality;
- appreciating vulnerability.

Trust and commitment

Trust implies some form of emotional investment in a relationship. At the same time, it implies thought. We make judgements about whom to trust, when to trust and what to trust these others with. In addition, we learn to trust (or not) as the trust we invest in others is confirmed or disproved. A pattern develops of trust at different levels, a product of both experience and the context of the relationship we are in.

Both thought and emotion, then, contribute to our decisions to initiate, persist with or end a relationship. They can enable us to make shrewd judgements and suggest when it is worth taking a chance. Recently, while hitch-hiking with my girlfriend on a Greek island, a small, battered old car stopped to offer us a lift. A large, elderly man with a handle-bar moustache drove us into town and invited us to tea later in the day. Over lunch we discussed his invitation. We both felt the man was somewhat strange, an eccentric of sorts. Despite our reservations, our curiosity got the better of us, and we followed his rather vague directions. There followed a wonderful afternoon being shown around one of the oldest houses in Corfu, set high on a cliff face over-looking the Ionian sea. I could tell further tales, but the example illustrates the complex mixture of emotions, fears and experience that inform decisions to enter into, sustain or end relationships with others. It might be worth adding that I was rather more fearful than my girlfriend. I could only put this down to an over-heightened sense of caution developed through several years of working in challenging inner-city areas.

To return to the context of learning relationships, certain features appear particularly important in establishing and preserving this trust.

One is what we might call continuity or reliability. The work of Salzberger-Wittenberg *et al.* (1983) draws attention to the importance of 'beginnings' and 'endings' in educational encounters. Beginnings are the initiators of trust and the foundations on which successful relationships are built. Endings involve the withdrawal of emotional investment. Implicitly, learning becomes more difficult the greater the number of beginnings and endings experienced by the learner. Each makes greater emotional demands, as trust has to be re-established and is subsequently withdrawn (and/or compensated for).

In practice, this might mean that we have to consider the potentially harmful effect of our absences from work, the implications of short-term (typically residential) work and even the ramifications of poor time-keeping. All pose a threat to the productivity of learning relationships.

These considerations apply equally to our own learning. We need to trust those we work with and those charged with facilitating our own professional development. Tutors and supervisors must create opportunities for students to analyse concerns and anxieties. They must protect those situations where interpersonal contact exists, including small group seminars, individual tutoring and informal association. It is through these avenues that we come to understand both ourselves and our fellow learners.

Support of this kind bolsters morale and provides an environment where problems and conflict in other relationships can be analysed and sorted out. Learning relationships, therefore, are characterised not only by trust but also by the opportunities for exploration and reflection which trusting relation-ships allow. Without these, the fundamental aims of education – developing abilities in thinking and understanding – are likely to prove elusive.

One might imagine from the above that a relationship underpinned by trust would be enough to facilitate the learning we strive for. But in addition, a level of commitment to develop and protect these opportunities for learn-ing seems essential.

Commitment suggests many things. There are few of us who cannot recall teachers, youth workers or other adults who made a significant impact on us. When asked to analyse this significance, our responses are often similar. Some of us might refer to their enthusiasm, to an obvious interest in their subjects or to their being animated in putting them across. All, however, demonstrated a commitment to us as persons. They showed a tangible inter-est in us and a desire to understand us for who we are. They identified with us as we would identify with those with whom we share more intimate relationships.

Mutuality

We have already mentioned the idea that learning relationships are mutual or reciprocal, involving give and take. But what does this mean in practice? Consider relationships that throw up uncertainties. If we respond to these in a positive way, as opportunities for shared exploration, there is a greater potential for both parties to learn from the experience. Learning becomes both a co-operative enterprise and a shared aim. Educators who suggest co-operative research in response to a question they cannot answer are also acting out this mutuality. The process of learning together becomes as important as the knowledge pursued. Being seen to defer to the greater knowledge or experience of someone else sends out a number of powerful signals: humility; the acknowledgement that you as an educator can also learn from the process in which clients are involved; and a commitment to the value of mutual engagement.

I remember having a discussion about escalating levels of race-related gang violence with young residents of an inner-city estate. I was keen to pursue conciliatory responses, but the debate was soon consumed by talk more of war than peace. The intervention of a young Somali man changed things completely. He described how he and many he knew had fled from the horrors of war in his homeland. Many young people had been put on flights to Europe by families who knew they were unlikely to see them again. They had made this sacrifice in the belief that it was the only way to ensure the safety of their children. These stories enabled many of the young people to put their local experiences into context. They became more appreciative of the reasons for the movement of some ethnic groups and increasingly aware of the often petty situations that acted as catalysts for their own conflict. For myself, I realised both the limitations of my own experience and the importance of embracing the contributions of others in achieving my aim of promoting learning. It became clear that when people have distinct and different bodies of knowledge or experience, mutuality is all the more important.

Mutuality is further evident when we are committed to change by virtue of this learning. Change is in itself powerful evidence of learning. If we are to pursue both learning and a greater understanding of our self and others, we need to be willing to see our views challenged and to seek out these challenges. At a more basic level, mutuality might simply mean respecting the desire we all have to feel part of the conversation we are involved in. This involves feeling that we are being listened to, having what we say valued and being respected as partners. It is this partnership that best exemplifies mutuality and its benefits.

Appreciating vulnerability

A further characteristic of a learning relationship is that educators appreciate the vulnerability of those that they work with. Vulnerability often comes from fear of failure. A positive relationship can encourage learners to take risks with learning they might otherwise not take. Conversely, a negative relationship can lead to complete breakdown, as the potential learner seeks to avoid both the relationship and the educational endeavour it is associated with.

Learners need to feel that they are being understood, that their feelings of trepidation and anxiety are appreciated and empathised with. Only then will they gain confidence to take risks with learning and to engage in new tasks. When feelings of deficiency, inability and a fear of humiliation surface, a complex range of commitments are needed from the educator. Rustin (1998: 38) describes this as the need 'to tolerate lack of knowledge and competence, invest effort in [enabling learners] to acquire these, and to bear with the pain of doing so'.

How must the educator behave to ensure these risks are taken, rather than avoided? Accepting and valuing learners as people with inherent vulnerabilities is important. This means showing interest in their lives outside of the institution we work in. How many educators have a good understanding of, say, the home life of those that they work with? Thereafter, encouraging participation, dispelling fears of being seen as stupid, tolerating and being sympathetic to misguided and 'naive questions' (Freire 1985) all become crucial. I remember suggesting to a nineteen-year-old man that I accompany him to the Careers Office. I was concerned that he would think this belittling. Instead, this support enabled him to do something he feared, due to the embarrassment of exclusion from school and later brushes with the law. The young man thanked me for going along with him. This was an acknowledgement that he would not have visited the office on his own. Our relationship allowed this to happen.

Committing in this way to a relationship with young people, or adults, can prove a powerful antidote to the disabling effect of the sarcasm and mockery that many have experienced. The importance of care and concern for the learner is self-evident. Weaknesses in relationships, indicated by a lack of care, concern and co-operation, will not only lead to negative feelings, but prove a threat to the success of the educational activity. To protect against this, learning relationships demand commitment and concern from all involved.

While we might strive for a relationship where all are equally committed, it is hard to imagine a situation where this happens. Despite this, our efforts can help to build the commitment of the learners we work with. In any case, we have a responsibility for managing an 'aura of concern and commitment' (Tiffany 1997: 29). This has the effect of drawing people into the dialogical process: 'It can bolster confidences, reassure those concerned about sensitive and personal issues and lead to a feeling of security' (ibid.).

There may be times when we misinterpret vulnerability. We may, instead, have exposed the issue of relevance. Put simply, are learners asking themselves, 'What has this got to do with me?'

Responding positively to this question of relevance comes from the wish to see the world through the eyes of another. Implicitly, a shift is needed – from imposing our own ideas of curriculum or programme to encouraging learners to generate their own. Making this shift shows us to be prepared to criticise our own values and to move beyond traditional authoritative structures and boundaries.

Professional ethics in learning relationships

It should be clearer by now that the kind of learning we are talking about takes place within the context of a practical, dialogue-centred relationship. It should now be possible to gather some thoughts about a code of ethics for learning relationships.

The work of Habermas (1984, 1990 and 1990a) has special importance for us in thinking about the values which should characterise learning relationships. Habermas challenges the predominance of 'instrumental reason' in industrial societies. He fears that this form of reasoning, based on technical and scientific thinking, fails to acknowledge the importance of human relationships. Instead, he makes the case for the value of social interaction and what he calls communicative action. He also identifies a number of rules that need to be applied whenever we enter communicative, and potentially educational, relationships. These are based on a series of commitments (many of which we have considered above) without which he argues that linguistic communication is unlikely to achieve either consensus or an effective critique of society. His 'ideal speech situation' also includes equality and reciprocity of participation. So if we accept Habermas's 'ethics of discourse', our working relationships are more likely to exhibit a commitment to listening without interrupting, concentrating on one issue before moving on to another and managing our competitive instincts, for example.

There is little space here to expand further on Habermas's work. It should, however, encourage us to identify the values which we see as important in fostering learning relationships and to commit to all they entail.

There is a paradox underlying this discussion of aims and values. Being obsessively focused on pre-determined aims, however worthy, can make us blind to the very evidence we need to consider in order to be objective about relationships. Our quest for quality can, ironically, divert our attention from the very processes that allow it to happen.

In conclusion

We have considered relationships in their many forms. In particular, we have looked at the characteristics of learning relationships. This discussion is located within a wider educational environment that appears to promote cognitive and instrumentalist agendas, especially in formal education. In contrast, we have examined the importance of affective and communicative components in the learning process. Rustin puts this succinctly. He sees learning as an:

> emotionally-charged process in which relationships in which persons feel themselves to be valued and understood are a key precondition ... [Furthermore] ... nothing can compensate for the absence of engagement in the learning task in a creative relationship with a teacher [or educator] and with fellow-learners.
>
> (1998: 34, 38)

This approach is founded on the belief that we learn best from other people, and they from us. This means that you have the obligation not to deprive others of what you can contribute to the learning process, and that you should expect others to contribute in turn. Learning, in this model, becomes a combined effort, something we do or make together.

Thus, our personal contributions – which for many of us are also professional commitments and responsibilities – become the most important learning resource of all. As informal educators, we are, invariably, in some sort of communicative relationship with others; it should be our aim and purpose to work with these others so that learning, ours and theirs, can take place. The idea that we are exchanging something might prove useful here. If we are exchanging something, we are working.

What are we offering for exchange, in our role as educators? Fundamentally, we must be prepared to give of ourselves. Our appreciation of the social and interactive dimensions of learning should lead us to prioritise our relationships with learners. In the wider scheme of things, if we are to commit to the aims and values of education, we need to argue for a more labour-intensive system, requiring more time and energy from those involved.

Time and energy is not all we need to give. Learning is mediated and facilitated through a range of skills and bodies of knowledge, cognitive and affective. In particular, we need to develop skills of gathering evidence that will allow us to analyse our work more objectively and at the same time develop a more intuitive, interpretative working style based on 'communicative action' rather than prescription. For this, an awareness of the specifics of our working relationships becomes all important. Simply suggesting that our relationships are characterised by openness, caring, sharing, honesty, doubt, fear etc. means that we fall into the trap of generality. Proper evidence of what these values mean in practice – our practice – gives us the tools to make individual judgements. This, it is hoped, will realise the potential our relationships have for advancing the learning of those we work with, and ourselves.

Further reading

Burbules, N.C. (1993) *Dialogue in Education. Theory and Practice.* New York: Teachers College Press. An analysis of what constitutes dialogue and how this can be used to enable learning.

Rogers, C.R. and Freiberg, H.J. (1983) *Freedom to Learn*, 3rd edn. Oxford: Maxwell Macmillan International. Especially Chapters 8 and 9, for a passionate account of the importance of the affective dimensions in learning.

Smith, M.K. (1994) *Local Education: Community, Conversation and Praxis.* Buckingham: Open University Press. Especially Chapters 2 and 3, which contain various references to the affective dimensions in learning, the complexity of 'real' conversations and some sense of normative aspects of dialogue.

References

Freire, P. (1985) *The Politics of Education: Culture, Power and Liberation.* London: Macmillan.

Goetschius, G. and Tash, J. (1967) *Working with Unattached Youth.* London: Routledge and Kegan Paul.

Habermas, J. (1984) *Theory of Communicative Action: Vol. 1. Reason and the Rationalisation of Society.* Boston: Beacon Press.

Habermas, J. (1990) *Moral Consciousness and Communicative Action.* Cambridge, MA: MIT Press.

Habermas, J. (1990a) 'Discourse ethics: notes on a program of philosophical justification', in S. Benhabib and F. Dallymar (eds) *The Communicative Ethics Controversy.* Cambridge, MA: MIT Press.

Kelly, A.V. (1994) *The National Curriculum: a Critical Review.* London: Chapman.

Rustin, M. (1998) *Learning and Relationship: A Psychodynamic Approach to Educational Practice.* Proceedings of the Philosophy of Education Society of Great Britain.

Salzberger-Wittenberg, I., Henry, G. and Osborne, E. (1983) *The Emotional Experience of Learning and Teaching.* London: Routledge.

Shuttleworth, J. (1989) 'Psychoanalytic theory and infant development', in L. Miller *et al., Closely Observed Infants.* London: Duckworth.

Tash, M.J. (1967) *Supervision in youth work.* London: YMCA National College.

Tiffany, G.A. (1997) *Dialogue as a Pedagogical Relationship.* MA thesis. London: Institute of Education, University of London.

9 Working with networks and organisations in the community

Alison Gilchrist

Introduction

One of the most important aspects of informal education is that it takes place in a social context. It involves people interacting and engaging in critical discussion. People learn from one another and they develop a view of themselves in the world by observing, questioning and thinking about the behaviour of others.

Informal education focuses, firstly, on individual development as a means of achieving personal growth. But in order to do this effectively, we need to understand and work with the political and cultural pressures which mould our lives. British society is characterised by diversity and inequality. This influences how we see ourselves and how we think and behave towards others. It also affects the choices and opportunities which are available to us. This means that informal educators need to be concerned not just with personal growth, but with change at a social and organisational level. This has political, psychological and practical aspects, some of which I will consider in this chapter.

In political terms, informal educators work with people to redress power imbalances and abuses: an activity often referred to as empowerment. Empowerment is about increasing the capacity of disadvantaged groups and individuals to express their own interests and influence decisions. This means having greater access to information, advice and resources that will enable them to make informed and sustainable choices. Empowerment also occurs through joint activities, such as the setting up of voluntary organisations and campaign groups.

Informal education thus has a particular emphasis on working with people who are disadvantaged or marginalised in society, and on fostering participation. Helping people to make connections with others enables them to share and compare experiences, learn new skills and organise on a collective basis. Informal educators also have a role to play in helping people to challenge the attitudes and barriers that make it difficult to form strong and diverse personal networks.

This chapter focuses on the ways in which informal educators create and use opportunities for shared activities to promote learning and to develop collective forms of organising. We can do this by working with informal social networks and community groups to develop their potential for learning and action; providing spaces in the community for diverse groups to encounter and learn from one another; working to help informal groups develop more formal structures; and linking groups and organisations with one another.

Social networks for learning and support

Over thousands of years, humans have evolved patterns of behaviour and ways of organising which have allowed the species to adapt and to survive. A key factor in this may be our ability to co-operate and to learn from one another's experience, using language and networks of relationships.

Humans are social creatures. We live, work and play amongst clusters of 'familiar strangers' with whom we may form emotional attachments. The relationships developed through informal networking are neither random, nor unconditional, nor always positive. They depend on personal preferences, prejudices and pragmatic choices. We tend to form connections with people whom we like, whom we meet regularly, and with whom we can exchange things that benefit us. These networks comprise the people we meet regularly in our everyday routines, as well as those who have made a strong impression and with whom we make a particular effort to stay in touch. Such relationships survive if they are reciprocal, reliable and based on some kind of shared activity (Miell and Duck 1992). Informal education is about the learning that occurs through these interactions.

Our individual learning takes place within a matrix of influences from the people around us. Our ideas about the world are formed and re-formed through endless observation, reflection and conversation (Smith 1994). We collect and check information from a huge range of sources in our lives – family, friends, books, TV programmes, authority figures, professional experts, the Internet, cultural icons, casual acquaintances. By comparing experiences, we come up with our own dynamic and complex view of how the world around us operates.

Our social identities are formed through interactions (Tajfel 1981). Whether we like it or not, our behaviour and thinking are influenced by others. We react to and learn from other people's expectations. Over the years, our personal belief system and patterns of behaviour adapt to 'fit' the conventions and circumstances around us. How we perceive and present our selves depends on both the social context and our personal needs.

If we are sensible and fortunate, our networks will include people who can provide us with access to useful resources, advice, information and support. These links are sustained through informal interactions, rather than bureaucratic or financial arrangements. They require an investment of time and effort and are usually based on feelings of love, trust, loyalty and respect.

Social networks can be a form of 'emotional insulation' buffering us against periods of hardship and trauma (Pilisuk and Parks 1986: 40). Our lives are enriched and often made easier if the links that we have with others are wide-ranging, dependable and generally sympathetic. It is also useful to include 'critical friends' in our networks, people who are prepared to challenge or contradict our own views, as this helps us to develop alternative perspectives. As Ledwith (1997: 46) argues, we need to develop 'an openness to exploring attitudes, values and beliefs. Out of this comes the courage to experience challenge and a willingness to understand different ways of engaging with the world.'

As well as providing all kinds of practical benefits, our networks are inevitably suffused with powerful emotions which bind us together. These can create difficult inter-personal dynamics which block or distort learning. Social networks are shaped by social structures and political forces, which tend to perpetuate existing inequalities and divisions within society. We make our networks but are also made by them.

Q1: Make a list of the networks which are important in your personal and professional life. Note down the benefits for you and your work. What are the disadvantages and limitations of these contacts? How do you maintain the links?

Hopefully you will have been able to identify a rich mix of connections with other individuals, groups and organisations, in which the time and effort needed to maintain relationships is compensated by the benefits to you as a person and as a worker.

Social networks, then, are important for individuals and for society as a whole. They provide support in times of need. They help us to develop common understandings despite a diversity of lifestyles. In a society which seems increasingly complex and fragmented, networks help us to adjust to rapid, often unexpected changes. Social networks also constitute a vital informal communication system and vehicle for mobilising collective action. They enable us to work together to solve shared problems and generally improve the quality of our lives.

Communities as environments for learning

Informal networks are created and sustained through habitual patterns of daily life and participation in joint activities. They, in turn, give us our sense of belonging to different and overlapping communities (Forrest and Kearns 1999). We are joined by these day-to-day relationships into larger communities, focused around different features of our lives, such as where we live or work, our religious faith, or some kind of voluntary activity, perhaps a hobby or political cause.

Early definitions of 'community' tended to be geographical. Sociological studies investigated social relationships by examining the patterns of interaction between residents of specific areas (Crow and Allan 1995). In Britain, one of the first and perhaps the most famous of these was Young and Willmott's (1957) research into family and kinship in East London. Later, sociologists came to realise that people's personal networks are actively constructed around dimensions of their lives other than where they happen to live. They discovered that people create and maintain significant links with individuals they meet at work or through religious and recreational activities (Wellman 1979). Shared values seem to be just as important to people's experience of community as shared living space.

The networks which make up people's experience of community also provide an important vehicle for collective learning and the accumulation of cultural memories and local knowledge. Much of this is dismissed as 'old wives' tales' or unscientific folklore, but it nevertheless becomes incorporated into family conventions and our individual notions of 'how the world works'. In this way, community networks can be seen as living computers, comparing information and ideas, testing out possible theories and checking out disparities between different versions of the 'life-world' (Dunbar 1996).

A community in this sense can be regarded as a kind of collective brain, processing information and organising responses to events in the outside world on the basis of current input and memories of past experience. What we think of as 'common sense' and traditional wisdom is stored in the web of relationships spanning generations, cultures and friendship groups.

We live, however, in a rapidly-changing world and this discourse of shared knowledge is neither accurate nor static. The 'collective brain' is useful only insofar as it is able to learn from experience, assimilating new ideas and revising its existing conceptual frameworks. Educators contribute to these dynamic and complex processes by identifying opportunities for informal learning and encouraging people to talk with others in similar situations. Mostly these conversations impose familiar interpretations on events, but occasionally they allow new formulations to emerge which challenge the old order, create fresh insights and generate innovative ways of working. This is what is meant by 'emancipatory education'.

Community networks operate on the basis of informal conversation, such as gossip, rumour, story-telling and hearsay. Non-verbal communication is a very important aspect, hence the importance of face-to-face interaction, in which raised eyebrows, grins, shrugs and body posture indicate emotional and moral responses.

> **Q2:** Think back over the past week and see if you can identify how you have been affected in your thinking or behaviour by informal or chance encounters. How have your opinions been reinforced or altered by these conversations? Have you been motivated or enabled to do something which you might not have done otherwise? Have you seen an issue from a new perspective? Have you been able to influence decisions to your advantage or gain access to facilities?

A sense of community is not simply a sentimental figment of our collective imagination. It emerges from the real experience of being connected into the flow of energy and ideas that characterise robust and vibrant networks. People who are actively engaged in social networks are able, individually and collectively, to learn from experience and to adapt to changing circumstances. Informal educators can play a role by helping people to make connections which are empowering and which combat typical antagonisms and dogma.

Communities for action

Discrimination and social inequalities have also generated new forms of community which are overtly political. These have been termed 'identity' or 'interest' communities (Willmott 1986). Identity communities often emerge in response to specific issues, such as the AIDS crisis or growing racial intimidation. In similar ways to locality-based communities, these networks are developed and maintained through sharing ideas, significant information or resources. They enable people to communicate and co-operate around issues of common concern or simply to enjoy one another's company. Discovering a social or political explanation for their experience can lead to increased

confidence. It can transform people from being angry, but helpless, victims to becoming agents of their own liberation. In recent years, identity-based networks have been important sources of political energy in the struggle for civil rights and equal opportunities.

Informal educators can support these processes by creating opportunities for people to meet. They can set up organisations to provide practical advice and assistance to tackle the problems created by discrimination and poverty. People who are neglected, abused or excluded by dominant social structures may need encouragement and assistance from outsiders, including informal educators, in order to make connections with others who share their experiences and to find the courage to challenge their oppression.

Intervening in community networks

As a profession, informal educators are employed to help people organise themselves at a local or community level. The worker is charged with helping people to develop their skills, confidence and knowledge, to work together around shared issues and to participate jointly in decision making. The focus of the worker's interventions is usually through direct interactions with individuals and the development of small-scale groups and activities.

These group activities may lead to a realisation that individual problems reflect broader patterns of cause and effect, arising from economic and political factors. This process of transforming private troubles into public issues is the key to social change. Freire (1996) developed an entire theory of emancipatory education based on the concept of 'conscientisation': the process of critical dialogue, through which people construct new understanding of their situations. By analysing the social and institutional forces which shape their current experiences, Freire (and others) argue that people come to recognise that many of their problems are the consequences of widespread exploitation and oppression. For radical workers, these are seen as fundamental features of a political system which promotes the interests and protects the privileges of those who enjoy economic and social power.

Informal educators help people to make, mend and maintain connections which enable them to obtain information, reach resources, influence decisions and find support. It is not enough, however, simply to urge people to be kinder and fairer to one another. The dimensions of discrimination and oppression are etched across society and its institutions, reaching into every aspect of our lives. They affect our social status, our health, our opportunities for advancement, our access to services, and the quality of our relationships.

Discrimination, exclusion and stereotypes distort and disrupt access to power and ideas, preventing people from making direct and productive links with one another. The professional commitment of informal educators to promoting equality and empowerment for disadvantaged groups means that we need to find ways of combating inequalities and prejudice and restoring an equitable flow of information and resources. Our strategies need to be flexible and appropriate to different circumstances, rather than rigidly imposed by external bodies. Additional funding may well be necessary in order to improve access for disabled people, to provide interpreters for speakers of other languages, or crèche facilities for parents, to name just a few familiar examples of positive action measures. Sometimes this entails a re-allocation of existing (and usually scarce) community resources to benefit previously excluded groups, or it may mean adjusting the 'normal' way of doing something to prioritise a different set of needs.

Inevitably, some people will be reluctant to support such changes. They may want to protect their own privileges and preserve the familiar ways. If they are in positions of power, they may use this to resist or undermine attempts to involve people who are different or 'difficult' to work with. There will always be conflicts and tensions within organisations and across communities. The task of informal educators is to promote mutual understanding, help people to find the things they have in common and to deal constructively with disputes and apparent incompatibilities in lifestyles or aspirations.

Because of the informal and voluntary nature of their relationships with people, informal educators often become aware of issues or discontent within communities that are not being addressed by the statutory services. The same themes crop up in conversations, but people are unsure what could be done to change the situation. As individuals their lack of understanding, lack of influence and lack of resources may leave them feeling powerless. Informal educators can help people to overcome this sense of apparent apathy by listening carefully to grievances, questioning assumptions, carrying out further investigations into the extent of the problem (perhaps using participative action research) and identifying potential sources of support. Informal educators are often in a position to bring together various 'stakeholders' to develop a joint strategy for solving the initial problem. They may also know about projects elsewhere which have successfully tackled similar issues and can introduce these examples of 'best practice' to help people think creatively about their own situation.

For example, residents may complain about minor acts of theft and vandalism occurring around the estate. Although they have no evidence, they accuse a group of boys who are seen off school premises during the day. These become generalised allegations about the nuisance and noise caused by young people hanging around the streets at night.

Informal educators will probably know most of the people who have an interest in this situation, or they will know how to contact key agencies. They are therefore able to use their connections to draw together useful skills, resources and advice. They will be able to communicate effectively with all concerned, but more importantly enable the different groups to co-operate in developing solutions which everyone can feel some ownership of (Holman 2000). This may well involve a certain amount of mediation and compromise, working through conflicts and misunderstandings until a settlement is reached. A prime function of the informal educator is to ensure that the resultant service or partnership is relevant and accessible to all intended users or participants. This is especially important in the current climate of community participation in social regeneration and other government initiatives. By assisting people to organise themselves into self-help and pressure groups, informal educators help them to have greater influence over decisions which affect their lives. This has both psychological and democratic advantages, and results in better and more sustainable policies.

Social networks can thus provide a foundation for informal co-operation and collective organising that cuts across organisational and group boundaries. They allow people to share information and resources in order to co-ordinate their activities. New organisations emerge from informal conversations and discussions, tackling old issues in innovative ways or bringing new perspectives to bear on familiar, but intractable problems. Professional intervention and initial funding may provide that catalytic spark which turns inspiration into reality.

However, social structures and informal networks also reflect power differentials, tending to perpetuate inequalities in status, opportunity and reward. Unless challenged, these can be reproduced at community level. Such biases must be actively countered, otherwise they will suppress or destroy emerging community networks which could promote social integration.

Q3: Think about an event that you were recently involved in. This could be a public meeting, a cultural or social activity, an informal gathering, anything which is intended to bring together a range of people. Make a note of incidents or practices which you think excluded some people (perhaps including yourself) from participating in activities or decision making. Were you aware of these at the time? How does this make you feel now? What could have been done differently to make the event more inclusive and accessible, more truly 'sociable'?

Such examples of exclusion need not be deliberate. Disabled children are often unwittingly excluded from holiday playschemes because 'special schools' do not receive the publicity leaflets sent to local mainstream schools. Similarly, an over-emphasis on 'English' cultural activities is likely to discourage people from other ethnicities from participating in supposedly 'public' events. You can probably identify actions which would help to include both these groups.

Bringing people together

Informal educators are able to facilitate communication and learning between those who experience oppression and those who might be in a position to eradicate it. This gives them an important role in helping people to fulfil their potential, sometimes in the face of resistance or antipathy from those in authority.

This will inevitably involve working with people who experience discrimination as well as those who benefit from it. This needs sensitivity, courage, perseverance and a strong sense of social justice. It requires a willingness to oppose institutional discrimination and an ability to deal with conflicts of interest arising among different sections of the community. In my practice as a community worker in a multi-ethnic neighbourhood, I found myself confronted by prejudices, assumptions and resentment from the majority population, while trying to ensure that different needs within the whole community could be addressed. I needed to maintain good relationships with a range of different people, and, perhaps more importantly, find ways of helping members of the community to develop these links for themselves.

But informal educators have limited formal power, and challenging others often feels uncomfortable and risky. We may ourselves need support and guidance from allies or professional advisers, especially if we have similar experiences of being excluded or oppressed. It is important to remember that discrimination may occur unintentionally, not as an act of deliberate antagonism or exclusion. And as practitioners, we need to be aware of how our own attitudes and assumptions, our prejudices even, affect our professional conduct.

As we have seen earlier, prejudices and resentment are often ingrained in people's perceptions of themselves and each other. These need to be challenged so that diverse cultures and lifestyles can be valued or at least tolerated. Bringing members of different communities together through social activities creates an enjoyable and educative shared experience, enabling people to interact informally and learn about each other's lives. It is important to make sure that these situations are welcoming for everyone and do not feel intimidating or exclusive. This means accommodating a variety of preferences or requirements, and acknowledging differences.

The community association I used to work for held an annual International Women's Day festival. We made sure that it took place in a building which was fully accessible to disabled women and that the activities happening during the day were representative of the range of cultures in the neighbourhood. The refreshments available were suitable for different religious requirements and the layout of stalls and seating space encouraged people to mingle. Through the outreach work and publicity material, we tried to ensure that all women's groups in the area felt that they could contribute and would persuade their members to come along on the day. This juxtaposition of very different lifestyles and moral values was deliberate, but not without its risks and tensions. For example, a lesbian drama society performed alongside the Punjabi dance class; the young mothers' group display might be situated next to women from the pensioners' club. Through sensitive and strategic networking, we managed to create a positive atmosphere which was vibrant with women's voices expressing the shared, but diverse, experience of living in that particular neighbourhood.

If handled with care, friction can provide a vital spark for change, but it can also cause the equivalent of painful grazes in tender places. The informal educator must be prepared, metaphorically speaking, to act as both fire fighter and nurse, able to 'dowse flames' as well as 'dress wounded feelings'.

Sometime more overtly educational strategies are needed which actively seek to change people's fears, assumptions and antagonisms. These may involve training workshops, for example, around disability equality or sexuality awareness. If this approach is being used, then informal educators need to make time to deal with a possible aftermath of hurt, recriminations and disorientation which often results when people are forced to examine their own attitudes and privileges. While our community association was transforming itself from a predominantly white organisation to a more multi-racial body, we did a lot of work around race equality and equal opportunities generally. For some of the older members, this was quite difficult, forcing them to reconsider their attitudes towards black people and to adapt to new ways of working within the association. Some felt that their previous hard work and commitment were being belittled, and were understandably resentful of this. It required a lot of home visits and one-to-one conversations to convince people that their contribution was valued and to persuade them to stay involved.

Change at a psychological level is never easy. It requires time, patience and a genuine belief that progress can be achieved through informed dialogue and reflection. In the meantime, there is much that can be done to facilitate greater access and equality through practical measures which need not involve extra costs.

> **Q4:** Imagine you are planning a neighbourhood consultation exercise to discuss proposals to regenerate the area. How might you go about this? What events and activities would you organise? How would you ensure that all residents had a chance to contribute their ideas and to participate in the debate? What difficulties might you encounter?

You will probably need to bear in mind the following: any significant religious or sporting events that might conflict with your chosen dates; school times and holidays; access and availability of public transport for those attending. In addition you will need to make sure that participants understand what is going on and are able to communicate with one another. What kind of preparation or interpretation might be needed? What wording and images in the publicity material would encourage people from different cultures to participate, and how should it be distributed? Are costs going to prevent some people from contributing? What kind of refreshments should be provided? And so on. With limited resources, it is not usually feasible to cater for everybody's needs and preferences, but by giving some thought to these questions it is often possible to overcome many of the obstacles and to convey a positive commitment to diversity and equality. You will probably also need to think about the psychological factors which might deter some people from joining in, such as low self-esteem, fear of appearing ignorant, and peer pressure.

Informal educators have a key role to play in encouraging people to question, challenge and learn from their social environment. Despite the prevalence of anti-discriminatory legislation and equal opportunities policies, not everyone in the community necessarily has access to situations which support shared learning or promote active participation. Many venues have a 'territorial' feel to them. Their reputation, publicity and appearance favour certain sections of the population and deter others from venturing in, or they might simply be inaccessible to people with limited mobility. Customary forms of communication similarly exclude people with sensory impairments or speakers of other languages. Overly-formal proceedings can be intimidating and official jargon may be incomprehensible except to those 'in the know'. Some people face prejudice, misunderstanding and outright hostility on a daily basis and may hesitate to seek out opportunities which could allow new skills and confidence to be developed. Without support, encouragement and practical assistance, people may be reluctant or unable to challenge the discrimination they experience, witness or indeed perpetrate themselves. A personal approach is often effective in these circumstances.

Developing groups into organisations

Studies of community and voluntary organisations indicate the importance of social networks in their formation and maintenance, a fact which is often overlooked by funders and managers (Milofsky 1988; Chanan 1992).

Informal networks are very important in helping people to co-ordinate their activities and organise collective ventures. They act as communication channels, the 'grapevine' which lets people know what's going on and draws attention to public events and campaigns. Networks are also useful in mobilising people to take part in collective action of all kinds and to learn from their own and others' experiences.

Informal educators, especially those employed in community settings, have a particular role in helping informal networks of like-minded people make the difficult, and sometimes contentious, transition to a fully constituted organisation with formal democratic structures and a legal status.

This process (which may take several months, even years) entails bringing together and advising a group on how they might develop and implement a shared vision. Informal educators are likely to play a number of roles, depending on specific circumstances and the particular capabilities of those involved. They may act as a focal point for people from a range of interests and agencies, convening and servicing meetings which enable people to engage in constructive discussion and to reach and implement collective decisions. Workers may help the group to obtain and manage resources effectively. They may also provide guidance on how the group can best be established on a more formal basis, with appropriate policies and a constitution. At every stage, informal educators endeavour not to undertake these tasks themselves but to enable others to acquire the necessary skills, confidence and motivation to take on roles and responsibilities within the new organisation.

Working across organisational boundaries

In recent years, there has been an increasing government emphasis on cross-sectoral co-operation, encouraging agencies to work together to deliver a range of welfare services and policy programmes. The 'Connexions' policy is a recent example. My own research with community development practitioners has revealed the pivotal role that informal educators play in linking different organisations and helping people with different cultures and interests to work together. I found that community workers were frequently concerned with helping people to co-operate in multi-agency initiatives. They were often the people who knew who to contact in the different agencies, and who acted as brokers between different sections of the 'partnership', making sure that the various stakeholders or participants communicated with one another and were able to work constructively together. Their activities and knowledge spanned conventional boundaries, and their role in 'networking the networks' provided an invaluable, but rarely recognised, contribution to effective collaboration. Informal educators are able to do this because they invest time and effort in developing personal links with key individuals in other agencies. This gives them access to unofficial, but incredibly useful, sources of information and allows them to make a more sophisticated appraisal of organisational dynamics within the overall context.

I have termed this aspect of professional practice 'meta-networking', by which I mean enhancing individuals' capacity to establish and sustain their own links and weaving a web of inter-organisational relationships to encourage and facilitate co-operation. (Gilchrist 1998). Meta-networking requires a broad analysis as well as skills in inter-personal communication and group facilitation. Informal networking can be an effective (but not always 'fair') way of crossing organisational boundaries and cutting through the 'red tape' of bureaucratic procedures. Such links offer short cuts to resources, advice and information which might otherwise cost considerable time and money.

This was illustrated for me in the mid-1990s when I was involved in organising a city-wide Festival Against Racism. This involved mobilising and then co-ordinating the participation of over 100 agencies, including faith-based groups, youth centres, schools, community organisations, trade unions and statutory authorities. Despite limited formal structures and resources, we were able to use informal networking to raise sufficient funds and contributions in kind across the private, public and voluntary sectors to put together a month-long programme of anti-racist activities based around the broad themes of Equality, Diversity, Justice and Solidarity. The Festival crystallised out of the social, professional and political networks linking key individuals involved in race equality work. Its success depended on shared values, trust and mutual respect that had developed over many years (Gilchrist and Taylor 1997). These are crucial aspects of what is sometimes termed 'social capital'.

Role of the informal educator in the community

Informal education can help people to develop and value their social networks, thereby making a contribution to the development of 'community'. This enhances individual well-being, social cohesion (not conformity) and creates a collective capacity to organise and manage shared resources. Being 'well-connected' is advantageous for everyone concerned. Your task as an informal educator is to work with individuals and organisations to render the networks as empowering as possible for those who are least powerful. This means having an awareness of the political dynamics of a situation and the impact that these have on different individuals operating within it.

Informal educators need to be versatile and professionally competent to operate across a range of settings. They should be aware of the barriers that prevent people from making useful connections, and work to overcome these. Sometimes this will involve acting as a 'bridge' between different sectors and communities. It might involve 'holding the door open' so that people can gain access to the support or resources that they need. Often informal educators are the 'go-between', interpreting and mediating between groups that are on the defensive and finding it hard to appreciate other points of view. Through joint social events, exchange visits, cultural or sporting activities, informal educators can assist people in making links with others who will support, extend and challenge their thinking.

It is a crucial principle of informal education that workers avoid encouraging other people to be dependent on them. The relationships that are necessary to promote participation and to support individual learning must be developed so that people are able independently to make and manage their own web of connections. In order to do this, informal educators work to create spaces for networking which are accessible (in every sense), safe and accommodating for a variety of needs and interests. They can do this by making physical places (activity rooms, community centres, café areas, etc.) feel welcoming and providing access to useful resources, such as local directories, noticeboards, photocopying, computer facilities, the telephone or simply space to meet.

Informal educators can provide background knowledge and information (names and addresses of other agencies) so that people can get in touch or be referred for appropriate advice or assistance. Occasionally, the worker may even make that first contact, suggesting and supporting the initial connections until people are confident or skilled enough to continue for themselves.

Conclusion

There is no doubt that we are affected by the rules and regulations which govern society. Social structures attempt to constrain our behaviour within acceptable limits, using moral pressure, sanctions and legal coercion where necessary. Our upbringing moulds our individuality, and perhaps we never quite shake off the mannerisms and values of the people we grew up with and were once dependent on. Nevertheless, through our encounters and relationships with people from different backgrounds and experiences, we can learn to question our beliefs and to acquire an alternative model of the world and our place in it.

In particular, we may realise that situations and opinions that we might previously have taken for granted can be challenged. We can change our own thinking, persuade others to change their behaviour and may also attempt to change the procedures and policies of organisations that we support or those who employ us. Usually we have been encouraged by someone (a teacher, a youth worker, a colleague or a friend) to question what is going on around us. As a result, we begin to see the world in different ways. As Jeffs and Smith (1996: 11) write, informal educators 'don't change people, people change themselves in interaction with others'.

Knowledge is never neutral. It is a source of influence and authority. As educators, it is vital to understand the context in which much of our thinking is formed so that we are able to work alongside people in creating new learning opportunities. Social development comes about through collective action and learning: combining skills, effort and resources in order to achieve a common goal. If people are able to connect and communicate with others from a diversity of backgrounds, abilities and outlooks, they are likely to respond more positively to different views and be better able to manage their lives within the complex and dynamic matrix of interactions which underpins our experience of society.

Tackling the barriers that prevent people forming these links for themselves is perhaps the most important challenge facing the informal educator. This involves working with people, working with structures and working to change the context. Informal educators contribute to these processes through skilled and strategic interventions to promote relationships based on equality, trust and mutual respect.

Further reading

Crow, G. and Allan, G. (1995) *Community Life*. Hemel Hempstead: Harvester Wheatsheaf. A useful introduction to the concept of community and an overview of relevant empirical investigations.

Gilchrist, A. (1995) *Community Development and Networking*. London: Community Development Foundation. An accessible guide to good practice in networking, with examples of how to be effective as a practitioner.

Hosking, D.M. and Morley, I. (1991) *A Social Psychology of Organising: People, Processes and Contexts*. New York: Harvester Wheatsheaf. An exploration of the scientific evidence on how attitudes, relationships and inter-personal dynamics affect organisations.

Ledwith, M. (1997) *Participating in Transformation: Towards a Working Model of Community Empowerment*. Birmingham: Venture Press. A lively explanation of the theory and practice of radical informal education, drawing on modern political thinkers and current experience.

Smith, M. (1994) *Local Education: Community, Conversation, Praxis*. Buckingham: Open University Press. Useful and thought-provoking analysis of the role of informal educators working in community settings.

Thompson, N. (1998) *Promoting Equality: Challenging Discrimination and Oppression in the Human Services*. Basingstoke: Macmillan. A guide to anti-oppressive practice based on an interactive model of different dimensions of social inequality.

References

Chanan, G. (1992) *Out of the Shadows: Local Community Action and The European Community*. Dublin: European Foundation for the Improvement of Living and Working Conditions.

Crow, G. and Allan, G. (1995) *Community Life*. Hemel Hempstead: Harvester Wheatsheaf.

Dunbar, R. (1996) *Grooming, Gossip and the Evolution of Language*. London: Faber and Faber.

Forrest, R. and Kearns, A. (1999) *Joined Up Places? Social Cohesion and Neighbourhood Regeneration*. York: Joseph Rowntree Foundation.

Freire, P. (1996) *Pedagogy of the Oppressed*. Harmondsworth: Penguin.

Gilchrist, A. (1998) *Connectors and Catalysts*, in SCCD Newsletter, Autumn, 1998, Sheffield.

Gilchrist, A. and Taylor, M. (1997) 'Community networking: strength through diversity', in P. Hoggett (ed.) *Ideas of Community*. Bristol: Policy Press.

Holman, B. (2000) *Kids at the Door Revisited*. Lyme Regis: Russell House.

Jeffs, T. and Smith, M. (1996) *Informal Education: Conversation, Democracy and Learning*. Derby: Education Now Publishing.

Ledwith, M. (1997) *Participating in Transformation: Towards a Working Model of Community Empowerment*. Birmingham: Venture Press.

Miell, D. and Duck, S. (1992) *Human Relationships*, 2nd edn. London: Sage.

Milofsky, C. (1988) *Community Organisations: Studies in Resource Mobilisation and Exchange*. New York: Oxford University Press.

Pilisuk, M. and Parks, S.H. (1986) *The Healing Web: Social Networks and Human Survival*. Hanover, NH: University Press of New England.

Smith, M. (1994) *Local Education: Community, Conversation and Praxis*. Buckingham: Open University Press.

Tajfel, H. (1981) *Human Groups and Social Categories: Studies in Social Psychology*. Cambridge: Cambridge University Press.

Wellman, B. (1979) 'The community question: the intimate networks of East Yorkers' *American Journal of Sociology*, 84, 1201–31.

Willmott, P. (1986) *Social Networks, Informal Care and Public Policy*. London: Policy Studies Institute.

Young, M. and Willmott, P. (1957) *Family and Kinship in East London*. London: Routledge and Kegan Paul.

Part III

Elements of practice

Introduction

Linda Deer Richardson

The six chapters in Part III, 'Elements of practice', highlight different and distinctive features of professional practice. The chapters can be grouped into three pairs which provide complementary perspectives on the main methods and processes of informal education.

Conversation, or dialogue, is a fundamental working method for informal educators. Mary Wolfe's 'Conversation' explores the nature of this everyday but complex process. She uses specific examples to illustrate the various stages and routines that are involved in conversation and argues for its central importance in promoting informal learning.

Place is another central aspect of informal education which is easy to ignore because of its ordinariness. To work as informal educators, we and those we work with normally have to be in the same place. This place forms the setting for our work, helps to determine the sort of work we can do and is linked in subtle ways to the identities which we and others bring to educational encounters. In 'Place, space and informal education', Mark K. Smith considers the varied spaces in which informal education can happen and suggests things we may be able to do to make our work settings places in which conversation and learning can flourish.

Apart from conversation, what are the ways in which we work with people, young people in particular? Pauline Riley is Senior Worker of a County Federation of Youth Clubs which offers a wide range of programme ideas and advice to affiliated clubs and young people. She argues that, 'in order to achieve the aim of delivering youth work using informal educative methods, a carefully planned programme is essential'. In 'Programme planning', she outlines factors to consider when designing an informal education programme, including agency aims, the developmental needs of young people, timescales, methods, priorities and resources.

But why do we use activities in working with young people? In 'Activities' Jean Spence questions the common assumption of the educational value of activity-based work. Her critique builds upon the historical overview provided by Tony Jeffs in Part I and returns us to questions of process and product which have run throughout the series.

Decisions to work in different ways with different groups or individuals may be determined by the worker's job or role, or made because they seem an effective way of working. Two methods which extend the boundaries of informal education are casework: a structured way of working with individuals which has grown out of social work models; and project work: a similarly structured and time-bounded method of working with groups. Alan Smith's 'One-to-one casework' outlines the skills, methods and values involved in this form of working, and considers to what extent these values are congruent with those of informal education. The question is an important one, because of the growth in government initiatives, such as the Connexions Service, which use casework as a tool for social change.

Project work is another method which is popular with funders because of its clear aims and limited timescale. In 'Doing projects: working with formal groups', Malcolm Payne considers what project workers need to know about working with groups; promoting learning within groups; and managing projects to support group learning. As with casework, there are questions about the appropriacy of this sort of formal learning within informal education practice. The advice of Smith and Payne is to proceed with caution and be aware of possible tensions between informal education values and methods which can support more controlling ways of working.

In this Part, our aim has not been to provide a comprehensive list of the methods of work used in informal education, but to focus upon those which, like chemical elements, are the basic building blocks of practice. We also seek to highlight those elements which invite careful thought or critical questioning. Such reflective approaches to our work are the surest way to foster good practice. Part IV considers aids to professional reflection and development which can be built into our working lives.

10 Conversation

Mary Wolfe

In this chapter I want to consider the importance of conversation to us as informal educators in our work with clients. I hope I can encourage you to think, and talk, about this seemingly quite ordinary and everyday human activity. Given the focus of this book, I shall be particularly exploring the importance of conversation in generating informal learning between participants. I have included a number of examples from discussions about different conversations which I have had with practitioners over the years. These are not exact transcriptions – most conversations lose their vitality in the face of a tape recorder. They are simply my recollections and observations – recalled here with permission. I shall be suggesting to you that conversation is of particular importance within informal and community education practices. For this reason, I hope that you will be able to add your own examples of conversations you have had which you continue to explore in your work as an educator.

Most societies have developed a range of terms for informal conversation: in parts of Ireland, we may refer to the craic, to scandalising in areas of the Caribbean or to blether in Scotland.

Q1: Think of as many examples as you can of words you use, or have heard, to describe informal conversation. Then, next time you are with colleagues or clients, ask them to add their own examples to your list.

Probably, most of us could add to any list of local terms to describe informal talk: the give and take of views, confidences, jokes or gossip which lie at the heart of so much of our social interaction. Indeed, this range of terms may reflect the importance we attach to the wide range of conversations which we engage in throughout our social lives. But I think we should not be fooled into thinking that because conversation is often an informal, everyday activity it is therefore straight-forward and easy to understand and to use successfully. On the contrary, like other apparently simple aspects of human activity, conversation is complex and open to different interpretations. After all, can any of us claim that we have never finished a conversation feeling confused, sensing some misunderstanding but unable to identify exactly what 'went wrong'? I hope not – because we need this sensitivity to the possible nuances and confusions of conversation to guide us into exploring critically the part which conversations play in our practice. As educators who seek to work effectively with the exchange which underlies any conversation, I want to suggest that we should aim to develop a particular sensitivity to how conversation works. After all, people at times risk opening up their emotions, ambitions or uncertainties to us in conversation. Although there is no guarantee against misinterpretation in such a human and inexact science, there is a responsibility upon us all as educators to make every effort to avoid unnecessary difficulties.

The extent of the literature around conversation may be some indication of its complexity (including Goffman 1981, 1990; Wardhaugh 1991; Smith 1994). As informal educators, we are constantly adding to this literature. Many of our professional recordings focus on our conversations: those which occur purposely in advice sessions or by chance in the streets, around other named activities such as a game of pool or a reminiscence workshop, those we have while collecting money or serving the tea. Such recordings offer a constant reference point to explore ourselves and our clients in practice, an opportunity to ask ourselves, 'What is going on here?' In their complexity, as much as their simplicity, they offer us food for thought and reflection.

It seems that in a wide range of areas, we seek to record and express our feelings about conversation. This is because it forms a central part of all of our relationships, of our making and sharing of culture and of our social identities. In preparing this chapter, I have found myself not only drawing upon writings from educational theory but also from fiction, personal experience and current affairs. Precisely because there is so much conversation going on all around us, we risk failing to notice its significance. All too easily, conversation blends, almost unnoticed, into the social background. For this reason, it can be a good idea to stop and take note of just how pervasive it is, of how we make and remake this warp and weft of our social connections.

Q2: Try and take note of the number of references to conversations which you come across, say, in one morning.

There should be quite a few! I noticed some in which I was an observer or audience and others in which I took an active part. In the first category, I included newspaper accounts of a number of conversations: formal discussions between Heads of State; alleged chat and gossip about public figures; anonymous briefings to journalists as well as that rather strange and formulaic conversation – the celebrity interview. Most of the conversations in which I had an active part themselves referred to other conversations which I variously had, and had not, been part of. We seem to talk about talk with significant enthusiasm and interest. In a similar way, perhaps, we sometimes use exclusion from conversation as a punishment – for example 'sending somebody to Coventry', or making young people go to their rooms or denying prisoners their association time. Being cut off in this way from the opportunity both to voice one's thoughts and to entertain those of other people can remain a peculiarly disturbing memory which I suspect some of us may still recall vividly. This is how Brodkey (1994: 536) recalls such a childhood experience:

> I can still feel the heat of my humiliation and recall my terror as I stood
> alone and in tears in the cloakroom, where I had been sent for talking
> ... The door that isolated me from the others may have terrified me
> more than it would have a child accustomed to closed doors. I was not in
> a dark or windowless room, but I could not hear what was being said in
> the classroom...

Perhaps it is because conversation offers a chance for us to give and take of
ourselves with others – a chance for social communion – that exclusion from
it is often such a painful process.

Defining conversation

I now want to consider whether there are certain identifiable features which
allow us to describe an exchange of words or signs as a conversation.

> **Q3:** Jot down three or four characteristics of a conversation.

I found myself expressing some of these characteristics negatively: not lectur-
ing nor reciting, not being entirely predictable. I included a focus upon a
dynamic relationship between participants – conversation involves negotiating an exchange. This may be an exchange of ideas, feelings or information.

Grice (1975) argues that for a conversation to happen, there needs to be
agreement to the 'co-operative principle' from those taking part. By this, I
take him to mean those behavioural norms which have to be accepted by
participants for an exchange to be described as a conversation. He concludes
that there are a number of significant features, which he refers to as maxims,
required in any authentic conversation. Among these features he includes
issues such as an agreement on the amount of information that individuals
should contribute or withhold, some accepted norms of politeness, and a
commitment to a degree of truthfulness and of relevance. Of course conversations can, and do, occur with markedly different degrees of, for example,
truthfulness; his point is that there are eventually limits to the degree of
truthfulness permitted for a conversation to remain sustainable. Wardhaugh
(1991: 63) sums up these maxims as a claim for *sincerity* between participants
for a conversation to take place.

So both Grice and Wardhaugh offer us a model for a specific quality of
conversation. As with any model which seeks to describe human behaviours,
it cannot account for the enormous range of interactions included in any
simple label such as 'conversation'. They are outlining a framework to locate
and explore our experiences of any one of those particular, and unique, conversations which we have experienced. So the level of sincerity in any given
conversation may have to be compromised, perhaps by participants' desire
for privacy, safety, approval – or mere brevity. I expect that few of us desire
complete sincerity in all our conversations, just as I expect that we assume
some degree of commitment or sincerity in most of them. If the members of
a conversation completely withhold sincerity, if they refuse to work with any
shared co-operative principles, then we may want to say that their exchange
is not a conversation: indeed that conversation has been made impossible

through some form of sabotage or breakdown of co-operation between participants. Conversely, if participants were to enter into an exchange demanding total and unambiguous truth, unarguable relevance or absolute politeness, there could be no scope for negotiation or exchange: and so the sabotage would be equally effective. We can see, then, that the co-operative principle itself is constantly being negotiated and is influenced by a number of factors. For example, where I work a number of people may ask me if I had a good weekend when they see me on Monday mornings. What makes for a sincere reply in this conversation? And is this the same as identifying what would be truthful and relevant? The reply I make will be partly informed by my judgement about what the other person may already know about my weekend, about the time available to us, the setting we are in (are we sitting down over a coffee in the staff room or crossing each other on the stairs?) and by my understanding of the purpose of the enquiry. Is this friendly social chat or have I already spoken to this person about a particularly challenging situation I faced last weekend? The quality, or lack of it, of my weekend may not be the only factor influencing my reply!

Read this extract from Samuel Beckett's play *Waiting for Godot* in which the two tramps, Vladimir and Estragon, are on stage engaging in a conversation with Pozzo and his slave, Lucky ... or are they? Does this meet your definition of a conversation?

Silence
Estragon: Then adieu
Pozzo: Adieu
Vladimir: Adieu
Pozzo: Adieu
Silence. No one moves.
Vladimir: Adieu
Pozzo: Adieu
Estragon: Adieu
Silence.
Pozzo: And thank you
Vladimir: Thank you
Pozzo: Not at all
Estragon: Yes yes
Pozzo: No no
Vladimir: Yes yes
Estragon: No no
Silence
Pozzo: I don't seem to be able ... (*long hesitation*) ... to depart.
Estragon: Such is life

(Beckett 1965: Act One, p. 47)

It seems to me that Beckett portrays little, if any, dynamism in the exchange between the characters. They seem stuck in a rut, programmed to make social noises. However, they do adhere to certain formulaic principles of conversation: such as turn-taking in their speech (a principle which itself is often found unnecessary or undesirable in actual conversation). Interestingly, since this is an extract from a play, the participants actually are programmed: the actors have to say the lines which the author has written; the characters are only real within the very limited boundaries of the stage, the text of the play and the audience's willingness to suspend their disbelief. Theatre provides us with a vivid image of the extremes of ritualised conversation. In this example, it seems that there is little engagement between the actors – or is there?

Q4: Read the extract from *Waiting for Godot* again. Then use those characteristics for a conversation which you noted earlier to decide whether you would consider this a conversation. Why, or why not?

I don't want to offer any simple answer here – because I do not believe there is one. Nor do I think should we be looking for one. If you agree that the ability to engage in conversation plays a key part in our social and human make-up, then I hope you will also agree that this is not a subject about which we should expect answers and certainties; rather we should be willing to work with all the mess, and all the richness, of human interactions. The challenge is for us to rethink the possibilities and potentials realised through conversation.

You may want to contrast the rather sterile interactions of Beckett's characters with more animated real-life discussion you have witnessed. For example, I participated in a number of heated debates about car parking at a Centre where I worked. These discussions, which frequently spilled over from the canteen to Users' Committee meetings and back again, typically involved Centre users and local residents in highly emotive debates. Participants brought their personal experiences, desires and proposals to the debate in an obviously engaged way. Often, there was little evidence of turn-taking in the contributions made! To what extent do you think these conversations were more 'real' – because they were more humanised – or simply more passionate?

Q5: Think back to any recent conversation. How did the participants show their agreement, or reluctance, to co-operate with each other?

When you analyse conversations in this way, you see how non-verbal signals can impact on communication. For example, signals such as looking at one's watch, failing to slow down to allow another person to keep up with your pace of walking, or deciding about leaving a door open or closed may all give clues to the degrees of co-operation extended. This recollection from an adult education worker also implies something about the importance of a sense of safety in authentic conversation:

> I was in the tea room talking to M. about the type of writing he had to do for his work and what he found most difficult when R. came in and joined us. We carried on for a few more minutes but pretty soon it felt that we'd lost it and I decided the conversation had ended.

It seems to me that here the worker is commenting upon the fragility of some conversations – their existence relies upon an awareness of confidentiality between the participants. The entry of R. into the established dialogue disturbs the balance and so ends the conversation.

At the enquiry into the murder of the young Black Londoner, Stephen Lawrence, the McPherson Committee heard how the five initial suspects answered each question with the words, 'I claim privilege'. Even when asked by the Lawrence family's lawyer, 'Is your name...?' the response came back: 'I claim privilege'. Such a response is allowed in the context of a court of law. However it seems to push the formulaic language of the courtroom to its extremes to the extent that, in line with Grice's maxims, we can again question whether this was a conversation. Did the participants share a principle of relevance or of authentic truthfulness in this situation?

From these examples, we can start to see that conversations usually involve participants demonstrating some shared commitment to accepted or agreed conventions for the exchange of information. The nature of the information which can be exchanged is, potentially, immeasurably broad. Each of us acts with unimaginable ingenuity and creativity to express or to present a constantly changing range of emotional, factual, social, personal, public or ideological issues of concern to us. We do so frequently and overtly (but not solely) through conversation. In conversation, we use spoken as well as unspoken language in our constant desire to make sense of ourselves and of our experiences.

Conversations and learning

At our best, through conversation we seem able to free our own particular ideas and thinking from the existing limits of our current understanding. In such instances, real, human participants build upon each other's contributions, acknowledging or refining the part each plays so that they work together with an increasingly shared resource. It is this quality of language which Morrison (1994: 22) describes as 'word-work'; as characteristically 'generative'.

We then work at the margins of our knowledge and understanding, allowing space for new thinking to flourish within the collective abilities of the pair or group taking part. It is in this marginal area of our understanding (which Vygotsky (1978: 84) terms the 'zone of proximal development') that most effective learning will take place – extending rather than simply reinforcing what we already know and experience. A monologue, were such a pure form of inner communication to exist, remains closed to influences from beyond itself, often unable to reach beyond its own limits. In reality, of course, an absolutely pure monologue would be difficult to achieve outside the spheres of literature or perhaps of the meditative experiences of hermits. For most people, our recordings and our inner conversations continue to be influenced by other people's ideas and actions, since we are social beings. Even as we reflect or analyse ourselves in inner conversation, perhaps especially as we do so, we also return to previous experiences and exchanges, we plan for future ones, we constantly check and recheck ourselves within a social context. Even as the drama played out on stage by Beckett's characters becomes a nightmare, still it offers an image of individuals living within a social world, albeit one of almost entirely ritualised and predictable social interaction.

The word 'conversation' is based upon two Latin words meaning 'to turn' and 'with'. I want to suggest that through conversation we turn around our ideas and experiences with each other on a formal, social or ritualistic level and we thereby also re-view those ideas and experiences. In fact, conversation provides us with one way in which either to revisit our experiences or to entertain possibilities of future experiences. Rather as I imagine a jeweller may turn a diamond around in the light, so we turn our thoughts around in order to cast them in a new light. For us as social beings this seems to offer an essential vehicle to articulate our often keenly-felt hopes and fears about our past and our futures.

Formal conversation, as the description implies, is generally quite obviously formed and carefully regulated. However, as conversations become characteristically more informal in nature, although they remain regulated by social and cultural rules and expectations, these regulations can often become hidden or less obvious. For example, the regulations within a formal conversation such as an interview for a job or a visit to the doctor are generally made quite obvious. Some participants in this conversation may sit together, perhaps facing the person who is to respond. Unlike informal conversations, there are predictable roles in this type of conversation – some people will generally ask questions while one other will answer. The questioners may well hide their own views while the respondent will try and present her's in an obvious and acceptable way. The questioners may even set out the rules about timing and turn taking – whereas the interviewee or patient should probably not risk doing so! We usually learn, or are taught, these social regulations consciously. This learning may occur formally in school or on work experience, less formally from our peers, from adults around us or perhaps from quite painful experience. Although we may feel ill at ease or disadvantaged, we are probably aware that there are certain rules in play which we would be well advised to try to work out.

Q6: Think about a typically formal conversation which has taken place in your work place – perhaps in a meeting or at an official event. Can you identify any particular social regulations which seem to be accepted as the norm? How obvious would these be to newcomers or to outsiders?

As informal educators, we may frequently find ourselves working in quite formal settings such as Committee Meetings. Usually, the formal expectations are made apparent through devices such as formatted agenda, the recognition of a Chairperson or the timing and siting of the meeting. Many of these conversations are with funders or stakeholders, rather than with people whom we may describe as clients. In such cases, the formality of the proceedings may serve a useful purpose. For example, having an agenda can help ensure that key points are covered and that seemingly awkward questions are addressed. A skilful chairperson can see to it that any less confident participants make their views and voices heard or that the dialogue is not monopolised by those apparently 'in the know'.

On the other hand, some informal educators may try to avoid such highly formalised contexts for their working conversations with clients. For example, an adult education advice and guidance worker may meet potential students in the mosque or the tenants' hall. A detached worker may spend time in the bus station. Both wait for comments and questions, responding to issues raised and encouraging ideas and suggestions. This is not to say that there are no regulations at work in the conversations here, but rather that there are different, perhaps less stated, ones than those we can see operating in formal settings.

Insidiously, although informal conversations may well be carefully regulated, the very informality of the conversation can serve to mask the regulations which are at play. For example, the reply to a casual, 'Hi, Mary, how's it going?' probably invites a similarly brief response: 'Fine' or even 'You know' (where the information may be given by a shrug, a grin or a groan as much as by words). In this case, it would be 'wrong', in the sense of being inappropriate, to respond as we may appropriately do to our doctor's enquiry about our state of health. The amount of information expected in these two examples is different. For the co-operative principle to flourish, participants need to share a view about appropriate levels of informational detail. We can say we liked the meal but, in many cultures, we do not ask how much it cost. In some cultures, an accepted spoken response to being given a gift may be: 'You shouldn't have'. In others, this seems a strange and ungrateful reply. Ideas of politeness, of social status or group identification can all influence and regulate our seemingly most informal conversations. The problem which we face is that many of the regulations which govern informal exchanges are, by their nature, inexplicit and thus hidden from the newcomer or outsider. It is easy to assume that everyone knows, and shares, social conventions for discussing issues such as personal well-being, money and present giving.

Q7: Think of a comparatively informal conversation which you have had with a group of clients. What expectations do you think you and the clients brought to the exchange (perhaps about turn-taking, appropriate language or timing)?

My own view is that because conversation is a social activity it is necessarily influenced by social regulations. Decisions around the use of gendered language or not, around whether 'swearing' is acceptable, about which topics get followed up by group members, distinctions between insults and jokes, all these have to be negotiated somehow. In informal settings, the norms which underlie these regulations may not be made obvious. This, in turn, can serve to exclude those not 'in the know' from taking part comfortably or successfully in these exchanges. As informal or community educators, we can choose to attend to issues such as who chooses the co-operative principles in each case, and how these principles may be learned, negotiated or agreed.

Kress (1996) has suggested that failing to recognise or question the social regulations which govern our (written) exchanges itself serves to assume a universal acceptance of our own particular cultural conventions. This assumption can, in turn, ignore possibilities for diversity. If we apply his thinking to our conversations, then we may try to start to question, or at least recognise, some of the unstated rules which we work to. As we become more aware of the expectations or assumptions which we bring to our conversations, so we become more able to problematise social conventions which may otherwise pass as merely 'normal' behaviour. Quite a trivial example of this may be the use of names. While working as an adult educator, different students have addressed me by my first name or by my last name plus Mrs, Miss or, very occasionally, Ms; I have sometimes been called simply 'Miss' or 'Teacher'. For me, these labels imply different connotations of status, age or formality. Although I believe that these assumptions are not universal, nonetheless I feel initially more at ease with some than others. Based upon my own experiences, I easily associate the use of first names with mutual respect and an adult relationship: 'Miss', on the other hand, reminds me of my schooldays. I could not, of course, be sure what meanings students associated with their use of names and titles – were they perhaps connected to notions of respect, formality or gender? So although I may try to judge the appropriate name to use in return, our conversation is likely to be affected by the different norms underlying these choices.

So should we aim to become more explicit about our conventions in conversation? ('Call me Mary...', 'We prefer to say Chair, not Chairman...' 'Please try to avoid offensive language...') Certainly this may increase the possibility that new participants will be able to adapt to those conventions. And by recognising our own assumptions, we may in turn become more open-minded to accepting different approaches or assumptions. Equally, the more we leave our conventions hidden or unexplored, the less can other participants challenge or negotiate them. We thereby tend to reinforce familiar group norms. However, such a thorough and painstaking re/negotiation of the norms or conventions for each, or any, conversation hardly seems possible. I am reminded more of a negotiation of a peace treaty than an informal and basically voluntary human exchange. Maybe we would do better to try to develop our sensitivity so that we become curious, rather than convinced, in our approach to what makes for a good or a normal conversation.

Q8: Think back to the informal conversation which you used in the last example. Who, or what, do you think influenced the expectations which you identified? How do you imagine these expectations may be changed in the future?

Here's how a drugs advice worker summed up her approach to acceptable language in her work with clients:

> At first, I tend to try and let the client set the tone. I mean, I don't bring out all my street talk from the start – mainly because it tends to be very local! I know when I first started, I used to really worry about not knowing all the language and that, but now I think they don't expect me to. In fact, in lots of ways I think it's better to wait and see how the client wants to play it. So I try and let them set the tone and then, afterwards, I'll often jot down the words that person has used and maybe come back to them myself in later sessions. At least that way I'm not always having to ask what you mean and I feel I'm not imposing too much. In this job, I think that's really important.

Context

In trying to understand or analyse our conversations more perceptively or sensitively, it can be helpful to think of them as (spoken) texts. We can then remind ourselves that they always occur within a context (again, based on the Latin *con*-text meaning *with* the text). Viewed alone, as a text somehow freed from any context, conversations tend to lose their meaning. Here are some features of context which can influence the meaning or impact of a conversation:

- time;
- place;
- professional roles.

You may well want to add more.

The importance of context may become more obvious if we consider a question like, 'What's your name?' and try to imagine some of the different meanings it may have in various settings or contexts – for example in a night club or in a police station, after a fight or between new Year–6 school students. Or think about any particular times or places which you, or your clients, use to signal an acknowledgement of your professional role. If you bump into Kay's mother in the supermarket and discuss her progress at school, is it different from discussing her in your office behind a closed door? Is it different again by appointment in her own home? I wonder what messages both of you may bring to those conversations based upon their different context?

Q9: Think about three different conversations which you have had about work – perhaps with a client, a colleague or a funder. What influence did the location have in each instance? How might the conversations have been the same, or different, if you had been in a different place?

You may have quite stark examples of conversations in unusual contexts – bumping into the Chair of the Community Education sub-committee at a party. Many people would then avoid discussing work precisely because of the ambiguities caused by the mismatch between a conversation with somebody responsible for your funding and the relaxed atmosphere of some parties. On other occasions, less than official circumstances can allow people to share insights which are otherwise rarely expressed. A train journey with the Chair of your Management Committee might allow either, or both, of you to speak quite warmly and openly about your reasons for working for the Centre. Such a discussion could be quite different in tone if raised in the context of a formal evening meeting.

Purposes

As educators, we work with our own and other people's abilities to learn about ourselves and our surroundings: conversation is a prime way in which we work together to make sense of our experiences. We use it to reach a provisional, at least, understanding of our surroundings. It serves a number of different purposes, just two of which I want to refer to now as placing and practising.

We use conversations to place our personal experiences in a wider social context by exploring them with others. This may be through so-called idle chatter, perhaps a quick grumble about the traffic on the way into the Centre (which itself may lead to a local campaign for another pelican crossing!). At the other end of the scale, we may seek reassurance by placing our own frustrations or ambitions into an apparently familiar setting where we anticipate they can be acknowledged or appreciated.

> I remember one time L., a young woman I know quite well, volunteered to do the coffee bar with me. She had to push herself forward because two other members had already said they wanted to. So I suppose – if I thought about it – I sensed something was going on for her. While we were clearing up, so we weren't looking at each other, she said she had come out to her mother at the weekend.

This brief exchange took place during a session for young lesbians and gay men. 'Coming out' is quite a frequent subject of discussion at the Centre. It seems that L. makes the chance to have a conversation with the worker over the clearing up in order to take a look at her feelings about her conversation with her mother. She thus opens up her own unique experiences in a place in which those experiences, in general terms, are familiar. She avoids having to rehearse the significance of coming out and so can 'cut to the quick' of exploring her own feelings. Other interest groups may well serve the same purpose. Another worker spoke of some time spent with a local oral history group in which the subject of wash day arose.

> Their conversation quite quickly became an exchange of nouns such as 'mangle', 'penny powder', 'wash board', 'Dolly Blue', all accompanied by increasing laughter and gesturing between the members. In the end, I was laughing with the best of them although I didn't follow half of what was being said. It just got infectious. Some of us had tears streaming down our faces by the end of it all.

The shared familiarity of their memories meant that members of the oral history group could succeed in placing their experiences perhaps just by using one word. The session allowed them to explore and enjoy them again without needing lengthy explanations. By placing our ideas or feelings in a broader context, we may seek or gain reassurance of their validity and significance. We can celebrate, or come to terms with, coming out or our memories of the old Public Baths.

Any conversation we have is contextualised (Bakhtin 1986; Wardhaugh 1991): each one is necessarily informed by previous conversations, and exerts an influence on future ones. In L.'s case, we could say that she had chosen to use this conversation to place herself since 'coming out' holds a peculiar significance within lesbian and gay culture. In the oral history project, the members were taking the chance to place their individual memories in the history of their now-changed local area. According to Bakhtin (1980: 94), all this forms a part of 'the chain of speech communication' with its past and its future; each conversation impacting upon any future ones – although, of course, we cannot say how. In line with him, we can argue that any conversation has a history and will therefore impact upon a future conversation – it will form history in its turn. If we return to the conversation between L. and the worker outlined earlier, here is the worker's view of how the exchange continued:

> I was caught on the hop a bit and I sort of laughed and commented, 'I bet she was pleased'. L. said yeah and then there was quite a pause. Then she added 'It will be all right, won't it?' She sounded a bit desperate and I remember wishing I hadn't been so off-hand, I felt I hadn't left us any space to say much.

It seems that the worker has here recognised that her contribution to this conversation was ill-judged. Her joking response may serve to influence future exchanges negatively – so its function in the history of this exchange may be to close down further exploration.

A further attribute of conversation is its potential use to practise or rehearse for our future. Once again, I want to link this back to our aim as educators when we make use of experience and understanding (see Kolb 1984), but importantly we do so in order to work for the social futures of those with whom we work. Often, for example, we can use conversation to face up to difficulties which we envisage in the future. For example, a client may want to practise for a job interview with you, or simply to talk over what he is going to say to his child's social worker. Rather as the worker below indicates, conversations like these can serve to prepare for situations which seem threatening. Of course they are not the situation and may indeed be quite different from it. We all know that, but we find in conversation a place to address concerns or hopes about what may happen and to manage our doubts or uncertainties.

> I knew that one of the young people at my centre was due for another operation shortly and I knew she knew that I'd been through the same sort of thing myself. I was quite surprised, then, when she told me she wasn't going through with it and I suppose my first thought was to try and persuade her. Luckily, though, I just let her talk and she was on about how she wasn't so much scared about the pain but worried that she wouldn't make friends on the ward. I think she'd been in with adults in the past for some reason. It seemed to me that the more she talked, the more she seemed to be coming round to saying she didn't want the op. – not that she wouldn't have it. It was as if she just needed to get some feelings off her chest a bit with someone.

Whether we are placing previous experiences in a new context or practising for significant future events, we seem to use conversations to shift our private experience into the public domain of that which can be said or debated. In this way, we achieve quite a fundamental, if commonly experienced, transformation. Conversations inevitably change us because they rework our experiences. In making public our thoughts, perhaps particularly when these thoughts are doubtful or disturbing, we tend to tidy up some of their more ragged, contradictory edges by focusing attention on particular issues. In this way, we seem to make more sense of them both to our audience and to ourselves. We can scrutinise, and perhaps understand, our uncertainties in the light of our social exchanges.

This capacity to engage in conversation, to make our thoughts public, seems one of our most human and sociable capacities. And because conversation is associated with change – with the transformation of experience from the private to the public, from the isolated to the contextualised, then it is rightly a central concern of educators. After all, education is all about change (Smith 1994); and as educators we work with a human capacity to develop, to 'be more' as Freire succinctly claims (1996: 146). Conversation can open up changes that affect both its participants and the experience which lies at its heart.

I expect that most of you are familiar with the shifting image which can be seen as alternatively either two people in profile or a vase. I think of the profiles as two participants in a conversation, and the vase/space between them as the topic of the conversation itself. Metaphorically, we can see how the two people together form or define the topic: were they to change, then the topic itself would be changed and differently fashioned. The participants set limits to the topic and give it a coherent shape. In the same way, the conversation, which I am likening to the space in the middle, itself serves to outline the speakers. They are shaped or defined by any changes engendered by the conversation. It is this potential for us to be changed and to develop through conversation that allows us to describe it as an essentially social activity. Conversation requires relationship: between participants and with experiences. It serves to unite us both with each other and with our social context.

Conclusion

As informal educators, conversations matter to us because they offer scope for unpredictable development and flourishing. They also share many of the characteristics of successful educational encounters. For example, they are voluntary, they can be entered into freely and then left open for some future development. They enhance, by humanising, the formal activities of our professions. For example, the chat in the Centre office, the remarks after the match or the discussion over a coffee can all give participants the chance to have their own say about an educational encounter. In that way, conversation serves to allow the client to become actively involved in their own learning. The potentially crude distinction between the educator and the learner is eroded: each may bring different skills, experiences and perceptions to a conversation but what will inevitably emerge are newly formulated views and questions. In most cases, participants in a conversation will lose sight of where a specific theme or idea was first raised – as understandings are pooled and developed, so the total exceeds the sum of the parts. They are the key currency of our social exchanges and relationships.

Further reading

Goffman, E. (1990) *The Presentation of Self in Everyday Life*. London: Penguin Books Ltd. This book explores some of the different ways in which people present themselves to each other in social situations, especially at work. The writer uses the metaphor of a dramatic performance throughout the study, using ideas such as roles, staging, performance and character. He draws upon a wide range of source materials to illustrate his points – including recordings from eighteenth-century servants and twentieth-century baseball umpires – in a study which has become recognised as a classic since its first publication in 1959.

Smith, M.K. (1994) *Local Education Community, Conversation, Praxis.* Buckingham: Open University Press. An in-depth study of the work of adult and community educators, of community and youth workers, in promoting democracy and human well-being within local groups and communities. The work is based upon the author's own professional experiences as well as upon those of over thirty workers whose words and experiences are recorded and analysed in this study.

Wardhaugh, R. (1991) *How Conversation Works.* Oxford: Basil Blackwell Publishers. A carefully argued and informative study which offers an approach to analysing, assessing and encouraging everyday conversation. The author considers the formal and informal rules of conversation, in a detailed and thorough study of the area.

References

Bakhtin, M. (translated McGee, V.W.) (1986) *Speech Genres and Other Late Essays.* Austin: University of Texas.

Beckett, S. (1965, first performed 1955) *Waiting for Godot.* London: Faber and Faber.

Brodkey, L. (1994) 'Writing on the bias', in *College English* 56, 5, 527–47. California: University of Santa Clara.

Freire, P. (1996) *Letters to Cristina. Reflections on My Life and Work.* London: Routledge.

Goffman, E. (1981) *Forms of Talk.* Oxford: Basil Blackwell.

Goffman, E. (1990) *The Presentation of Self in Everyday Life.* London: Penguin Books Ltd.

Grice, H.P. (1975) 'Logic and conversation', in P. Cole and J.L. Morgan (eds) *Syntax and Semantics, Volume 3, Speech Acts.* New York: Academic Press.

Kolb, D. (1984) *Experiential Learning.* Englewood Cliffs: Prentice Hall.

Kress, G. (1996) *Learning To Write,* 2nd edn. London: Routledge.

McPherson, W. (1999) *The Stephen Lawrence Enquiry.* London: The Stationery Office Limited.

Morrison, T. (1994) *Lecture and Speech of Acceptance, Upon the Award of the Nobel Prize for Literature.* London: Chatto and Windus.

Smith, M.K. (1994) *Local Education Community, Conversation, Praxis.* Buckingham: Open University Press.

Vygotsky, L.S. (1978) *Mind in Society.* Massachusetts: Harvard University Press.

Wardhaugh, R. (1991) *How Conversation Works.* Oxford: Basil Blackwell Publishers.

11 Place, space and informal education

Mark K. Smith

As informal educators we operate in a wide variety of settings, often not of our making. Our work place can be wherever people congregate or spend time. This takes us into shopping malls, people's homes, the corridors of schools and colleges, clubs, cafés, classrooms – the list goes on. Each has its own characteristics and these have a direct bearing on the work we can do. What is more, our identities are wrapped up with the places we inhabit. How we see ourselves as educators, and how those we work with come to understand themselves, are linked to a sense of place.

On spaces, places and identity

If, like me, you live in a city or a town, then encountering wide, open spaces comes as a bit of a shock. It is something outside my everyday experience. I'm used to buildings, the constant sound of trains and cars, and to other people being around. Walking in the hills, where all that is before us is sheep and grass we may experience a sense of space. The hills probably encourage this – they allow us to draw a line on the scene, a distant boundary. Yet such landscapes are more than spaces – their features have names – and naming things locates them – they become places. We can attach meanings to them. We may feel we belong (we are not 'out of place'); the absence of clutter and sense of space may bring us closer to God or allow us to ground ourselves (we find our 'place in the world' and see the 'bigger picture'). It is not surprising, then, that many educators try to create opportunities for others to share these experiences and to engage with them.

Part of the attraction of such places is the way they contrast with our daily experiences. Increasingly we have to conduct our interactions with others at a distance. We use the phone to keep in touch with friends and family and to deal with business and personal matters. Many look to the Internet to get information or to shop. Yet the local is still important. Many of us still live much of our lives within a relatively small area. While we may travel to work, we still tend to use local schools, shops and food places, belong to community organisations and so on. Crucially, if we look at things from the point of view of children and young people, then it can be seen that much of their lives are wrapped up around the local – home, school, streets, fields and parks.

Particular places have strong meanings for many people. To be attached to one is seen as 'a fundamental human need and, particularly as home, the foundation of our selves and our identities' (Eyles 1989: 109). In this sense they are 'profound centres of human existence'. Through growing up in a place, or perhaps by living there for a long time, we can come to name ourselves as Mancunians, Cumbrians, Glaswegians and so on. This attachment is not surprising at one level. The urban experience of children and young people up to the age of 14 or 15 years is largely confined to their immediate neighbourhood (Taylor, Evans and Fraser 1996: 266). As a result, discussion by 13–15-year-olds about their own neighbourhood often involves, 'a quite elaborate and affectionate display of knowledge with respect to local police, local "characters" and so on' (*op. cit.*). Through their experience of local schooling, family and social networks, and of making their way around the neighbourhood, they come to know local ways of life and perhaps to develop some sense of belonging. This might be added to by knowledge of places beyond the immediate area. However, such knowledge tends to rely on second-hand sources, fleeting impressions, local stereotypes (e.g. around the roughness of an area) and reports and stories in local media.

In this way place can be understood as space which people in a given area 'understand as having a particular history and as arousing emotional identifications, and which is associated with particular groups and activities' (Watt and Stenson 1998: 253). However, things are not always that cosy. Places 'can provide not only a sense of well-being but also one of entrapment and drudgery. To be tied to one place may well enmesh a person in the familiar and routine from which no escape seems possible' (Eyles 1989: 109). Place, then, has to be central to our work as educators. The feelings associated with place, and the impact on identity and opportunity, surface in many of our conversations as educators. We need to explore what people may be experiencing.

Q1: Consider your own relationship with place.

- What place do you describe as home? Is it where you live now, or, if it is different, where you spent some of your childhood or youth?
- When asked about yourself, do you talk about place when describing yourself?
- Where are the main places in which you spend time? What do they say about you?

Geographies of childhood and youth

To help us in this I want to begin by examining the significance and nature of place for children and young people.

For most children territorial range increases with age. The range can also alter suddenly following events such as changing or starting school, moving house or having a new friend (Hill and Tisdall 1997: 107). The activity spaces they inhabit provide a map of their everyday lives – home, school, park, friend's houses and the paths between them. We can quickly see the impact upon them of weather, landscape, the range of local facilities, and distance from family and friends.

Where do young people spend their time? In the UK, home-based forms of leisure – watching television, reading, using PlayStations and so on – are by far the most common non-work activities that young people engage in

(OPCS 1995). The other place in which children and young people spend much of their time is school or college. Since 1974 the school leaving age has been 16 and the proportion of 16- to 18-year-olds in education and training has expanded significantly. For example, in England around 74 per cent of that age group were in education and training at the end of 1998, having increased from 61 per cent some ten years before (DfEE 1999).

If we then turn to leisure activities outside the home and school for 13–20-year olds, the most popular activities are visiting friends (85 per cent); hanging about with groups of friends on the street (56 per cent); discos (47 per cent); sports clubs (40 per cent); youth clubs or groups (31 per cent); cinemas (31 per cent); and pubs (29 per cent) (Hendry *et al.* 1993: 42). Again each of these involves particular activity spaces – people's homes, streets, clubs, etc. Each has its rules and norms which, in turn, are conditioned, in part, by the physical location and what people make of it. An example here might be the street. It can be seen as a place of danger. Traffic threatens the very young, the possibility of attack or unwanted approach may worry the older. However, such 'hazards' may attract as well as repel – being in a 'dangerous' place can bring status. Such rules, norms and expectations are of fundamental significance to informal educators. They have to attend to them if they are to establish relationships with people in different places.

> **Q2:** Consider the lives of one or two of the children you either work with or know.
>   First, think about the *territorial range* they are familiar with:
>
> * *habitual range* – where they spend most of their time;
> * *frequented range* – places they go that are further afield;
> * *occasional range* – locations that are encountered once or rarely (Moore 1986, in Hill and Tisdall 1997: 107).
>
> Second, consider the activity spaces they inhabit – the paths and routes they take, and the places (or territories) in which they spend time.

Geographies of power and exclusion

Relations of power and exclusion are, perhaps, one of the most difficult aspects of place for educators. There is an obvious geography of power as soon as we look at where major economic decisions are made, and who gains and suffers as a result. Large, multinational corporations usually have their headquarters well away from where the bulk of their employees work. Important decisions are made elsewhere, and usually look to questions of profitability and political cost/gain rather than the impact on local people. Furthermore, sometimes it is difficult to know exactly where power is.

At a more local level, a geography of power also exists. 'The human landscape', David Sibley once wrote, 'can be read as a landscape of exclusion ... power is expressed in the monopolization of space and the relegation of weaker groups in society to less desirable environments' (1995: ix). Particular areas may well come to be perceived as being 'white', 'Asian' or 'Black'.

Many public spaces are experienced by women as being 'male-dominated' and seen as being risky places to be on your own. In this process, those labelled as 'others' are placed as outsiders. Their presence in a place can then be seen as threatening the norm (and are therefore in need of exclusion) or as making them 'fair game'. The experience of children and young people is a good example of this phenomenon.

Parents often try to negotiate or impose rules on children as to where they can, or can't, go (especially when they are younger). Rules generally flow from a concern that they stay close to home (so that they can be located and supervised); to avoid 'dangerous people' (paedophiles, gangs); and steer clear of dangerous objects and events (traffic, lakes, railway lines). Children can also be put off going to the places they see as defended by custodians like park-keepers, janitors or watching neighbours (Moore 1986, in Hill and Tisdall 1997: 107). We can also see this geography of exclusion appearing in a much more blatant way with regard to children and young people in many North American cities through the use of curfews. In the United States most curfew regimes apply to those 17 and under and run from 22.30 through to 06.30. A growing number are supplemented with daytime curfews operating during school hours – usually 09.00 to 14.30 (Jeffs and Smith 1995).

The geography of informal education

While we, as educators, can do some work at a distance via telephones and the Internet, mostly we have to be in the same place as those we are working with. Being centred around conversation, informal education entails talking, and joining in activities with others (children, young people and adults). Obviously, to do this we have to be close physically to those we want to work with. This leaves us with two basic strategies – either we go to where people are, or we set up some sort of facility that encourages people to come to us. In youth work this has led to the classic division into club- or centre-based work and detached or outreach work; and previously in community work the split between community centre and community development work.

As we have already seen, with increased rates of participation in education and training, the development of home-based entertainment and the expansion of commercial leisure opportunities, youth centres and clubs have had a hard time attracting customers. There has been a marked drop in the average age worked with, and a near abandonment in many centres of work with those over 18 years (Fitzpatrick, Hastings and Kintrea 1998). Specialist forms of provision, for example around arts and adventure, have had some success in bringing in older groups, but for the most part it is the pre- and early-teens who go to youth centres and clubs. Younger people's leisure 'career' appears to take three stages:

- organised – youth groups, sports clubs and so on (up to age 14 years);
- casual – hanging about (ages 14 to 16 years);
- commercial – clubs, pubs, cinema (post-16 years).

Young women are more likely to be involved in 'casual' and 'commercial' leisure, and young men in 'organised leisure' (Hendry *et al.* 1993: 43). This has had profound implications for the geography of practice. It has forced many agencies concerned with the informal education of young people into working where young people can be found, rather than attempting to draw them, initially, to centres. If we look simply to where people in the 14–18-year age range spend their time, then our priorities as informal educators would run in the following order:

1   Developing learning activities within the home.
2   Working within schools and colleges – both in social situations and in more formal settings.
3   Streetwork – making contact, and developing work with people 'hanging about'.
4   Exploring the possibilities of work within commercial settings – pubs, clubs, cinemas, bowling alleys, etc.
5   Working in 'youth provision' such as clubs, centres and cafés.

Q3: Think about the work of some agencies that seek to work with young people.

- What is their basic strategy – to go where people are, or to attempt to attract them to provision?
- If they do seek to work where people spend their time, how does their approach match up to the above priorities?
- What problems are they experiencing in attracting and making contact with young people?

A very similar set of questions and issues arises with regard to work with adults. Just as the home is the centre for leisure for young people, so it is for adults. For example, there has been a substantial shift away from the use of public houses and bars for the consumption of alcohol to the home. Current government strategies around lifelong learning have similarly turned away from the traditional classroom, towards exploiting the more individualised learning opportunities of television, the Internet and distance education (Smith 1999). However, this trend should not be overstated. A large number of people remain involved in local community groups, voluntary organisations and enthusiast groups. In Britain around 12 million women and men are currently involved in running some 1.3 million voluntary groups, teams and organisations (over 25 per cent of the adult population). In addition, well over half the adult population belongs to a local voluntary organisation (Elsdon *et al.* 1995: 47). Voluntarily joining together in companionship or to undertake some task can bring both personal satisfaction and social benefit. Such association can also be a major educational force and the site of intervention by informal educators (Doyle and Smith 1999; the informal education homepage 1999). As Dickie (1999) has concluded with regard to local community organisation, more systematic approaches to the educational aspects of campaigning can consolidate collective learning processes (see also Foley 1999).

Issues for informal educators

All of this poses significant problems for informal educators. First, *access* to a number of these environments is difficult. We have to satisfy various 'gatekeepers' as to our credentials before we can get into many places. In the case of the school this might be the headteacher, in commercial settings the manager, and in the home this could mean young people and parents. Entering local community groups can be especially difficult as we can be reliant on individuals who may rather not have us there (seeing our presence as a threat to their position) (Francis and Henderson 1992: 32–4). Many gatekeepers will be suspicious of us. For example, parents or carers may well have worries about our intentions or ways of working if we seek to come into their houses.

Second, there are questions of *purpose and possibility*. Some settings are obviously good for making contact, but may not be so good for deeper work. We may well look to commercial settings, for example, for making contact, but find that people have other priorities than to talk with us. Different environments will open up, and close down, various avenues of work.

Third, and linked to the above, are questions of *appropriateness and safety*. Certain behaviours will be appropriate to one setting, others will not. If we return to the example of working in people's houses then simply 'being around' – hanging about with people – is likely to be viewed with suspicion, whereas work with a clear focus will generally help people feel more at ease. There are certain situations in which 'hanging about' in this setting might well be appropriate – for example, where a person's home is communal, as is the case in YMCA hostels or children's homes. Going into private houses requires us having and declaring a clear focus for our visit. For example, we may come into the house because someone wants to talk about a particular issue, or to do some tutoring around literacy, or to work on some project such as doing the community association accounts. In doing this, we must have a care that we do not put ourselves, or those we work with, at risk. For example, it may not be advisable, as an individual worker, to spend time alone with a lone man or woman in their home. In some situations it is appropriate, for example working with a tenants' association committee member you have known for a time; in others it is not. It is important that we make a proper assessment of the risk.

Fourth, we need to think carefully about the groups we are *targeting*. We have already seen how age range is significant. We can attract significant numbers of children to organised provision such as groups, clubs and centres. Similarly, it is possible to make contact with large numbers of young people in schools and colleges. We can meet a lot of people by simply going door-to-door around a neighbourhood. However, we need to think about who may not be present in those settings – for example, those who have left, or those who are no longer attracted to schooling and, thus, try to avoid spending much time there.

Fifth, there are issues around *scale*. Some settings allow for work with large numbers of people; others are more suitable for individual and small group work. We need to think about the shape and nature of the physical environment. For informal educators concerned with community development, for example, there can be nothing more dispiriting than getting issues of scale wrong with regard to public meetings. Having a small number of people in a large hall is generally far less conducive to conversation and exploration than a large number in a small room. A similar 'rule' applies to youth club and project work.

Sixth, there are questions around the relative degree of *control* people have over the different spaces. Here we come across one of the great misconceptions concerning 'detached' or 'outreach' work – that it takes place on people's 'home ground'. People do not own the pubs they drink in, or the shopping centres they spend time in. They may attempt to colonise areas, to alter their physical appearance (with graffiti, etc.) and to work social relationships to gain influence, but they often have little or no 'legitimate' power over the setting.

Last, there is the problem of our own *attitudes*. For example, many of those who see themselves as youth workers have a problem with the idea of working in schools (with the various rules, compulsory attendance and so on); and in making contact with people in their homes. The latter in part flows from a fear of outreach work, but it can also be linked to the concerns about entering such a private world as the home. Other informal educators have had less of a problem with this. Here we only need to look to the work of those concerned with traditional approaches to community development or with health promotion to see something of the possibilities of work in the home.

Working so that spaces become places

In an earlier book, *Local Education* (1994), I explored the work of educators who engage with local networks and cultures, and who build ways of working which connect with local understandings. Calling ourselves local educators is not simply to do with our working in a certain area, it is also to say that we belong in some further way. Our identities as educators are wrapped up with the place or type of place in which we work. This can build up from simple things like clothing – in street work we may have to dress in one way, for operating around a college or school another.

However, having a concern for place goes further than identity and process – it also links to questions of purpose. If, as informal educators, we are concerned with working so that all may share in a common life (Dewey 1916: 7), then it is clear that we need to look to:

- questions of identity;
- the ways in which people make sense of place;
- how people deal with distant systems and bodies; and the impact of exclusion.

Running through all three elements is a concern that informal educators should work so that spaces can become, or can stay, places with particular qualities. We look to create and sustain the conditions for encounter and conversation – so that all may share in a common life.

On the street, in people's homes, or in the supermarket, our main points of intervention concern the social setting or context and the subject for conversation. There is only so much that we can do about the physical setting. We can work in a way that can influence people's experience of the space; or, if it seems appropriate, encourage them to move to another place where conversation can happen. In contrast, when working in space that we manage, we can make use of the usual array of tools. There is no shortage of guidance for workers in this area. In youth work, for example, setting out rooms, the use of equipment and the design of settings has long formed part of the standard textbooks (e.g. Russell and Rigby 1908: 40–52). As Josephine Macalister Brew rather quaintly put it:

> A club is a community engaged in the task of educating itself. It therefore follows that a youth organization can meet anywhere. There are only three necessities – light, preferably the sort that cannot be turned off or blown out by the practical joker – warmth, and if you cater for boys this means a 'fug' – and comradeship.
>
> (Brew 1943: 67)

We work in physical surroundings and contribute to the interactions that are going on. Teachers, especially those in primary education, have long appreciated that both are necessary – hence the care that is often taken with the organisation of classrooms, the pictures on the walls, the various materials and pieces of equipment that are to hand. Many informal educators also take care with the atmosphere that can be generated in buildings or areas that they have some responsibility for. By working on things like lighting, seating arrangements, music, dress, we try to create physical environments which communicate warmth, friendliness, community.

Q4: This may be a good moment to review the places in which you work.

The most important questions concern the extent to which they foster conversation. For example, do they:

- provide a stimulus for conversation? Are there things like posters, leaflets, papers, a television showing almost any of the daily soaps or magazine programmes?
- have comfortable spaces to sit or stand?
- have somewhere for a quiet word?

Whatever the setting, our first and obvious step as informal educators, is to work our way into being close enough to people to talk or communicate. Our second is to operate in such a way as to move from simply being around in a place and part of the scene, to being present in a more direct way to people. Informal educators tend to use one of four basic moves or tactics to make such openings (Smith 1994: 44–5):

- Greeting or speaking to a member or gathering to whom they are already known or can legitimately speak. This can then be used to gain an introduction to the other people present.
- Becoming recognised as someone who is routinely around, who is part of the local scene – basically 'being around' (see Jeffs and Smith 1999: 95–7).
- Going up to people, saying who they are and what they are doing and then asking questions or offering information. Here various direct means can be involved, such as giving out leaflets or making a straight introduction ('Hello, I am a new worker at...'). Other approaches can be more indirect such as 'making friends' with someone's dog.

- Doing some activity that attracts attention or interest. When people come to see what is going on, you can then 'catch' them.

These moves may happen within a setting we are responsible for (such as a centre, café or 'drop-in') or in a place where we are one amongst others, such as in street work.

Space, place and informal education

Informal education is a practice of place. Our fundamental purpose is to work for forms of living that foster conversation, democracy and learning (Jeffs and Smith 1999). Some of the time we work with a clear objective in mind – perhaps linked to some broader plan, e.g. around the development of reading. At other times we may go with the flow – adding to the conversation when it seems right or picking up on an interest. For this reason, informal education tends to be unpredictable – we do not know where it might lead. In conversation we have to catch the moment where we can say or do something to deepen people's thinking or to put them in touch with their feelings. To do this we have to connect with place. We need to attend to physical surroundings and how they are experienced and reworked by people.

Further reading

Jeffs, T. and Smith, M.K. (1999) *Informal Education. Conversation, Democracy and Learning.* Ticknall: Education Now.

Massey, D. and Jess, P. (eds) (1995) *A Place in the World? Places, Cultures and Globalization.* Oxford: Oxford University Press with the Open University. This Open University course explores the meaning and significance of place in the context of globalisation.

Smith, M. (1994) *Local Education. Community, Conversation, Praxis.* Buckingham: Open University Press. An exploration of the processes that informal educators engage that attends to place.

Visit the informal education homepage: www.infed.org

References

Brew, J.M. (1943) *In the Service of Youth.* London: Faber and Faber.

Department for Education and Employment (1999) *Participation in Education and Training by 16–18 Year Olds in England 1992/93–1996/97 – Release 7/991.* London: Department for Education and Employment.

Dewey, J. (1916) *Democracy and Education.* New York: Macmillan.

Dickie, J. (1999) 'Neighbourhood as classroom', in J. Crowther, I. Martin and M. Shaw (eds) *Popular Education and Social Movements in Scotland Today.* Leicester: National Institute of Adult Continuing Education.

Douglas, T. (1991) *A Handbook of Common Group Work Problems.* London: Routledge.

Doyle, M.E. and Smith, M.K. (1999) *Born and Bred? Leadership, Heart and Informal Education.* London: YMCA George Williams College/Rank Foundation.

Elsdon, K.T. with Reynolds, J. and Stewart, S. (1995) *Voluntary Organizations. Citizenship, Learning and Change.* Leicester: NIACE.

Eyles, D. (1989) 'The geography of everyday life', in D. Gregory and R. Walford (eds.) *Horizons in Human Geography*. London: Macmillan.

Fitzpatrick, A., Hastings, S. and Kintrea, K. (1998) *Including Young People in Urban Regeneration: A Lot to Learn?* York: The Policy Press.

Foley, G. (1999) *Learning in Social Action. A Contribution to Understanding Informal Education*. London: Zed Books.

Francis, D. and Henderson, P. (1992) *Working with Rural Communities*. London: Macmillan.

Goetschius, G. and Tash, J. (1967) *Working With Unattached Youth*. London: Routledge and Kegan Paul.

Hendry, L.B., Shucksmith, J., Love, J.G. and Glendinning, A. (1993) *Young People's Leisure and Lifestyles*. London: Routledge.

Hill, M. and Tisdall, K. (1997) *Children and Society*. Harlow: Longman.

The informal education homepage (1999–) 'Association and Civic Participation', www.infed.org/association.

Jeffs, T. and Smith, M.K. (1995) 'Getting the dirtbags off the streets', *Youth and Policy*, 53, 1–14.

Jeffs, T. and Smith, M.K. (1998) 'The problem of "youth" for youth work', *Youth and Policy* 62.

Jeffs, T. and Smith, M.K. (1999) *Informal Education. Conversation, Democracy and Learning*. Ticknall: Education Now.

OPCS (1995) *General Household Survey 1993*. London: The Stationery Office.

Russell, C.E.B. and Rigby, L.M. (1908) *Working Lads' Clubs*. London: Macmillan.

Sibley, D. (1995) *Geographies of Exclusion*. London: Routledge.

Skelton, T. and Valentine, G. (eds) (1998) *Cool Places. Geographies of Youth Cultures*. London: Routledge.

Smith, M. (1994) *Local Education. Community, Conversation, Praxis*. Buckingham: Open University Press.

Smith, M.K. (1999) 'Lifelong learning', on *the informal education homepage*, www.infed.org/lifelonglearning.

Taylor, I., Evans, K. and Fraser, P. (1996) *A Tale of Two Cities. Global Change, Local Feeling and Everyday Life in the North of England. A Study in Manchester and Sheffield*. London: Routledge.

Watt, P. and Stenson K. (1998) 'The street: "It's a bit dodgy around here". Safety, danger, ethnicity and young people's use of public space', in T. Skelton and G. Valentine (eds) *Cool Places. Geographies of Youth Cultures*. London: Routledge.

12 Programme planning

Pauline Riley

The need for formal structures in informal education

If youth workers are committed to educating young people informally any time, any place, anywhere (rather like the old Martini advertisement) then the question must be asked why do we have the need to use a traditional formal educative process – that is – a carefully thought out, planned, structured programme with clear, well-defined aims and objectives?

I propose to examine this apparent contradiction by looking at how my work as a county-wide youth worker involves detailed planning to ensure a favourable environment for informal education while taking into account the needs of the young people and how these needs can be married to the aim of the association.

My organisation's aim is: 'to help young people so to develop their physical, mental and spiritual capacities that they may grow to full maturity as individuals and members of society.'

This aim is rather vague and wide-ranging, but nevertheless conveys, I suspect, the ethos of youth work generally. It is not tightly defined or prescriptive and therein lies its strength. It gives scope for creative and imaginative planning and the implementation of a wide variety of learning experiences and opportunities for informal education.

To give an example – several years ago we planned a mountain walking residential in the Lake District. I encouraged a worker friend to bring a group who had never been away from inner-city Bristol before. One day as we sweated and toiled through the snow up Red Pike and over the ridge above Buttermere the sun came out, mist swirled up from the gulleys below us and we witnessed a completely circular rainbow; one lad held his arms outstretched and his elongated shadow pierced through the mist and rainbow. We were individually, and as a group, strangely moved and reduced to a wondering silence (quite an achievement!). Someone tried to explain the meteorological reason for the circular rainbow but no-one was interested – for us it was a spiritual moment. It is something I will never forget and I know had a profound effect on each member of the group. The experience moved one of the lads from Bristol to take up mountain walking and he regularly travels independently to the Lake District after that day.

This example gives an insight into how a residential programme item can address issues which are in tune with an agency's aim of 'developing physical, mental and spiritual' capacities. This experience fitted very snugly into our aim. However, I would also suggest that the smallest behavioural change can also be effective. For instance, a young man I work with who is usually disruptive and has been barred from several local agencies offered to make me a cup of coffee when I was feeling unwell. He showed kindness and consideration. I felt he was starting to adopt a caring attitude and I could quite legitimately claim that he was beginning to fulfil my agency's aim of 'growing into full maturity as an individual and member of society'.

Trying to grasp the concepts of devising a programme to fulfil agency aims may be somewhat daunting for new practitioners but it is crucially important to realise it is not necessary to produce an 'all-singing, all-dancing' event in order to deliver practice that is in harmony with your organisation's aim.

I find it helpful to think of the overall aim as an island. The programme content should provide the informal educative practical learning experiences or 'stepping stones' towards that 'island' or aim. The 'stepping stones' are fundamental core considerations that need to be taken into account when planning a programme to meet with your aim. In my experience these core considerations are:

- the *needs* of the young people taking part;
- *timescale* and *programme* content;
- the *environment* in which the programme will take place;
- the *constraints* there are in terms of resources;
- *flexibility* within the programme to allow for and encompass deviations from 'intended' outcomes;
- provision for the further *development* of young people;
- effective, user-friendly *monitoring, reflection* and *evaluation* of work;
- *health* and *safety* procedures.

Let us examine how each of these considerations is taken into account in order to plan and deliver a programme which is in tune with our aim of encouraging young people's personal development through informal education.

Needs

Providers should understand that their perceptions of young people's needs are not necessarily those of the receivers of the programme.

If, as workers, we are aiming to intervene positively in young people's lives with the purpose of educating them informally, then we must ensure that we establish what their needs are. It is our responsibility to make sure that programmes are designed to stimulate and encourage meaningful learning and feelings of self-worth and confidence among the recipients, and to give scope for further involvement to help with their development.

It follows therefore that it is worth taking time to talk with young people to establish what their real needs are. It may seem elementary but if, for example, there are literacy problems in the group it would be insensitive and non-productive to ask them to write a report of a particular experience. The programme should be flexible enough to suggest alternative methods of relaying young people's learning – options should be given for a video, audio-tape or photographic display. Programmes should ensure that people take part on a 'level playing field' regardless of their academic abilities.

A colleague and I are currently working with a group with mixed abilities

on a peer health education project. Several members are articulate but have difficulty with the written word – others are very capable in that field. We purposely designed the training programme using informal educative methods introducing discussions, role-plays, videos, practical exercises and so on. We write up the group findings on flip charts so that no one is asked to perform a task they are not comfortable with. This project, in my view, is a good example of the value and strength of informal education – the group members feel confident in delivering their own learning to their peers without embarrassment about any academic weaknesses they may have.

The area of fund-raising can be a minefield where 'needs' are concerned. If practitioners working for voluntary groups need to apply for funds to enhance the programme it is tempting for organisations which are hard-pressed financially to lose their way. It is critical that workers apply for funds to fit the 'needs' and not for 'needs' to fit the funds. For example, a worker I know was invited to apply for funding from the Health Authority to deliver work around HIV/Aids. She felt this was in line with her objectives for the group and planned a six-week programme with visits from health specialists and got the funding. Her young people had been involved in an intensive HIV/Aids programme at school. The last thing they wanted in their leisure time was to repeat the whole thing again and so they voted with their feet. The worker was left with feelings of inadequacy and embarrassment when no one turned up to meet the invited speakers. Had she taken time to talk with the young people the whole debacle could have been avoided.

Time scale and programme content

If we go back to our aim of 'developing young people' and are committed to working with them using informal educative processes it follows that there should be a progression in terms of their levels of responsibility, involvement and development.

A way of achieving these goals is to plan a programme of short, medium and long-term projects within the overall framework. Let us look at these in greater detail.

Short-term activities

Pool tournaments, quizzes and discussion groups are available on a 'take it or leave it' basis for everyone and very little prior commitment is required from the participants; they are relatively easy organisationally and involve minimal time commitment from workers. Large numbers of young people are usually involved.

These 'short-term' activities are a useful means for workers to begin to get to know young people who are new to them and vice versa. This is a 'testing out' time. They give the worker opportunities for appraising situations, developing conversations, and starting to assess needs at a fairly basic level. Occasions will arise for the worker to intervene informally; ground rules can be established; youngsters will learn what behaviour is acceptable and what is not. Issues around fair play, bullying, being civil to one another can start to be addressed at this stage. The worker is able to evaluate sessions and plan future interventions around areas of concern. The young people decide whether they want further involvement or not. They are free to come and go without any firm commitment.

Medium-term projects

These might be monthly trips, discos, ice skating, special events. They need more thought, preparation and planning. They can be designed to promote involvement from members and require a firm commitment before the event can take place. Young people should be encouraged to contribute their ideas and help with planning for these events while the worker has overall responsibility for making sure they happen. There will be smaller numbers involved in the planning processes. This involvement presents opportunities for the worker to assess needs in greater depth and plan intervention strategies where appropriate – for example, particular responsibilities can be allocated to individuals who have low self-esteem and have a need to feel valued or 'important'. Involvement in the planning and execution of projects develops self-confidence and feelings of self-worth among young people; they start to assume responsibility and ownership for what happens. It is absolutely crucial that the worker gives support and guidance.

Sometimes the planned event may not happen for whatever reason. Again it is vital that the worker takes the time to work through the difficulties and point out the positive learning experiences for the young people involved so that they are not left with feelings of inadequacy or worthlessness.

Long-term projects

These can include peer health education, drama, annual camps, residentials. If a worker is committed to the personal development of young people there are plentiful opportunities for concentrated involvement and participation. These events involve detailed planning and work. They are specific projects within a specific time scale where small groups of young people can start to take on responsibility, leadership and organisational roles. A lengthy time commitment is required from the young people while the worker is able to draw back somewhat. The worker's role will be largely supportive and practical – making sure of legal or health and safety implications. The worker has to learn to 'let go' of responsibility to a degree and this is not always easy!

There will be difficulties and blockages to overcome which can seem insurmountable to an inexperienced young person but present little difficulty to an adult. This is where the skill of the worker can and should be brought into play; a timely intervention can overcome difficulties and prevent disillusionment and feelings of inadequacy for the young people concerned. There are arguments for letting young people make, and learn from, their mistakes and I am not suggesting that this should not happen along the way, but I would argue that if we are concerned with supporting a young person's development an occasional timely intervention is not necessarily a bad thing. Mutually preparing and working through the process of making a check list of 'things to do' with a young person at the outset of a project is good practice and hopefully will circumvent any major disasters along the way.

In summary the programme content is a useful tool for the development of a young person's progression through to adulthood, underpinning tried and tested activities and events with informal educative processes.

Environment

The environment in which a particular activity takes place is another crucial aspect to consider in programme planning and fulfilling agency aims.

The layout of a room can affect behaviour and what happens during a session. I run a weekly club in a building which is two temporary offices joined together. The ceiling is low, the hall is big, bleak, noisy and impersonal. As the evening progresses the noise level rises; the room echoes and by the end of the night conversation is conducted at a bellow. Introducing a thoughtful structured programme in this environment is difficult and challenging, but we tried...

We acquired screens and sectioned off a corner of the room around a few easy chairs and a coffee table. We introduced quizzes, quiet table games and discussions and tried as far as possible to keep this a quiet(er) area. To some extent it has enabled us to introduce a more structured educative approach to the club programme. By having this quieter space we are able to foster conversation, discuss needs and make positive interventions into the lives of the young people present. Through conversation which developed we have embarked on a process, within the programme's structure, to give opportunities to develop and encourage self-confidence and esteem in a young woman who I learned was being physically abused by her father. Without making a determined effort to change the environment in that club it is highly unlikely that the opportunity would have arisen to learn of this young woman's problems or do anything positive to try to address them.

I am a great believer in getting the best possible environment for whatever event you are planning. It is my experience that young people (like the rest of us) respond more positively to whatever is on offer if they feel they are being valued as individuals.

Each year I run a Fashion Show in which our club members are models. This programme item is very much concerned with our aim of improving young people's sense of self-worth, confidence and esteem using the medium of dance and giving opportunities to wear the latest High Street fashions.

It is an event that is extremely popular with young people. Last year the venue was a community centre with the catwalk constructed from tables; rehearsals took place in youth club rooms. The show went well but the behaviour during rehearsal times was not good. This year the venue was a prestigious theatre in the centre of Chester; the behaviour of the young people was first rate, they worked hard, didn't drop litter and were totally co-operative – so what was so different to bring about this marked behavioural change?

The difference between the two events was the environment in which the activity took place – the choreographers and workers worked in exactly the same way on both occasions. The change in behaviour exhibited by the young people was, in my view, because they felt valued. The theatre space was professional; the set had been designed especially for them; the lighting technicians worked closely with them to show them off to the best possible advantage and the young people responded to the respect they were shown by showing respect for people and property themselves. I think this example demonstrates the powerful effect the environment can have on a programme activity and underlines how young people's behaviour can be affected quite dramatically by their environment.

Constraints

My main constraint in developing a programme is time. Constraints such as money, buildings, equipment and transport are hurdles and blockages which can by and large be overcome, but time is finite.

We are seen as an organisation that works closely and actively with young people and are perceived by some as having achieved a measure of success with many of our projects. As a consequence we are frequently approached to pilot new projects or undertake specific pieces of work. Very flattering, challenging and time-consuming.

Time, therefore, is a precious commodity. You will need to be careful not to enter into situations without assessing the timescale involved properly. To give an example, one of our long-established voluntary clubs went through a difficult patch which resulted in the local authority worker being withdrawn. We were drafted in to rescue the club, recruit volunteers and then withdraw. This we have done to an extent and the club is now flourishing, but the recruitment of volunteers has been difficult. We have one enthusiastic young woman. We now have a dilemma – do we pull out, disappoint the youngsters and the volunteer that we have nurtured and fostered; or devote a disproportionate amount of time to this one club? (Answers on a postcard please!)

Constraints to our work are often beyond our control. Our area has undergone an enormous change recently. The shire county has been reduced by one-third as two new unitary authorities have been formed. This situation placed constraints on what we felt we could offer, as workers felt unable to make any long-term commitment. Anxious that young people should not be the losers in this situation, and in an effort to address this issue, we introduced a new dimension in our programme whereby our staff offered six-week projects in clubs around specific areas, i.e. health and fitness, volunteer training and arts. We went out to clubs rather than expecting them to come to our events.

From a young person's perspective one of the greatest constraints in gaining access to what our programme has to offer is transport. Public transport is expensive, unreliable and, in rural areas, non-existent. We have developed several different strategies for addressing this particular constraint. Events take place at different venues around the county; we apply for transport costs for young people in bids to funders; we transport small numbers in our minibus; we encourage club workers and parents to transport youngsters. None of these solutions is totally satisfactory and again they take up that most precious commodity – time – but there is no easy answer to this age-old problem.

Lack of effective communication by adults is another constraint which affects young people's participation in our programme. It is one of my greatest concerns. We are totally dependent on workers passing on information to young people. Often our material is not displayed and opportunities we can offer are not discussed. I would argue that if we are committed to doing the very best we can for our young people we do not have the right to withhold information and opportunities from them.

It might be considered odd that funding is towards the end of my lists of constraints. As I mentioned earlier, I tend to look at money as a hurdle to be overcome rather than a barrier to work taking place. There is funding available in tune with our aims for wide varieties of work, but again it is my experience that it is the constraint of time which prevents a worker from filling out many different application forms and reports to meet funders' differing criteria.

Flexibility

Opportunities for informal education in youth work happen all over the place through informal conversations, on a mountain top, in a coffee bar, in a camp, in a minibus, and that is its great strength. It is important for a worker to develop coping mechanisms for different situations – things don't just 'happen', and sometimes the environment is beyond your control. It is always advisable therefore to have 'emergency back-up' strategies for such an eventuality.

I recently booked a room in a multi-purpose youth centre for a group meeting. It was to be an intensive peer education session. When I arrived at the centre we had been double-booked and were sandwiched between a practising heavy metal rock band and a disco. It would have been pointless to attempt to work through our planned session and would have been fruitless and frustrating for both the young people and ourselves. It was essential therefore to alter the session 'on the hoof' to something more frivolous – in this instance drama games and team-building exercises which were less intense but noisy and great fun. This change of strategy enabled the continuation of the session without the loss of the interest of the young people concerned.

If we accept that our planned programme is structured within an overall framework, i.e. short-, medium- and long-term projects to fulfil our aim, we must be prepared for deviations from the intended outcomes. A short-term project can reveal all manner of issues for workers to address. For example, a pool tournament, the perceived outcome of which is to determine a competition winner, can unearth concerns around bullying, aggressive behaviour, insecurities (youngsters unwilling to take part in case they might make 'fools' of themselves) and so on. The tournament as a 'formal' activity gives workers the opportunity to begin to tackle these issues through interventions using conversation and dialogue. Therefore, what can appear superficially to be a routinely boring pool competition can, in fact, be a useful tool for informal education and an aid to working towards agency aims.

Development

A well-structured programme should be planned to accommodate and encourage the personal development of the individuals who participate. There is no doubt in my mind that informal education is a lifeline for many youngsters who are not academically inclined or are not able to cope with the discipline of 'formal' education.

One of the most striking pieces of evidence of the value of this informal way of working manifested itself when one young man who had been excluded from school said to me, 'I worked harder on this three-day residential than I did in the whole of my last year at school.' Why was that? What was there about the formally-planned sessions with structured learning outcomes (just as in a lesson plan in a formal class room setting) which captured that young man's imagination and enabled him to work so hard and gain so much self-confidence?

I would suggest that the blend of formally-structured sessions with an allowance for varied interpretation of session content together with the informal setting (comfortable rooms, fun exercises, challenging discussions, good food, nice place, mixing with people of his own choice) created an atmosphere in which he actually wanted to learn. As workers on the project we, in turn, gained confidence in our work by witnessing each young person's increased self-confidence as the training progressed. Even the quietest lad at the outset became quite vocal and self-assured by the end of the training package using this formal and informal educative method.

An experienced worker will spot a young person with potential for further development and hopefully will encourage, stimulate and nurture that growth. This can happen in a number of ways by giving that young person added responsibilities: for example, assisting with Junior clubs, taking subs, organising pool/table tennis tournaments, helping in a coffee bar, undertaking senior member training. These added responsibilities are tried and tested ways of developing social skills and personal growth and fostering leadership qualities.

Monitoring, reflection and evaluation

Youth workers have traditionally been poor at explaining to the 'outside world' the value of informal education. If we are achieving our organisation's aim with regard to young people's development, is it not our responsibility to be able to convey this message in clear and simple terms that people unused to informal educative processes can understand clearly?

It follows, therefore, that it is useful to have a method of assessing work in terms of statistical information, reflection on the work itself and evaluation of programme content.

Monitoring in terms of statistical information, i.e. numbers and ages of young people involved, gender breakdown, ethnic origin; suitability of venue, length of session, etc. (useful for funding applications) can be gathered relatively easily on user-friendly forms designed by the worker personally so that relevant information is gathered effectively. (There is no point spending huge amounts of time following rigid forms and gathering sheaves of irrelevant statistical information given the time constraints faced by most workers.)

Recordings are, in my view, the best possible way of reflecting on face-to-face work. It is crucial to find a way of recording that a worker is comfortable with. I like to write up using narrative accounts at the end of a session or the next day – a colleague uses short sharp bullet points, another uses a tape recorder. There is a danger that if things are not recorded soon after the event they become inaccurate and distorted by the passage of time – looking back through rose-tinted spectacles or maybe imagining situations to be much worse than they actually were. It is important to find a way of recording that you are comfortable with, otherwise it can become a chore which tends to be put off!

By referring to previous recordings it is possible to monitor the progress of young people in terms of behavioural change; progression in terms of personal development; issues to be tackled; strategies to be worked out; future programme planning and so on and so forth. For instance, if we go back to the pool tournament, by consulting recordings of concerns at the time, future programme items can be planned to incorporate training sessions on bullying, dealing with aggression, etc.

It is also important to record feelings. There will undoubtedly be young people who you do not and cannot like or those that you are really fond of. It is important to recognise these feelings and work with the young people in a non-judgemental way.

Recordings are personal to the worker but the evaluation from those recordings in terms of how future programmes can be planned and the reasoning for programme changes can be produced as hard evidence if necessary.

Evaluation of an event or programme activity should take place ideally with the staff team, or if a person is working in isolation, with a line manager or supervisor. It is helpful to have constructive criticism from someone who is slightly 'removed' from the face-to-face work and who can be truly objective. Simple questions like 'What worked well?', 'What did not?', 'What would I do differently again?' are useful.

It can also be helpful to give young people evaluation forms after an event. These need not be complicated or off-putting but again can be a useful tool in evaluating an activity. If a medium- or long-term project is being undertaken I usually ask young people to fill in a 'Before' and 'After' survey. This again is an effective way of recording what a young person has learned, particularly in terms of personal and social skills, and can be a valuable piece of evidence for both the young person and worker.

Health and safety

This is not an area I want to dwell on at length but, nevertheless, it must be taken into account for the well-being of those taking part in activities and events if, as responsible workers, we are to comply with our overall aim.

It is normal to become so familiar with your place of work that you don't notice potential hazards. It is advisable to look objectively at your working environment from time to time. If workers are building-based, the buildings should be regularly checked by the Fire Brigade.

By and large health and safety is a matter of common sense and a series of 'do nots'. Do not leave wires trailing; position trampolines near plate glass windows; have dodgy electrics; wet floors; have sharp objects sticking out; climb on chairs, and so on – the list just goes on.

It is advisable to get some basic first-aid training and a well-stocked first aid box that only the worker has access to. In my experience I have never found a youth club first aid kit with any plasters in it!

Conclusion

I would argue that, in order to achieve the aim of delivering youth work using informal educative methods, a carefully planned programme is essential. The programme should be designed to take into account the *needs* of young people; the *timescale* involved; the *environment* in which the work is delivered; the *constraints* within which planning takes place and the *health and safety* of the participants. Within the programme should be the built-in provision for *reflecting, monitoring and evaluating* work and allowance for *flexibility, growth and development* of the individuals and groups concerned in order to fulfil a worker's aim of helping young people to realise their full potential as valued and responsible members of society.

Further reading

Lothian SMIT Co-ordinating Group (1992) *Pyramid Programme Planning – SMIT Handbook – Hand Out 10.* Lothian Region: Lothian SMIT Co-ordinating Group. SMIT (Senior Member Involvement Training) was established in 1985 to help young people to develop skills and understanding which would enable them to become more active in their own club situations. The Pyramid Programme Planning condenses the idea of short-, medium- and long-term planning into a simple but effective diagram.

Brierely, A. and Dutton, S. (1998) *Practical Ideas for Junior Clubs Volume 3.* Chester: Cheshire and Wirral Federation of Youth Clubs. This helpful booklet was written and produced by Sam Dutton (youth worker) with contributions from Anne Brierely (youth arts worker) as a result of a series of hands-on practical training days aimed at volunteers working in junior youth clubs. As well as a comprehensive section on programme planning there are sections on drama, printing and useful resources.

13 Activities

Jean Spence

Introduction

Youth work has always provided recreational opportunities for young people through programmes of activities. Whatever its other purposes and concerns, the organisation of activities seems to be one of our most straightforward means of engaging young people in youth provision. In the creation of new youth projects, the nature of the activities to be provided is often a primary consideration. For example, concerned adults will sometimes organise a regular disco or a local football team. Their motivation is usually towards giving young people something to do, partly for the sake of the young people themselves, but also partly in order to bring them under the supervision of adults and away from the freedom and threat of the streets.

> **Q1:** Think about your own early experiences of youth work.
>   Which activities did you use to help you make contact with the young people?
>   Can you remember why those activities seemed most useful to you as a worker?

It is quite unusual to hear from workers, especially those new to the work, who do not use some activities as a basis for their work with young people. Of course these may vary from board games to team sports, from residentials to Go-Karting. Initially at least, they all seem to provide us with an obvious way to approach young people. In starting their careers in youth work, many adults will admit to having relied on their enthusiasm for a particular activity as a basis for communicating with and befriending young people, and it is only with experience, training and professionalisation that long-term and more complex methods, goals and explanations are brought into their work (Brew 1957; Foreman 1987).

Often, the organisation of activities is such a self-evident part of the work that it is taken for granted. Common sense dictates that anyone who wishes to work with young people in a systematic manner will, of necessity, be engaged in activities with those young people. This common sense acceptance of activities may not be problematic in its own terms. However, since – like all common sense understandings – it seems *obvious*, it can also prevent us from thinking through the more complex implications of activities in practice.

This chapter will address the omissions within the common sense view of activities. The intention is to progress towards a more critical perspective on the use of activities in youth work as informal education practice. I shall identify five main concerns which allow us to question more carefully the obvious, or common-sense, approach.

- First, activities are taken for granted and therefore it seems that we do not need to define them.
- Second, the everyday reality of activities involving youth workers and young people can obscure the range of different perspectives and purposes involved in organising and participating in particular types of activity.
- Third, activities are obviously practice, and this often prevents us from developing a theoretical understanding of their place in practice.
- Fourth, activities are task-centred. They keep us busy and they often involve the application of skill. They therefore seem to be justification in themselves for the educational claims of youth work. This is a superficial view of education.
- Fifth, the common-sense approach to activities suggests that their meanings are straightforward and obvious in the nature of the activity itself. This deflects our attention from some of the complex historical and social meanings attached to particular activities and so contributes to a naive use of activities in practice.

Defining activities

The term 'activities' usually refers to those aspects of youth work which can be programmed. They are the most visible aspects of the work and they directly involve young people. Yet even if they are the central focus of an organisation, individual programmed activities do not comprise the whole *activity* of youth work (Smith 1988).

Some youth work activity, such as networking, is not necessarily associated with programmed activities. Other work, such as timetabling, might be essential to providing activities and yet is not usually thought of as a part of those activities. In terms of the activities themselves, each one might be a component of another activity, and might itself comprise a range of smaller activities.

Q2: Think of an activity which you enjoy organising within youth work. What do you think might be the range of activities associated with organising that activity? Break down the main activity into its component activities.

Can you now define 'activities'?

For example, a project might include 'art' in its programme. Within this, the favoured activity might be 'mural painting'. The creation of a mural may in turn involve seeking permission to paint in a particular place, researching and planning and creating the design, raising funds for the materials, mixing the paint, and only finally, painting the mural.

In the common-sense view, 'activities' are usually understood as those operations which can be included in a programme. However this definition of 'activities' is actually imprecise and unstable. 'Activities' might be those actions and events which can be programmed, which involve the participation of young people and are most visible, yet the associated and component work is often of equal, if not greater, significance in youth work.

In the common sense understanding, activities are reified. They become 'things in themselves'. They are self-evident, with their own obvious characteristics. Within a critical understanding, the definition of 'activities' shifts and changes according to our perspectives and purposes.

Perspectives and purposes

As workers, you make decisions about activities; so do organisational representatives, such as managers, and so do the young people themselves. Each group has a different perspective and the activities which are eventually chosen for a programme will be those which most effectively combine all interests. These interests might vary widely.

Activities enable youth workers to use practical personal skills. This facilitates self-confidence and authority in the professional role (Brew 1957; Foreman 1987). When you are interested in the activities which you organise for the benefit of young people, you are more likely to bring an element of your personal identity into the professional arena and this contributes to your enthusiasm for the work.

> **Q3:** List those activities which you organise most often in your work.
> What is your personal interest in those activities?
> Do these activities help you to enjoy your work?

Anyone engaged in activities with young people can be *seen* to be doing. The work can be easily described and explained. For instance, organising dancing teams might involve raising sponsorship to fund the cost of competitions, involving parents in making outfits, encouraging and training the dancers and arranging performances. All this can easily be understood by participants and observers. Meanwhile 'outcomes' can be easily measured in terms of numbers of young people involved, competitions entered or performances undertaken, and trophies, medals and certificates won. This can provide copy for the family album, the 'record of achievement', the local newspaper and the annual report. Thus the activity of dancing can help justify continuing financial support for a youth organisation.

From the perspective of organisations which are under-resourced, visibility and self-justification are important. When youth workers are increasingly being asked to measure service delivery in order to maintain their financial support (Jeffs and Smith 1999) the range of activities on offer and the number of young people involved in these activities can be crucial to organisational survival.

From the perspective of young people, participation in activities serves a number of purposes. It can be simply a means of relaxing or of directing and absorbing physical and mental energies. It can provide opportunities for developing, using and demonstrating personal skill. It can be a medium for associating with and creating friendships with others with similar interests. As a first principle, whatever the interests of the youth worker, whatever the policies of the organisation, the activities provided must appeal initially to young people.

Some activities, such as dancing, drama and football are perennially popular (Henriques 1933; Brew 1957; Rose 1998). They provide the staple ingredient of youth work programmes. Other activities are more ephemeral. Who today plays bagatelle? Yet during the Edwardian period, access to the bagatelle board in a Sunderland Boys' Club had to be rationed (Lambton Street 1902) in the same way as today there might be a time limit on access to a computer. Youth organisations which do not respond to the newest popular activity will fail to attract style-conscious young people. A combination of stability and flexibility in the range of activities on offer is a necessary feature of successful youth provision.

Q4: Identify what you think is the latest popular (legal) activity among young people.

Is it possible to organise this activity within your work?

Would there be any value in doing so?

Sometimes young people participate in activities in order to gain new experiences, to test themselves and to demonstrate their developing maturity. Within the context of youth work, it has been possible to encourage such motivations through the provision of opportunities which include travel, adventure and service. Youth organisations and schemes such as the Scouts and Guides, the Woodcraft Folk, the Duke of Edinburgh's Award and The Weston Spirit are based upon the understanding that, although fun is important, it is only one aspect of the desire of young people to participate in activities (e.g. Baden-Powell 1922; Paul 1938; Burke, Hand and McFall 1999).

Once you begin to consider these motivations, you can think beyond the recreational aspects of activities in relation to young people. In devising and implementing programmes of activities aimed at challenge, personal development and social responsibility, you will be considering questions of process as well as content. You will be addressing educational issues. The idea of youth work as *social education* encompasses the notion that youth work is about both recreational *and* developmental activity with young people, and that its aims include the creation of active and responsible citizens. Since its very earliest days, most youth work has embodied these principles and the activities introduced into the work have been chosen to reflect this (Russell and Rigby 1908; Henriques 1933; Brew 1957; Davies and Gibson 1967).

The interest in some activities by particular groups of young people reflects their identity and self-perceptions. Age, gender, ability, ethnicity, class and subcultural allegiances all play a part in the willingness of young people to engage in particular activities. Part of the skill of youth work is to be able to understand the connections between identity and interest in particular activities. Acceptance of an educational brief for the activities base of youth work requires a consideration of which activities are acceptable, which activities reinforce or challenge stereotypes, and which activities encourage attitudes and behaviour appropriate to the aims and objectives of the worker and the organisation. Thus, as a youth worker choosing activities, you are involved in making moral, ethical and political decisions (Banks 1999).

Q5: Are there activities which you would wish to particularly encourage or discourage in the youth work setting? What are your grounds for making these decisions?

The literature produced by the movement for work with girls and young women provides a useful example of moral, ethical and political decision making in practice. Particularly during the 1970s and 1980s, some women workers attempted to use activities to encourage young women to use the resources of youth organisations. At the same time they wished to raise questions about the role of girls and women in society (WWG Newsletter 1982). The workers involved attempted to use traditional feminine activities in a manner which attracted young women and affirmed female identity without reinforcing the secondary status of female activity. They also worked to encourage young women to participate in non-traditional activities without undermining self–confidence or reinforcing the primary status of masculine activity. As a reflective practitioner in any practice context, you will be involved in similar considerations in relation to the particular groups with whom you work.

Q6: Identify a group of young people with whom you have worked.
   Are there any particular activities which they associate with their personal and group identity?
   How could you use these activities in a way which encourages them to ask questions about their identities?

However you negotiate your own interests with the interests of the organisation and with those of young people, you must eventually make choices about which activities are offered. These choices are based upon your perceptions of the purposes of youth work in general. As a worker, you are here assessing the place of particular activities within the whole agenda of possible activity. The choices you make reflect your understanding of the relationships between particular activities and your own professional beliefs and values. It is important to make coherent decisions at this level. In order to do so, we all need to develop a well informed theoretical awareness of the significance of activities.

A theoretical understanding of activities

The range of the activities associated with youth work seems potentially limitless. To the casual observer it might appear that through their involvement with youth organisations, young people merely camped, climbed, trekked, canoed, danced, acted, painted, played and discussed their way through the twentieth century (Foreman 1987). Involvement in organised activities signifies purposeful engagement and a willingness to become involved in socially approved behaviour on the part of young people. A full programme of activities and the involvement of a wide range of young people in activities presents youth work itself in a positive light in the public imagination. Indeed, for some people activities and youth work are synonymous; they are the same thing. It is therefore not surprising that in various types of text, a discussion of activities is central.

Introductory manuals, reflecting recreational and controlling aspects of youth work, and adopting fairly mechanistic approaches to education, simply consider activities in themselves. They tend to predict the type of young people and situations which youth workers might encounter and suggest a range of possible activities which might suite that context. Typically, this will be followed by a description of the skills, organisational points, resources and safety checks needed to undertake that activity successfully. Any discussion of outcomes will be read off directly from the form, content and method of the activity in question (Hedges 1948; Dearling and Armstrong 1980; Mountain 1989).

More sophisticated texts move into social educational concerns and discuss the underlying possibilities and messages which can be mobilised in the *choice* of activities. They understand adolescence to be a difficult transitional life period which youth work attempts to alleviate. Activities are assessed in terms of their contribution to young people's progress towards mature adulthood and responsible and active citizenship. Such texts will discuss, for example, whether an activity promotes co-operation or competition, individualism or teamwork, independence or interdependence, and which activities encourage the type of behaviour associated with the ideal adult citizen. Many of the long-standing voluntary organisations, such as the scouts, have historically adopted this approach. Social education in this sense has been a dominant theme in youth work (Baden-Powell 1922; Henriques 1933; Brew 1943, 1957; Matthews 1975; Merton and Parrott 1999).

During the 1920s and 1930s, activities in themselves very much came to dominate the youth work agenda, to the detriment of wider welfare and educational questions (Lambton Street 1914–29; Eager 1953). Partly in reaction to this mechanistic approach, as the statutory youth service was developed, and particularly after the publication of the Albemarle Report (1960), theorists were at pains to stress the social and informal educational principles of the work (Brew 1957; Davies and Gibson 1967).

Finally, the more theoretical texts tend to adopt a more critical approach. They take social educational principles rather than recreational activity as their starting point, and so present us with what they consider to be more liberal democratic, educational or 'emancipatory' approaches. In some of these texts, the power of activities to dominate thinking can be gauged by the strength of opposition to them! They raise questions about the meaning, purpose and implications of engaging young people in programmes of activity. They argue that the thinking behind such programmes is typically conservative and underdeveloped, encouraging *character-building* rather than a questioning understanding (Davies and Gibson 1969; Butters and Newell 1978; Foreman 1987; Smith 1988). From this perspective, it can also be argued that situating activities-based youth work within a 'character-building' context simply reinforces the predominant image of activities as things in themselves.

Q7: Consider any text about youth work which you have read recently. What is the author's view about the place of activities? Can you identify any problems with this view?

The place where the image of youth work as little more than activities for young people is lodged most enduringly, is within annual reports and promotional material. Why? Although these texts claim to represent reality, they are produced for particular purposes, with particular audiences in mind. Their aim is to show the youth organisation in a positive light. This often means playing to the common sense stereotypes, emphasising the breadth and quality of the activities on offer. The following quote from Macalister Brew in 1943 is dated, but many a youth worker today could no doubt echo its sentiment:

> what hope would a club leader have of securing funds who stated, 'last year my boys learned nothing except how not to cheat at games quite so often, to wash their hands occasionally, to take their caps off in the club, and to enjoy being together'? No, in order to secure funds you must have a class in civics, or some vigorous P.T., a house system, and a public school spirit!...
>
> but to quote a very wise leader, 'fortunately life in the clubs, whatever may be the language of the annual reports, is generally ruled by common sense'.

(Brew 1943: 49–50)

Brew seems to be suggesting that the differences between annual reports and practice does not really affect what happens 'on the ground' in youth projects, that 'common sense' will prevail. Yet the language of annual reports *is* important because it provides one aspect of the *discourse* of youth work.

Discourse involves the language and the imagery which act as terms of reference for practice. It helps us to describe, explain, discuss and understand the reality of practice. However, discourse is more than just language and images. It also serves to form our professional practice. The language and images of youth work describe the *relationships* involved in practice, and in particular the relationships of power. However, they do not simply *reflect* reality and relationships, nor do they float free, in a separate sphere. They influence our practice and become part of it. Language and imagery inform us. They explain to us what we are doing and what is possible. They tell us what is happening, what is allowed and not allowed. They therefore affect practice, but they do not do this in a direct way. Some things happen in practice which are either taken for granted, or are common sense, or are not really noticed. Other things happen which are slightly 'under cover'. These aspects of the work are silent in the discourse. Discourse, as a system, both *excludes* as well as *includes*. It reproduces itself and makes it difficult for us to explore some practices and ideas. In particular, it makes power relations seem normal. Thus to privilege programmed activities in the written and visual discourses of youth work (Chaplin 1994), both reflects and reinforces the power and the dominance of activities-based work in practice. The consequences of this are that the other developmental, supportive and educa-

tional aspects of the work are eclipsed. Yet it is often those less tangible elements which define youth provision as something other than a leisure
service. The confusion in the discourse between programmed activities, or
activities *in themselves* and the more complex and less tangible aspects of
youth work activity has serious consequences for the value attached to the
work and for its status as a meaningful service.

Q8: Collect some annual reports. Assess the way in which activities are
represented within them. How are activities shown with reference to
other parts of the work?

The 'dishonesty' within annual reports of which Brew speaks in 1943 (p. 49)
is still apparent today (Spence 1996). There is much within youth work practice which is not 'activities' in the traditional sense and which, by its very
nature, is more difficult to represent. For example, think about any conversation between a youth worker and a young person which takes place during a
countryside walk. It probably cannot be represented in the same way as the
walk itself. It may be more difficult to describe the conversation than to
record the number of young people participating in the walk, the number of
miles covered, or the scenery and weather encountered. The temptation,
then, is for the youth worker to recount the walk in terms of what is tangible
and to focus on what is valuable *in the walk itself.* Yet the conversation might
be of much greater importance than the fresh air, exercise and countryside
experience to the young person concerned or to the future interactions
between the youth worker and young person. The walk provides the context
and facilitates the conversation, but although conversation is an *activity,* it
does not fit neatly into the stereotyped conception of *activities.* It cannot be
planned, structured, counted, measured or easily assessed in terms of outcomes and achievement (Smith 1994). It is difficult to represent a conversation visually. It is therefore undervalued and displaced in the descriptive
texts. This does a disservice both to the potential value of the presenting
activity – in this case walking, and to the less concrete activity, in this case,
conversation. To organise a successful walk in the countryside with a group
of young people might involve a great deal of background educational work;
the activity which takes place during the walk, and the manner in which
participants relate to each other during the walk, are equally important.

Within promotional material, descriptions of activities undertaken and
photographs of young people actively engaged are everywhere. For example,
a recent publication from the National Youth Agency, describing a number
of projects with a variety of aims and methods, most of which seemed to be
not activities-based in the superficial sense, used nearly forty images which
included or suggested activities and their outcomes as though the activity
itself was the only concern. The activities illustrated included motorbike
riding, car maintenance, canoeing, rafting, climbing, an assault course, art-
work, cooking, erecting a tent blindfold(!), and the perennial table tennis. A
number of these photographs showed young people receiving awards for
achievement. Although other images were included, the most powerful
photograph in the booklet is that of a young man in a safety helmet struggling up a cliff face, clearly suffering but concentrated and determined, put

Figure 13.1
Source: Burke, Hand and McFall (1999)

in a situation of risk where he can only go forward through his own efforts
(Burke, Hand and McFall 1999).

The implication of many youth work images is that, through engaging in
the activities offered, young people learn to strive, to overcome difficulties
and to achieve. Hopefully, in the process, they will also enjoy themselves,
because this, after all is what attracts them to the opportunities in the first
place. But pleasure, after all, is not the goal. The goal is the possibility of
each young person reaching the top of their own individual mountain.
Exploring the processes through which young people can be helped to reach
the top of this mountain takes a secondary role in the discourse. The image
is often left to speak for itself, as a metaphor for the best in youth work. Yet,
as youth workers, most of us understand that climbing the mountain itself is
only a part of the process of youth work.

Activities and education

Youth workers are able to claim that their activities-based work differs from
that of teachers, social workers and the police because of the *voluntary* participation of young people and because the informal educational processes of
the work do not involve *fixed* outcomes. The consequences of informal educational interventions depend not only upon the aims and objectives of
workers and organisations, but also upon the level of engagement, the expectations and the purposes of the young people themselves. Therefore,
although any given activity within youth work might be well planned, well
structured and explicit about its aims and objectives, and this requires technical skill, the art of youth work involves creativity, adaptability, responsive-
ness, sensitivity and open-endedness. To develop successful informal

educational youth work requires qualities which cannot flow directly from activities in themselves. The educational possibilities of activities can only be processed through the medium of the worker in dialogue with young people (Freire 1972).

How activities are delivered is just as important as the activities themselves. For example, if young people are involved in the processes of decision-making, fund-raising, and planning around an activity then their expectations and experiences of that activity will be entirely different from those young people involved in a similar activity which has been entirely organised by youth workers. In the latter situation, the educational aspects of youth work will be focused narrowly and mechanistically within the activity itself, whereas in the former situation, the processes of engagement and dialogue surrounding the activity become the primary arena for pursuing educational possibilities.

There are some activities which lend themselves easily to the objectives of social education. Such activities might involve group co-operation, problem-solving, communication, dialogue, conflict resolution and personal reflection, development and achievement. This has resulted in a great deal of emphasis being placed on those activities which appear to include within themselves the widest range of social educational experiences. While such activities are useful, over-reliance on them diverts attention from the responsibilities of youth workers as *informal* educators and re-inforces the misleading representation of youth work as an activities-dominated profession.

The approximation between social educational objectives and the outcomes of engagement in activities is particularly apparent within the field of outdoor activities. Within mainstream activities programmes, these are perennial favourites with workers and young people alike. Outdoor activities seem to encapsulate in concentrated form the whole range of possibilities inscribed within a recreational and social educational approach to youth work.

In this spirit, 'outdoor activities' are now usually described within youth work as 'outdoor education' (Wild 1988, Hunt n.d.). A whole range of learning possibilities can be identified as implicit within outdoor education. For example, a group building a raft and sailing it, might learn construction skills, might develop resourcefulness, creativity, rationality and teamwork. At a deeper level, participants can learn about themselves, their possibilities and potential and about the significance of human interdependence and co-operation.

From this perspective, all that seems necessary to encourage young people to develop the attributes of maturity is to encourage them to participate in activities appropriate to their particular interests and developmental 'needs'. Intervening to influence the behaviour and attitudes of young people is at the heart of social education. It teaches young people what is expected of mature adults in society. This is important; but what this type of activities-based social education does not do, is encourage a questioning of that society. (Davies and Gibson 1967). There are also a number of other problems in the assumption that experience in organised activity is the most effective basis for the pursuit of the educational objectives of youth work.

- Firstly, there is an implication that, in order to learn the lessons embodied in activities, it is necessary to introduce contrived experiences. As Smith (1988) suggests, this indicates an unwillingness to accept young people as they are at that moment in their lives.

- Secondly, although a range of skill and understanding *can* be gleaned through participation in activities, there is no guarantee that the learning achieved will be necessarily transferred appropriately into other contexts (Davies and Gibson 1967). Learning lessons under contrived and sometimes unfamiliar conditions does not of itself lead to the self awareness, sensitivity and connectedness which are the general aims of humanistic education. In other words, learning which is purely experiential is unprocessed. It leaves the learner to make of it what they will.
- Thirdly, any given activity carries associated and contextual meanings which can communicate powerful messages. These meanings can run counter to the educational objectives of youth work.

Q9: Think about some of the different activities which you associate with youth work either currently or in the past. What messages do you think these carry, in terms of assumed cultural assumptions?

I thought about boxing, dancing, music, team games and archery. It seems to me that the meanings and stereotypes attached to any activities are rarely neutral. They may well be contested and contradictory, but they nonetheless impact upon the potential for engagement and participation by young people in our work. Is football ever simply football? In choosing activities, youth workers must consider not only the likely messages inherent in the activities themselves, but also whether or not these complement or contradict the purposes of their youth work, and whether or not they can be used to raise other questions and issues. The following section continues to use the example of outdoor activities to understand the power of contextual meanings.

Historical and social meanings

Grand claims have been made for the efficacy and attractiveness of outdoor activities work with young people:

> A sense of adventure has its roots in the beginnings of the human race, and this innate spirit of quest has been manifested throughout our own nation's history. At times, it has given rise to great achievements: the voyages of the Elizabethan adventurers, of Cook, Shackleton and Scott, and many others in more recent times. These deeds have been a source of great inspiration to our people, and in particular, to our youth.
>
> (Hunt n.d.: 11)

This introductory statement of a report on Adventure Education for young people at the end of the 1980s could have been written at virtually any time during the last century. It suggests some of the more problematic themes in activities-based youth work where the activity *in itself* is expected to encompass most of the educational aims. These problems include an overarching conception of human essence – of a natural human spirit most in touch with itself when it is closest to nature, to the land, and away from urban culture. There are elements of this philosophy within socialist, feminist and 'green' movements, reflected in youth groups like the Woodcraft Folk. However, historically it has also been powerfully associated with nationalism, imperialism, male heroism, female maternalism and youth as the unspoiled hope of the nation (Springhall 1977). In the earlier years of the twentieth century, fascism frequently employed the imagery of the outdoor life and of 'keep fit' to emphasise how the ideal nation could be achieved and this association continues to be communicated particularly via historical film footage.

The association with imperialism and nationalism is only one of the meanings associated with outdoor activities. However, it is indicative of a dominant tradition running through the history of activities-based youth work which has its roots in the nineteenth-century origins of youth work practice.

Firstly, youth work grew out of concern for the condition of young people in the poor and overcrowded urban slums of Victorian and Edwardian Britain. Outdoor activities, open-air sports and games, drill (or later, 'keep fit') were organised by early youth workers and community workers as an antidote to the cramped, unhealthy conditions within which many young people lived and worked. Women workers in particular were keen to use the rural environment for the purposes of relaxation and recuperation for women, young female workers and children (Pethwick-Lawrence 1938; Montagu 1941; Bell 1943). Excursions into the countryside were designed to improve the physical health of those participating, and that indeed has remained a value in itself.

Less positively, this concentration upon health slipped easily into the ideology of 'Muscular Christianity' in work with boys and young men. The idea of muscular Christianity, which was fashionable in the public schools, suggested that athletic pursuits and the building of character were as important, if not more important, than intellectual learning and knowledge in the creation of the whole *man*. These ideas were imported directly into the youth work situation by early youth workers (Eager 1953), who were largely public-school educated. Their approach included the objective of imparting to working-class boys some of the advantages which they had gleaned from the games and outdoor sports practised as a significant element in their schooling.

Female use of the outdoors was relatively unstructured with mainly the quieter activities of walking and reading encouraged. For men, on the other hand, the outdoors was a context for action. Away from the artificialities of the city, unclothed for swimming and running, pitting themselves against the elements, men and boys could indulge in male bonding. Activities and games, particularly in the outdoors, were believed to facilitate masculine and racial identification, dulling the significance of the class differences which divided the nation. The boy scout movement pursued the logic of this masculinism to the full. In Baden Powell's 'Venture Scouting' one of the illustrations shows a very upright white man, dressed only in shorts beside a smaller, admiring black man dressed in the full regalia of male formal dress, including top hat and tails. The narrative tells of the admiration which a group of black visitors expressed for white gymnastic instructors. The caption reads: '*A white man and a man*'. Developing a fine physique through activities was an imperial duty (Baden-Powell 1922).

The meanings incorporated within outdoor activities in particular, at a very early stage in the history of youth work, promoted the centrality of the white, physically perfect, mentally alert, God-loving Englishman. It was

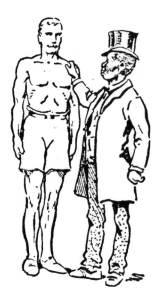

Figure 13.2
Source: Baden-Powell (1922)

around his recreational interests that the social, educational, activities-based programmes were constructed and it was towards the values of citizenship of Imperial Britain that the educational motif in these activities was pursued and standardised within youth work.

These meanings have been overshadowed with the passage of time. Most people enjoying outdoor activities today are unaware of the associations and cannot be held responsible for them. A wide range of social groups now enjoy outdoor activities and education. Nevertheless, while the activities in themselves carry no bias, it can still be argued that the ambience and culture of these activities remains male, and white, with a strong emphasis upon physique and prowess.

When other groups of young people participate, they do so within terms of reference which are not their own and therefore begin at a disadvantage. There is thus an ethical responsibility on the part of the youth worker who believes in the value of outdoor education, to understand and work through these issues, as well as to simply deal with practical instruction and the social educational possibilities which derive directly from the activities themselves. As a youth worker, you carry responsibility for the situations which are encountered by young people through the activities you organise. If the meanings and associations of these activities are not considered fully, then your educational principles are at risk. Far from being a straightforward and unproblematic aspect of youth work, the organisation of activities is full of complexities and pitfalls for the unwary. Activities might be an easy option on one level, a diversion on another, but as an integral aspect of an informal educational approach, they require your knowledge and critical understanding as well as your skills.

Conclusion

The range of activity which can be integrated into youth work is extensive. In theory all legal and moral activities are possible within its structures and processes. Choosing which activities to use in a given situation will involve you in considering a range of issues which are much wider than the activities themselves.

Activities-based youth work has never been the full story of youth work even though it occupies a central place in its history. If you wish to become a reflective practitioner then it is insufficient to simply provide programmes of activities or to describe and publicise the work through the activities framework. All activity, including the decision-making processes, the timing of arrangements, the organisation of space and the methods of communication, is linked to, and has consequences for, the educational possibilities of youth work. Informal educational activity is not simply something which is undertaken on Saturdays or during a week in July. It is the culture and processes of the everyday life of the project.

For informal educators, activity within youth work is purposeful, contextualised and open-ended. Projects and programmes do not simply fall out of the sky; they are situated in particular places and times and relevant to particular groups of young people. Within informal educational activity young people must be the subjects rather than the objects of your intervention, and the activities you adopt should create opportunities for those young people to grow, learn and act in a manner which is meaningful to them in their social context.

Activities are a framework around which the educational aspects of the work with young people are structured but as a youth worker, you are responsible for their educational value. While the nature and inherent possibilities of any given activity in itself is significant, nevertheless, it is the interventions which you make in association with the activity, or in the spaces in the timetable, which provide the most important opportunities for pursuing your objectives as an educator.

As long as significant, unstructured interventions remain unquantified and un-named within a discourse which inflates the common sense value of activities, then youth work as informal education will itself be undervalued and threatened with extinction. Is informal education worthy of being defended as a key aspect of youth work? If you think so, then you will have to work against the grain of the privileging of activities as such within the standard discourses of policy and practice. You will take upon yourself a responsibility to describe, analyse, defend and represent the value of the whole range of the work and to situate activities within their overall context.

This raises the whole question of what is considered legitimate youth work. What do policy makers and funders expect and how can organisations survive if they refuse to prioritise programmes of activities? The only answer to this can be that as a worker you need to have the courage of your convictions. You must strive to ensure that you identify educational moments and processes in your work and represent this effectively within annual reports and promotional materials. Those who write training manuals and theoretical texts must also celebrate this. Such a change in perspective will expand the discourses of youth work. It implies risk-taking, but after all, that is what we are asking of young people when we ask them to climb mountains!

Further reading

Bennett, A. (1998) 'The Frankfurt "Rockmobil": a new insight into the significance of music-making for young people', in *Youth and Policy*, 60, Summer. Leicester: Youth Work Press, pp. 16–29. This article provides a useful case study of an activities-based project which uses the 'fun' element of activity to engage in developmental work with young people. Practical music-making is presented as the basis for the development of personal and social skills. However, the author also considers questions of gender and racial inequality in his analysis, providing opportunities for the reader to consider differences in relation to the organisation, purposes and uses of one given activity.

Gair, N.P. (1998) *Outdoor Education: Theory and Practice*. London: Cassel. Gair uses the activities of mountain walking and expeditions as the focus for thinking reflectively about outdoor education. The author is aware of practical and policy concerns and theoretical analysis is grounded in practice examples. This text would be of interest to readers who are enthusiastic about outdoor education and wish to develop their understanding of the conceptual issues raised by such activities.

Greenaway, R. (1998) *Growth Through Activities*. Lyme Regis: Russell House Publishing. This is a handbook rather than a theoretical text. The author has a broad definition of what constitutes an 'activity' and is keen to encourage practitioners to consider purpose as well as skill and technique in the use of activities. This text provides the opportunity for the reader to consider the possible value of a range of activities in themselves.

Wilson, J. (1988) *Politics and Leisure*. London: Unwin Hyman. For any reader interested in pursuing further contextual influences upon the development of activities within informal educational practices, this book provides a well-researched overview. It offers a historical and social analysis and addresses structural difference and inequality between different groups. It would be an excellent text to use to begin the process of thinking generally about the role and use of activities within any given political or organisational arena.

References

Baden-Powell, R. (1922) *Rovering to Success:* London: Herbert Jenkins Ltd.

Banks, S. (ed.) (1999) *Ethical Issues in Youth Work*. London and New York: Routledge.

Bell, E.M. (1943) *Octavia Hill: a biography*. London: Constable.

Brew, J.M. (1943) *In the Service of Youth: a practical manual of work among adolescents*. London: Faber and Faber.

Brew, J.M. (1957) *Youth and Youth Groups*. London: Faber and Faber.

Burke, T., Hand, J. and McFall, L. (1999) *Moving on up: how youth work raises achievement and promotes social inclusion*. Sheffield: DfEE/NYA.

Butters, S. and Newell, S. (1978) *Realities of Training*. Leicester: NYB.

Chaplin, E. (1994) *Sociology and Visual Representation*. London and New York: Routledge.

CYWU (1999) Paper delivered by Paddy Tippin, MP, March 1999, Gateshead Civic Centre. Unpublished. Reported in *Rapport*, April 1999.

Davies, B. and Gibson, A. (1967) *The Social Education of the Adolescent*. London: University of London Press.

Davies, B. and Marken, M. (1998) *Towards a Youth Strategy: The Sunderland Youth Review*. Leicester: Youth Work Press.

Dearling, A. and Armstrong, H. (1980) *The Youth Games Book.* Edinburgh: Intermediate Treatment Resource Centre.

DfEE (1999) *New Start: The journey for everyone helping young people to stay in learning.* No. 5, March 1999, London.

Eager, W.McG. (1953) *Making Men: Being a History of Boys' Clubs and Related Movements in Great Britain.* London: University of London Press.

Freire, P. (1972) *Pedagogy of the Oppressed.* Harmondsworth: Penguin.

Foreman, A. (1987) 'Youth Workers as Redcoats', in Jeffs, T. and Smith, M. (eds) *Youth Work.* Basingstoke and London: Macmillan.

Hedges, S.G. (1948) *Youth Club Activities.* London: Methuen and Co. Ltd.

HMSO (1960) *The Youth Service in England and Wales (The Albemarle Report).* London: HMSO.

Hunt, J. (ed.) (undated: probably 1989) *In Search of Adventure: A Study of Opportunities for Adventure and Challenge for Young People.* Guildford: Talbot Adair Press.

Henriques, B.L.Q. (1933) *Club Leadership.* London: Oxford University Press.

Jeffs, T. and Smith, M. (1999) 'Resourcing Youth Work: Dirty Hands and Tainted Money', in Banks, S. (ed.) *Ethical Issues in Youth Work.* London and New York: Routledge.

Lambton Street (1902) *Minutes of the Sunderland Waifs Rescue Agency and Street Vendors' Club.* Sunderland: Unpublished Archive.

Lambton Street (1914–29) *Minutes book of the Sunderland Waifs Rescue Ageing and Street Vendors' Club.* Sunderland: Unpublished Archive.

MacDonald, R. (ed) (1997) *Youth, the 'Underclass' and Social Exclusion.* London and New York: Routledge.

Matthews, K.R. (1975) *A Guide to Youth Club Leadership: Principles and Practice.* London: Elek Books Ltd.

Merton, B. and Parrott, A. (1999) *Only Connect: Successful practice in educational work with disaffected young adults.* Leicester: DfEE, NIACE and NYA.

Montagu, L. (1941) *My club and I: The story of the West Central Jewish Club.* London: Herbert Joseph, Ltd.

Mountain, A. (1989) *Lifting the Limits: A handbook for working with young women at risk or in trouble.* Leicester: NYB.

Non-aligned Working Group (1997) *Young People as Citizens Now: towards more inclusive and coherent policies for young people.* Leicester: Youth Work Press.

Paul, L. (1938) *The Republic of Children.* London: Allen and Unwin.

Pethwick-Lawrence, E. (1938) *My part in a changing world.* London: Victor Gollancz Ltd.

Rose, C. (1998) *Touching Lives: A Personal History of Clapton Jewish Youth Centre 1946–1973.* Leicester: Youth Work Press.

Russell, C.E.B. and Rigby, L.M. (1908) *Working Lads' Clubs.* London: Macmillan and Co. Ltd.

Smith, M. (1988) *Developing Youth Work: Informal Education, Mutual Aid and Popular Practice.* Milton Keynes and Philadelphia: Open University Press.

Smith, M.K. (1994) *Local Education: community, conversation, praxis.* Buckingham and Philadelphia: Open University Press.

Spence, J. (1996) 'Feminism in Youth Work Practice', in *Youth and Policy,* No. 52, Newcastle.

Springhall, J. (1977) *Youth, empire and society.* London: Croom Helm.

Wild, S. (1988) *Women into The Outdoors.* Unpublished Dissertation. Edinburgh: Moray House College.

Working With Girls Newletter (1982) *Activities Issue* 12, Nov/Dec 1982. Leicester: NAYC.

14 One-to-one casework

Alan Smith

Introduction

This chapter considers the skills, methods and values involved in the type of work with individuals which has come to be known as casework. The first part of the chapter defines the casework method and compares it with less structured forms of work with individuals which informal educators may undertake. You will be able to assess the extent to which the work you do with individuals is similar to casework. Understanding the implications of the values underlying classic casework methods is important for educators, because changes in Government policies and agency practice mean that casework has come to prominence as the method of choice for engineering social change. As a result, more and more informal educators are being asked both to use casework methods and to accept the values which these often imply. The second part of the chapter looks at the implications of the Connexions policy in particular for workers who are, or wish to be, involved in this sort of work.

Methods or values?

Often when we talk of education, informal or formal, we are thinking of the experience of working with groups. We may recognise differences between externally-driven curricula and aims negotiated with learners, between formal and informal learning environments, and between different ways of measuring outcomes; but almost certainly we will focus on group-based activities.

However, if we consider the process of learning, we are more likely to think about individuals and the activities that they engage in: reading a book, watching television or taking part in conversation, for example. Here again, though, we might identify internal outcomes, in terms of individual growth and development, or external ones based on specific measurable achievements.

As Tony Jeffs and Mark Smith have suggested (1996) the skill of the informal educator lies in creating opportunities for learning, by managing the environment in which the worker engages with the learner. Informal educators consider this process as the core of their work, and will reshape the task they are engaged in to develop learning opportunities that are meaningful to the learner.

Informal education, then, involves working with individuals, alone or in groups, to promote their learning. A wide range of employing bodies and

Government initiatives also recognise the benefits of this ability to facilitate learning through informal education methods. Health services; information, advice and counselling services; schools, colleges and universities; social work agencies; regeneration initiatives and the Government's 'Connexions' service have all recognised the usefulness of this approach. However, agencies which value, and even rely heavily upon, the knowledge and skills that informal educators bring may not share the client-centred values of informal education or recognise the principles on which the profession is based. This is a particular danger for Government initiatives, such as the Connexions policy, which seek to encourage youth and community workers, and other professionals working with young people, to take a casework approach. Equally, workers may adopt casework methods without fully realising the value base within which they were developed. One-to-one work therefore highlights particular moral and educational dilemmas and possibilities for role confusion, which this chapter seeks to explore. I shall argue that, while casework methods can be valuable to informal educators, the values that underlie much casework are not congruent with those of education.

Q1: Think about the role you currently undertake. What tasks within that role involve work with individuals? What outcomes are expected from this work by:

- you?
- the individuals you work with?
- your employer/funder?

Are these expectations similar?

What is one-to-one casework?

Casework, or at least work with individuals who are seen to require professional intervention in order to solve their problems or meet their needs, has become a growing area of practice for youth and community workers. This work clearly builds on informal educators' skills in working with individuals and groups. Whether casework can be seen as part of informal education is perhaps less easy to determine.

We need to consider, first, what part of our work is casework and what differentiates this from more general work with individuals or groups. Once we have identified the point at which informal education becomes casework, it may be possible to draw a professional boundary between the two, thus helping employers and workers distinguish between them. In looking at the crossover between casework and other forms of intervention used when working informally with individuals, we also need to identify any factors that clearly distinguish one from the other.

We can start by looking at the stages and activities of 'classic' casework.

Casework methods

Smalley (1967) states that one of the earliest theoretical models of social work to be identified was 'social casework'. It was concerned with the one-to-one relationship between a person seen as in need – the client – and the person responding to that need – the caseworker (Richmond 1917).

This form of casework follows an established pattern of referral, interview, recording, diagnosis, treatment, evaluation and ending.

Referral

The initial referral may be imposed through a legal/statutory process, or may be a self-referral as a result of an individual identifying a need. The basis of the referral, and the way in which it is carried out, will have a significant impact on the relationship between the worker and the client.

Interview

While the interview may be carefully structured, based on a referral form, questionnaire or set questions, it can also follow a counselling format, in which the worker identifies the range of issues to be addressed with the client, often over several sessions.

Recording

Casework methods require that the worker keeps detailed records, usually while the interview is taking place. Recording after the interview may mean that crucial information is missed, but in some cases it might be necessary to avoid frightening the client.

Diagnosis

For many youth and community workers engaged in one-to-one casework, the diagnosis of a client's problem(s) is their biggest dilemma because it requires an assumption of professional superiority and the labelling of the client as 'in need'. However, casework also acknowledges individuals' 'power' and 'rights' to make decisions about themselves throughout the process of treatment.

Treatment

The worker's intervention (or 'treatment') is intended to help clients solve their problem or satisfy their need. This is a more difficult issue if the client is not self-referring. Treatment may take many forms, often dependent upon the philosophy of the agency – therapeutic, developmental, educational, psycho-dynamic, behavioural – or on the nature of the problem.

Evaluation

As treatment is dynamic, any evaluation of the work must be continuous. Has solving a practical problem resolved the underlying social or psychological problem? Could alternative strategies achieve a better outcome?

Ending

In all casework relationships, there should be a clear ending: a solution to the problem, a response to a need, or a redefining of the issues. In terms of referrals that are the result of a legal order, the end date may be pre-determined; this needs to be taken into account when planning the treatment process (adapted from Obbo: 1990: 95–128).

Q2: Perhaps the best way to take this comparison forward would be to ask yourself what is actually going on when you work with an individual young person or adult. Can you recognise any of these typical casework processes or stages? You may of course use different terms.

Referral   Are the people you work with referred to you by other professionals or agencies (e.g. social workers, the courts)? Or do they come to you because they have identified a need for themselves (e.g. literacy difficulties, skills gaps)?

Interview   Do you interview (formally or informally) those you are intending to work with?

Recording   Do you have a daily log or account of your work? Is it recorded against individual names or merely incidents? Do you keep an information sheet or membership file on each individual? How do you inform colleagues of significant issues that are affecting members?

Diagnosis   Do you assume that you know what is best even before you are given any information? Have you already made a diagnosis of the presenting problem(s) based on previous experiences?

Treatment   Do you somehow consider the work you do as offering a solution to a problem, either individual or more general?

Evaluation   How do you measure and record the outcomes of your work? Are you required to justify the actions you have taken? Does the person you are working with have a part to play in the evaluation process?

Ending   How do you know your involvement has ended? Do clients stop attending or change the nature of the relationship?

Casework theories and values

Your answers to the above questions will help you to decide to what extent the work you do uses methods that are typical of casework. However, the process we have outlined above ignores the fact that there are several different models of casework, which differ in their aims and values. One of the earliest theories of casework was set out by Richmond (1917), writing for social workers. Her model of social diagnosis had two central themes:

- that clients and their problems have to be individualised, and
- that successful casework requires careful diagnosis.

Richmond's view was that a clear understanding of what needed to be done would emerge from a systematic study of all the 'facts' of the case. If the case-worker amassed enough 'facts', the intervention plan would follow logically (see Barber 1991: 15–16).

As a model of practice, Richmond's theory was based on a theory of diagnosis and treatment, rather than seeking to promote growth and development through shared experience (see Obbo 1990).

An alternative model, based on the writings of Otto Rank, saw casework in terms of the relationship between the client and the agency (Taft 1937 in Barber 1991). In this model, individuals may still have an identified need, but their relationship with the agency is based on its mission in a particular field (e.g. child protection, welfare benefits) which leads it to work with a particular category of 'needy' individuals. The key focus here is on the function of the agency, or its primary task, rather than response to an individual need. While this still retains a view of the agency's function as remedial, or 'putting things right', it recognises that a problem, or need, can affect more than one individual. Clients are, however, still dealt with on an individual basis, and, as in social diagnosis casework, the starting point for the relationship is the presumed need of the client.

The work of Helen Harris Perlman (1957) tried to draw on both these schools by bringing together some of their key ideas. Perlman's basic premise is that 'human living is a continuous problem-solving process and therefore that the goal of casework is not "cure" but facilitation of an individual's capacity to cope with current problems' (Barber 1991: 19). According to this definition, all of us would benefit from a caseworker to facilitate our problem-solving.

As you can see, in all these models the focus is on the individual, ignoring the social factors that impact on specific groups. Casework in this sense is rarely 'political' and seldom moves beyond a 'help the victim' mentality. This reductionist view fails to recognise or acknowledge a social dimension, the broader economic and political context, or the inherent discrimination that exists within Britain today.

Casework in informal education

Within informal education, casework can be seen, at one level, as a systematic approach to working with individuals (or indeed with groups). In this sense, we can try to identify stages which we might go through in working with an individual, without necessarily adopting the assumptions or even the specific processes of social casework.

Suggested stages or phases might be:

- problem exploration/assessment;
- contracting;
- intervention;
- monitoring and evaluation;
- termination phase.

A number of these stages can be found in other methods of working with individuals or groups, and also appear in theories of relationship building, team building and problem-solving. Barber indeed acknowledges that this approach is so general as to make no distinction between casework, group work and community work (1991: 27). However, using these stages as a diagnostic tool, we may be able to demonstrate a systematic approach to practice which acknowledges casework methodology, while retaining the principles and practices of informal education, youth or community work.

Two specific examples may illustrate this more clearly.

Intermediate Treatment (IT)

Since the development of the Intermediate Treatment (IT) initiatives of the early 1980s, one area of informal education practice has been work with young offenders. This form of work created tensions among workers' professional values as educators, the rationale and purpose of the employing agency, and the broader principles of youth justice. However, for those of us who chose to work in such a setting, it provided us with an insight into a casework approach that used our knowledge and skills and, depending on who employed us (usually the local authority or a voluntary agency), offered us an opportunity to consider the compromises we would have to make.

In working with young offenders, all five stages of our systematic approach to casework are clearly identifiable, and are shown below in Table 14.1.

The Young Adult Learners Project

In other cases, work may not so obviously follow a casework model, but may still draw on casework practice. A Government-funded initiative aimed at helping 'young adults with low self-esteem acquire the state of learning readiness that will enable them to take advantage of the increasing number of programmes and projects...' (Merton and Parrott 1999: 2) goes some way towards demonstrating this. The project workers identified five stages:

1. Reaching Out: recruitment, targeting and retention;
2. Bringing In: programmes of activity that work;

Table 14.1

Problem exploration/assessment phase	Referral, initial enquiry, risk assessment, court report
Contracting phase	Designing the programme, caution, supervision planning
Intervention phase (formal/informal)	Supervision, groupwork, reparation, mediation, life and social skills work
Monitoring and evaluation phase	Case review, case conference, record-keeping, case supervision
Ending	Revocation of a court order

Table 14.2

1.	Problem exploration/ assessment phase		
2.	Contracting phase	1.	Reaching Out
		2.	Bringing In
3.	Intervention phase	3.	Putting Across
4.	Monitoring and evaluation phase	4.	Achieving Together
5.	Termination phase		
		5.	Working With

3. Putting Across: effective approaches to teaching and learning;
4. Achieving Together: assessment and accreditation methods;
5. Working With: professional partnerships and inter-agency support (1999: 10).

We can see some general similarities between these stages and our five-stage model. These are listed above in Table 14.2.

The stages are therefore similar to those in the IT example, but the nature of the relationship between worker and clients differs. In this case, the participants may have exhibited a need for professional intervention, but the outcome is intended to be self-development. Casework-type methods are used to help young people to develop their future employment or learning potential, in ways that suit them.

A key factor, then, seems to be the motivation lying behind the processes or methods that we may describe as 'casework', and the nature of the relationship it encloses. Are the aims of the work negotiated within that relationship or externally imposed? Is the intention to meet and clarify the client's own agenda, or that of some outside agency? These questions will become central to our discussion in the next section, of casework as an instrument of social policy.

Q3: Think about the language you would use to describe work you are undertaking with an individual. Is it similar to the five stages we have identified, or those identified by the Young Adult Learners Project workers? Ask yourself:

*   Is there a problem exploration/assessment phase?
*   How do you and the other person engage in the process?
*   What methods do you use?
*   What aspects of the work are negotiable?
*   How do you measure success?
*   Who judges it a success?
*   How will you know when your role has ended?

If your work matches the key stages we have identified, can it be defined as casework or are there other factors that make your work different?

Based on this chapter and any additional reading, can you identify what aspects of your work you might now describe as using a casework approach?

Casework as an instrument of policy

In considering the range of settings in which informal educators may be employed as caseworkers, we now need to examine changes in social policy and the development of Government-led initiatives aimed at 'putting right' some characteristic of an individual or group. As your answers to the last question might have revealed, policymakers have identified a wide range of social 'problems', based on personal deficit models of social welfare, and assuming a need for state intervention. These, in turn, are creating new professional roles for informal educators, often based on casework models.

This trend can be seen in the Government's concerns about social exclusion and the disaffected, and in initiatives, such as the Connexions Service, which present casework-style interventions as a response.

Connexions

Work with the disaffected has been given a significant emphasis in the political debates of recent years, particularly as the result of two key reports published in July 1999 and January 2000 which focus on the 'socially excluded'. They are *Bridging the Gap* (Social Exclusion Unit 1999), offering new opportunities for 16–18-year olds not in education, employment or training; and *Learning to Succeed* (DfEE January 2000), a new framework for post-16 learning.

Both reports acknowledge the impact of exclusion and recognise that education, life chances and levels of participation in society as a whole are central to a healthy, equal and fair society. The research that informed the two reports clearly identifies the range of problems facing the socially excluded and the areas of need that might exist for them. However, it doesn't itself offer a model for practice, instead suggesting the range of services that might be needed to support an individual facing such difficulties. Such projects and services seem to be based on notions of 'need' which require professional intervention to combat isolation and exclusion. We can see some similarities here with the values of the casework models, particularly the diagnostic model, we discussed earlier.

Following from these reports, the Connexions (Youth Support and Development) Service has been developed to address these problems. Its stated aims are broad and focus on educational outcomes:

[6.2] The key aim of the Service will be to enable all young people to participate effectively in appropriate learning ... by raising their aspirations so that they reach their full potential. The new service will play a central role in helping to deal with problems experienced by young people, removing any wider barriers to effective engagement in learning that young people are suffering.

(DfEE 2000: 32)

One proposed method of meeting these aims is a 'casework' approach, with the appointment of Personal Advisers for all young people. If this plan goes ahead, the new Service will be delivered by a network of Personal Advisers and Mentors – in the first instance primarily youth and community workers and careers advisers – who will engage with all young people in order to help them achieve their full potential in terms of education, employment and lifelong learning opportunities. Workers in this 'new' professional role will:

[6.10] take responsibility for ensuring all the needs of a young person are met in an integrated and coherent manner. Personal Advisers' work will range from: ensuring school attendance pre-16; to the provision of information regarding future learning and work opportunities; to more in-depth support in gaining access to education and training and the brokering of access to, plus co-ordination of, specialist services. Personal Advisers will be deployed in a variety of locations, including schools, FE Colleges and community settings so that young people can have access to them in an appropriate way.

(DfEE 2000: 35)

This approach will require Personal Advisers to work in partnership with various agencies and groups in the community. Their tasks will also include assessment, planning and review, keeping in contact with clients and monitoring their progress (DfEE 2000: 40–1). In this context, the use of a casework approach seems to be intended to ensure that each 'client' is successfully engaged with education or employment and can be 'supported' and 'tracked' through that process.

Connexions and the informal educator

Although youth and community workers may have reservations about some aspects of their proposed role within the Connexions Service, most of us would accept that the intended aims of the Service, and many of its core principles, are closely allied to those of informal education. It also makes use of established youth work skills. For instance, the Government has identified a very clear role for outreach and detached workers to engage disaffected young people with the Service.

However, the scheme's proposals raise a number of major concerns for youth and community work practitioners and other informal educators. In accepting that youth and community work is an educational service, it is obvious that it will logically form a core element within the Connexions Service. To work within this system, however, existing youth and community work will have to change to a more bureaucratic system. In the process, it could lose its distinctive, informal character: arguably the very reason why the socially excluded have chosen to engage with the youth service in the first place. Alternatively, youth and community work will have to become an aligned (and potentially marginalised) provision to whom young people can be referred – but on what terms?

Against the stated commitment of the Connexions Service to every young person, and to the principles of learning and participation, informal educators will have to balance a number of ethical dilemmas. Two major issues are especially relevant to the theme of this chapter: confidentiality and the voluntary nature of the informal education relationship.

In many ways, the dilemmas are similar to those faced by caseworkers in areas such as IT. Workers within the Youth Justice system are required to police the activities of young people, and to administer forms of intervention which may or may not be right for the young people involved. How much should they tell young people about these job requirements? Youth and community workers involved with Connexions programmes may feel that they need to explain the full implications of their role, prior to engaging any young person with the Service. This could create questions about confidentiality and cause problems in working with other professional groups who are less willing to disclose their positions.

As part of this same initiative, the language that previously described the 'voluntary' nature of the worker's relationship with clients is being re-framed. Connexions seek to ensure that 'all the needs of a young person are met' in the most effective way. As we have seen, one aspect of classic casework is the assumption that clients have needs which workers can identify and meet. But the relationship between a young person and informal educator is on a more open and equal footing, in which needs may not be a driving force, or may emerge in the course of the relationship. The requirement to take part in the scheme, and the need to meet an external agenda, changes the nature of this relationship and will limit the freedom of choice for young people.

The reports that set out the Connexions policy also reveal a particular attitude to education. In this way of thinking, the growth and development of an individual through education can only be justified if that education is going to make each recipient a more active and valued citizen. Similarly, it is no longer sufficient to describe informal education work in terms of the learning process. Some sort of outcome, which is both measurable and agreed, is necessary.

Concluding thoughts

Using the Connexions Service as a model, it is possible to identify a new form of casework. Multi-disciplinary teams, by co-ordinating their efforts, can offer a coherent approach to working with the individual. Bringing together different disciplines acknowledges that social exclusion is the result of a combination of factors that require varying models of intervention – a clear example of the Government drive for 'joined-up thinking'. However, philosophical differences that exist among the agencies involved, for instance on the question of confidentiality, may mean that such teamwork is going to prove problematic.

Many of us involved in the discussions and debates that are informing this new development have a sense of re-inventing the wheel. Youth and community work has traditionally worked with the very groups being targeted by the Connexions Service and has engaged them with some success;

yet we acknowledge that we could do better. At the same time, informal educators are likely to be uneasy when they consider what is expected of them and the values that underlie it.

This new development clearly outlines the Government's expectations of caseworkers. It seems to be based on the philosophy of the market place – competitiveness, customer choice, cost-effectiveness and public accountability. All of this may cause problems for the informal educator, particularly if young people's knowledge, attitudes and skills are to become quantifiable measures of a successful intervention.

Further reading

Barber, J.G. (1991) *Beyond Casework*. Basingstoke: Macmillan. Offers a contemporary account of 'politically progressive casework', building on a broad theoretical base and offering practical examples. It moves beyond the social work definition of case-work and considers principles that underpin informal education, youth and community work.

Department for Education and Employment (DfEE) (2000) *Connexions. The Best Start in Life for Every Young Person*. Sheffield: DfEE. Seldom has a Government report acknowledged the value of youth and community work practice in such a positive light. It is such a shame that it fails to draw on the underpinning values and principles of the work, or to acknowledge the benefit of practice which promotes and engenders growth and development for individuals and their communities.

Huskins, J. (2000) *From Disaffection to Social Inclusion: A Social Skills Preparation for Active Citizenship and Employment*. Bristol: John Huskins. An updated account of how to use Huskin's material in a way that meets many Government agendas. A useful resource (together with its earlier counterpart).

Merton, B. and Parrott, A. (1999) *Only Connect. Successful Practice in Educational Work with Disaffected Young Adults*. Sheffield: DfEE/NIACE/NYA. An account of research drawing on twelve projects funded through the Young Adult Learners Project. It offers a model of curriculum development which can be transferred to other similar initiatives.

References

Barber, J.G. (1991) *Beyond Casework*. Basingstoke: Macmillan.

Burke, T., Hand, J. and McFall, L. (1999) *Moving On Up: How Youth Work Raises Achievement and Promotes Social Inclusion*. Sheffield: DfEE/NYA.

Department for Education and Employment (DfEE) (2000) *Connexions. The Best Start in Life for Every Young Person*. Sheffield: DfEE.

DfEE (2000) *Learning to Succeed*. Sheffield: DfEE Publications (White Paper).

Huskins, J. (1996) *Quality Work with Young People: Developing Social Skills and Diversion from Risk*. Bristol: John Huskins.

Huskins, J. (2000) *From Disaffection to Social Inclusion: A Social Skills Preparation for Active Citizenship and Employment*. Bristol: John Huskins.

Jeffs, T. and Smith, M. (1990) *Using Informal Education: An Alternative to Casework, Teaching and Control?* Buckingham: Open University Press.

Jeffs, T. and Smith, M. (1996) *Informal Education: Conversation, Democracy and Learning*. Derby: Education Now/YMCA.

Johnson, D.W. and Johnson, F.P. (1987) *Joining Together. Group Theory and Group Skills*. London: Prentice-Hall International.

Merton, B. and Parrott, A. (1999) *Only Connect. Successful Practice in Educational Work with Disaffected Young Adults.* Sheffield: DfEE/NIACE/NYA.

Obbo, D.K. (1990) 'Methods, techniques and skills of youth and community work: Social case work, community development, and Supervision', in Osei-Hwedie, K., Mwansa, L.-K. and Mufune, P. (eds) *Youth and Community Work Practice: Methods, Techniques and Skills.* London: Commonwealth Secretariat (pp. 95–128).

Perlman, H.H. (1957) *Casework. A Problem-solving Process.* Chicago: University of Chicago Press.

Richmond, M.E. (1917) *Social Diagnosis.* New York: Russell Sage Foundation.

Smalley, R.E. (1967) *Theory for Social Work Practice.* New York: Columbia University Press.

Social Exclusion Unit (1999) *Bridging the Gap.* London: Social Exclusion Unit. www.cabinet-office.gov.uk/seu.

Taft, J. (1937) 'The relation of function to process in social case casework', *Journal of Social Work Processes* 1, 1–18.

15 Doing projects

Working with formal groups

Malcolm Payne

Starting points

Working with groups as educators is a complex task. It demands of us that we bring together in our practice three areas of experience, skill and knowledge: understanding groups; working to promote learning; and project management.

First, we need to understand about groups themselves and how they work. We need to recognise and understand patterns which are common to groups in general (theory) and to transfer our understanding to working with particular groups (practice). Choosing to work with a group (rather than with individuals) involves a number of decisions; choosing how to work with a particular group involves yet more. Practice also involves me – the practitioner. So I need to understand how I work with and behave in groups, so that I can understand how I am working with this particular group. For however much we know about groups, we are likely to be faced at some time with something new in every group with whom we work. And at that point, we need to be able to choose how to move on, based upon some clear principles about who we are as workers.

Next, there is the question of learning. In group settings we have the chance to enable people to learn from one another and from the task or activity in which the group is engaged. In order to do this we need to know how to use the group setting to promote learning. Education is a conscious process: it implies that the educator, acting with intent, has some purpose in mind. Purpose is closely connected with values – what we believe in. In groups, people are 'acting out' their beliefs and values in how they treat one another and how they express themselves. Every group is a micro-version of our world. It can be a more or less democratic place, a more or less fair place, a more or less creative, satisfying place for those who are part of it. It may confirm 'who they are' in helpful or unhelpful ways, or it may offer opportunities for change. How we work with groups also reflects our own values as educators – the way we see the world and how we wish it to be.

Finally, educators pursue different activities and projects when working with groups which demand a wide range of skills and knowledge to do with defining goals and managing tasks. These management skills need to be integrated with educational purposes and values, and with group processes.

Projects are usually time-limited: they have a beginning, a middle and an end. They may be short-term, lasting only a few hours or days, or be sustained over weeks or months. Taking on a project means that we have chosen to use our resources in a particular way. It implies that a decision has been made to try to meet certain educational goals by, for example:

- running a residential;
- offering a training course;
- helping people to mount a campaign;
- forming a new community group;
- working with a group of excluded students; or
- raising awareness about local environmental concerns.

These are just examples; you can probably think of many other aims which might lead you to decide to work with groups on a project. The list is endless, reflecting the very wide variety of contexts, agencies and tasks within informal education. Often, a project arises from everyday contact – from 'being around' people in the places where we work (Jeffs and Smith 1996: 67). Listening to their concerns and ideas may lead to the decision to develop a project.

To sum up, then, three broad questions form the basis for this chapter:

- What do we need to know about groups and working with them?
- What do we need to know about learning in groups?
- How can we design and manage projects with groups so that their members can achieve and learn?

Case study 1: The dance group

The idea to form a dance group had emerged from two or three of a larger group of teenage friends in a conversation about being bored, not having anything to do. For a while, it had just been a 'bright idea' but no more than that. They were unsure about what they could achieve. They met often as a group and there was a shared interest in dance – but could they really become a dance group? Could they perform in front of others?

There would be a lot to think about if they were to become a dance group. No longer could they just turn up at the youth centre and chat. They would need to get organised. Everyone needed to play a part – it could not be left to chance. Decisions needed to be taken – how often they would practise, what music they would dance to, who would take the leading roles and who would be less prominent. And, when they reached a crisis point – and groups often do – where some key members threatened to leave, they had to find a way to talk about what was going wrong and how they would begin to mend some of the relationships which had become damaged. This meant going back over the group's life: did they all want to be there, or was the goal less important to some than others? Some members felt left out – that their views were not being heard. They began to resent the more vocal members who, in turn, felt that the quieter ones were not fully committed.

What was to be done? In the simplest terms, the group needed to learn how to *sustain* itself. That meant giving themselves a regular opportunity to talk about what was going on in the group – their relationships, how they were communicating, how decisions were being made – so that members could learn and practise all of the skills that are required for group life. Before, they had simply focused upon the *task*: putting on a dance performance. Now, they had learned that the *process* – how that task was tackled – was just as important if they were to succeed. The *primary goal* for the group was to dance and to put on a performance. But in order to achieve this, the group had taken on a secondary goal: group *maintenance*.

Working with groups

In many ways human nature is co-operative. We are more like ants and wolves than like cats. We readily join groups and form attachments, and receive powerful biological and emotional rewards for doing so.

(Argyle 1991: 247)

Case Study 1 illustrates some familiar features of group life that we are likely to encounter when we work with formal groups. To begin with, however, we need to understand what we mean by a group.

Whenever three or more people come together we can call them a group. Three people standing at the coffee bar together, having a chance conversation as they wait to be served, constitute a group in this simple sense of the word. But to work with groups we need a better definition than that. For the purposes of this chapter we will ignore these sorts of groups – except perhaps to say that such informal groups may be the start of something more. That conversation might lead to an idea, to them meeting again, to the group beginning to have some sort of life of its own, as we saw in Case Study 1. In the day-to-day work of many informal educators, such beginnings can be very important – but they are not our primary focus in this chapter.

Defining these chance groupings as *informal* groups begins to throw some light onto what we mean when we speak about *formal* groups. By formal we do not mean that the group behaves in formal (or conventional) ways, but that the group begins to take on a *form* of its own: its own distinctive shape or identity. In a formal group, we might, for example, know who are its members (and therefore, who are not). And we might begin to see some particular patterns of behaviour – whether we feel these are good or bad. So, relationships in the group might be seen as close, supportive or co-operative; or they may be felt to be distant or competitive. Each of these features of a group's behaviour will affect what the group can achieve. The pattern within a particular group is unique to that group, but the study of human behaviour in groups suggests that most groups exhibit similar patterns.

Q1: Think about a recent group with whom you have been working. What features about it might suggest that it is a formal group?

Hare, writing in 1962, attempted to define the five features of groups which are likely to interest us as informal educators:

> The members of the group are *in interaction with* one another. They share a common *goal* and set of *norms* which give direction and limits to their activity. They also develop a set of *roles* and a network *of interpersonal attraction* which serve to differentiate them from other groups.
>
> (Hare 1962: 5; my italics)

Taken together, these five features of a group represent its unique culture and identity and serve to distinguish it from other groups. They also suggest questions which we can use to think about the group:

- *Interaction:* how are people communicating in this group? What patterns can be seen for different group members? Is there more interaction between some than others? Are some members silent or marginalised?
- *Goal:* what is the group trying to achieve? Are all members equally interested? Does motivation change at times? Are some more confident than others? Is everyone satisfied with the group's progress? What does the group need to learn and do in order to achieve its goals?
- *Norms:* what norms and values have the group adopted, for example about how decisions are made, or who is listened to? How do those affect its members? Are they helping the group to achieve its goals? Might it wish to adopt different norms?
- *Roles:* what roles exist in the group? Are some members more powerful than others? How aware are members of their own and others' roles? Are they happy with them or do some want them to change?
- *Relationships:* what sorts of relationships are there? What patterns, e.g. of dominance, dependence, friendship or hostility (Argyle 1972) can be seen? Are some members popular while others appear less valued? Are relationships helping or hindering the group?

For educators, formal groups present a range of opportunities for members' learning: about themselves; about themselves in relation to others; and about whatever it is the group is engaged in. This familiar triangle of *individual, group* and *task* can be said to define a fertile arena for learning, if an environment is created to enable that learning to take place.

In Case Study 1, the group is attempting to make a difficult transition: from simply being a group of friends (what is sometimes known as a natural group) to becoming something more formal. The group wants to take on a purpose or goal (the task). This will make all sorts of demands upon its members which did not exist before. Some examples of the challenges they face are offered in the case study: getting organised; paying attention to who is to do what; giving themselves time to reflect.

Q2: Think about the group in Case Study 1. If you were a member of this group, what suggestions might you make to other members about what might be done to keep the group going successfully?

Learning in groups

> We never educate directly, but indirectly by means of the environment.
> Whether we permit chance environments to do the work, or whether we
> design environments for the purpose, makes a great deal of difference.
>
> (Dewey 1916: 16)

As informal educators we are concerned with enabling people to learn.
Research suggests that we learn a lot from being with others in groups. For
some, working with groups is a – or even *the* – primary means of encouraging
learning, because those with whom we work are able to learn from and with
one another, rather than simply from us as the worker. Learning in groups
can therefore promote what Mullender and Ward (1991: 11) call 'self-
empowerment' – people's ability to make choices for themselves. However,
we as educators are still important to this process. The choices we make
about how to work with a group will make a difference to what is learned.
These decisions represent our attempt to 'design the environment' as Dewey
suggested – where the group itself is a central feature of that environment.

Promoting learning by working with groups rather than simply with individuals is probably as old as education itself. The history of what has come to
be known in the helping professions as 'group work' is much more recent.
Much of the literature which focuses upon such work – and there is a great
deal – has been developed in the field of social work since the 1920s. Practitioners have tried, through careful study and reflection about its purposes
and methods, to identify how group work can be used, and to what effect, in
order to establish this form of work with people as a discipline.

Another origin of this sort of work comes from educational work with
groups which 'developed from the need for mutual aid and support' (Kunstler 1955: 40). This was a way of working which challenged traditional ideas
about the 'giver' and 'receiver' of help, and instead recognised people's abilities to support one another and to achieve social change. These philosophical ideas remain important. Original forms of this work were found in
informal education settings: self-help groups, playgrounds, summer camps,
settlements and neighbourhood centres.

Informal education work with and through groups is not a universal
method, however, to be applied in all circumstances. Its use in a disciplined
way implies that we must decide when and how to apply the range of
methods generally referred to as group work. A decision to pursue particular
educational goals by such methods should mean that we think that they will
be effective – that they will achieve certain purposes and fit with the ethics of
our practice.

Why should educators work with and through groups?

There have been a number of attempts to identify the benefits of working
with and through groups (see for example Brown 1992: 12–27).

- Being part of a group is a normal and everyday experience for most
  people. Group experience matters for virtually everyone and therefore
  provides a potentially fertile learning environment.

- Being part of a group makes a number of demands upon people: negotiating what will or will not be done; performing tasks; taking on roles and responding to those of others; sharing thoughts and feelings. Each of these features of group life contains the potential for personal development and growth, if the group environment is conducive to it.
- Many people with whom we work experience a sense of isolation. This may arise from their home situation (living alone, bringing up small children, a family where they are the main carer, for example) or from other aspects of their life – for instance if they are disabled, suffer from illness, or face discrimination. Being with others, especially if they share some of the same experiences, can reduce people's feelings of being alone in their world. New friendships and support networks can be built.
- People often want to create change for themselves – to find new ways to react or behave, to understand themselves better, or to learn new skills. Being part of a group with others who also wish to change can support learning.
- People seeking to bring about social and political change, particularly those facing oppression, have long seen the potential for groups to raise consciousness among members and confront oppressive social structures. Feminist groups, for example, have an important place in the history of modern social change (see Butler and Wintram 1991).
- Doing things – whether taking up a leisure activity, pursuing some local political issue, or building a new community group – frequently depends on finding others who share a similar passion or interest. From an early age we learn that there are many things that can be achieved only by co-operating with others.

These ways in which group experience offers opportunities for learning also hint at the wide range of group tasks and projects which educators might pursue. If we were to attempt to mention them all, a very long list would result. Drawing upon Jeffs and Smith (1996) we can see, however, that what they all have in common is that the worker is using the medium of association (people being with others) to enable people to gain and provide mutual aid, a sense of belonging, identity and self-esteem; and to foster learning, change and development. As educators, we must attend to all of the features of groups which might serve to promote these ends. Conversely, since being in a group with others can also confirm feelings of isolation, reinforce oppressive structures or behaviour or damage self-esteem, we must also establish ways of working which avoid – or at least limit – these risks.

Contemporary group work practice, then, drawing upon the history of informal education and social work, attempts to establish a systematic *methodology* to guide our work with and through groups in order to promote learning and growth.

Q3: Think back over your own experiences of being in groups. Jot down some of the things you have gained, and the ways in which you have learned from particular groups. What group experiences have had negative consequences for you?

The educator's role in the group

People take on roles when they belong to or work with a group. It is helpful to think about two types: *functional* and *behavioural* roles. As educators, both aspects of our role are important. There is no one role which can always be applied in whatever group we are working; we need to be flexible and adaptable. In one group, we may need to be much more assertive than in another. Or we may need to be prepared to take the lead until the group's confidence has grown. These should, ideally, be conscious decisions. We must be aware of and be able to choose the roles we perform, based upon our judgements about what is appropriate, ethical and effective. What is constant is the functional role we perform as an educator. In order to perform this, we must adjust the ways we behave and the tasks we take on.

As workers we often hold a lot of authority, power and influence – based upon our knowledge and expertise, our position in the community, our age, gender, or race, or our ability to offer resources to the groups with whom we work. How we exercise such influence in groups is a key aspect of professional practice and goes to the heart of questions about learning and democracy. Gibson and Clarke (1995: 64), discussing the role of youth workers in groups, identify three styles of working:

- *authoritarian:* the worker makes the decisions and presents or sells them to the group;
- *consultative:* the worker offers tentative decisions, invites discussion but reserves the right to decide;
- *enabling:* the worker sets boundaries, shares information, initiates discussion and supports decision making by the group.

It is clear that it is the third style, that of the enabling worker, which is likely to be most empowering to those with whom we work. It most closely accords with the democratic ideals which have shaped group work practice and informal education, because it encourages participation by group members and a climate of support and co-operation. It also reminds us that, when we are able to, we will want to encourage groups to adopt a similar style of decision-making themselves. But not all groups will be ready or able to work in participative or co-operative ways. As Gibson and Clarke point out (1995: 47), good practice in informal education will sometimes mean that we have to exercise our power, to set the boundaries, to persuade or cajole. For example, if we perceive that a group might come to harm, or harm others if we allow it to continue to do something, we need to be prepared to step in, perhaps even to become authoritarian. We cannot avoid such responsibilities at times, although we would want the group to understand why we had to act in such a way.

Davies reminds us that workers may adopt non-directive techniques, trying to appear as self-effacing and uninfluential as possible, but can never succeed in eliminating their own impact. They will see themselves, and the group will see them, as 'the worker' (Davies 1975: 107). The role itself inevitably brings with it some power and authority, whatever style of working is adopted.

In our first case study, young people were trying to develop a dance group. Below, the same case study is revisited in order to examine the role of the worker.

Case Study 1 Revisited

The youth worker is employed by a local authority to develop work under Local Agenda 21. She sees that there might be an opportunity to support the group to achieve what they want and, at the same time, by working with them, to promote some of Agenda 21's objectives concerned with young people's involvement in their community. Her intentions as a worker, the aims of her agency and the young people's interests are, she judges, congruous. Offering the group her support involves exploring with the group what she is able to offer and what might be their needs and expectations. She is not an expert in dance, but she feels that dance provides a useful vehicle for informal education.

The worker begins by talking with the group about their intentions: what they want to achieve. They want to form a dance group; they want to perform in front of others. She asks why, thinking through with them what the project will involve. She explores some of the possible benefits: for example, that it might show young people in a positive light in the community, as well as lots of opportunities for learning new skills. Worker and group consider what will be needed if they are to be successful: the time that will be required, a place to practise, things to be organised.

The worker needs to take care at this point. It is *their* idea and she must not 'take it over'. She must support, but not lead. She must not push the pace faster than the group wishes to go, but at the same time, she wishes to encourage. She can offer help, but she must do so in ways which they will find acceptable, and which will allow them to retain control.

Q4: Look at Case Study 1 Revisited. Imagine yourself in the position of the young people. What might you want from the worker? And what might you *not* want?

Now put yourself in the position of the worker. Try to write down as clearly as possible (a) what you will offer the group and (b) what role(s) you will adopt.

We need to ask ourselves some sharp questions about our role, and the power and influence we bring to our work. Notice how, in Case Study 1 Revisited, the worker's role is partly defined by the fact that she is employed to pursue the objectives of Local Agenda 21 for young people. That means that she is concerned with such things as citizenship, participation and democracy, and environmental issues. At the same time, she is working from informal education principles. This is a common enough scenario: the agency, job title or funding source provides the focus for the work; our profession (as youth workers or community educators) offers the framework of principles, values and methods. Similar situations may also occur in health education, 'community safety' or school exclusion projects.

It is not always easy to bring these two sets of expectations together. For example, we may be expected to work more quickly than we judge that a particular group is capable of, or we might be expected to take some decisions on behalf of the group which we would prefer the group to take.

> **Q5:** Identify a couple of examples of different funding sources (or agencies) which might be paying for (or employing) informal educators. What tensions might arise? What are the sources of these tensions?

It is clear that, as informal educators, our intentions to promote learning are never value-free. We believe certain human values to be important, and this gives rise to an agenda for the learning we want to promote. Indeed, some would argue that the informal education task *is* the promotion of learning about values (Young 1999: 3). For youth workers, Young argues, this gives rise to a learning agenda which is intended to give young people opportunities to examine their own values, think about the principles on which they are based, and make informed decisions and choices.

The choices we make will strongly influence the group learning environment: what and how group members learn, and our relationship with them. Smith refers to this as a choice we make about our *disposition* (1994: 77): how we conceptualise and approach our task as educators. Will we choose to be an expert or teacher, ready to pass on our knowledge and expertise? Or a kind of 'group parent' who will set the boundaries and rules of behaviour? Or perhaps a manager: the person who ensures that the task gets accomplished effectively? The basic disposition we choose will be recognised by those with whom we work. And they are likely to react to us by adopting a reciprocal role, as pupil, child or subordinate.

Group work texts and manuals are not short on lists of roles which workers and members take in groups (see, for example, Harris 1994). Perhaps the usefulness of these suggested roles lies in what they say about the practitioner's overall task – to work in such ways as to support the group to achieve the objectives of the project in which it is engaged. As with the choice of 'dispositions', this involves the worker making sensitive decisions about what is needed at a particular time. None of these roles is owned only by the worker however: any group member may take any of them on. Indeed, Davies (1975: 106) suggests that interventions by the worker are only justified when they are unlikely to be made by another group member. And the more the worker says and does, the fewer openings there are for others to do what is meaningful for them.

How then can we find a suitable approach and role for ourselves in promoting learning in groups? Despite the arguments put forward in the curriculum debate (see, for instance, Jeffs and Smith 1996, Chapter 5) there is not a single answer to this question. The debate centres upon whether informal educators can or should employ a curriculum to define the learning processes and outcomes of what they do. On the one side there is an expectation that the outcomes of the work can be clearly demonstrated in terms of the learning which people have gained as a result of the projects and activities practitioners organise or involve themselves in. The opposing camp argues that learning cannot be specified by simple descriptions of objectives, content and outcomes. It arises mainly from the conversations which take place in the course of informal education activity (Jeffs and Smith 1996).

> **Q6:** Jot down some examples of recent work you have undertaken with groups. Do they seem to you to represent formal or informal, curriculum-led or conversation-based approaches?

In responding to the curriculum debate, we might recognise that most educators engage in both formal (curriculum-led) activities *and* informal (conversation-based) learning. Depending upon the precise role they perform – and this may change from activity to activity as well as from job to job – the balance between the two forms of education will vary. Some agencies emphasise the outcomes-led aspects of their work, for example in providing health education through outreach work with young people and adults. Or, as part of the role of community worker where much of the work is informal, practitioners may respond to a need for more formal approaches to learning – for example by organising a residential or workshop.

Case Study 2: The anger management project

A youth work agency wishes to offer young people an opportunity to learn how to manage their anger better. Put simply, the experimental project is based upon the idea that, for some young people, becoming angry and aggressive leads to confrontations – at school with other students and with teachers, and outside school with peers, parents and authority figures. The agency's workers have done some analysis of this issue and want to pilot a project to tackle the problem. They work closely with schools, education welfare, youth justice and social services in order to develop the proposed scheme. Subsequently, they will undertake a careful evaluation of the pilot scheme to judge its effectiveness.

Six young men between thirteen and sixteen are invited to participate in the project, which will consist of an intensive course during school time. All are in contact with welfare agencies, where concern about their anger has been expressed by the young people themselves as well as those working with them. The group project is intended to supplement individual educational work being undertaken with each of the participants by the agencies involved.

Clear aims and objectives are set for the course by the agencies. A conversation is held with each of the young men before the course begins, so that they are fully informed of what it is about and able to decide for themselves whether to attend. The programme reflects what could be achieved by working with a group rather than with individual work. For example, participants are asked to work in two groups and helped to devise a script to be performed by the other group, based on an example of the sort of situation in which they become angry, and how they had dealt with this. The performance was followed by discussion of what had happened and whether there were alternative actions open to the characters.

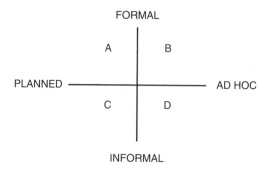

Figure 15.1

(based upon Payne and Scott 1982)

> **Q7:** Think carefully about Case Study 2. What aspects of the work suggest that it is an example of informal education? And what aspects suggest that it is formal?

In working with groups, we can map our educational strategies using a matrix, as shown above.

The vertical axis of the matrix represents a continuum from formal activities at the top, through to informal activities at the bottom. Instructing people in the safety requirements of rock-climbing is an example of formal education. A spontaneous discussion about a topic in the newspaper might be an example at the informal end of the scale.

The horizontal axis shows another scale. Activities on the left are planned, such as organising a health and safety workshop for new committee members. At the other end of this continuum, we might respond to an incident which takes place in a group by encouraging members to 'take stock' of what is happening. This cannot be planned for, although we must be ready to use the *ad hoc* opportunity it presents.

We can now begin to map some of our educational interventions on this grid. Those in the quadrant marked 'A' are formal and planned. They may often have a curriculum associated with them. So, for example, we should be able to state what learning outcomes are required for our new committee members if they are to take responsibility for health and safety: they need to understand the various rules and regulations, and what their role is in implementing them. We will also have thought about the best methods for achieving the learning they might need. We may decide that it would be helpful to test whether the learning outcomes have been achieved.

Quadrant 'B' represents formal but *ad hoc* learning activity. Responding to a learning need as it arises, the worker takes the opportunity to present information or demonstrate a skill to group members – or to encourage another member of the group to do so. Examples might include information about how the local council is organised, or how to use a particular computer program.

Quadrant 'C' represents learning which is informal but planned. By engaging a group in an activity, the worker can predict that certain issues will arise and can become the prompt for exploration and discussion. 'If I was to look at all the residentials I do then I could name all the issues that I know will crop up over the weekend . . .' (Smith 1994: 73). Here, the accent is on planning an environment which creates the potential for informal learning.

Quadrant 'D' maps an area of educational activity which is both informal and *ad hoc*. Opportunities are seized, ideas floated, opinions aired, concerns, needs and aspirations are uncovered in the course of on-going contact. Here, informal education practitioners work from the broad purposes and strategies which attend their roles: the education may be informal and *ad hoc*, but it is not accidental. In a recent conversation with a school nurse, she described how she works: 'I do more useful work with these children in the course of repairing a cut leg or a bruised forehead than I ever do when I am working in the classroom teaching them about oral hygiene. They learn when *they're* ready, not when the timetable says they're ready. That means *I have to be ready all the time* by making myself available to them.' Notice here that her relationship with students – her availability – is central to the learning.

Most informal educators need to be able to operate in all four quadrants. And indeed, many formal educators (teachers for example) also use informal methods to achieve some objectives, particularly in those subject areas where the learner's own opinions and values are important. Which takes precedence will be determined by the requirements of the worker's agency and role, and the opportunities these present. However, if the way we work means that formal methods take precedence most of the time, it is unlikely that we are really acting as informal educators.

> **Q8:** Look again at Case Study 2. Imagine that you are part of the youth work team which is running the anger management course. Now, using the matrix, identify the learning activities which you will wish to pursue in each of the quadrants A, B, C and D.

Does a framework for learning – a curriculum – imply formal education? Put the other way, we might ask: 'Can we operate a curriculum and nonetheless work from the agendas of those with whom we work?' I believe that the answer to that question is both 'no' and 'yes'. The absence of curriculum must not be allowed to become equated with absence of learning. Similarly, the presence of curriculum must not squeeze out opportunities to respond to the here and now.

On the positive side, there are a number of advantages to being more explicit about what are the intended outcomes of our work, whether we call this a curriculum or simply a project aim. First, it makes our agenda clear to those with whom we work. As a result, they may be able to decide whether or not to engage with us. Second, it may lead us to be more purposeful in our work. For example, in planning a particular project, a curriculum may enable us to build in activities or approaches which will enhance participants' learning in more clearly-defined areas. So, in relation to the anger management course, we will be able to plan activities, and create an environment, which will enable the young people involved to think about what are likely to be very sensitive issues, and not just rely on our reactions as workers to situations as they arise. This is the idea of curriculum primarily as a planning tool (Payne and Merton 2000). Rather than prescribing outcomes, such a curriculum offers a broad framework for learning. Third, even where we are operating in the informal and *ad hoc* arenas, there are circumstances where a curriculum may be helpful. In settings such as residential centres for care-leavers, or semi-independent living projects, where practitioners work with a relatively small number of people on a sustained basis, a curriculum can be a useful tool to identify learning needs, design learning events and assess progress. Operated sensitively, and carefully negotiated with learners, such a curriculum does not need to restrict – and may even broaden – opportunity.

Designing and managing projects for learning

In this section we will consider how we set about devising projects in ways which fulfil their potential for learning. The main focus is on two aspects: deciding whether and how to pursue a project, and agreeing project objectives. The section ends with a brief consideration of project management.

As informal educators, we are concerned with what Brookfield (1986: 233) refers to as mutuality: the idea that we are engaged with learners in collaborative activity. Young (1999: 69) uses a similar idea, that the youth work relationship is based upon reciprocity. This leads to two important observations. First, the more we take the lead role as educators in defining needs and designing learning, the less space we leave for those with whom we work to do it for themselves. Second, that in designing learning, the more closely we specify objectives, content and methods, the less emphasis is likely to be given to all of the learning which might arise informally and in response to people's own identified needs and reflection.

Why a project?

When as educators we become involved with people in designing, supporting or running group projects, we will already have made a number of decisions about how we will work. As suggested at the beginning of the chapter, projects are by definition time-limited. Doing a project suggests that the intentions we started out with will be met by the time it is complete. This might suggest that project work is straightforward and predictable. In my experience, however, projects rarely follow a purely logical and text-book process. In theory, the steps might look something like this:

1 Identify a need and examine whether or how this need can or should be met.
2 Decide whether meeting the need identified fits the purposes of your agency.
3 Decide whether meeting this need is a priority when compared with other work.
4 Draw up a draft project plan including the objectives to be met, the timescale and, ideally, the success criteria.
5 Identify the resources which will be required to implement the plan.

6   Gain agreement for the project plan from those who will be involved or affected.
7   Carry out the planned project.
8   Evaluate the process and its effects and decide what (if anything) to do next.

The trouble is that what appears as a relatively straightforward process is much more complex when applied to real life. We cannot always see clearly what a 'need' is, and others may have a different view. Agency purposes are not always so clearly defined that, when a new situation arises, we can make a decision about whether we should pursue a course of action. Priorities change: what seemed important yesterday may be overtaken by something more urgent. People may become enthusiastic and we will want to avoid disappointing them; or they may lose interest.

Because of the ways in which we work, projects will come about in a variety of ways, for example:

•   someone has a 'bright idea' about which they are enthusiastic and we latch on to their idea;
•   in conversation with those with whom we work, we begin to see a way in which a project might create an opportunity or meet a particular need;
•   in developing a programme for our centre or club, we try out some ideas for a project which we hope will catch members' imagination;
•   a source of money becomes available and we try to think about a useful way of using it;
•   we attempt to extend the work of our agency by undertaking some research and developing a project;
•   we work with other agencies who have identified an issue or problem they wish to tackle.

Doing projects has to be a mixture of science and art: we must be both rational and creative, logical and reflective, analytical yet opportunistic, prepared to lead and able to 'go with the flow'. So we need some adaptable tools and techniques for thinking our way through the complexities. Perhaps we should return to the two projects we considered earlier in order to illustrate the process.

Case Study 1 involves a group of young people following a dance project that they have thought up themselves. The youth worker responds to the idea. What then, is the 'need' to which she is responding? We can subject her decision to support their project to some analysis. Some of the observations and questions in the chart below may serve to uncover the processes involved.

A number of points arise here that we can apply to other projects. First, our practice is guided by the way in which we, and our agencies, view our purpose. In this case, as we saw earlier (Case Study 1 Revisited), the worker's intentions arise partly from policy (Local Agenda 21 and its intentions for democracy and participation), and partly from her own professional knowledge, skills and values.

Second, we have to think ahead in order to see what will be needed for the project to work: the resources (skills, money, time, equipment); the motivation of those who will be involved. Can we do it? Will their interest be sustained? Have we helped them to think about the consequences?

Table 15.1 Analysis of Case Study 1, the dance group

Worker's observations	Questions
Young people do not have a strong voice or presence in the community. Their achievements are not recognised. This leads to the community ignoring their concerns and aspirations.	What are the reasons that young people are not heard? Does the agency believe it should be attempting to advocate on their behalf?
	How might a dance project have an impact and on whom? The young people involved? Other young people? The wider community?
	Will the intended impact be helpful? What messages will the project convey about young people? For example, might it unintentionally confirm in adults' minds that young people are only interested in 'trivial' things like dancing to pop music? Or might it deflect attention away from other important issues?
	If the intended project is to bring benefits to young people in the town, what will need to be done in addition to simply helping them to form a dance group? Is that what they want – or do they just want to dance?
This group of young people appears enthusiastic to learn to become a dance group. They would like some help from me and my agency.	How real is their enthusiasm? Might it just be fleeting?
	As well as learning to dance together, what else might they gain from the project, e.g. a range of other skills?
	I can help them simply by offering some space at the youth centre. Should I be offering more? What do they really need? Am I the best person to help – or could I just put them in contact with someone else, e.g. a dance teacher? What resources will I need?
In order for the project to achieve some useful objectives, I will need to make some agreements a) with the group, and b) with my agency.	How might helping the group further my agency's objectives?
	If the project is to have wider impact, how will it need to proceed? For example, who does the group need to have contact with, how will it need to present itself? What are the implications for the way I would need to work?
	What will be my role? How much time should I offer? Can we agree a basis for my involvement – at least to begin with – with a possibility of reviewing my role in a few weeks' time? If not, can I at least be helpful so as not to dampen their enthusiasm?

Third, we need to be clear about the role we will take in the project. What will the group need from us if the project is to succeed? What is our judgement about the group's readiness – its internal resources of skills, knowledge and ideas, its ability to maintain itself? How can our involvement enable the group's resources to grow?

These initial questions guide our decision to develop (or support) a project:

- What is the need as we perceive it?
- What purposes and policies will be fulfilled?
- What are the intended benefits, including learning?
- What opportunities are available (or can be developed)?
- What resources will be required (and can be obtained)?
- What will be my (and my agency's) role, and who needs to agree?

Q9: Return to Case Study 2. Draw up your own chart, as in the example above, listing the observations which might have guided the decision to develop the programme, and the questions that need to be asked, based on the list above.

Case Study 2 is an interesting example. Here, the youth agency concerned did not simply have to ask itself critical questions about the need identified, the intended benefits and impact, but also to think hard about the approach it would adopt and the resources required. This led the agency to pilot the programme in one or two schools before proceeding. From its evaluation, it learned that its first idea was not sufficiently developed: if it was to make a difference to young people's lives, the programme needed to be longer and there had to be opportunities built in for the young people to be supported after the initial course.

The agency also needed to ask questions about its role: what does a youth work agency bring to this issue which means that it is best placed to intervene? Its decision to go ahead was based on the conviction that it could promote learning for these young men that might not otherwise be available to them. This raised questions about how schools would use the programme: for example, did the young people come to the programme under pressure from teachers? This had implications for how the project was designed, as well as raising fundamental questions about whether it should be offered at all.

We need to think critically about the nature of need: what are its causes, whose perceptions are at work? And if we have doubts about a project but still wish to proceed, can we do so in a way that allows us to adjust plans or change tack once we know more? For example, we might agree that there will be a review point after a few weeks, or that we will only commit limited resources in the first instance. The bigger the project, the more important it is to get things right. This is one aspect of what is often referred to as 'cost–benefit analysis'.

Planning the project and setting objectives

Let us assume that you have now made a decision to go ahead with your project. This means that you have:

- a clear analysis of a need;
- a clear purpose and aim;
- an idea for pursuing the project.

How good our idea is will be central to the success of our project. This is the creative side of our work. It doesn't matter how careful is our analysis of need, or how clear our aim. If people are not attracted to the idea, if it does not win their enthusiasm, it is unlikely to work. Sometimes, we will be able to hitch our plans to their enthusiasm (as in Case Study 1); at other times, we might need to stimulate them to come up with a good idea, or enthuse them with our own. Whichever way we do it, though, a 'trigger' for the project will be needed.

At the same time, we have to recognise that the idea is not in itself the purpose, only the *medium* through which the need identified is to be met, and the aim to be fulfilled. It is the *how*, not the *what* or *why* of our plan.

Before we go much further, we will want to try out our idea to see whether it is likely to get support: from the people we are working with, from our colleagues, and perhaps others too. We will want to encourage as much talking about the idea as we can. There is little point in devising a detailed project plan if the idea turns out to be a dud, so a little 'market-testing' may save a lot of wasted time and energy. In testing the idea, it will usually get better as others' ideas begin to be included.

By now we can assume that there is a viable project idea: we believe it will work. So we are ready to undertake some detailed planning. That will mean devising the objectives which the project will meet: the specific things the project will achieve. Who is going to do this and how will it be done? These are important questions because they demand that we think both about the outcome of our work (in this case, the outcomes of the project), as well as the process by which it will be achieved. We can think back to Case Study 2 in order to illustrate this issue. The youth work agency involved devised the anger management programme with other agencies concerned with young people's welfare. A project group drawn from the agencies devised the objectives.

In this sort of project, there is a strong emphasis upon curriculum. The objectives define what participants will learn – and will reflect perceptions and values held by the agencies and their (adult) workers about young people. In this case, young people themselves are not closely involved in devising the project and setting its objectives. They may have been involved at an earlier stage, but the project is essentially adult-led (i.e. educator-led). This further illustrates my earlier point: the central idea of the project is only the means by which purposes are fulfilled. There may be many other ways that the same overall aim of helping young people to manage their anger could have been tackled, for example through a peer-led project. The agency's view is that the approach it has agreed is, in some way, the most likely to achieve its purpose.

In devising project objectives we are enacting the principles and values by which we work. In Case Study 2, young people are involved by ensuring that they have a clear idea about what the programme will offer, and by trying to ensure that their participation is voluntary. A contract or agreement with each young person is made before the programme begins. Once they are involved, the programme then gives the young people some control over its content: a broad and agreed framework is set for the learning, then particip-ants choose its focus so that it best meets their particular needs. Dialogue and negotiation is built in to what are broadly pre-defined parameters.

Contrast this with Case Study 1. There, the worker might help the group to identify the objectives to be met. Some may be identified only once the project is under way, for example when the group realises that in order to maintain itself, members need to think more about group processes. It is a much more fluid and organic project. Learning opportunities arise from the task (developing a dance group and putting on a performance), rather than learning itself providing its basis. In Case Study 1 the worker is asking: how can I enable learning to arise from the task? In Case Study 2 the workers are asking: what tasks can we devise which will enable learning to take place?

From this discussion it should be clear by now that in pursuing projects we are likely to use a range of educational interventions, and that these will be reflected in any project plan we devise. There may be an educator-led or learner-led emphasis, but we will wish to pursue approaches which offer as much opportunity for learner autonomy as possible, consistent with our intentions and purposes. This has implications for the approach we take to planning: the extent to which we can engage people in the devising the project, or setting the objectives.

Each of the six questions we used in creating a plan (p. 201) can be approached so that group members take primary responsibility for following them through. Or the educator may do the planning, with learner influence designed to occur at a later stage. So, in planning the project we can ask:

Who will:

1 identify need and examine whether or how this can or should be met?
2 decide whether meeting the need identified fits the purposes of the agency?
3 decide whether meeting this need is a priority when compared with other work?
4 draw up a draft project plan including the objectives to be met, the time-scale and the success criteria?
5 identify and obtain the resources which will be required to implement the plan?
6 gain agreement for the project plan?

And *how* will we assist them?

Asking these questions at the planning stage says much about whose project this is and the educative role we are adopting.

Managing the project

Much of this section of the chapter has been about thinking through purpose, role and task: what we are attempting to do, and how we will approach it. Managing the project is about following these through, paying attention at each stage to the same questions. Just as in project planning, we are attempting to build mutuality – shared ownership – into the process, so we will wish to do this in project management.

Of course we want to ensure that projects are completed satisfactorily, but not at the expense of people's learning, growth and autonomy. We will want to adopt a role which reflects what we are trying to achieve, including learning about core values of virtue, equality and fairness, caring for others, identity and self-esteem. That means striking a careful balance between completing the project task and paying attention to questions of process and learning: *how* the task will be completed. We are reminded of the triangle mentioned earlier – the balance between maintaining the *task*, the *group* and the *individual.* An enabling role does not mean paying less attention to task completion, but thinking through how it can be achieved in ways which build confidence and maximise learning for those involved. This is the balance between what Herschel Prins referred to as the *enabling* and *ensuring* functions (in Marken and Payne 1987: 37), and there are potential conflicts between them.

The chart opposite summarises this balance.

The left side of Table 15.2 shows a simple management process. Although it appears as a series of linear steps, in reality we may need to revisit earlier steps as the project proceeds. So for example, questions raised about resources may mean going back to adjust the objectives. Or if we discover that problems are arising for some members of the group, we may need to stop one part of the task while we pay attention to process.

Each of the steps on the left is necessary for a project to be managed successfully. Depending upon its nature, time-scale and complexity, some may be more important than others, but all will need to be present in one form or another, even in simple projects. Think of a relatively straightforward project such as running a workshop on 'young women and the media'. You might expect it to take quite a bit of *planning*, but there may be few opportunities to *monitor and adjust.* Nonetheless, when participants begin to show signs of boredom, or an unanticipated issue emerges, the project managers will need to make a quick decision about how to respond. In more long-term projects, monitoring and adjusting will take place regularly and may result in revising plans and possibly even rethinking the purpose.

We must not assume, however, that for management to take place, we (informal educators) must do all, or indeed any, of the managing. Again, it is a question of role: what responsibility are we to take for the project's success? Can we fulfil the ensuring function without taking control and undermining the core principles and purposes of informal education? How best can we perform our educational role?

The right side of the chart suggests some of the questions we might ask of ourselves in planning and running a project. The key idea is simply this: ensuring (a management function) does not have to mean *doing.* I can choose to ensure by *enabling* instead of controlling. In doing so I do not relinquish my responsibility to try to make things happen successfully, but choose a role for myself which gives the group as much control over its own destiny as I can. I support group members' growth and development most by recognising that:

> People . . . learn social and political responsibility only by experiencing that responsibility . . . by actively participating.

> (Freire 1974: 36)

Table 15.2 The balance between enabling and ensuring

Ensuring function	Enabling function: think about
Clarify purpose	Whose need? How is it to be defined, and by whom? What benefits? Whose perceptions will inform our intentions? How will the project fulfil the purpose? How does the project purpose fit with informal education principles? What values are reflected? Who needs to own the project? How can I act to enable their ownership? Have I negotiated a clear role for myself/my agency? How will my role support the group's learning? How will policies, e.g. equality, confidentiality, health and safety, be enacted?
Set objectives	What objectives? Who will set them and how? Who else needs to be involved, and how? Do they reflect the right balance between task and learning-related objectives? Are they achievable? By when? Can we develop a useful learning framework or curriculum?
Identify resources	What resources will be needed? What resources are available? What resources does the group have? How can these be enhanced, e.g. through supporting group learning? How can I help the group to use its own resources? How can I help it to identify what further resources will be required? What do they need from me?
Plan	What steps are required in order to complete the project? How can I support the group to do its own planning? Does the group make clear, shared decisions? What decisions might I need to reserve for myself? Can these be negotiated? How does the plan allow for learning to take place?
Organise and develop	What skills in organising does the group have? Are the group's own roles clear and helpful? Are relationships in the group helping it to achieve? In what ways are power issues being dealt with? Is the group communicating well? How best can I support them?
Monitor and adjust	How will the group measure its progress and make decisions about next steps? Is the group on track? Is the group creating space for itself to reflect? Can mistakes, issues and problems be aired? In what ways can I assist?
Evaluate	How will the group know what it has achieved? Is there a clear end-point in sight? How can I assist the group to gain a sense of achievement? How can individual and group learning be recognised and acknowledged? What next? How can I help them to build on their achievements and to move on? What next for me and my agency? What have we learned? What impact on the need? What should we do as a result?

When we work with people we become part of the complex web of roles within the group. The role we adopt as informal educator sits alongside and interacts with their roles. If the educator's management role is to be complementary, it must enable group members to assume responsibility for what happens, to take as much control as possible. We can then attend primarily to the opportunities for learning which the project presents: by encouraging group members to reflect upon and learn from and about themselves, other group members, and the task in which they are engaged. In that way we build in the mutuality and reciprocity that we seek.

Further reading

For the original research on groups which gave rise to some of these ideas about patterns of group behaviour, read Argyle, M. (1972) 'The nature of social relationships 1–1', in *Social Relationships*. Buckingham: Open University Press.

For a more recent discussion of group processes and dynamics in the social welfare field you could read Chapters 1 and 2 in Vernelle, B. (1994) *Understanding and Using Groups*. London: Whiting and Birch Ltd.

For an extended discussion of groupwork methods you could again read Vernelle (1994) *Understanding and Using Groups*, Chapter 4; or Brown, A. (1992) *Groupwork*, 3rd edn. Aldershot, Ashgate Publishing Ltd, Chapter 1.

For a detailed discussion of project planning in the field of adult education you could read Brookfield, S. (1986) *Understanding and Facilitating Adult Learning*. Buckingham: Open University Press, Chapters 7 and 9.

References

Argyle, M. (1972) *Social Relationships*. Buckingham: Open University Press.

Argyle, M. (1991) *Cooperation. The Basis of Sociability*. London: Routledge.

Brookfield, S. (1986) *Understanding and Facilitating Adult Learning*. Buckingham: Open University Press.

Brown, A. (1992) *Groupwork*, 3rd edn. Aldershot: Ashgate Publishing Ltd.

Butler, S. and Wintram, C. (1991) *Feminist Groupwork*. London: Sage.

Davies, B. (1975) *The Use of Groups in Social Work Practice*. London: Routledge and Kegan Paul.

Dewey, J. (1916) *Democracy and Education*. New York: Macmillan.

Freire, P. (1974) *Education: The Practice of Freedom*. London: Writers and Readers Publishing Cooperative.

Gibson, A. and Clarke, G. (1995) *Project-Based Group Work Facilitator's Manual: Young People, Youth Workers and Projects*. London and Bristol, Pennsylvania: Jessica Kingsley Publishers.

Hare, A.P. (1962) *Handbook of Small Group Research*. New York: Free Press, quoted in Douglas, T. (1976) *Groupwork Practice*. London: Tavistock/Routledge.

Harris, V. (ed.) (1994) *Community Work Skills Manual*. Newcastle: Association of Community Workers.

Jeffs, T. and Smith, M. (1996) *Informal Education: Conversation, Democracy and Learning*. Derby: Education Now Publishing Co-operative Ltd.

Kunstler, P. (1955) *Social Group Work in Great Britain*. London: Faber and Faber.

Marken, M. and Payne, M. (eds) (1987) *Enabling and Ensuring*. Leicester: National Youth Bureau/Council for Education and Training in Youth and Community Work.

Mullender, A. and Ward, D. (1991) *Self-Directed Groupwork*. London: Whiting and Birch Ltd.

Payne, C. and Scott, T. (1985) *Developing Supervision of Teams in Field and Residential Social Work*. London: National Institute for Social Work.

Payne, M. and Merton, B. (2000) *Louder Than Words: Youth Work and Learning for Sustainable Development*. Leicester: Youth Work Press.

Smith, M. (1994) *Local Education: Community, Conversation, Praxis*. Buckingham: Open University Press.

Vernell, B. (1994) *Understanding and Using Groups*. London: Whiting and Birch Ltd.

Young, K. (1999) *The Art of Youth Work*. Lyme Regis: Russell House Publishing.

Part IV

Developing professional practice

Introduction

Linda Deer Richardson

This final Part, 'Developing professional practice', considers aids to professional development which we can make use of in order to be effective and responsive educators. The main 'helps' discussed in this section are managerial skills; participative research; supervision; and evaluation. All of them involve workers joining with others to develop their own practice in different ways.

'Managing work' looks at the varied modes of work undertaken by informal educators and suggests ways in which they can be managed so that workers can meet their commitments and produce quality work. Professor Ted Milburn uses his own experience and research into the ideologies and attitudes of youth workers to offer practical advice which, unlike most management models, is based on the realities of work with people.

Researching your own practice is an obvious, but often neglected, method of seeking understanding. It need not be a solitary task. Using her own research as a case study, Alison Tomlin explains in ' "We become experts": working with basic education students as researchers' how her students came to be involved in her research, as experts in what it meant to be students. The result was that they developed a clearer understanding of their role as students and she learned things that she could not have learned in any other way about student expectations of her as a tutor.

The next two chapters, 'Using line management' and 'Using supervision for professional development' compare the aims and advantages of managerial and non-managerial supervision. Annmarie Turnbull places the supervision which workers receive from their line managers within the wider context of learning organisations and of personal and organisational change. She considers the needs of the supervisee and outlines the purposes and processes of managerial supervision. Janet Woods explores the principles that underlie the model of supervision used by the YMCA George Williams College in its qualifying training and emphasises the importance of effective supervision for trainee and practicing informal educators. The chapters share a practical emphasis on helping readers to evaluate their existing supervision arrangements and decide what changes, if any, are needed.

In the final chapter, 'Evaluation of informal education', Alan France argues that evaluation should be seen as an essential component of 'reflective practice'. His own research has revealed the fears and resistance with which educators often view evaluation, seeing it as an intrusive requirement imposed by outside bodies. Turning this argument around, France argues for the benefits of evaluation to educators themselves and those they work with, and explains what evaluation is, why we should evaluate, and how we can do so effectively.

Particular opportunities for professional development will vary with the work setting. But these chapters provide a checklist of the support mechanisms which should be available to every worker. Such support shows a practical commitment to the value of educators as learners and to the principles of informal education as a whole.

16 Managing work

Ted Milburn

The work of the informal educator with young people is demanding and challenging. It is conducted in a range of contexts and covers person- and group-centred processes, organisation, administration and project development.

In this chapter we look at the modes of work of the educator and consider their implications for managing our commitments.

This item uses some quotations from workers.

Introduction

Whether you work in an agency where you are the only full-time informal educator, or in a project where you have responsibility for the management of others, the importance of managing work satisfactorily is central to your success. You will want to do this well, in a way which seems natural and in keeping with the ethos of your profession and agency. If it is your own work which you are managing, you will be eager to ensure that you plan for effectiveness, progress and growth. Where you are responsible for the support and supervision of others, you will have similar aims in mind to negotiate with them. In both cases, these will need to be set within the stated aims and ethos of the organisation or agency with which you work.

Unfortunately many of the models which appear in the literature concerning the tasks of management and the skills required are aimed at and borrowed from industrial and commercial settings. They can appear over-formalised, embedded within complicated systems, and bureaucratic in the extreme. The essence of my own approach to managing work is to locate it within a series of intentions:

- looking ahead;
- identifying where we are going;
- balancing competing work demands;
- achieving results together.

These management intentions fit closely to the nature and style of our work with people, and are sympathetic to its unique nature. We explore the implications of this approach in the following sections.

Looking ahead

If you are driving a car on a relatively long journey, it is prudent to check a road map to identify the junctions and roads which you will need to take in order to reach your destination efficiently and, hopefully, on time. You may even predict that on stretches of narrow road you will travel slower and on dual carriageways you might be quicker. Some may even check the motoring organisations for weather forecasts and road reports in order to predict potential hazards. If you have vision, you will also check to see if you can make the journey as well, or better, by public transport. Do you have enough money to make the journey as planned? Can you, or should you, take others with you?

The same principles apply to managing work within your own agency or organisation. On a regular and on-going basis we have to engage in the debate concerning the nature and range of our 'destinations'. This will involve consideration of the significant trends in the communities we work within, changes in population, housing, social conditions; and changes in need amongst those with whom we work. Other 'players' may enter the same work as ourselves, in the same communities. All of these will and should have implications in relation to the work which we feel we ought to be doing and what it is we are trying to achieve. In addition, even if we are still convinced that the 'destinations' are the same, ought we to continue to use the familiar methods to get there? To use the travelling metaphor again, there is a story told of a tourist, driving in the Northumbrian countryside who loses his way. Stopping a shepherd by the roadside, he asks for directions to Alnwick. The shepherd replies, 'I can give you directions to Alnwick, but if I were you, I wouldn't go from here!'

As a result of this periodic examination of purposes and direction, hopefully conducted with colleagues and others in your management committee who have lively, innovative and challenging opinions, you may need to adjust or significantly change the work you do. This has obvious implications for you managing your work.

Identifying where we are going

By carrying out the analysis above, your organisation should have clear and relevant statements about the aims, policies and strategies it is planning to pursue. Hopefully your job remit will in some way exemplify these by specifying tasks and roles for yourself and other workers. This job remit will clearly prescribe the areas of work for which you will be responsible, but they are notorious for including the catch-all paragraph at the end saying something like 'and all other duties which from time to time may be specified by the Director of Education (or Management Committee)'.

The identification of where we are going is therefore likely to be partly enshrined in policies and statements of organisational objectives. In all social organisations involved with informal education, there are always more than a few 'destinations' or organisational work targets. Organisational objectives characteristically concern such desired outcomes as meeting needs, creating programmes, raising funds, building the organisation, recruiting staff, training and supporting volunteers. There are many pieces of work to be achieved, some larger than others in scale. Some are different in kind. One objective might relate to the practical development of a counselling service for young people, whereas another might concern the creation of a welcoming atmosphere for young people, parents and members of the community.

It has been my experience that, too often, statements of objectives have

been seen as presentational documents, required by higher levels of management as evidence of planning activity. I suspect that sometimes there is an intention to control and to use them as a device to ensure accountability. Having said that, there is precious little evidence to show that many organisations use them as working documents for the purposes around which they are going to be most useful – for managing work and achieving desirable outcomes!

Some who work with people in social organisations reject the use of objectives, often because of the criticisms highlighted above. I believe that by writing and working to objectives, we achieve a number of significant advantages.

- It is a way of making clear to a wider audience what we intend to do, and of recruiting fellow travellers.
- It is a way of dividing your intentions into work-sized sections which relate to timescales and your available resources.
- Your line managers agree your work schedule – disputes about priorities are avoided or minimised.
- You can see the extent and degree of progress on each objective and determine whether you are falling behind.
- If well written, they specify outcomes, necessary tasks, timescale and which workers are responsible for which sections.
- Monitoring and evaluation of success or otherwise is facilitated.
- Once written, they protect you from going off course, or from having to take on new work which has not been agreed within the approved plan.

In order to achieve these advantages, objectives have to be SMART (Specific, Measurable, Achievable, Realistic and Time-limited) and the ability to write good objectives comes with practice. Anyone can write objectives which are easy to achieve. Conversely, objectives which are too demanding and do not take the capabilities of the worker/s or resource issues of the organisation into consideration can be crippling and will be counterproductive. It follows that you therefore only write the number of objectives which you and your colleague feel it is realistic to achieve in a given timescale. They are central to managing work successfully (Leigh 1985: 3).

Objectives are particularly helpful in managing work, where a colleague or line manager uses these as the basis for periodic meetings with you to review progress, the methods being used and what support and assistance you may require.

Balancing competing work demands

Managing work is not something over which we have total control ourselves. It is not an activity which happens in a vacuum, separated from other organisational behaviours around us. It is achieved within a cultural context where people have ideas, beliefs and values concerning the way we should undertake our work. Most importantly we have very strong ideas ourselves. One of the most significant areas in the study of the sociology of work and organisations is the way in which the values and attitudes which workers hold about their job interact with other cultural factors in the work place (O'Donnell 1997: 267). There is considerable evidence to support the view that where there is discontinuity between deeply-held professional ideals of individual staff and the culture of the organisations within which they are obliged to work, there is fall-out. Observe the debates about teachers, nurses and other professionals leaving their jobs, burning out and in some cases adopting defensive work practices.

For these reasons, it is imperative that the main modes of working around which informal educators organise should be embedded in the job remits for youth workers which we discussed earlier. Inappropriately conceived and written job remits make the management of work more difficult. Management committees, managers and those employing educational youth workers require to have an understanding of the nature and styles of work which are intrinsically linked to the values and principles of education within youth work settings.

Smith (1994) highlights six modes of work, which emerged from research which he undertook with practitioners working in local communities. These modes of work were described as ways of doing or being which arose out of the way in which local educators interpreted the interaction between purpose, roles, issues and strategies (Smith 1994: 92). The modes were:

- being about;
- being there;
- working with individuals in groups;
- doing projects;
- doing administration and research;
- reflecting on practice.

These modes of work are different from each other in substance and in context. Those which rely upon relatively informal and unstructured contact with young people, such as being about and being there, are more susceptible to unplanned calls upon the time and attention of the worker. By their nature they are not so easy to structure in advance. The outcomes can lead to even more demands upon the worker's time, to support, encourage and help young people in a number of ways, at the time or in the future. To a lesser extent the same applies to working with individuals in groups. Link these facts with the likelihood that many workers see these modes as being central inspirations for their own entry into work with young people, and we have a profound incentive for them to emphasise these aspects of their work over other competing claims for time. A detached worker in my own research indicated:

> *This is where I like to be, on the streets, meeting kids. This part of the work gives me a buzz and I would rather be doing this than anything else. Recording, admin, writing letters are things that I tend to leave till the last minute . . .*

The requirement for sufficient time

Accepting that preference for types of work might in some way affect our capacity to effectively balance competing demands, it is important to remember that the educational aspects of our work require substantial periods of commitment. Without this allocation of time, we cannot do our jobs effectively, as the nature of our work with socially excluded young people requires a particular quality of relationship.

The importance of 'being around' and 'being there' cannot be over-emphasised. Apart from demonstrating openness to young people and inviting their conversation, opinions and views on a number of issues which are important to them, it helps you to stay in touch. Being around and there in this manner ensures that you are picking up on clues relating to peer group understanding, emerging friendships, young peoples' concerns, and ideas for potential projects. It is also an invaluable opportunity for young people to better understand you as a person – itself an integral part of a growing relationship about mutual learning (Furlong *et al.* 1997: 45).

Everything we do in this aspect of our work is geared towards processes which assist young people to grow in self-esteem and self-confidence and to become empowered (Hendry *et al.* 1993: 58). It is a matter of fine judgement as to how much you actually do *for* young people and how much *with* them. Central to the whole process is the objective that they will also be empowered to do things for themselves, when they are ready. In being there with young people you will clearly be making judgements about the extent to which you will, for example, accompany young people to courts, colleges, housing departments or to meet public officials. For many adults, let alone young people, these situations are frightening and challenging. There is a role for the educator to help young people to develop strategies which they themselves can use in these contexts. There is also the need for you to be there with them in many settings or situations. All of this demands a substantial allocation of time to allow these processes to develop.

Working with individuals in groups also takes time. It almost always involves a more prolonged relationship with individuals and groups than 'being there' and 'being around'. It is at the heart of the learning process, and you may not be able to predict in advance the journey which you will travel with the young person. Because of this, it also has to be managed in the work setting. Time out taken from everyday working activities such as administration or project development has in some way to be predicted and managed. Because of this you will want to maximise your time by working collaboratively with other full-time, sessional and volunteer colleagues to cover for each other when new opportunities are deemed to arise which unexpectedly require a quick response. Over time, the planning of counselling sessions, group work opportunities and the assisting of young people to follow new enthusiasms, activities and learning can be pre-planned. You also need to be able to respond to the unexpected opportunity for learning. Some excellent practical examples of managing competing demands of this kind of work can be found in Jeffs and Smith (1996).

Doing admin and research

In my current research concerning youth workers, ideology and practice, a number of workers express concerns about managing this aspect of their work:

> *I'm pressed all the time for returns and reports. These are not only for the youth work that I am doing. I'm asked to make comments upon grant applications by voluntary organisations; attend area liaison committee meetings and act as secret-*

ary; submit statistics; contribute to departmental reports on the social strategy; write numerous proposals for extra funding. We become clerks for the Chief Executive!

I came into this work to be with people. Admin keeps me away from group work. For parts of some evenings I am forced to work in the office and this must give young people the feeling that I am unapproachable or not available to contact. It worries me.

Although Smith's research points to respondents indicating that admin takes up a relative small amount (20 per cent) of the overall time spent by the educator (Smith 1994: 97), there is some impressionistic evidence in Scotland that this figure is higher. Community educators report that, following the disaggregation of large regional councils to smaller, relatively underfunded local authorities, there has been an overall cutback in staff and resources. With the growth of contracted work for voluntary youth organisations there has also been an increase in the demand for administration and management of resources.

All of this points to the fact that administration and management are essential aspects of the work of the educator. The results of that management and administration can also be used to persuade funders, line managers, elected officials and others in the community of the importance of the work. It can be the vehicle for advocating on behalf of young people.

It is a mistake to see administration and management as an unfortunate interference in our real work 'which is with people'. If carried out efficiently and effectively, it can be a very persuasive vehicle for transmitting the true nature of our work. It can often be the bedrock upon which group relationships are either enhanced or, in some cases, diminished or destroyed. I well remember as a youth worker on the South Coast taking part in a canoeing weekend on the River Wye with fifteen young people, where the organising staff member had forgotten to book the canoes at our destination point. From an atmosphere of positive and relaxed expectation as we travelled in prospect of a good weekend, the mood deteriorated into one of dismay, conflict and recrimination. Good group work is not all about personal relationships!

Careful planning is important if you are to carry out these tasks efficiently and allow yourself both time and the appearance of being available for young people. Administration should be conducted as far as possible when young people are not usually around – perhaps in the early morning of each day. Larger scale administrative tasks which you know about should be timetabled in advance so that you deal with them over time. They should not be left as crisis tasks which block out large periods of time and availability. It is a testing challenge, but well worth the effort, to develop the skill of one-touch administration. Instead of reading letters or reports and putting them to one side to be dealt with later, you should try to reply to them at once. The use of hand-held dictation machines is a time-saving skill to develop. While word processing and typing for ourselves is of value, it is wasteful of time if dedicated secretarial support is made available elsewhere.

Achieving results together

This requires you to find productive ways of working with others to save time, work more effectively and maximise your combined skills so that the work is managed more appropriately. Businesslike and time-limited meetings and appointments; divisions of labour; recruiting volunteers; finding quiet places where detailed work can be undertaken without interruption are key aspects. It is also important to find someone to reflect with you on your current practice in work management and other aspects of your role.

Unless we reflect upon the professional practice we undertake, the other modes of working which we highlighted earlier are increasingly likely to be lacking in direction and focus. While reflection implies 'thinking about' the activities and processes of our professional life, it also relies upon a record. Most of us are pretty good at thinking about our job. As we drive or walk home from work, in quiet moments while reading or listening to music and often at night – we think about our job! We sometimes feel we wish we could release ourselves from it! This form of thinking, however, is haphazard and often related to the present importance of pressures or problems. The kind of reflection we seek from the educator would be something which is much more systematic. It is based upon the keeping of a written record of key aspects of our work – not just those which are causing us difficulty.

These recordings need to be written in a reflective and analytical way, refreshing our memory about the circumstances and the details of social interactions and the development of our work. When used to reflect over a period of time, they are a constant reminder of the inadvisability of making judgements on first impressions! They allow us to consider our intentions, the methods we use, the way we balance the competing demands of our work and the observed results and outcomes of our relationships and professional behaviour. It is possible to reflect upon our effectiveness and where, in future approaches, we should change.

These reflections upon recordings can make significant differences in the way we sharpen our professional capability. They are enhanced even further if we can do that in the company of another colleague who might bring an alternative point of view, a degree of challenge, and an understanding but critical judgement. It is unlikely that such a supervisory relationship will be suggested by our employers, except for normal line management purposes. We should choose this colleague personally. In this manner we have the opportunity of reaching someone who is emphatic, objective and who can bring some independent reflection to the discussion.

Most importantly, this action/recording/reflection discussion can be the power house for an on-going analysis of your work and the management of time and professional commitment. Competing demands upon your time can be explored; new directions entertained; unhelpful work habits identified; tricks of the trade shared. Most of the management techniques I have learned have been from other colleagues whose opinion and example I valued.

Emphasising performance

The burden of my argument so far has been that it is essential to manage the contrasting elements of our work so that we can carry out our role as an informal educator. Emphasis upon managing work is, however, worthless if the result is that you become effective at producing systems and managing your time, but the work which you do is of low or mediocre quality. Our aim is therefore to manage work for effective performance.

In fieldwork at present there is a culture of development planning and of the evaluation of work through the measurement of performance indicators (PIs). Performance indicators are one approach to evaluation (McConnell 1996: 319). Early examples of written PIs have been somewhat formalised statements of quality, which often do not seem to sit easily in many of the informal contexts in which we work. In addition, they have tended to emphasise measurement and until recently have not touched seriously upon ethos, atmospheres or the affective domain.

There has been considerable fear that this emphasis would place an inordinate pressure upon workers to do things whether they were relevant or not. Secondly it has been feared that in the measurement of activity, it would be numbers, project size and public relations acceptability which would be the governing indicator of value, rather than process, quality and group and individual learning. The modes of work which are highlighted earlier in this chapter start at the opposite end of the managerial spectrum to those procedures which lead easily to development planning and pre-set performance indicators. For me, however, they are not mutually exclusive or impossible to combine. Faced with a managerial climate within which development plans are required, the skilled worker can write objectives which deal with the affective domain and with qualitative dimensions of the work. These will reflect the requirement to 'be around', 'be there' and 'work with'. The early performance indicators were invariably quantitative and measurable in size and volume. We are now writing qualitative performance indicators which deal with personal growth and development, ethos, process and group formation. When well written and used properly, they can assist us in managing work for effective performance.

Good practice is not represented as often as it should be in journals and books. Another way in which we can impinge upon the management of work is to write in more considered detail about our work, its difficulties and its high points. Reflective and critical writing of this kind not only helps us to be more certain about professional modes of working which are positive and bearing results. It informs a wider audience and encourages a debate within which ideas are refined and developed. All of these dimensions of reflection should not prevent us from seeking opportunities for reflective discussion with colleagues.

The work of the informal educator is often lonely. It is regularly conducted within a professional atmosphere inhabited by teachers, social workers, the police and others who have different challenges in managing work and may have incomplete understandings of the principles and values which underwrite our practice. Discussions with colleagues who are co-workers can clearly help in building and establishing confidence in our methods of work. In the same way, discussions with colleagues from other professions can help to develop an evaluative dimension to our contribution which ensures more realistic assessments of our work and role.

Conclusion

In all jobs there are moments when crisis overtakes the most effective planning. This can happen at times of organisational change, when new government policies are introduced, when funding is cut or when forward planning is revised. Accepting that is the case, it is still necessary to have a close understanding of the nature of the work of the informal educator and an understanding of the implications for managing it. By keeping yourself informed you can often predict the arrival of these crises and their potential outcomes – and plan for the changes in work demand.

In managing work, we have to ensure that in normal circumstances there is an appropriate balance between the competing modes of work. The appropriate balance is likely to vary with the post and the setting. Each mode is likely to have differential allocations of time. It is apparent that they are all interlinked and that 'working with individuals in groups' and 'doing projects' rely intensely upon those times you will spend 'being around' and 'being there'. Without the emphasis upon communication and conversation, you are in a much more vulnerable position in relation to the development of a 'working with' philosophy and the move towards projects which are meaningful and relevant to young people.

It is clear then that in managing your work you have to ensure that certain conditions are in place. You need to go to the places where young people are. It is important that you make yourself and your work known, and that your purposes are clear. You will plan and manage programmes and projects which demand time. Administration and management tasks have to be handled effectively and efficiently and there has to be space to respond to situations as they develop (Jeffs and Smith 1996: 61). These modes of work are interlinked. Each has its place in the thoughtful way the informal educator will work with young people. An energetic approach to managing your work will order these competing demands and make your work more effective.

Further reading

Leigh, A. (1985) *20 Ways to Manage Better.* London: Institute of Personnel Management. Many of the books on management theory and practice deal in considerable depth with the functions of management and overlook the opportunity to offer clear, succinct, practical advice to the manager. This text is a practical guide which also encourages the manager to think about processes and workable systems. There are twenty sharply written chapters on most aspects of management, but for me the sections on Setting Objectives, Recruitment and Selection, Appraisal and Review, Problem People, Delegation, Controlling your Time and Project Management relate most closely to the informal educator.

Fontana, D. (1993) *Managing Time.* Leicester: The British Psychological Society. Skills in managing work are closely related to our capability in managing time. Fontana presents an interesting and entertaining selection of exercises and case studies to help us make an analysis of the ways we perceive, use and manage (or mismanage) time. A range of professional situations are highlighted and supported with some challenging insights into ways to work and plan productively, differentiating between urgent and marginal tasks, professional aims and objectives, and delegation. This book has helped me to make a detailed analysis of my own use of time and encourages thoughtful practice.

Jeffs, T. and Smith, M.K. (1996) *Informal Education: Conversation, Democracy and Learning*. Derby: Education Now Books. Most readers will know this book for its very effective and succinct exposition of the concept and practice of informal education. I am listing it in my reading recommendations because of the practical and helpful final chapter on 'Organising the Daily Round'. This offers a sympathetic but challenging discussion on the issues surrounding balance and emphasis when managing the six basic work modes of informal education. Each is important, and surrounded as they are by competing expectations from young people, colleagues and management committees, they have potential as central influences upon the possible development of role conflict. Jeffs and Smith give helpful ways to manage work in settings where there are multiple demands upon the worker. There are suggestions for relatively straightforward and practical planning steps which improve the management of work.

References

Furlong, A., Cartmel, F., Powney, J. and Hall, S. (1997) *Evaluating Youth Work with Vulnerable Young People*. Edinburgh: SCRE.

Hendry, L., Love, J., Craik, I. and Mack, J. (1993) *Measuring the Benefits of Youth Work*. Aberdeen: Aberdeen University Press.

Jeffs, T. and Smith, M.K. (1996) *Informal Education. Conversation, Democracy and Learning*. Derby: Education Now Limited.

Leigh, A. (1985) *20 Ways to Manage Better*. London: Institute of Personnel Management.

McConnell, C. (1996) *Community Education: The Making of an Empowering Profession*. Edinburgh: Scottish Community Education Council.

O'Donnell, M. (1997) *Introduction to Sociology*, 4th edn. Walton: Nelson.

Smith, M.K. (1994) *Local Education – Community, Conversation, Praxis*. Buckingham: Open University.

Material in this chapter includes unreferenced quotations from workers which are from unpublished research by Ted Milburn into youth worker ideologies and peer group responses.

17 'We become experts'

Working with basic education students as researchers

Alison Tomlin

This chapter will give three stories from research with adult numeracy students in London. First, I will say something about myself, so you know the dilemmas that led me to the research project from which the stories are drawn, and I will describe how the research got started. After that, the stories, with students' and my own comments; and I will be trying to open up the issues and ask how they are relevant for you, in your own context.

I started working as a tutor in adult basic education about twenty-five years ago. I have always hoped I was a radical adult educator – someone who

> aspire[s] to a progressive social and political purpose in their work, who wants change in the original meaning of 'radical', 'from the root'.
>
> (Coben 1998: 3)

Most basic education students have quite different backgrounds, lives and knowledge from mine, and I try to use their knowledge and 'build on strengths' (a slogan from adult literacy work), for example using people's own language or ways of calculating. I invite students to share parts of their personal histories which might be relevant to the course; for example, their experience of schooling, and use students' writing as a basis for group discussion. I negotiate the curriculum, working with students to find topics of common interest for group work, and use teaching materials which directly address issues we might broadly call 'political': wages for manual jobs (a cleaner, say) and high-flyers (footballer, industrialist), the levels of state benefits for single parents, local planning issues (for example, the conversion of a women's hospital to a supermarket), police racism, housing policies.

This kind of agenda is supported by Freirean educators (see, for example, Freire 1985; Mayo and Thompson 1995) but left me (and, of course, students) with a problem: what if their 'topics of common interest' are not the same as mine? Like many tutors, I organise groups so that there is time for individuals' more personal work (for example, writing a letter or appealing against a benefits ruling) – but I still felt uncomfortable.

> *I get bored with your political worksheets.*
>
> (Sandra)

The discomfort came partly from remarks like Sandra's. How could I answer? Do I tell her she 'should' be interested? Do I try to make the worksheets jazzier, better laid out, work harder at finding out what is a 'relevant' topic for her? All these approaches assume that Sandra's lack of interest in political worksheets is a problem, and that the solution is in my hands. That's a key issue in this chapter: who defines the problem? Whose responsibility is it to find the solution?

I was also worried when I felt I didn't really know what was going on in the group. Sometimes people dropped out from courses without letting the group know why. There are endless possible reasons; people's lives may be difficult and complicated, and the course may be much less important to them than whatever else is going on. But it could be my fault – maybe I had failed them in some way. Some people came to the groups but I (and other students, often) felt they were not 'really there': they did the work but didn't seem to be enjoying themselves or committed to group work.

Our commitment to a radical agenda is reflected in our aim to 'strengthen students' voices' and 'empower' students. There have been strong critiques of these positions from poststructuralists and feminists. This is a summary by Carmen Luke:

> [W]e cannot claim one method, one approach, or one pedagogical strategy for student empowerment or for making students name their identity and location ... [W]e are not politically and ethically justified to assume positions of authority on 'negative identities': to assume that we have the power to empower or the 'language of critique' with which to translate student speech and give it back to them in politically correct terms.
>
> (Luke 1992: 48)

Let's unpack this in terms of my teaching, through a rather crude example. If I try to persuade Sandra to be interested in political worksheets, I might say, 'But you're Scottish!' (That is, you come from a 'minority'.) 'You're working class! A single parent! Poor! Exploited at work! And you've got disabilities!' Of course I wouldn't do it so directly – but I think the Freirean version of radical adult education (which has overlaps with 'critical' education) would suggest I should steer the conversation so that Sandra comes to connect these 'truths' about herself with other examples of oppression, and accepts a 'correct' political position.

My description of Sandra is factually 'true'. It's an example of my assuming a position of authority on Sandra's 'negative identities', to quote Luke. Positioning Sandra like this suggests I have authority to decide what educational agenda is 'good for her', and that her own understanding of her situation is inadequate, naive or too personal; she understands her life, perhaps, but not how she fits in the wider political picture. (An aside about the research process: after I wrote the previous paragraph, I read my description aloud to Sandra and asked if I could use it. She said, 'You wouldn't dare say that to me!' She agreed to its inclusion in this chapter when I explained the point it was helping me to make.)

How does a radical adult educator reconcile her politics with her authority in the classroom? A tutor is paid to be 'in charge'; for example, twice during the research I had to decide what to do about accusations of sexual harassment in the classes. To take a less politically loaded example, when I say, 'Shall we look at page three?' everyone does. That particular example will come back in one of the stories I shall tell.

Starting research

For three years I had a grant while I 'gathered data' (more on this later) for a research degree. My first research question was: 'Can writing in basic maths (numeracy) groups help students learn maths and contribute to strengthening students' voices?' and I started by asking all the students I was teaching whether they would be willing to take part. Everyone agreed, but every time I wrote about the data – say, analysing the themes in a tape transcript – I checked whether those particular students agreed both that the material was accurate, and that I could use it. Most students have at some stage refused permission. This is frustrating for me – wonderful nuggets of information, jokes, life stories and so on will not be included in the thesis. But it is extremely important that people trust the researcher not to exploit their experiences – particularly when we claim to 'empower' people.

I soon moved on from my first question about writing. I had found what seemed to be an answer: firstly, 'writing' is not separate from talking, reading or listening; and secondly, writing in maths groups helped some people but not others (an example is that if you have problems with spelling, having to write makes learning maths even harder). The interest in writing, and the data I collected, led me to an interest in classroom *discourse*. Discourse means the ways people use language, but it's a term which includes the power relations behind the language. Thinking in terms of discourse leads, for example, to questions about why everyone agreed to take part in the research – was it because I was their tutor, with considerable control over whether they achieved maths qualifications, for example?

The data was based on my own notes of teaching, copies of students' work, and quickly noting down things students said. Meanwhile I was reading, and the reading helped me identify what I wanted to write down (I didn't expect to be as interested in tea breaks as I later became, for example). Other data includes tape transcripts from classes, interviews with students, and things students told me, or wrote for me and each other, because they thought it useful for the research. I kept a diary where I wrote down anything I thought interesting. As the work continued I fed back my ideas to the students, and invited them to become co-researchers. That step – or series of steps, since it's not easy for me or the students, and is a continuing process – has of itself become a key theme of the research.

> **Q1:** Empowering or stereotyping? Giving a voice or seeking to understand silence? Critical or democratic?

The three stories I shall tell are selected from many. The names are as students wanted – some are pseudonyms, some real. The stories come from two groups, each about eight students meeting once a week for two hours, and from a conference and magazine organised by students from several groups meeting together. Although the stories may seem to be self-contained, the way I tell a story now is informed by all the rest of the research process. Learning to be a researcher has involved reading and re-reading all the data, time and again, to check whether the themes I find are consistent or not; and also searching to see whether I have missed out something just because it didn't neatly fit. Because I was working for a research degree, my data and writing are also discussed by my supervisors and fellow university students. Meanwhile I was also talking to the students in the research project, for example showing one group what another group had said, so they also were able to reflect on the developing pictures and check that my interpretations were consistent with theirs.

Pat and Cathy

The students in this group had been keeping maths diaries each week. Pat and Cathy agreed to be interviewed about their diaries for my research (at the stage when I was interested in *writing*), but I couldn't find time to fit the interview into the class, so they borrowed a tape recorder, spare batteries and a tape and interviewed each other at home. I gave them a list of questions, with a more open one at the end: 'Any advice for tutors or other students?' I meant the advice to be about diary writing, but Pat and Cathy took the opportunity to talk about wider issues.

In the following class, Pat suggested they play the tape to the group. This is part of what we heard:

Cathy: I have enjoyed the course, but sometimes I think it is a bit wishy-washy.
    You get told that you have done very well because you're *almost* right, or on the right tracks.
    But in maths I think you're either right or you're wrong.
    I wish you were told you had got it right, or you had not got it right.
    It's kidding yourself.

Pat: But you are gaining more than you thought you would.
    I think the confidence I do have is because of the teacher.
    Being adults, and having children of our own, and feeling inadequate when our kids come home and we're not able to help them – having the right teacher and being in the right atmosphere and company, it does help.

Cathy: Yes, and maybe that's why the teacher never says, 'You've got that all wrong'. What would be the point?
    You probably wouldn't come back.
    And it's only Basic Maths, perhaps at this stage it's not all that important.

Pat: You feel like you're in the winning *team.*
    Like me, I'm generally a quiet person, but because of the confidence that I feel, from the teacher and the other pupils, I feel it's refreshing my memory.

It was a shock to hear my teaching described as *wishy-washy* (and when other students heard it, there were some appreciative chuckles), but the issues raised here are much deeper than any tutor's discomfort at hearing criticism.

Cathy's description of how I taught was pretty accurate, I thought. My approach to teaching maths was intended to reflect my view of maths itself: that it is socially constructed; there are different ways of getting to solutions; and you are *not* always either right or wrong, as Cathy put it (for more about the social construction of maths see Benn 1997).

Listening to the tape I realised I hadn't got all that 'across' to them. Cathy understood it as tutor kindness (or patronage); and my teaching confirmed for her that she is 'only' at the 'basic stage' of maths. Before the interview, I had thought that both Pat and Cathy were reasonably happy with the class – their diaries seemed content with the teaching, though they were not always pleased with their own work. Playing the tape to the group meant this was not a private word in the teacher's ear; now I wondered what they said about the class in private, with no tape running.

The tape also recorded Pat asking other students to be more regular in attendance, so the criticism was not addressed only to me. We discussed the tape for a few minutes, and it seemed most people agreed with Cathy. We then carried on with the maths class; I had mentally resolved to be less patronising.

Marjorie showed some of her calculations to the group, on the board. She had worked out a conversion from 5 kg to pounds (or lb, a British 'imperial' measurement). One kilogram is 2.2 pounds, and she worked out her calculation like this: $2.2 \times 5 = 10.10$. I started saying, 'Well you're nearly right' – because it's true that 5 kg is about 10 lb. I changed it to, 'No, that's wrong, because…' and I talked about multiplying decimals (the 'correct' answer is 11). Marjorie protested: 'But I'm nearly right!' and the whole group laughed. We then talked more, about my feelings on hearing the tape, Marjorie's feelings when working in front of others on the board, and about right and wrong in maths. So what had I learned?

- We can make available space and time that is not controlled by the tutor, so students can raise their own issues.
- Sharing participants' comments in the group widens the discussion; it changes the discourse of the group.
- It is important that the group should have space to talk about group processes as well as content.
- We should not assume we know 'the truth' because participants tell us something directly (in this case, through diaries). What is said is determined by our relationship (including the authority of the tutor or facilitator); and meanings are not transparent.

How does this fit with the notion of students as researchers? Pat and Cathy knew that I was asking students to take part in the research because I saw them as *experts* – they knew more about students' experience than I ever will. The interview question had asked them for *advice*, so it positions them as knowledgeable people. Extracts from the interview were later included in a magazine called *Global Maths*, which was edited and produced by student researchers, with the hope that the article would raise questions in other groups – so the interview is seen not just as advice to Pat and Cathy's group, but a means to raise the questions more widely and explore other students' views (you can tell even from the short extract here that Pat and Cathy did not entirely agree with each other, so it makes clear that difference of opinion is welcomed).

Q2: How do you know what participants think of your work?
How do you feel if you overhear adverse comments?
How do you make space for people to develop their critiques of their group?
How can participants share their experience with other groups or organisations?

Group class observations

One group needed to do 'data handling', including some sort of survey, for their course certificate. They chose to observe their own class – so this data was not produced directly for the research, but it turned out to be much more useful, for all of us, than just answering the needs of passing the certificate. I brought in some observation schedules, mostly drawn from other researchers' work, assuming the students would perhaps pick one and amend it. In fact they chose to use all six, at the same time, over two classes, I think partly because it seemed 'handy' – there were six students and six schedules. Trevor opted out of doing the observing, and I was given one of the sheets. The schedules were *Tutor's questions*; *Who does the talking?*; *Students' questions*; *Teacher/student interaction*; *Students' responses to the class*; and a timed observation sheet, noting what was happening at ten minute intervals. In the third class, the students amalgamated the tally sheets from the first two. Table 17.1 below shows the collated results of the *Tutor's questions* schedule:

There were four women and two men in the group, yet I asked the men twice as many questions as I asked the women. The next table (Table 17.2 on page 228) shows: *Who does the talking?*

We can see that Theresa, Carol and Joyce all have a higher score for 'talking in a small group': in the group discussion about the observation results, they said they enjoyed working together and helping each other.

I copied all the sheets for the group to read and discuss. The results are not accurate, of course (did you notice how many times I talked to myself?). We had spent most of both classes laughing, as we observed each other observing the group. We taped one of the classes and I transcribed it; that showed up immediately that we all talked far more than the observation

Table 17.1

Tutors questions to . . .	Group	Women	Men
Genuine question – wanting to know the answer	1	8	6
A question to find out if the student knows something		2	11
A question to help the student work something out		3	6
Other sorts of questions	3		3
Totals	4	13	26

Table 17.2

Names	Andy	Alison (Tutor)	Priya	Trevor	Theresa	Carol	Joyce
Talking to the whole class		3		1	1	1	
Talking in a small group or a pair	6			2	9	11	7
Talking to the tutor	4	6	6	6	2		1
Totals	10	9	6	9	12	12	8

schedules had shown. 'Accuracy' in the sense of detailed statistics is not the point, though. Observing the class changed the discourse of the class.

Andy! Write it down – Alison asked Priya a question!

Changes in the discourse of the group

The observation of how much more I talked to the men than the women was right in spirit if not in detail. Both the men had missed a class, and my plan included spending time with them to help them catch up (the group had a tight timetable for completing portfolios of work for examination). But that plan was mine, not the students', and when we discussed the findings of this research, the women said they think men talk more than women, in maths classes. So the research gave them the opportunity to raise issues about gender which they already had in mind, but had not before been able to raise openly. In a later class Carol directly reproved Trevor for taking too much of my time.

Trevor! You're a man! Consider your teacher!

The students noted that Priya didn't seem to talk much. In reply, she said she used to go to speech therapy and is not a talkative person; she also said she doesn't mind others talking, but prefers not to be pushed into group discussions. That was helpful to everyone, I think; I, at least, had wondered if she thought the group work was a waste of time. I had seen Priya as a student who was not 'really there', but it now seemed she saw herself as fully committed to the group, but entitled to her own different ways of expressing herself (her own discourse, in James Gee's terms (1999)).

The *Teacher/student interaction* schedule asked the observer to grade the teacher and student according to various criteria: moving about the room or sitting at a desk, for example, and participative or distant. Andy, the observer, had listed me as *dominant* – not his word, but the one he chose from the sheet. I was horrified – and, as with the Pat and Cathy interview, I was horrified in public since the whole group went through the sheets together. However, the students could not understand my reaction to the observation. Since I was the teacher, they saw a dominant role as entirely appropriate, as distinct from *authoritarian* – a word Andy had not selected from the list.

We became much more self-conscious about the use of questions in the classroom, and particularly tutor's questions. I was already aware, from my own reading, that many 'questions' used by teachers are not seeking information – the common sense idea of the meaning of the word *question*. For example, if someone is stuck on multiplying 24×4 and asks me to help, I might ask one of these questions (depending on my knowledge of the student): 'What's 25×4?' What have you tried so far? What would four lots of £24 be, roughly? (For discussion of patterns of classroom talk, see Cazden 1988.) I expected the students to notice and comment on this. In fact it seems it was so naturalised in the classroom discourse that such questions were often not noted (they showed up more clearly in the transcript, with all the question marks). What they did notice was a quite different kind of question – one that functions to disguise my authority. When I 'ask', 'Shall we look at the worksheet now?' what I mean is, 'Look at the worksheet' – it's an instruction. You probably do the same kind of thing in your own practice; it's not, I hope, a deliberate attempt to manipulate people but something we have grown up with ourselves. Noticing this in our group changed it – so when I asked, during the next few weeks, 'Shall we look at page three?' people laughed and said, 'Is that a question? What happens if we say no?'

Alison: Shall we have a tea break?
Students: You mean you're having a tea break now.

The observations were funny and entertaining, and led to serious and important discussion of group discourse: who can say what, when, and how it is interpreted? These issues revolved around questions of classroom control and authority, and were now up for discussion in the group. I am still 'dominant', but we all became more aware of the ways the dominance works, and of its justification and possible abuse.

This particular piece of research also problematised 'official' research: who does the observing? Is the observer biased? Who decided the questions to address in the research? For example, the students asked why the table showing *Tutor's questions* groups the students by gender. It came from my own view (supported by research I had read, and by the women in this group) that women and men have different relationships to maths and talk differently in classrooms. After doing this research, the students were more critical and inquiring about data used in my teaching materials – so, for example, when I brought in a newspaper report of a government crime survey they wanted to know whether the survey had open or multiple choice questions.

> **Q3:** How would the observation change if the students were divided by:
> - age group;
> - first language;
> - length of participation as a student;
> - ethnicity?
>
> ...and you will be able to think of more categories.

> **Q4:** If you set up observation-based research in your work, how would you decide what to observe?
> What kinds of things might change as a result of the observation?
> Who would write the observation schedule – you, or other participants?

Meeting for maths students for beginners

This was the name of a conference organised by about eight students ('the organisers'). I will give first some information about how the conference was planned, then some of the data from the event itself. The process started when I distributed a leaflet to all the students I knew, because I wanted students to come together to discuss writing (still my central theme at that time); the leaflet invited people to 'help' organise a meeting. It was held in South London; to advertise the conference, the organisers wrote a letter which I distributed to basic education workers in local colleges and community centres, and to other students I knew. The organisers negotiated free use of a community hall, and I used some money from the research grant to pay for food and a crèche, and transport costs for anyone who needed it. Some adult educators have said to me, 'It wouldn't work – basic education students don't see themselves as going to conferences' or 'You must know some amazing students'. I think the conference worked partly because *I gave up feeling responsible.* Because of that, the conference organisers took the decisions – and because they have so much in common with the people they wanted to come, they had the experience on which to base their decision-making.

Compare these two texts:

> **A conference
> for maths students?**
>
> Get involved!
> Help organise a meeting
> for maths students to get together

I hope to organise a conference/for people in adult maths classes.

What use is a conference?
I am working with maths students as a tutor,/and as a researcher.
I am looking into whether writing can help people/learn maths.
A conference would mean/that students could meet each other/and share ideas...

MEETING FOR MATHS STUDENTS FOR BEGINNERS

Please come and join us to discuss your ideas and views on maths. We have discovered that there is more to it than numbers! We have so far learnt some of the inventers who have discovered maths; where maths was discovered; [...] the different ways in which other countries used maths, e.g. Egyptians, Russians. We have found many ways which suit us when we are doing maths. We are no longer afraid of maths. It is now fun to do. Maths is everywhere you go; you deal with it every single day and you might not know it...

I wrote the first to invite students to join the planning group, so it's written by a basic education worker: plain typeface, big print, and line-broken to help those who have reading difficulties. The organisers wrote and typed the second leaflet, to invite people to the conference. It has smaller print, more formal font style and it's also far more positive and inclusive.

From the organisers' leaflet:

> *Maths is in politics; when you go shopping; when you look at the time and when you plan your day.*

From Alison's leaflet:

> *Don't worry if you have never done this sort of thing before . . . As you don't need to be good at reading, writing or spelling.*

I assumed literacy difficulties would hold people back; the student organisers just got on with writing, checking each other's spelling and punctuation as they wrote. At the first of the three planning meetings I had a hand-written agenda, on big paper, including date, venue, crèche, food, topics for discussion and so on. I thought it would take us about two hours; in fact it took 30 minutes, because *everyone agreed with each other* and *everyone volunteered for tasks*. They were better placed than me to make the decisions. For example, two of the organisers were crèche workers; two had disabilities and knew what was needed in a venue; one knew the café workers at the community centre. Professionals, in my experience, take much longer: we have been to conferences before and expect problems as much as success. In my research 'field-notes' after the meeting I wrote to myself, 'Just shut up'.

Students' comments during and after the conference:

> *There was a lovely sort of atmosphere, and warmth. It was as though we all knew each other.*

> *They were very surprised when I told them that one of the trainees did the cooking.*

> *We felt welcomed and comfortable.*

> *The conversation was very interesting and intellectual.*

> *It was useful for both students and tutors to hear the valued ideas and opinions of other students from across the country.*

I didn't learn much about writing in maths groups. The organisers had written their own list of questions to use in small discussion groups, and they didn't mention writing – that is, the agenda for conference discussions was the students' own (though I expect I influenced it). We all did learn a huge amount about what maths students, given an opportunity, say about their past maths experience and their classes. Here I want to mention what I learned about tutors' roles. One tutor (apart from me) came to the conference. The students' invitation had been addressed to students, but she assumed, as many of us do, that she could attend in a support role. These are some comments from organisers after the conference:

Tutors, I thought there was no tutors! At the back please, keep quiet, just take notes, I felt like saying ... [A tutor] kept on asking questions, she was directly looking at me, and do you know what I mean? I felt really intimidated.

(Shazia)

I think the tutor should have took a back seat and let the students interview the students, and just listen to what's being said.

(Jeremy)

Tutors are sort of loudly spoken.

(Lorraine)

I, a tutor, did not see any evidence of domination by the tutor, other than the anger and anxiety generated in the students. Our role as tutors makes us intimidating, however democratic our intentions. The message from the students is that to discuss how maths education should be organised, students need space without tutors there.

> **Q5:** In your work, what 'counts' as research?
> How is it shared, and with whom?

That message, like Pat's and Cathy's interview, has been passed to other groups through the *Global Maths* magazine, which included reports from the conference discussion groups. It has gone as far afield from London as Ghana: one of the organisers, Violet, went on holiday to her home village, taking the magazine. At the village meeting she was invited to talk about what she had found through her research in London, and she chose to compare it to her schooling in the village. Schoolchildren, she said,

> *are getting the answers [in mathematics] but they don't have the understanding. Because of the treatment we had [at school] we couldn't pursue it further.*

What we hear is a 'basic education student' who had been 'failed' at school returning home as a researcher.

Students as researchers

The process of 'writing up' the research for me has involved writing a university thesis. But the writing up of analysis has been a continuous process, sharing and changing texts as we go along. Here is one example. I taped a class in which students read and discussed each other's writing about percentages and fractions. I brought back the transcript for the group to read and check, they approved it, and some will be used in my own writing about students' work on fractions. The tape also included discussion about how to manage the conflicting demands of homework, childcare and paid employment. I edited that section and made it into a new text, again checked and edited by the group, which I then distributed to other students to read and discuss. Later the conference organisers edited it again (with the group's participation), and put it into *Global Maths*. In research terms, we were all engaged in analysis of the original data, and using that to develop new ideas. We have followed this process of returning students' words to them in a wide range of work, from discussion of how to do subtractions to renegotiating course content. In some ways it is similar to the practice of some literacy groups, where the group uses for reading material what their own members have written. It is a central part of the research process, for two reasons.

Firstly, it means our findings are more securely based. Secondly, it helps students get to know each other's opinions and experiences. As tutor I am inevitably 'dominant' ('loudly spoken'); sharing students' spoken or written words helps them develop mutual support networks.

I also brought in examples of outside research into adults' mathematical experience and learning (e.g. Knijnik 1997), to widen the basis of discussion and to make clear that other opinions than mine were welcomed. Having material to discuss from quite different circumstances can offer new ways of considering our own experience.

I have told just three research stories from many. I have learned things about my own and students' practice that I could not have learned through doing the research alone. This work shares some ground with participant action research (Merrifield 1997, 1997; Mulenga 1999), and with New Literacy Studies, where ethnographic research is used to study the practices, including power relations, behind texts (Hamilton, Barton and Ivanic 1993; Barton and Hamilton 1996; Prinsloo and Breier 1996; Barton, Hamilton and Ivanic 2000). The 'action' here is changing the discourse of the learning groups themselves, and the 'literacy' being studied is that of the group themselves. The focus is on processes, ways of talking and power relationships – the discourse of the group.

How does this help with the problems facing radical adult educators? This research with students does not necessarily produce 'radical' courses; some students want to pursue quite traditional learning goals, because they want to do well within the system. It certainly doesn't suddenly make everything alright: aside from anything else, it has been difficult for me to hear criticism (from 'Wishy-washy' to 'Tutors are sort of loudly spoken'). But working with students as researchers means the problems are no longer just mine. It offers a route between two political positions. In the first, the tutors are the radicals and intellectuals, and have responsibility for empowering students. In the second, tutors recognise the different positionings and relations to authority of people in the group, and may be immobilised by wanting to avoid abuse of their own power. Positioning students as researchers challenges these prevailing values. 'Researchers' are experienced in their own field yet want to know more; they build on their expertise to formulate new questions; they share their findings with others; they make proposals for change. Above all, they are intellectuals. Tutors, too, are knowledgeable and inquiring; but rather than somehow donating that knowledge, whether of maths (in my case) or of politics, to students, we can look on the project of developing democratic practices as a shared endeavour with no preset template.

Some of the student researchers have gone on to lead workshops at conferences and university seminars:

> The students in this project are researchers, and have a free hand to organise everything. . . . Sometimes the tutor is a friend; but in some situations the tutor is an authority. At the students' conference and at [the

Research and Practice in Adult Literacy conference] we organised how the group discussed things, and what questions we asked. For example, one older woman at the students' conference was quiet and we wanted to be able to learn from her, so we asked her some questions, and she talked and talked. The room went silent – it was intense listening. We learned so much from her. We become experts listening to students from other centres, and students relate more easily to each other than to a tutor. We are in the same situation.

(Gray *et al.* 1999)

These stories have come from someone working as a maths tutor in London. Your personal histories and politics, institutional settings and personal identifications are different. I don't know what categories are used to define you and the people with whom you work – worker and young people? officer and users? facilitator and participants? Whatever the labels, they position people in the second category as less authoritative than you. Positioning all of you as *researchers* doesn't remove the differences (I am still 'dominant' in groups), and nor should it; our roles give us different responsibilities. What changes is the discourse of the group itself, so that all those problems I started with – empowering or stereotyping? radical, critical or domineering? taking part in the group, or 'not really there'? – are up for debate within the group. We also find out about participants' issues which otherwise may have been discussed only privately, without you there.

There isn't a recipe for how to work with participants as co-researchers. As I have said, we all work in different circumstances, with different resources and above all, different experiences – not only among you, the readers of this book, but among the people with whom you work. However, here are some suggestions which probably apply to all of us:

- *Listen* very carefully, to what you don't like to hear, as well as what you do.
- *Keep records* ('collect data'), somehow – take notes, make tape recordings, keep a diary, take photos.
- *Ask questions* – and it is essential that those questions reflect the interests of all the participants. New questions come up all the time; they will shape how the research develops and what data you gather.
- *Respect confidentiality*, but don't *assume* people want to be anonymous, or to keep their stories private. They may want their stories to be told to other people, as part of developing a bigger story; they may want their stories told, but with a pseudonym. Ask them what they prefer.
- *Share ideas* and themes as they develop; argue over them; go back to the data and check; if some people are not sure they agree, together work out ways to start a new line of inquiry.

It's everyone's responsibility to search for solutions, and there is a chance that participants' huge pool of experience and knowledge can be made available to all the group.

Further reading

Gee, J.P. (1999) *An Introduction to Discourse Analysis: Theory and Method.* London: Routledge. James Gee's book is a readable and up-to-date discussion of discourse, including spoken and written language and other ways in which people create and maintain social identities.

Merrifield, J. (1997) 'Participatory action research: knowing, learning, doing', *Focus on Basics* 1(A), Website http://hugse1.harvard.edu/~ncsall.

Merrifield, J. (1997) 'Participatory action research: knowing, learning, doing', *RaPAL Bulletin*, 32, 23–7. The two articles by Juliet Merrifield give examples of participant action research, mostly from the United States.

Mulenga, D. (1999) 'Reflections on the practice of participatory research in Africa', *Convergence* XXXII, 1–4, 33–46. Derek Mulenga discusses the work of the African Participatory Research Network, with an analysis of its political contexts and consequences.

References

Barton, D. and Hamilton, M. (1996). 'Putting the new literacy studies into practice', in S. Fitzpatrick and J. Mace (eds) *Lifelong Literacies.* Manchester, UK: Gatehouse Books.

Barton, D., Hamilton, M. and Ivanic, R. (eds) (2000) *Situated Literacies.* London: Routledge.

Benn, R. (1997) *Adults Count Too: Mathematics for Empowerment.* Leicester: NIACE.

Cazden, C.B. (1988) *Classroom Discourse: The Language of Teaching and Learning.* Portsmouth, NH, USA: Heinemann.

Coben, D. (1998) *Radical Heroes: Gramsci, Freire and the Politics of Adult Education.* New York and London: Garland Publishing, Inc.

Freire, P. (1985) *The Politics of Education: Culture, Power and Liberation* (Donaldo Macedo, trans.). London: Macmillan.

Gee, J.P. (1999) *An Introduction to Discourse Analysis: Theory and Method.* London: Routledge.

Gray, J., Kattah, V., Lesley, Sandra, Tomlin, A. and Tracy. (1999). 'Maths – our ideas all came into one', *RaPAL Bulletin*, Spring 1999, 38.

Hamilton, M., Barton, D. and Ivanic, R. (eds) (1993) *Worlds of Literacy.* Clevedon: Multilingual Matters.

Knijnik, G. (1997) 'An ethnomathematical approach in mathematical education: a matter of political power', in A. Powell and M. Frankenstein (eds) *Ethnomathematics: Challenging Eurocentrism in Mathematics Education*, pp. 403–10). New York: Suny Press.

Luke, C. (1992) 'Feminist politics in radical pedagogy', in C. Luke and J. Gore (eds) *Feminisms and Critical Pedagogy*, pp. 25–53. London and New York: Routledge.

Mayo, M. and Thompson, J. (eds) (1995) *Adult Learning, Critical Intelligence and Social Change.* Leicester: National Institute of Adult Continuing Education.

Merrifield, J. (1997). 'Participatory action research: knowing, learning, doing', *Focus on Basics* 1(A), Website http://hugse1.harvard.edu/~ncsall.

Merrifield, J. (1997) 'Participatory action research: knowing, learning, doing', *RaPAL Bulletin*, 32, 23–7.

Mulenga, D. (1999). 'Reflections on the practice of participatory research in Africa', *Convergence* XXXII, 1–4, 33–46.

Prinsloo, M. and Breier, M. (1996) *The Social Uses of Literacy.* Cape Town: Sached Books (Pty) Ltd.

18 Using line management

Annmarie Turnbull

This chapter begins by defining what we mean by line management supervision. It places this in the wider context of learning organisations and personal and organisational change. Your individual needs as a supervisee are then considered, prior to a more detailed outlining of the purposes and processes of managerial supervision. The chapter ends by asking you to evaluate your own existing arrangements for line management supervision and to plan any changes you need to make in them.

What is line management supervision?

To answer this question, we need to look at the two terms, 'supervision' and 'line management' separately.

Supervision

What is supervision? What does it mean to supervise? One dictionary definition says that it is 'to superintend, oversee the execution of a task etc. and to oversee the actions or work of a person'. Chapter 3 considers a different form of supervision, which is especially relevant to informal educators, but for the moment let us use the term in its generic, everyday meaning.

> **Q1:** Can you think of two times in your life when you have been supervised, in the way described by the dictionary definition, while undertaking some task? What did it feel like?

Below are some responses to that question.

When I was about seven my mother let me make some scones. I felt a bit frightened but excited and very proud when I'd made them.

If I get stuck with something I go to my boss and ask for her views. It makes me feel supported and responsible.

My boss went through a weekly checklist on my work every Monday. I hated it. It was so cold and seemed to be about getting things off the list, not the hows and whys of the work. It was unreal.

I was about ten and my dad supervised my painting a figurine. I felt we were a team achieving something together.

A friend who's a DIY buff checked each stage when I tried to assemble a wardrobe. At first it annoyed me, it seemed so slow, but I really needed it. It showed me what I usually do wrong and made me a bit more confident.

You too might have found that whatever the activity that was being supervised, there were strong feelings associated with it, both negative and positive. It is helpful to monitor your own feelings about supervision in a wide range of contexts, as this can have a powerful effect on how useful the line management supervision you receive at work can be to your learning, and to the learning of the organisation for which you work.

Line management

Line management responsibility is represented by vertical lines, joining managers and those for whom they are accountable, on what is often called an organisation chart. The chart diagrams the roles of the people within the organisation and the formal avenues of accountability that exist. While ultimately the head of the organisation, whether called the Director, Principal or Manager, is responsible for what happens in the work place, line management produces a chain of responsibility. A sensible organisation will ensure that measures are in place that enable the work to be done both efficiently, for example with clear boundaries of responsibility, and effectively, for example to the standard the agency has set itself. Line management is one method of strengthening these measures. It enables all workers to be clear about whom in the organisation they must answer to about their work performance.

> **Q2:** Draw a diagram of the line management arrangements in your own work place or an organisation you know well.

If this was an easy exercise, it is likely that the organisation has thought carefully about how it uses line management. If it was complex and confusing and you were not sure about the chains of responsibility, then it is likely that the organisation is not making the most effective use of line management and that the workers may be unsure about the standard of work expected from them or the limits of their responsibilities.

If line management supervision is linked to responsibility for a person's work, as it usually is, its primary purpose is to help to manage the work and achieve the organisation's goals. Effective managerial supervision provides an opportunity for an organisation to get the best from its staff, who, after all, are its major resource. But it is also concerned with your development as an individual professional worker. We will consider the purposes of line management supervision, for the organisation, the worker, and the manager, next.

The learning organisation

All the people in an organisation are potential resources for learning. Knowles' comment on learning in organisations draws attention to the potential of every work setting for learning.

> No educational institution teaches just through its courses, workshops and institutes; no corporation teaches just through its in-service education programs; and no voluntary organisation teaches just through its meetings and study groups. They all teach by everything they do, and often they teach opposite lessons in their organisational operation from that which they teach in their educational program.
>
> (quoted in Hughes and Pengelly 1997: 77)

From this perspective, it is apparent that line management needs to be evaluated to ensure that it constantly meets the needs of the participants. How far and in what ways your work place is meeting its obligations to its clients can, in part, be discovered by assessing what is happening in supervision. Are the needs of all the participants (employee, manager, client(s)) being met appropriately?

In 1967, Joan Tash described a project that aimed to train the supervisors of youth workers. Her book is every bit as valuable today as it was three decades ago, because it looks in detail at the processes of supervision at work and measures their outcomes. Tash concluded that supervision was a valuable learning forum. Among the sorts of learning it facilitated were: learning to use theories (that is, to relate theories to practice); learning to use feelings; learning to use values; learning from practical situations and learning to manage time better. But Tash also acknowledged that the supervisory relationship often has limitations. Mistakes were made within supervision and it was not a panacea for bad practice elsewhere in organisations.

One of the key thinkers on learning in organisations, Argyris (1982), pointed out that we only learn in environments where we are encouraged to be responsible, productive and creative, and where errors are seen as the vehicle for learning. A good learning culture needs to provide opportunities for risk taking and for experiential, practical and reflective learning; and this is what we want to enhance, not only in our line management supervision, but throughout the organisations we work for.

Supervision and the informal education worker

As Christian and Kitto have recognised, the work of informal education offers particular challenges:

> The worker functions in relative isolation, often alone and in the evenings when other professionals are at home; works within a framework where there are few restrictions on the kind of activity; and meets situations charged with emotions. All this means that the worker is more prone to confusion, and more subject to chaos, than those working in more structured ways.
>
> (Christian and Kitto 1987: 1)

This potential for isolation and lack of clarity in the work of many people, including adult educators, youth and community workers, advice and health education workers, teachers and social workers, is reason enough for making the best use of any available line management supervision.

It is also an opportunity to broaden or deepen your professional skills. In fact, the activities involved in line management supervision can make this one of the most useful learning forums in our working lives.

It may be that you have only a baseline knowledge and experience of some areas of work. Perhaps you have helped people in distress and have used some rudimentary counselling techniques. Your manager could help you to identify different levels of expertise in helping those in distress and increase and deepen the repertoire of knowledge and skills you use.

Again, if you have never acted for and on behalf of young people and your job requires you to work as an advocate, you will inevitably lack all the knowledge and skills you need to undertake that role proficiently. Managerial supervision is the arena in which to specify and evaluate your learning goals.

Finally, while some people think that a professional qualification magically bestows the ability to operate successfully at work without feedback from your manager, this is rarely the case. As individuals we are constantly changing as we age and gain new experiences. We are also frequently working in settings which themselves are, as Christian and Kitto remind us, demanding and confusing. Our agencies may be undergoing profound changes in terms of their values and orientation, their priorities or their operating systems. And of course all this is set within a constantly changing wider society which impacts constantly on our selves and our work. All these changes are the backdrop to the line management supervisory relationship.

Q3: Needs Audit

At this stage in your professional training, you will have an enormous number of learning needs. As a rehearsal for the kind of learning agenda you might make for future sessions with your manager, list your current five main learning needs. Next specify the sort of work activities that would meet these needs over the next six months and note some concrete learning goals or milestones that you can set yourself to check your learning needs are being met.

This exercise is very demanding, but you'll be returning to it at the end of the chapter, by which time its purpose should be clearer to you.

The manager's aims for supervision

Line management supervision can be a microcosm of the wider management of the agency or it can operate in apparent isolation or even conflict with the organisation as a whole. It may be regulated by rigid policies and procedures, by form-filling and checklists, just as the wider work of the agency is. It can be an apparently unstructured and informal activity within an agency that prides itself on non-hierarchical structures and easy-going, non-judgemental working relationships. Or, in contrast, a vague commitment to managerial supervision may operate in a highly regimented work place and a careful, regularly monitored supervision process may exist in an apparently chaotic work place. Ideally, however, this relationship at work needs to be part of a wider management strategy to enhance the support, learning and individual accountability of all the agency's staff and, by extension, of its clients.

In managerial terms, the overall aim of the relationship is to maximise your competence and confidence in order to help you to be more proficient and self-determining as a worker in the organisation. Kadushin (1976) has developed a model of supervision for social workers, but it is equally applicable in many fields of 'people' work. He identifies three distinct managerial goals for supervision.

1   To share responsibility for work standards and practice

The line manager has to protect the reputation of the agency in relation to your work. This entails ensuring that you understand the agency's philosophies, policies and priorities and are using them successfully in your practice. The norms that operate in the organisation in relation to culture, values, boundaries, control, accountability, planning, objective setting and standards are all involved in this goal. Line managers also have to ensure that work is correctly resourced and that staff are informed of and, where appropriate, involved in, changes within the organisation.

2   To develop skills, knowledge and attitudes in relation to the work

Managerial supervision also has a role in facilitating learning at work. To meet this goal, line managers need to discover how you learn best and what motivates and demotivates you. They need to be aware of the specific skills needed for your work and, if these are absent, to find ways of developing them.

3   To support workers in their work

Line managers are one source of support for you at work. They can give clear feedback on your work and help you to develop realistic work programmes

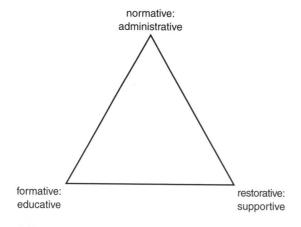

(Based on Kadushin 1976)

and time management systems. The work we do is sometimes stressful. The supervisor needs to understand your stressors and offer appropriate assistance. This might mean giving you uninterrupted time and space to talk, sending you home to sleep, or insisting that you take the risk of trying a new piece of work.

These three goals can be summarised as normative/administrative, formative/educative and restorative/supportive. The three are connected and interdependent in practice, however, and Kadushin represents them as three corners of an equilateral triangle (see page 240).

Q4: Imagine that you asked your line manager for feedback on a piece of work you had undertaken: arranging a sports day for sixty young people. This was part of the reply.

'You know how hard it has been to get the girls fully involved in the past. I think you did really well to keep so many of them practically involved in the detailed work of the planning stage. You also seem to have grown much more confident and efficient in dealing with the paperwork that needs to go to head office, though it was disappointing that you didn't manage to involve Jane [a volunteer] in any of that. In fact, I'd be happy for you to plan the next sports day without my directly monitoring each stage, although it would be a good idea if we discussed how Jane might contribute.'

Can you see how the administrative, educative and supportive functions of supervision are combined in this reply? Try to differentiate between the three areas.

Administratively it is apparent that the manager has an awareness of what was achieved, not just by the event, but in its planning and in ensuring head office have been kept appropriately informed. The manager has also flagged up your *learning* in relation to paperwork and direct work with the girls around planning the day, as well as suggesting an area that needs more attention in future – your work with the volunteer. The final comment is a clear message of *support* for your continuing professional development.

The line management supervisory relationship

In your work place, an important concern will be how the relationship with your manager can work successfully. The supervisor/supervisee relationship is just one aspect of the relationship you have with your manager. Both of you will have expectations of that relationship, which need to be clarified. Managers will need to be clear on the extent to which they agree with the triangular model of supervision presented above, or the version of it which they wish to use.

Research on the qualities of an 'ideal supervisor' has produced awesome lists which it would be impossible for anybody to display consistently. You may not have a clear idea whether you see the role of line manager supervisor as that of a tutor, teacher, counsellor, colleague or boss. It is important to clarify your own expectations of this relationship.

> **Q5:** List some of the things you regard as essential for a successful supervisory relationship in your work. Differentiate between what you will need and what your line manager might need.

The relationship contains a number of implicit duties and obligations for both parties. You might have noted that you will need to be able to describe your work fully and accurately and to identify issues with which you need help. This will mean preparation. You will need to be able to ask for guidance and support and to be open to feedback. Here you will have to be mindful of any tendencies you have to justify, explain or defend your actions needlessly. The relationship also works best when you adopt an active role. You may want to challenge assumptions and restrictive thinking you face in your work or in managerial supervision itself. You need to be able to assess what feedback is useful to you, to implement and monitor changes agreed, and, over time, to identify areas where your work has improved. You also need to be able to take action if you receive inadequate supervision from your manager.

Managerial supervisors usually acknowledge a responsibility to find a space where you can talk freely about work and to negotiate sufficient time for supervision. They usually help workers to explore, clarify and improve their work practices and share their own knowledge, experience and skills. Because of their normative role, they must challenge work they judge incompetent, inappropriate or unethical. But they will also acknowledge change and progress in work proficiency.

Do these ideas accord with your own? It may be worth reflecting on the areas of omission or addition you have identified and what these tell you about your expectations.

Line management supervision is inevitably a dynamic process. As one of its key functions is to facilitate change for the workers, the clients and ultimately for the organisation, its content and processes itself need to develop over time. Both you and your manager have to be aware of the range of knowledge and skills necessary to operate as competent reflective professionals.

Setting boundaries

It is impossible to be prescriptive about a relationship which, as you will see, can be so variable. There is no set pattern for line management supervision. But it is worth clarifying some of the boundaries of a supervisory relationship, with regard to some simple practical matters, as soon as possible.

> **Q6:** Reflect on a previous line management relationship in which you received supervision. (If this is your first post, consider the arrangements for supervision in your current job.) Note down the agreed procedures you followed in relation to the purposes of the supervision and the basis on which your work was assessed. Where, when and for how long were meetings held? What was considered confidential? Were these procedures clear and consistent? How satisfactory did you find them?

Lack of clarity about the limits can be a powerful deterrent to a productive learning relationship.

In examining purposes, your previous experiences and current expectations can usefully be discussed with your manager. Any agency documents dealing with staff support and development will also be valuable. Your organisation might have appraisals and performance reviews, but these have different purposes and need to be distinguished carefully from the supervisory process. Whether you work with, or near, your manager on a day-to-day basis may have an important impact too. The more managers see staff at work, the more accurate their assessments and observations are likely to be.

Clear arrangements for the site, frequency and timing of programmed sessions are important, but there may also be a need for brief, unplanned contact. Confidentiality is of critical importance. Vague assumptions about the boundaries here are inadequate; apparent breaches of confidentiality are a frequent criticism of poor managerial supervision.

Q7: Briefly note your own expectations regarding the confidentiality of your discussions with a line manager.

While I am sure many of your points will be sensible, and cover issues such as keeping personal matters, disclosed failings and the opinions of colleagues confidential, it is not always possible to ensure the confidentiality we would wish. In managerial supervision, the supervisor has a responsibility for good practice in the agency and may therefore have to pursue issues disclosed in confidence, on a 'need to know' basis. Managers may also need to discuss their supervisory practices with their own supervisors. They may have taken notes of your meetings. Who will have access to these and what is their status within the organisation? The bounds of confidentiality are complex and therefore need to be discussed early on in the relationship.

Contracts

One way of helping to systematise and formalise managerial supervision is to contract for effective supervision meetings. Specific work situations will require different contracts, but perhaps at the initial meeting with your line manager, and at regular reviews, you can develop an explicit contract. This might usefully cover agreements about your agenda, the meeting space and notes of the meetings. Will you use an agenda? Who will set it and when will it be set? Will there be any regular items appearing on it? Will the meeting space be private? Will there be interruptions? When will dates and length of meetings be established? Who will make notes? Will they be signed? Who will have access to them, and what happens when you or your manager move on?

Making line management supervision work

However carefully planned, the process of managerial supervision may encounter various blocks. If you and your manager are aware of these, they can be more easily avoided. Possible blocks includes organisational factors (for instance, overwork); misunderstandings caused by differing backgrounds or management styles; restrictive thinking and assumptions; and perceptions of power and authority. The examples in Questions 8 to 10 illustrate some potential threats to successful line management supervision.

Q8: In the following scenario, what *organisational* blocks appear to be inhibiting the supervision? For which of Kadushin's three functions is supervision operating effectively?

Manager – We're very over-stretched here. I manage eight staff and it's hard to keep track of them. What I like to do is to go through their work programmes to check they are on line and tell them when I can see potential problems ahead. I do prioritise supervision but it has to fit around other, more pressing, things.

Worker – Supervision's all right. We just go through the list and check I'm on target and I let her know if there are any problems. She's a bit aloof though. I don't know what I'd do if I had a real problem.

The three goals of managerial supervision are difficult to manage. As in this scenario, it is often the case that the triangle becomes skewed, with more emphasis placed on one aspect of the process (here the normative function) than on the other two. It may not be feasible or even desirable to always keep the weighting of emphasis equal across all three areas, but beware of a situation which gets stuck in one corner of the triangle. Here, there is no indication that the supervisee uses managerial supervision for learning or support. This seems to reflect both the manager's priorities and her 'over-stretched' position.

Styles of line management supervision

You may be working with someone whose background, training and experience are markedly different from your own. For example, managers may have been trained in a particular form of counselling or in formal education, and this will inevitably influence the style of their supervision. It is also likely that their style will be affected by the character of the rest of their work. Whether they are practitioners or simply managers, for example, may influence how they operate in supervision.

While you need to share enough of a common language and value system to be able to learn together, diversity need not be a hindrance. Indeed, the more conscious you are of the diverse experiences both of you bring to the relationship, the richer the process can be. Ideological, cultural, sex, sexual orientation, class and personality differences all inevitably complicate managerial supervision, but if they are recognised and acknowledged, they can also enrich it enormously. But it is true that both participants will have to work much harder if aspects of their background and attitudes are affecting their work adversely. Sometimes our own patterns and behaviours prevent us from seeing situations clearly. Or it may be that we are ignorant of what it means to be in the position of those we work with. For example, we may not understand what it means to be homosexual or to have a disability.

Q9: In the following two scenarios, can you identify some of the issues that are affecting the *style* of the supervisory encounter? Are *assumptions* or *restrictive and limited thinking* operating?

1 *Manager* – I know she has problems writing, so I take the opportunity in supervision to correct her work. Last time we had to totally restructure her piece for the annual report, so I didn't get anything else on the agenda done.

Worker – I suppose she needs to know that everything we produce here is of a good standard. Luckily I don't have to worry too much about recordings and evaluations because she sorts that out in supervision.

2 *Manager* – She can be really aggressive. I think that's pretty common with some African-Caribbean workers. Sometimes it's just in the look she gives me when I'm trying to explain how I see something. An example was the way in our last session she reacted to my questioning what she meant by 'encouraging respect' in her girls' group.

Worker – I've never had a black manager before. At first I was really pleased, but she's so wishy-washy. I don't know where she's coming from. You'd think she'd never had any problems at work.

Many unspoken assumptions might be hampering these relationships. They include stereotyping on the basis of ethnicity, the expectation that management must involve a powerful and assertive authority figure, the confusing of teaching or coaching with supervising. You may also have suspected that restrictive thinking around issues of ethnicity, literacy and accountability in the organisation are affecting how line management supervision is being used here.

Power

It is also important to acknowledge the power dynamics of the supervisory relationship. In line management supervision, the authority of supervisors is underlined by the legitimate power they hold in the organisation. However, other power dynamics often operate as well.

Q10: After reading the following scenario, note what the participants' perceptions of power and authority seem to be. In what ways is this hampering the supervision?

Manager – I think he likes me but I get so frustrated with him. We never seem to have enough time. It takes him over half the session to sort out what the issues are. I try not to be at all prescriptive, but he seems to think he has to tell me about everything that happens every time he's with his group. I try to reassure him, but usually I feel like an encouraging father. I think he needs to be a lot more independent.

> *Worker* – Supervision's OK. He's really good in some ways, gives me loads of time and is really interested in my group. The sessions fly by, but afterwards I don't really think I get much out of them. Maybe it just reassures him to know that I'm doing OK.

If you can see that both are insecure in this relationship and appear to be stuck in an impasse over who holds what kinds of power or authority, you will have grasped how these dynamics can be very destructive. The supervisor is trying to be supportive and encouraging, but this is not helping the supervisee, who doesn't need a father figure, but some concrete professional development. It is inevitable that our individual attitudes to authority will impinge on the process. If, for example, you have an internal image of an authority figure you respect, you may seek for that image in supervision and judge the supervisor accordingly. Try to be aware of this possible dynamic to prevent it from affecting the relationship adversely.

It's also worth remembering that a core aim of line management supervision is to enhance your self-directedness. The development of your own personal authority is therefore at the heart of supervision. In the scenario above, this function has been lost and is clouded by the game-playing and evasions of the participants.

Managerial supervision as dialogue

The most important aspect of line management supervision is the dialogue between you and your manager. For this to be as fruitful as possible, you will need to develop the skills of active listening and giving and receiving feedback.

> **Q11:** We all have failings and weaknesses in our professional work. How do you deal with your failure, or weakness, in a particular task or area of work when you discuss it with your manager? Identify two or three of your typical methods of dealing with your failures.

There are all sorts of methods for protecting ourselves from the negative impact of failing. Perhaps you try to cover up, blaming problems, events or other people. Perhaps you minimise the failing and try to focus on what you regard as your compensating successes. Maybe you justify the failure as part of the plan, a necessary step to success. Or perhaps you admit it and try to learn from it. You would not be very usual if you typically used the last method, but by receiving feedback skilfully you can avoid evading your responsibility for failings and you are more likely to have your strengths recognised. Feedback may be uncomfortable to hear, but that may be less of a disadvantage than not knowing what others think and feel. Your manager will have opinions about you as well as perceptions about your behaviour, and it can help to be aware of them. However, it is important to remember that you are entitled to your opinion. You may choose to ignore information if it is of little significance, irrelevant or refers to behaviour you wish to maintain for other reasons.

When receiving feedback, it is useful to listen carefully to precisely what is being said about your work performance and your professional judgement. Ask your manager to explain anything that is not clear. Later, if possible, check the comments with observations made by others – to see whether the feedback has general agreement.

If you do not receive feedback at all, you may have to ask for it and, indeed, help your manager to provide useful feedback to you. Sometimes you may get feedback restricted to one aspect of your behaviour and may need to ask for comments on other areas of your work. Providing feedback, whether positive or negative, can be uncomfortable and difficult for managers; they may need help from you.

Having received feedback, it is important to assess its value, the consequences of ignoring it or of using it. Then you can decide what to do as a result of it. It will be wasted if you don't make active decisions. Your objective is to communicate constructively with someone who is offering you feedback on something that you need to consider doing differently. In that way line management supervision can become a vibrant part of your professional development.

Mapping your support needs

You should now have some of the tools to evaluate your own experiences of managerial supervision. How far is this process currently helping you to monitor your practice and to develop proficiency? To what extent is it supporting and encouraging you? If it is not meeting your learning goals and support needs, you need to assess the situation and take some action.

One possibility is to look for sources of professional supervision outside the line management relationship.

Q12: Look back at Kadushin's three functions of supervision. Which is likely to diminish or disappear if a line manager is not involved? What might be the benefits of this change?

You'll have recognised that it is the normative aspects of supervision which diminish in non-managerial supervision. This has advantages and disadvantages. It may be that involvement in a different model of supervision will enable you to shift the focus from work performance to exploration of personal needs and goals. However, you should recognise that, without line management supervision, your work is not being managed directly. This leaves both you and the organisation in a vulnerable position, with no-one taking responsibility for you and your work when difficulties arise.

Q13: Look back at the learning goals you identified for Question 3 (p. 239). Are there any that seem unlikely to be met through managerial supervision? Can you think of ways of changing this situation, or alternatively identify other sorts of supervision for professional development that you could use? Try to think of several possible solutions.

It may be that you can see areas where none of your learning needs are being addressed. Consider if there is the potential to change or develop your supervisory relationships at your work place. If you cannot alter the current arrangements, you may need to look towards colleagues or role models within the organisation for support. Are there potential mentors, or colleagues, who could work with you in a supervisory relationship? If there are, ask them. Look carefully at your methods for self-supervision. Perhaps you can now see ways that these can be improved. If you can see that there are still barriers to getting what you need, or gaps in its provision, you will have to look beyond your organisation towards the wider professional networks in which you operate. As we learn best by doing, look for activities and organisations where you can become directly involved. You owe it to yourself as a professional worker to start to make time and space for supervision.

Further reading

Hawkins, P. and Shohet, R. (1989) *Supervision in the Helping Professions. An Individual, Group and Organizational Approach.* Milton Keynes: Open University Press. Written by two psychotherapists, this book is useful for its focus on a broad spectrum of supervision issues. It goes beyond reflection in the individual roles of supervisor and supervisee to examine self, group and peer supervision and how the helping professions can develop working cultures that support learning.

Pritchard, J. (ed.) (1995) *Good Practice in Supervision. Statutory and Voluntary Organisations.* London: Jessica Kingsley Publishers Limited. While this book is aimed at line managers, it contains much of interest on the supervisor/supervisee relationship in a range of work settings relevant to the informal educator. The cumulative force of the chapters reinforces the idea that it is unwise to be too generalising or prescriptive about work place supervision; a wide variety of models can be effective.

Tash, M.J. (1967) *Supervision in Youth Work.* London: YMCA National College (reprinted 2000, YMCA George Williams College). Although this book is now over thirty years old, it is still extremely useful. Seeing supervision as a form of on-going training for the youth workers, it outlines both the potential and the limitations of supervision and draws valuable lessons from an empirical study of supervision in practice.

References

Argyris, C. (1982) *Reasoning, Learning and Action.* San Francisco: Jossey Bass.

Briscoe, C. (1977) 'The consultant in community work', in C. Briscoe and D.N. Thomas (eds) *Community Work: Learning and Supervision.* London: George Allen and Unwin Ltd.

Clough, R. (1995) 'Taking supervision work in residential care', in J. Prichard (ed.) *Good Practice in Supervision. Statutory and Voluntary Organisations.* London: Jessica Kingsley Publishers Ltd.

Christian, C. and Kitto, J. (1987) *The Theory and Practice of Supervision. Occasional Paper 1.* London: YMCA National College.

Hawkins, P. and Shohet, R. (1989) *Supervision in the Helping Professions. An Individual, Group and Organizational Approach.* Milton Keynes: Open University Press.

Hughes, L. and Pengelly, P. (eds) (1997) *Staff Supervision in a Turbulent Environment. Managing Process and Task in Front-line Services.* London: Jessica Kingsley Publishers Ltd.

Tash, M.J. (1967) *Supervision in Youth Work.* London: YMCA National College (reprinted 2000, YMCA George Williams College).

19 Using supervision for professional development

Janet Woods

This chapter is written as an introduction to what we sometimes called non-managerial supervision. It is written for both students training to be informal educators and for workers in the field. It will explore the principles that underlie the model of supervision used by the YMCA George Williams College in its initial training courses for informal educators. The focus will be on your experience as a student or worker who is being supervised (the supervisee), and how you can most effectively use supervision to improve your learning about your practice and therefore be more effective workers.

Supervision and informal educators

Why do we see supervision sessions as an important part of your work as an informal educator? Let us start by looking at the nature of informal education and see how this relates to the process of supervision.

Informal educators work with people in a particular way. You are expected to be able to work without resources other than yourselves, using your abilities and skills to form relationships with others. Through these associations you endeavour to foster opportunities for others that make for human flourishing. The relationship is voluntary, in that you engage with people who choose to associate with you and work to provide an environment of mutual respect and active involvement. You are often called to work with people at times of tension and vulnerability. You often have to work on your own, sometimes in isolated situations. You are expected to be able to take decisions that are underpinned by the values and aims of the work you are doing and take responsibility for the work done.

These factors make for work that Schön (1982: 39) describes as demonstrating 'complexity, uncertainty, instability, uniqueness, and value-conflict'. However, these situations demand that you make decisions, often 'on the hoof'. The complex nature of each situation means that there are not always obvious solutions to problems and there is not always an opportunity for you to go away and think about what to do. The processes involved in having a conversation with another person mean that some decisions have to be made, at least in deciding what to say and how to say it. Schön (1982: 49, 69) calls this type of thinking 'reflection-in-action', where you reflect on what is being said and think, on the spot, about how you might respond.

This type of thinking, reflection-in-action, is not of course restricted to informal educators. It is a very common way in which we all obtain new insights, learn new theories or revise old ones about how the world works. We learn through doing a task and by reflecting on it at the same time, whether it is bathing a new baby, or taking some young people bowling or chairing a committee meeting. We reflect on what we are doing all the time, often without consciously thinking as we change our theories from one experience to another.

But what about the times when we might not find it so easy to recognise at the time what was happening? We might feel confused and unsure of ourselves. We might feel so angry or upset that we find it difficult to think clearly about the situation. How do we learn to see more accurately what we had experienced?

Q1: Think about a situation in your work where you felt confused or upset. What did you do afterwards to try to make sense of what happened?

One possibility is that you discussed it afterwards with a colleague or friend. Or you may have written about it in your recording of the session and pondered over it. Schön calls this form of reflection 'reflection-on-action', the looking back on a situation after it is over, rather than thinking about it as it was happening. You may have discussed it with a colleague who had been there and who was able to give you their view of the situation. You may have found this helpful or you might not have agreed with their perception of what happened. In this case the picture may have been more confusing with two versions of the event instead of one!

You may have found that when you tried to discuss it with a colleague, that the *timing* was not good. You may have had to interrupt the conversation to continue with your work or your colleague may have had to go to a meeting or go home. Similarly, the *place* where discussions take place may also not have been helpful. The usual office space may not have been suitable to discuss a sensitive issue, as somebody else might have overheard your conversation. These issues about time and space mean that, while not dismissing the 'conversation over the teacups', you can find the results sometimes damaging to the work. At the very least, you might find them frustrating, as you may not be able to achieve clarity; it might turn out to be a 'hit or miss' situation.

You may therefore have decided that it is important to create the time and space that can facilitate deliberations without interruptions or worries about confidentiality. This is the focus of what we call 'supervision'.

The history of supervision

To some extent the history of supervision is as old as the human race itself. We all need to talk to other people at some time or other about things that confuse or concern us. We welcome possibly a different outlook on the situation or the giving of support. This need to discuss with others has gradually became more formalised for certain professions. Psychoanalysts, for instance, found difficulty in handling the complexity of the work they were doing so the profession decided that trainee psychoanalysts should have regular sessions where they could reflect on their work with their patients. These sessions were needed, firstly, in order to enable the trainee practitioners to understand why they were responding to their patients in a particular way, and secondly, to receive help and support in their work. The sessions were therefore seen as being both educational and supportive. The sessions were on a one-to-one basis with a supervisor who would offer support and help in both analysing the work and relating it to theoretical models.

Psychoanalysis was not the only profession where it was recognised that supervision would be helpful, particularly to the trainee practitioner or to the newly-qualified worker. Other people-related fields such as counselling and social work also adopted the method. Social workers particularly found supervision useful when looking at casework and social group work. Later, the introduction of social group work into youth work 'naturally brought with it the possibility that supervision would also be valuable' (Tash 2000: 13). Nowadays supervision is seen as being helpful in all areas of the work of the informal educator.

Although formal supervision might have started with the profession of psychoanalysis, the supervisor in informal education is neither a psychiatrist nor a counsellor. The supervisor's role is an educational one where the holistic nature of the supervisee is recognised. We have both achievements and problems and both are important to our view of ourselves. This is echoed in a book written over thirty years ago by Joan Tash about a supervisor training project. The book is called *Supervision in Youth Work* and is still the standard work on supervision in this field. Tash said that in the supervisory process we are 'neither patients nor people in distress' (Tash 2000: 24). The focus in supervision is work-centred not problem-centred.

The function of supervision

We have identified the type of problems inherent in the work done by informal educators that can be clarified by the kind of support that is provided by supervision. Let us look more closely at the model of supervision that the college offers to its students. I will start by looking at a definition of the word 'supervision'.

The word 'supervision' comes from two words: super – meaning 'above', and 'vision' – meaning 'sight, or seeing', hence 'overseeing'. The word 'supervisor' is commonly used for a person, maybe in an office or factory, who has some managerial responsibility over other staff.

Some supervisors working in the field of informal education also have a managerial responsibility over their supervisees. This is often called 'line management' or 'managerial supervision'. There is further information about this model in the chapter by Turnbull.

But the model used at the college is slightly different and is sometimes called 'non-managerial supervision'. In order to look at the differences between the two models, we can look at the supervision model offered by Kadushin in his book, *Supervision in Social Work* (1992). Here he identifies three elements in supervision, the educational, the supportive and the administrative. The educational element is the focus on the learning of the supervisee about their practice. The supportive element is the recognition of the affective side of human beings and the need we all have to be recognised as being of importance. The administrative element concerns the supervisor who is also the line manager and, therefore, has the responsibility for the overseeing of the work of the supervisee. As line manager, the supervisor may have to forbid or instruct the supervisee to do something.

In the college model, or non-managerial supervision, the administrative element is not present, only the educative and the supportive. The responsibility for the management of the work would not belong to the supervisor.

The values of supervision

The supervision process is also a relationship between the supervisor and the supervisee. Christian and Kitto call supervision 'a particular kind of working relationship' (Christian and Kitto 1987: 2). In order to see what kind of relationship, we will look first at the values that underpin the work.

All relationships are affected by the values held by the people involved. If I value going out for meals whereas my partner wants to always eat in, then this will affect how the relationship is conducted between us. We may both have to learn to compromise. If my friend does not value spending time with me, then maybe my values about friendship may be different to hers. I might decide to give up on the friendship because my expectations of the association were not being fulfilled. In this way, values can inform the expectations and the behaviour of both participants in the relationship.

So what are the values that inform the supervisory process? The college sees the following values as the foundations of the supervisory relationship:

- autonomy;
- relatedness;
- confidentiality.

Autonomy

The dictionary defines autonomy as 'self government', the freedom to determine one's own actions or behaviour. Kitto (1986: 67), in her book *Holding the Boundaries*, extends the definition to include not only the freedom to choose but also the 'ability to make a choice and to act on the basis of that choice'. McNair argues that 'it is as immoral to restrict another person's autonomy as it is to restrict their freedom of movement' (McNair 1996: 233). But autonomy does not mean doing what we like when we like. We live and work in social situations with others, and there are not many decisions that we make that do not affect or are not affected by other people. We might say that part of being human is to recognise our relatedness to others.

Relatedness

What do we mean by 'relatedness'? It is the invisible thread that binds us humans together. We allow people to get off the train before we get on to it, we form a queue and take our turn to get our food or pay our bill, we cook for our family or earn wages to take them on a holiday – all these actions (including our negative actions) suggest explicit or tacit ways in which we relate to people. Just as autonomy informs us about what we should do in relation to ourselves, relatedness informs us what we should do in relation to other human beings. Although autonomy and relatedness seem to be two different concepts, they are really two sides of the same coin, and they help us regulate our behaviour to ourselves and to others.

Confidentiality

A value that is also significant in supervision is that of confidentiality. The word 'confidentiality' comes from the Latin 'con fid' meaning 'with faith'. Having faith in somebody or trusting somebody is a state of mind, an attitude towards somebody than informs our expectations of the association.

For instance, we would have expectations about how a doctor should behave. We would not expect our doctor to gossip to others about any medical problem we might have. We would expect the doctor to hold that information 'confidentially', that is to keep faith with us about how we would want this information to be used. This is not to say that this information would therefore be treated as a secret between the doctor and us. A secret implies that the doctor cannot talk about us to anybody else whereas this might need to be done in order to help us get better.

But confidentiality implies that the doctor handles the material in a way that respects us as a separate, autonomous individual and acknowledges our common relatedness. Thus confidentiality can be seen as a value naturally arising from the two values of autonomy and relatedness.

These three values – autonomy, relatedness and confidentiality – inform the process of supervision. Let us look at how this happens in practice.

Autonomy in supervision

> **Q2:** How do you think the value of autonomy might be demonstrated in your relationship with your supervisor?

I expect you may have said something like 'my supervisor would recognise that I am an individual' or 'I decide what to do about my work'. This means that you expect to be able to exercise your autonomy, to make choices and to take responsibility for them. The way you would exercise your autonomy as supervisee would be influenced both by the situation and the role you could play. In the situation of supervision, the focus of the work is on the education and support of you as supervisee in your practice. McNair would argue that educational processes are more likely to produce 'efficient learners' if the person being educated has a sense of ownership about what they want to learn (McNair 1996: 233). In this case you would demonstrate your autonomy and your ownership of the learning by choosing the piece of work you wished to bring to the session for discussion.

I would also expect your supervisor to behave autonomously, but within the role. It would not be the responsibility of your supervisor to tell you what to bring but it is the responsibility of your supervisor to work with it, whatever it is. Tash, in her book, *Supervision in Youth Work,* says that supervision sessions are:

> to help the worker to learn more about his [sic] work and himself in it, and that for this to happen they (supervisor and supervisee) would need to explore the areas in his work in which the worker wanted help or needed to understand more. This meant that the material discussed would be brought to the sessions by the worker and would be about his

work. The supervisor would help him to look at what he was doing, to think about it and to learn about it.

(2000: 23)

It is also your perception as supervisee of the incident under scrutiny that is the starting point of the supervision process. It is how you saw the situation, what feelings you had, what actions you took and what motives you had for taking such actions that are significant. It is only by enabling you to reflect on the situation as you experienced it that you will be able to understand more fully what was happening. Therefore your supervisor 'works with the account of the events and not with the events themselves' (Christian and Kitto 1987: 8).

This is not to say that your supervisor does not exercise his or her own autonomy. Your supervisor does not merely reflect back to you like a mirror what you have said but is an active participant in the process, thinking about what is being said and making choices about how to respond. The supervisor's role is to 'show that the questions that the worker has brought can be thought about, and maybe to show ways in which they can be thought about' (Christian and Kitto 1987: 7).

Your supervisor's role is not to interpret what was happening for you or to say 'it was really like this'. The valuing of autonomous behaviour means that the aim of supervision is to support you as supervisee in your thinking, not that you become dependent on your supervisor's interpretation. It is necessary for the effective use of supervision that you do not see your supervisor as an omnipotent person with all the answers nor, conversely, that you see yourself as an impotent person without any capacities.

This is not to say that your supervisor will not learn anything through the sessions. We might expect your supervisor to learn as well, but this will be a by-product, not the main aim. Christian and Kitto, in *The Theory and Practice of Supervision*, also emphasise this important distinction. They see supervision as 'enabling the *worker* to see more, and to see it more accurately' (Christian and Kitto 1987: 9).

Relatednesss and supervision

Q3: How would you expect the value of relatedness to be demonstrated in the supervisory relationship?

One of the ways I think that relatedness would be shown is in the way both parties accept their responsibilities in the partnership. If you, as supervisee, do not bring material to the session to be discussed then the work that can be done by your supervisor will be affected. You will also need to be prepared to look critically at your work, otherwise the learning may not happen. If your supervisor does not respect your viewpoint when talking about your practice, then the supervisory process, and therefore the work itself, may suffer. So both you and your supervisor need to take responsibility for the success of the relationship.

Supervision also gives you a chance to receive individual training and support, whereas often training takes place in groups. There the focus is on what the group needs to learn, not necessarily on your needs as an individual. In supervision, you can look at your work in some depth and incidents can be discussed which you might be reluctant to look at in a group setting.

Confidentiality and supervision

Confidentiality, as I have said, arises naturally from the other two values of autonomy and relatedness. You and your supervisor must have confidence (another word coming from the same source 'with faith') in each other to handle the process in a way that demonstrates these values. These are manifested by the way these roles are held within the relationship.

> **Q4:** In what way do you think you and your supervisor could demonstrate a belief in the value of maintaining confidentiality with each other?

I thought of three areas:

- setting;
- use of time;
- handling information 'with faith'.

The setting

Your supervisor normally provides a suitable environment in which the sessions can take place and where the importance of both the learning and the support that is being offered is demonstrated.

The material that is discussed is confidential, and you and your supervisor need to feel confident that you will not be overheard. The corner of a coffee lounge or a table in a café can make for an anxious session. It also needs to be quiet enough not to distract thinking. Next door to where the drama group is rehearsing might be too noisy!

It also needs to be somewhere where interruptions are unlikely to happen. Small children running in and out, other workers coming to ask for keys, telephones ringing are all things that are not conducive to quiet reflection. It is also the message that is being given to you as supervisee. The accommodation of interruptions by your supervisor implies that the session itself is secondary to other demands on the supervisor. There are times when emergencies occur, of course, and the session will need to be interrupted, but these should be just those, emergencies. A notice on the door saying 'Do not disturb' and the phone switched off give the message that this work is important.

The use of time

The use of time is not usually connected with confidentiality but it does arise if we consider it as being associated with 'maintaining faith'. This means meeting the legitimate expectations of others. In terms of the supervisory process it means turning up on time for meetings and endeavouring not to

cancel meetings without good cause. Again, emergencies do arise and meetings get cancelled at the last minute but you and your supervisor need to have confidence that both are equally committed.

There should be time enough during the session for both of you to reflect in some depth and also to come to some conclusions about what you have learnt. On the other hand the session should not be so long that concentration lapses or it degenerates into social chat rather than work.

The sessions should also happen regularly so that you get into the habit of using them. The variety of the work, the isolation of the worker and the feelings and emotions involved mean that supervision is very important. By taking regular supervision you will develop the necessary skills and emotional reserves to be able to use the sessions most effectively.

Handling information 'with faith'

The material that is discussed should be handled by both parties in a way that keeps faith with the expectations of both. This means that your supervisor will try to understand where you are coming from and how you see the situation in which you are working. This does not mean that your supervisor will never challenge what you say or offer another way of looking at what happened. These things will be done, but with the aim of extending the understanding, not predicting what that understanding might be.

You, as supervisee, meet the expectations of your supervisor by your open attitude to learning and your willingness to critically look at your practice. As the relationship continues you will hopefully show a confidence in it by maybe taking risks in the material you bring – something that you find difficult to talk about or that does not reflect well on you.

Handing the information 'with faith' refers to outside the session too. What is said in the session should not be used as gossip amongst colleagues or friends. This is not to say that what is said is treated as a secret. Your supervisor may need to discuss the session with another worker in order that she might learn to be a more effective supervisor to you. The focus here will be on the work of your supervisor not on the work of you as supervisee. 'Handling with faith', of course, also applies to any written recordings that are made about the sessions that should not be left around for anyone to read.

All these areas – setting, using the time, and handling information from the session – should demonstrate to both you and your supervisor that you have confidence in each other.

The supervisor

In this part we look at what qualities, background and skills you would need in your supervisor.

> **Q5:** What skills, experience and background would you want in your supervisor? For instance would you want your supervisor to be an informal educator? Do you think it important that your supervisor is the same race, gender and age as yourself? Would you prefer somebody you already know?

Let me give you my thoughts concerning these questions.

Should your supervisor be an informal educator? You might see this as your first priority – that your supervisor should be from the same profession. You might have thought, 'I need someone with similar experience to me in informal education if I am to learn more about how I practice'.

Tash found, in looking at the process of learning by supervisees, that the professional background of the supervisor was not the main concern. She argues that the skills and attitudes that supervisors brought to the relationship were more important than their professional qualifications or experience. The qualities needed in all supervisors were that they should be able to demonstrate their 'flexibility, and ability to feel, learn, think and analyse...' (Tash 2000: 164). You might say that these are the qualities in all informal educators but it might be more difficult to argue that these abilities and attitudes are exclusive to this profession. These qualities are also in workers in allied fields – such as social work, teaching, the ministry and other people-related professions.

However you might argue that even though the skills are available in other professionals, the lack of previous experience of informal education could be a disadvantage to the supervisee. You might well ask, 'How is my supervisor going to understand what I am talking about when their experience is different?' To look at what this might mean, let us go back to an earlier point – it is your account of your practice that is under exploration. This experience will be unique to you. Even if your supervisor is also an informal educator, they only have their own experience to look back on. If their role was to talk about their experience or to give advice to you, then it might be a help to have somebody with similar experiences. But this would still be limited help as nobody's experience or situation is exactly the same. But the role of your supervisor is not to give advice or talk about their experiences but to try to help you to think more clearly about *your* situation. The aim is to enable you to learn more about *yourself* and how *you* work.

Indeed, sometimes you might find it an advantage to work with a supervisor who doesn't instantly seem to understand what you are talking about. If you work with someone from another profession you might find that you couldn't take for granted your supervisor having a similar experience or understanding. This might mean that in talking about the situation you will have to explain more fully and carefully what you want to look at. In this way a more accurate picture of your own perceptions about what happened emerges and, hence, more productive learning. Your supervisor may also find it easier to put aside their own feelings and judgements in order to understand those of the supervisee.

Attitudes and feelings do play a part in the supervision relationship as in any other relationship. If the situation seems a similar one to the one experienced by your supervisor it might be tempting to give advice and say, 'I did this when this happened to me'. But situations are never exactly the same and certainly the people involved are not. By giving advice your supervisor might be ignoring the differences and indirectly suggesting that their practice be followed. This could undermine your autonomy.

Same race, gender or age?

You might have said that the background of the person supervising you was also important and argued that you need to be supervised by someone with a similar cultural and social background to you. For instance, if you are female then you are given a female supervisor. In this way your supervisor would be able to understand your experience of being female. A similar case could be made for working with somebody from the same racial or age background.

I think the same arguments against matching backgrounds could be made as for those with the same employment experiences. Even if your supervisor were matched to you by all the obvious points of difference, for instance, race, gender, professional experience, class and age, it would be difficult to guarantee that you would be two people of like mind. We are all unique and even within these four variations, there are numerous different experiences and attitudes, knowledge and skills, values and beliefs.

Being too similar in ways of thinking and attitude could also be seen as being a hindrance to learning in that it might narrow the path of exploration. Your supervisor is expected to help you to bring out different aspects of the situation that were not obvious before to you. This might be easier if she is coming from a different experience to you.

This is not dismissing any feelings that might be around for you at the beginning of the supervisory process concerning differences in background and experience. Kadushin certainly found that 'in each instance of age or race, or gender, different stereotypes may tend to shape *initial* behavioural responses in the relationship' (1992: 320). However as the supervision sessions continued and people experienced actually working together, these differences became less important. He found that:

> The relationship between supervisor and supervisee established over time may be more significant than the factors of age, gender, and race.
>
> (ibid.)

Somebody I know or a stranger?

It is a professional association, not a social one. This can be difficult if you feel that you must know something about your supervisor on a personal level before you can work together. We might say this is natural curiosity and we are all guilty of it. However it might be that it says something more about the anxiety we all have about starting a new relationship. We want to know more about the other person because it makes it easier to place ourselves in the relationship. We like to know about common areas of interest or belief. In the supervisory process, however, the areas of common concern are the pieces of work that you bring to the session. It is through working with these that you and your supervisor will get to know each other. But these understandings will be in terms of what needs to be known in order for the relationship to function. The problem with social contact is that it could interfere with or stop the work. Tash when writing about the supervisor training project, said that supervisors resisted getting to know the supervisees socially as they felt it could be 'used as a substitute for a working relationship', or it might block 'a worker's understanding of the possibilities within one' (Tash 2000: 23).

The one area that was not included in the question about the qualities of a supervisor was whether your line manager could also be your supervisor. I have already touched on this earlier.

In the supervision model used by the college, the supervisor allocated to the student or worker will not have any managerial responsibility. In this way your supervisor will be detached from your working situation and not subject to all the constraints that being a line manager as well will bring. This means that as supervisee you will be able to make your own decisions about the work and of course to be responsible for the consequences.

Your supervisor will also not be encouraged to visit you at your practice or to talk to your line manager about you. This means that your supervisor is not then 'subject to all the detail and flux of experience that surrounds the worker every day at work' (Christian and Kitto 1987: 14). For instance, if your supervisor had observed the situation you want to discuss, she might be tempted to say but 'it wasn't like that – I saw it like this'. The supervisor's interpretation may be quite comforting to you if you are unsure that what you did was appropriate but it doesn't necessarily help you to understand more clearly what was going on. It might even end up increasing your dependence on your supervisor, and thus make the process counter-productive.

This separation of the role of line manager from that of supervisor can give added strength to the supervisory process. It can be a helpful division particularly to people new to supervision, for instance trainee practitioners.

This is not to say that a line manager cannot be a supervisor, but that the managerial role may be better dealt with separately from the supervisor role. If the line manager and the worker are both competent and recognise the boundaries to each role, then there may be no problem. It will also depend upon the nature of the relationship between both parties. There may be barriers that are felt by the supervisee no matter how understanding the manager tries to be. If the supervisee feels 'tentative and inadequate, or ambitious and determined, the barriers are likely to go up to the person with power, however understanding he [sic] is' (Tash 2000: 162).

The process of supervision

Now let us look at what Christian and Kitto (1987: 2) call the 'particular kind of work', the supervision process itself. In order to look in more detail at how supervision works, I am including an account of a piece of work written by the worker. This is followed by a transcript of the supervision session where the worker discussed the incident with his supervisor.

Q6: Please read the process recording of the work and also the transcript of the supervision session.

Looking at the supervision session, how does the supervisor help Tom to identify and work on the questions he brings? Identify any of the three values, autonomy, relatedness and confidentiality, that you think inform the supervision process here.

The first thing I notice is that the supervisor asks Tom to identify what he wants to look at. Tom, however, seems a little uncertain at the beginning and answers in rather general terms. The supervisor does not challenge this and Tom seems to realise that he needs to be more specific (line 64). The supervisor helps him to put his thoughts into words more clearly and identify what he wants to focus on.

I think the supervisor is recognising that Tom is an autonomous person and is in charge of what he wants to look at. Her role is to accept his autonomy but also to demonstrate how she is also part of the process (her relatedness) by helping Tom to identify more clearly what he wants to look at.

Tom picks up on the problem of his role (71) and asks the supervisor what he should do. The supervisor does not answer the question directly but asks Tom to say more about what happened that afternoon. By doing this the supervisor is enabling Tom to look in more depth at the incident. This brings the focus then back on what Tom experienced rather than on what might happen in the future. In this way the supervisor is not assuming that the problem has already been correctly identified but is helping Tom to concentrate on analysing more clearly what happened.

Again the supervisor does not attempt to take away Tom's autonomy by making decisions that are his to make. She also does not throw away hers by giving up the role she has to help the learning and instead to offer advice. She may feel that to answer Tom's question would encourage his dependency on her rather than develop his own skills in reflection.

Tom goes on to describe how he sees the situation and how he views the two young men (78). He sometimes asks the supervisor a question (82) but again she turns them round and puts them back to him. By her questions he is helped to think more deeply about his relationship with the two boys. The supervisor gives her opinion at one point (101) about what she thinks the problem might be, but gives her evidence from what Tom has said.

I think the supervisor's role might be seen as passive by Tom who might have become quite frustrated by not having his question answered. But I think the supervisor is not passive but quite active in choosing her questions carefully and by altering the focus of what is being said when she feels it appropriate. The supervisor in asking her own questions is not providing answers for Tom but opening up areas for him to consider. In this way Tom's and the supervisor's autonomies are both preserved.

I think that as the session goes on Tom is getting more confident about the nature of the partnership between him and the supervisor (113). He seems to have faith that he will be supported and accepted for what he is, his autonomy is recognised and the supervisor is working with him not against him. This confidence enables him to look more deeply into his practice and to accept more direct questions from the supervisor (121).

This active relationship is continued later in the session when the supervisor goes on to pick up on other areas that she judges important. For instance, why Tom used the word 'accept' (133). This gives Tom a chance to consider aspects he might not have thought of and to extend the interpretations with further evidence (141).

This seems to me to be quite an equal association in that both parties exercise their autonomy to say what they believe within the boundaries of the supervision session. But the two people also show their relatedness to each other by listening carefully, by responding to what was said by the other, by being aware of the other.

The supervisor seems to be only interested in the young men as they affect Tom. She is not interested in them as themselves. The questions she asks about them concern their association with Tom (139), how they affect him, how he sees the relationship (146). In this way she helps keep the focus on Tom and how he feels and functions in this situation (152).

As the session goes on, the supervisor's questions seem to help Tom to focus in more depth on his work. He talks more about his feelings (178) and the values (185) that underpin the work he was doing with the two young men. He also explores in more depth the dynamics between them and himself (200). The supervisor's questions also become more direct as she challenges him about his role as worker (207–12). By the end of this part of the supervision session Tom is able to articulate some of the things he has learnt about himself and the work, and has cleared up some of his confusion (238).

Tom seems to have received both education and support from his supervisor. His autonomy has been recognised and the session has been one that demonstrated interaction and a sense of commitment between him and the supervisor. From these his confidence in the supervisory process grew and he was able to finish by identifying for himself the learning he had achieved.

The nature of the relationship between Tom and his supervisor

The session seems to have been a journey undertaken together; not that one person had all the insights but that they arrived at the end at a similar time. This is an important point in that it implies that the end point, in this case the supervisee's learning, is not predictable by either person. The supervisor is not the person who knows what the problem is and informs the supervisee. This is not to say that the supervisor is merely a passive recipient of information. We have seen that the relationship is a working partnership where both have a role to play.

Conclusion

We have looked at the nature of supervision, what is involved in it and explored an example of a recording. We have looked at the values of autonomy, relatedness and confidentiality that underpin the work, and how they determine the methods that are used in the sessions.

I would like to finish with a quotation from an OFSTED discussion paper on *Spiritual, Moral, Social and Cultural Development*. The words relate to the spiritual development of school pupils but I think they relate equally well to development through supervision. I have therefore taken the liberty of replacing the words 'spiritual development' with the word 'supervision' and changed 'pupils' for 'supervisees'.

> *Supervision* relates to that aspect of inner life through which *supervisees* acquire insights into their personal existence, which are of enduring

worth. It is characterised by reflection, the attribution of meaning to experience, valuing a non-material dimension to life and intimations of an enduring reality.

(adapted from OFSTED 1993: no page quoted)

How worthwhile to be involved in such a creative process, either as a student or as a worker!

Case Study

Process recording – Thursday 3.00 pm

Was around the market. By the Post Office ran into Chrissie, Jean W. and talked about the application to the Housing Department, then saw Phil and Ted and chatted about things for about 5 minutes, last night's International and so on. They are keen to arrange a match with Southview. All this took a good half hour. Went into Joe's for a coffee 5 feeling I needed to take the weight off my feet. Logie and Buster (age 15 and 16) came in. They saw me and I saw them say something to each other. I wondered what they would do (school-time). Then they went up to the counter. I kept my eyes on them so that I could signal I had seen them but they didn't look up. I wondered if they would ignore 10 me. They didn't look at me but brought drinks over to my table. I was quite pleased about this. Then said 'Hello then,' they were behaving almost as though we had an arrangement to meet. They sucked their drinks and I think there was a bit of a silence. I said 'How's it going then? Been let off school?' I felt I was taking a risk but felt awkward 15 about the situation. There's a few kids I regularly expect to find around during school hours but not these two. They grumbled about school, didn't like the afternoon classes, complained of being picked on, the usual. I talked a bit about my school experience, the things I didn't like (French) and how I tried to get off, and how good the craft workshops 20 were, some pretended enthusiasm here I think, I wasn't much good at craft. Boys were being a bit cagey, silent. When I mentioned French, they went off into giggles and behaved as if they were performing to me. Coarse remarks about French tarts etc. They rather took over and I relaxed and listened. Really they were quite funny. I find them a 25 couple of bright boys. They said they thought Allie and Sue would be coming. A bit 'man of the world' or guys waiting for their bit to turn up. I suddenly thought of Dina and asked Logie if she had managed to keep her job. He said vaguely he thought it was OK, didn't seem very inter- ested. Buster said quite angrily that she was a fool and deserved to 30 lose her job if she couldn't keep time. I was a bit surprised at how angry he was. They went on talking about jobs they might get in the market and the sort of money they might earn, rather boasting I thought, saying how you had to work hard. Buster did most of the

talking, Logie a kind of chorus. Buster said his dad only paid him for 35
cleaning the car if he did a proper job.

I felt I wanted to get a bit further with the question of school. I was a
bit uncomfortable leaving it where it was. Asked Buster if he didn't think
he ought to be in school because someone was paying. I tried to keep
it a bit joking. He dismissed my remark. 'I don't have to go. Teachers 40
can't do anything to you. They're suckers.' Feeling a bit daring I asked
what he would do if he was a teacher. 'Belt them', he said, and laughed
and they both laughed. Logie said Buster's dad would belt them if he
knew he was off school. By this time the two were falling about. They
talked for a few minutes about work in the market and then left. 45

The Supervision

Tom: I picked this piece for supervision because it is easy to
identify this as work, and that is not always easy, I find.
Also it left me with some questions about my role. 50

Supervisor: Yes.

Tom: How would you like me to start off?

Supervisor: Well, I take it that what you want to explore today is what
happened between you and these two lads.

Tom: Yes. 55

Supervisor: And they're 15 or 16 and you are worried about them
being out during school-time.

Tom: I think I'm worried about my role as worker when I meet
them when they are away from school. I feel if they
choose to be away, in a sense, they take the respons- 60
ibility for it, but what do I do if I meet them in the middle
of the afternoon in public?

Supervisor: What did you do this time?

Tom: We had a conversation, and I swizzled from sitting and
listening to them – they were horsing around quite a lot – 65
and there was a part of me that felt I ought to put the situation to them, not being in school. They're club members,
very reliable, useful members, Buster plays in the football
team. They are not the regular school truants, **you** know.

Supervisor: Yes, (laughs). 70

Tom: The sort of people where you can make it a joke. So,
here they are in the middle of the afternoon, and I
suppose I didn't know what I was supposed to **be**. Should
I sort out why they are off school and try to get them
back? 75

Supervisor: Did you want to get them back to school? Is that what
you had in mind?

Tom: I don't think I was as certain as that. I think I would have
liked them to go back to school. (Wondering to himself)

| | I think they are fairly able boys, could do some GCSEs at least. Of course, I am not certain. (Hesitant) And there is another thing which is about authority. What is my position in relation to the school? Should I back the school? | 80 |
| Supervisor: | How well do you know these boys? | |
| Tom: | Well, I've seen them quite a lot and we have chatted a lot. Not problems. They're not the sort I expect to have problems. (Realising he doesn't know them as well as he thought) I suppose, I **feel** I know them fairly well because I've seen them around the club quite a lot, and outside, and I've met Buster's father. He turned up one day giving the boys a lift to a game. To be quite honest, they are not two boys that I've spent a lot of time thinking about. They are just there, and they don't create a problem. | 85

90 |
Supervisor:	And yet there is a problem, because you were saying you didn't quite know what to do, and you are not sure about your authority, and what's going through my mind is that perhaps **you** see a problem, which is about the boys not being in school.	95
Tom:	You mean, because they aren't in school it's a problem for **them**.	100
Supervisor:	And then it's a problem for **you**, with the boys there and you not knowing what you should do.	
Tom:	Yes. I think I see what you are getting at. Are you saying that there might be two problems?	
Supervisor:	(Firmly) Yes.	105
Tom:	There **might** be a problem for the boys and there **is** a problem for me.	
Supervisor:	Yes, because they are not where they are supposed to be, as you say. So, something is wrong. And you pick it up very quickly. In your record you say right at the beginning 'been let off school?' You are aware of something going on, aren't you?	110
Tom:	Yes, I am. (Pause). It did rather hit me, because if I'm around in the afternoon there are some people I am not a bit surprised at meeting. But these two came in and it gave me a little jolt, and I didn't know why and suddenly I realised; they are not the people I meet in the afternoon.	115
Supervisor:	So you were surprised. What sort of conversations do you have with people you are not surprised to see in the market place in the afternoon?	120
Tom:	(Pause for thought) It could be almost anything. We talk about... well, sometimes we talk about school. It depends who it is. If it's Bill, well, Bill's been away from school so long now that it's not worth talking about it. It's almost a	

| | joke. And, (a bit defiantly), I'm not going to do the educa- 125 tional welfare officer's job. So, we usually talk about other things. We have talked about school. He knows that I know that he's not there, and I suppose he must know that I would prefer it if he was able to use school, but he's not and I accept it and so we will talk about the next disco 130 or something like that. |

Supervisor: You used an important word there, you used the word accept'. It seems to me that because you accept it with Bill you are very much more comfortable in your relation-ship with him, at least how you describe it. 135

Tom: Yes. (thinking) I feel we have got over the difficult bit, which is what is my reaction going to be about him not being in school.

Supervisor: Yes, whereas with these two you don't really accept it that they're not in school. 140

Tom: (Long pause) I think I don't accept it because of what is behind it. I've talked to Bill a lot; he isn't really for school, his family aren't behind him. He's earning some money, he's the sort of kid who wouldn't be in school, if you see what I mean. 145

Supervisor: I don't, actually. What do you mean?

Tom: (Long pause) I sometimes feel with 14- or 15-year-olds that they have outgrown school, partly. They are earning money, getting jobs, making their way in the adult world, being men. I really feel that school doesn't have very 150 much for them. They're learning things somewhere else.

Supervisor: So you have made certain judgements which make you feel more comfortable about accepting truancy from Bill?

Tom: (Pause) Well, there's nothing I can do about Bill. No effort of mine is going to get him back to school. I mean, if any 155 kid comes to me and says he thinks school is a waste of time, and he is doing other things and they are of some use, I'm not going to turn myself inside out to get him back to school. It's not my job. At least, **technically** it's not my job, (pause) but I'm an adult and I suppose it's not 160 so simple. (laughs)

Supervisor: Well, what's going through my mind is the sense of dis-comfort you feel about your authority with Logie and Buster. I wonder if it is not **your** discomfort and insecurity you feel, around your authority. You say they are not bad 165 boys and here you are almost suggesting to me that they **ought** to be in school.

Do you think that these boys know that you think they ought to be in school?

Tom:	I should think that most kids think that most workers would expect them to be in school, because they're adults. Unless you actually say 'I don't mind whether you are in school or not.'
Supervisor:	Right.
Tom:	I think they felt a bit uncomfortable when they came in. They didn't look at me until they came across. We really have a very friendly relationship, quite an equal relationship. I like them. (Pause) You know, I suppose I felt almost as if I was sorry I was there. I felt I caught them out or perhaps I felt they caught me out. A bit unfortunate; I caught them with their pants down.
Supervisor:	Yes, yes. So both sides are feeling that perhaps there is something wrong, that some sin has been committed, perhaps.
Tom:	Yes, sin! (Both laugh)
Supervisor:	And also, perhaps, there's the feeling you have that you ought to do something about it.
Tom:	Yes, and I also feel that **they** feel I ought to do something about it.
Supervisor:	Yes. Perhaps that's why there's a bit of a silence. You know, 'they behaved almost as though there was an arrangement to meet. They sucked their drinks and there was a bit of a silence', in your recording. In other words, it was not a free and easy meeting, there was some guilt here. I wonder if you feel you helped to increase the guilt or to hold it.
Tom:	(Long pause) Well, I made a reference to school right at the start, feeling a bit daring, taking a risk.
Supervisor:	(firmly) Yes.
Tom:	Taking a plunge. I felt uncomfortable about it. I felt, I really can't go on meeting these two and pretending it's not school time. Of course, they may have had a perfectly good reason for being out of school, but I guess they hadn't or they would have said so. (pause) I think if I had said nothing – I don't think I could have done that – pretended.
Supervisor:	You couldn't have pretended very well though, because, unlike with Bill, you immediately felt some question about your authority, so if you had tried to pretend you would have communicated something about what you were feeling, wouldn't you? Or are you very good at pretending?
Tom:	I don't really approve of pretending, you can't do that. (Pause) Well, that's a very easy thing to say. (Pause) I

	suppose it's what I was saying earlier about Bill. With him it's all out. So, no pretence is necessary.	215
Supervisor:	Yes. You meet him as a **person**.	
Tom:	Yes, as a person, who happens to be breaking the law, of course.	
Supervisor:	Yes, but you have accepted the limitation with Bill. Whereas with these two, you seem to expect that they should be in school and you should do something. In other words, I wonder if you saw these boys as boys or whether you saw them in terms of your expectations, as schoolboys who were not in school?	220 225
Tom:	Yes, I suppose so. I've always thought of them as boys who do go to school.	
Supervisor:	Why didn't you ask them more directly, then?	
Tom:	Yes. (thinking) You are saying then, that I should have put it on the table more directly, or could have done. Certainly I could have done. Why didn't I? (Pause) Maybe that was to do with the way they were talking. They went into this conversation about the girls they were going to meet. It was a social situation, a chance meeting, having a drink together. I wonder if my problem was that I didn't want to spoil a friendly chat.	230 235
Supervisor:	But were these your friends, and were you on your job?	
Tom:	Well, I think you've got a point. I did want to keep it friendly. I was a bit anxious about it turning into a healthy chat from the head of house at school. (Both laugh)	240
Supervisor:	On the other hand, since it is your work beat and it is work time, you have the worker's hat on. I agree that you wouldn't want to do any work with friends but this situation seems to me to be different.	
Tom:	(Protesting a little) Well, I did open it up in the end.	245
Supervisor:	Yes, so I see. And you got them to relax quite a bit because your recording says **you** relaxed and listened and they were quite funny. 'I find them a couple of bright boys.' But, the interesting thing to me in your recording is that you say '**you** relaxed and listened.'	250
Tom:	Yes, I suppose I was talking about school, because – well, we've all skipped off school. Who hasn't, who hasn't wanted to? (Both laugh) I didn't skip off school a lot. Some people were hardly there. I think I would have liked to have skipped off more than I did. I was a bit afraid when I was talking to the boys that they might think I was on the side of the goodies.	255
Supervisor:	Yes.	
Tom:	Saying 'look, you ought to be at school.' I stayed at	

	school and look where it got me. (Laughing) But I was	260
	anxious that they would just tell me to eff off.	
Supervisor:	Yes, and what seems good is that your relationship	
	remained intact even if you were feeling a bit tentative.	
	You and the boys seem to have got on well. It seems to	
	me that the early worry you had, has subsided.	265
Tom:	(Pause) You know, I think I was more worried than I	
	realise about keeping the relationship intact. Talking to	
	you now makes me think that I could talk about not being	
	in school on another occasion. You know, if they came	
	into the club one evening. I think there was a bit of a	270
	shock when they came in. We weren't expecting to see	
	each other.	
Supervisor:	Yes, yes.	
Tom:	I mean, there may be nothing to it, they just skipped off	
	one afternoon. So what! But I do think it's a problem for	275
	me when these things happen. About perhaps, the sort of	
	responsibility I have and keeping the relationship intact.	
Supervisor:	Yes, so I suppose if you met them again you would be a	
	bit better prepared.	
Tom:	Yes, if I met them again I might well make a joke about	280
	'starting an out-of-school club?' or something like that.	
	(laughing)	

The session continues with a short exploration of the worker's relationship with the school and ends with a further and deeper exploration of   285
the worker's feelings when the boys came into the cafe and how he
may have imposed his own values on them.

References

Christian, C. and Kitto, J. (1987) *The Theory and Practice of Supervision*. London: YMCA
    National College.
Kadushin, A. (1992) *Supervision in Social Work*, 3rd edn. New York: Columbia Univer-
    sity Press.
Kitto, J. (1980) *Holding the Boundaries*. London: YMCA National College.
McNair, S. (1996) 'Learner Autonomy in a Changing World', in R. Edwards *et al.*
    Boundaries of Adult Learning. London: Routledge and Open University.
OFSTED (Rev. edn 1993) *The Framework for Inspection*, as quoted in OFSTED (1994)
    Spiritual, Moral, Social and Cultural Development. London.
Schön, D.A. (1982) *The Reflective Practitioner: How Professionals Think in Action*. Educa-
    tion Basic Books.
Tash, M.J. (2000) *Supervision in youth work*. London: YMCA George Williams College.

20 Evaluation in informal education

Alan France

Evaluation is sometimes viewed with fear and resistance because it is seen as being both imposing and intrusive. Yet its strengths and benefits are normally ignored. In this chapter I want to suggest that evaluation should be seen as an essential component of the 'reflective practitioner'. Not only does it offer workers new opportunities to develop our practice, but it can also create new and exciting ways of working with young people.

In this chapter I will cover three key questions: What is evaluation? Why should we evaluate? and How can we evaluate?

What is evaluation?

In this section I shall be making three main points:

1   Evaluation is something we do as a part of our everyday lives. Usually it is quite informal and in many cases unconsciously undertaken.
2   Evaluation is about making judgements, usually against explicit or implicit standards. These are then turned into action.
3   To make these judgements, we usually need to have information or knowledge. If we do not have this information, we may have to go out and find it.

When I was planning to write this chapter, I wanted to give some thought to how I could introduce you to the notion of evaluation. What I normally do in these circumstances is go down to my local café, with paper and pen, find a nice quiet space and order a cup of coffee. While I was sat there, I drifted off in my thinking and started to ponder about why I came to this particular café. I concluded that I kept coming here because I found the food quite reasonable and cheap, it was convenient and the service was very good. I also liked the fact that it has a no-smoking room and that they just let me sit here with a pot of coffee without disturbing me.

What I realised was that I had made a judgement about the suitability of this café. I had identified what my needs were (quiet, no-smoking café near my home) and made a choice or judgement based upon my previous personal experience. I had also judged it in comparison to some other cafés I had visited in and around the local area. What I had done, therefore, as a part of my everyday activity, was make an evaluative judgement.

Making judgements is also something we do in our daily work. As professional informal educators you will have to continually make judgements about priorities and resource allocation. Let me create a scenario to illustrate this.

You are a worker in a full-time youth centre and over the past two years you have noticed that fewer and fewer girls, aged 14–17, are using the centre. As you and your local youth service have a policy of equal opportunities you are concerned that resources and energy are going into young men but not young women.

Your own thinking is that the local pub, which has a night club attached, has more attraction than your youth centre. Girls, you think, are voting with their feet and going there instead of your club. You therefore decide to investigate. Your first stop is this local pub but you cannot identify what girls might be within your age range or who might live within your catchment area. To find out what is going on, you decide to write a short questionnaire and approach Year 10s and 11s at the local school to get them filled in.

After you get the results you discover three things. First, that the girls are not going down to the local pub. Second, that many of the local young women do not know about the youth centre. Thirdly, that many of those that do know about it are intimidated by the presence of older boys and a small group of dominant women. Finally, many do not come because they have too much homework and their time is limited.

As a result of these findings you decide to:

1   produce a leaflet targeted at young women giving them information about the centre (designed and written by young women?).
2   explore with workers and users of the centre how the centre can change to attract these young women (young women's night? peer-led projects in schools?).
3   create a homework club for young women where they can meet other young women.

After six months of implementing these programmes the club has increased the number of young women involved by 50 per cent. After talking to the young women you discover that they are finding the youth centre friendly and usable and the introduction of a young women's night and homework club something that is helping them with their study and self-esteem.

So what does this tell us about evaluation? First, evaluation is a vital part of being a 'reflective practitioner' and an essential component of informal education. Planning, monitoring and measuring our work are essential if we are to meet young people's needs and provide quality services. Secondly, our own 'common sense views' and judgements about why something might be happening cannot always be trusted. Sometimes we need to broaden our knowledge base. Thirdly, evaluation is about making changes and achieving improvement. Finally, by monitoring progress we are able to ensure that the service provided works and gives maximum benefit to young people.

Q1: Are there any aspects of your own work that raise questions that might benefit from a similar evaluation process to the one in this example? Can you think of areas where you are relying on 'common sense' rather than going and finding out?

I now want to introduce a more formal definition that brings many of these points together. At one level evaluation, as we have shown above, is nothing more complicated than 'assessing the value of something' (Feuerstein 1986), but it does involve a number of key practices which require a more complex definition. The one I have chosen is taken from a book by Carol Weiss and goes like this:

> Evaluation is the systematic assessment of the operation and/or outcomes of a programme or policy, compared to explicit or implicit standards as a means of contributing to the improvement of the programme or policy.
>
> (Weiss 1998: 4)

While this definition is focused on programme evaluation (something we will return to later) it is also relevant in explaining evaluation at the practice level. For example, let's break it down and use it to explore the example we have just discussed above.

The systematic assessment of the operation and or outcomes. This means more than just relying upon 'common sense' beliefs to assess how things work and the results. It was important for our worker to collect information from young women (both before and after the changes) and then to assess the operation of the club against it. After the operation (the way the club was organised) had been changed (by introducing a new structure of girls' work) the outcomes were assessed. After six months young women were approached to find out if the changes had been a success. Systematic assessment required the worker to broaden his knowledge of events and not to rely upon his own perceptions of what might be happening.

This assessment takes place against an explicit or implicit standard and contributed to the improvement of the programme. For example, the broader policy context is the local authority's commitment to equal opportunities. This is confirmed at the local level by the recognition that young women are invisible and not using the club's facilities. The actions of the youth worker to change the structure of the club and increase provision aimed to ensure that equal opportunities were offered. Equal opportunities policy was the broader standard being used. But at a club level the standard was the number of young women attending. Improvement was measured against this standard.

Such a definition therefore gives us a better understanding of what evaluation means and enables us to draw out the complexities. If we think back to my earlier example of evaluation you can see that such a definition works at both the personal and work level. The explanation given by Weiss thus captures both the simplicity and complexity of evaluation.

Why should we evaluate?

I now want to turn our attention to the question of why we should evaluate. At one level the previous discussion shows why it is important (the 'reflective practitioner'), but as others have suggested there are many reasons why we should evaluate (Feuerstein 1986).

Q2: What reasons can you think of in favour of evaluating your work?

When it comes to youth work I think there are two main reasons why we should embrace evaluation and see it as important to our everyday practice.

1   As professional workers we are accountable for the quality of service we provide and we need to be accountable for the spending of funds.

Youth workers and other professionals employed to work with young people should be accountable for the service they provide and the funds they spend. This is not just an issue for those working within the public sector; it is also important for those working in the voluntary sector. Many decisions about youth resources are made by policy makers and funders with the objective of improving the quality of life (and services) of young people. We might not always like some of the agendas we inherit, but it is the professional worker who is the guardian of these resources. We therefore have a responsibility to ensure that resources and funds are used in the most effective and efficient manner. Evaluation gives us the tools to achieve this.

2   Evaluation gives us the opportunity to identify what works and what does not work.

This has three dimensions. First, we need to be sure that what is done, in the name of young people, has a positive outcome. Traditionally it has been assumed that youth work is good and that having been 'youth worked' results in positive outcomes. But how do we know this? The reality is that we do not have a clear view of what impact youth work has on the lives of the young people we work with. It has always been assumed that youth work and youth work methods, such as informal education, are good and any contact will be beneficial for that young person. We may have anecdotal evidence but we do not know the true impact of our work. Building in evaluation will give us the answer to this question and will ensure that the work we are doing has value to young people.

Second, evaluation offers us the opportunity to clarify our aims and purpose; to set clear objectives concerning the boundaries of our work and to clearly state what our work is, and is not, about. This is important not only at a political level but also in our practice with young people. Youth workers are not always open about their agendas. Many young people do not know what they are 'signing up for' when they get involved with youth work. They are not always clear about what outcomes they want or what youth work can offer. For example, Love and Hendry (1994) asked both youth workers and young people about their perspectives of youth work. The research showed a clear mis-match between what workers thought youth work was for (education) and what young people thought it was for (leisure). Evaluation offers us opportunities to set down clear boundaries for our work and also enables us to be clear with young people, about our (and their) roles and responsibilities.

Third and finally, evaluation can support funding claims. Youth work has never been good at showing value for money or why it should receive external funding. It desperately needs to be able to show policy makers and fund holders why they should financially support youth work. It is no longer good enough to claim that youth work works. Politicians of all persuasions are asking, 'Is youth work value for money and how do you know it works?' Unless workers can demonstrate its effectiveness it is likely to continue to suffer from underfunding.

Youth workers' concerns over evaluation

> **Q3:** Are there any considerations that make you reluctant to evaluate your own work or the work of your agency? Jot them down now.

While there is good reason for youth workers to evaluate their work I am aware of a number of concerns workers have about doing evaluation (France and Wiles 1996). Some of these arise from a lack of understanding about what evaluation is and how it can be useful. Others are concerned with more practical questions about the implementation of evaluation methods. I now want to discuss some of these issues and explain how I think they can be overcome.

1   Evaluation is just a mechanism that is used by management or policy makers to reduce funding and the role of youth work within either a national or local service framework.

This concern about the way evaluation is used is based upon youth workers' real experiences (France and Wiles 1996). Clearly, youth work has been through a period of erosion (Maychell, Pathak and Cato 1996) where services have been cut and reduced. Evaluation has been seen, in this context, as a management tool used to help find ways of saving money. But if this is how workers have encountered evaluation then the problems are not with the process but with how evaluation is being used by management. As Everitt and Hardiker argue, 'The task we have set ourselves is to retrieve evaluation from being employed as a tool of social control to one that will contribute to the development of "good practice"' (1996: 1). We have to be aware of the political nature of evaluation and how it can be abused but we therefore have to be more pro-active in designing methods that reflect the nature of our work and challenge the management approach. As I shall argue later, evaluation provides us with the opportunity both to produce clear evidence that youth work has a positive contribution to play in work with young people and to develop more 'participatory' approaches. Evaluation also gives workers political power in that it can show politicians that youth workers are reflective and responsive to the needs of young people; that they have a clear set of aims and objectives that reflect local and national policy; and that the money invested in youth work is money well spent. Clearly, such evidence can only advance the cause of youth work and ensure its continued survival.

2   Evaluation is time-consuming and of little practical use to workers on the ground. There are major worries by workers that it takes away time from young people and makes more administration.

Good practice in this area should eliminate this problem. Evaluation is concerned with informing practice and ensuring that objectives are being met and that outcomes are achieved. This means that it has to be useful on a day-to-day basis and be of value to workers. If this is not the case then either it is not being implemented correctly or it is being managed ineffectively. Evaluation, as I have suggested, is nothing more than a formal and systematic method of monitoring and informing practice. In many ways workers are already engaging in a reflective form of practice and the move to a more informative and effective form of evaluation may only be a short step away. Evaluation should formalise this process and provide valuable evidence to explain why the work is being done, what it is aiming to achieve and what the final outcomes have been. This does not mean that the process of evaluation has to be complicated and time-consuming. Methods have to be designed that allow the minimum of effort but provide clear information. Being efficient while also being effective is essential if evaluation is to be of value to youth workers.

3   Youth work cannot be evaluated because of its qualitative nature. Notions of measurement miss the context of youth work and devalue the importance of relationships between young people and youth workers.

Such an argument is self-defeating in that it stops any attempt before it is started. Clearly youth work, like any services that attempt to improve the quality of people's lives or the personal development of individuals, will have difficulties in capturing the complex processes and outcomes of interaction between workers and users. This issue is not unique to youth work in that similar questions are being asked within the disciplines of education, social services and the health service. Yet if we are going to show funders and policy makers the value of youth work, then attempts should be made to try to capture this aspect of the work. Such an approach is not beyond the abilities of youth workers; in fact such practices involve simple processes of talking and engaging young people within a research and assessment process. This is something that does not have to threaten or undermine the relationship between young people and workers. For example, Cheetham *et al.* (1992) outline how social work can go about evaluating itself. They argue that even though social work is concerned with 'people' and the quality of interaction there remain a number of techniques and approaches that workers or evaluators can use to explain both the process and outcomes of social work. Others working in the evaluation of programmes have also shown how qualitative measures can be developed to assess the quality of provision and learning outcomes of programmes (Cook and Reichardt 1979; Feuerstein 1986; Patton 1986; Blackburn 1997; Weiss 1998). As I shall argue, this can (and should) offer exciting opportunities for workers that put young people's needs and voices at the centre of any practice.

> **Q4:** Look back at your answers to Question 3. Did you raise any of the same concerns? Do you feel more positive about evaluation now?

How do we evaluate?

In this section I want to start by giving you a short history of evaluation and to locate its recent development within a number of key changes taking place in society. Second, I want to suggest that there are certain aspects of these developments that we should and can learn from. Finally, I want to discuss alternative ways of thinking about evaluation (more 'bottom up' approaches) that open up opportunities, not only to provide some of the management information being requested of us, but also to design methods that actively engage young people in the processes.

The growth of evaluation

So far we have explored the notion of evaluation at the level of practice but, as the quote from Weiss indicates, evaluation is used in a number of different contexts. I now want to outline some of the history of evaluation and show how it exists at a number of levels.

Although there is a complex and debated history about the 'birth' of evaluation (see Weiss 1998) it is clear that developments in America have been a major influence on our understanding (and experience) of evaluation. But not only has the development of evaluation been driven by events in America, it has also been greatly influenced by scientific and management approaches (Everitt and Hardiker 1996) where measurement is achieved through 'scientific research methods' (such as the collection of statistical data and analysing it on computers) as opposed to more 'natural' or qualitative approaches (such as observing events, and interviewing participants) (Weiss 1998). For example, much of the early developments in America draw upon 'scientific approaches' such as experimental design where control groups are used as a comparison to assess if social change has taken place (see for example, Campbell and Stanley (1966) as an example of this approach).

In Britain, evaluation has a shorter history (and one that has not been catalogued) although it can be seen at three levels. One of the major areas where evaluation has become popular is at the level of policy.

In the 1990s, the commitment to evaluating policy has grown and become a central feature of British policy making. A good example of this can be seen in the recently-published document, *The Evaluation of the Hamilton Child Safety Initiative* (The Scottish Office 1999) where three pilot projects were run in Scotland to see if they could reduce crime. A number of other examples are also evident within recent policy changes being developed at national level. For example, two policy changes within youth justice have evaluation built into them as a method of assessing their success. First, under the new Crime and Disorder Act, the new Youth Offender teams have set up eleven pilot projects. These are being evaluated to examine the impact of the new teams on youth justice. Secondly, the new Youth Courts have attached to them a Home Office-funded evaluation that aims to explore the impact of these new changes on young people's experience of the youth justice system. Such developments are not unique to criminal justice; they are also taking place in health, education, social work and in many other areas. Evaluation is becoming a key term (and requirement) in terms of policy.

But the growth of evaluation has also taken place at another level. As the state attempts to target its resources more effectively, we have seen a massive increase in programme funding. In England, this has been seen through the introduction of programmes such as Safer Cities, City Challenge, and the most recent, the Single Regeneration Budget (SRB). All of these require local authorities to bid and compete with other authorities. All aim to be targeted at particular groups (usually at the poor or those involved in criminal activities), and all are funded from central government but run locally by QANGOs (non-elected organisations that have authority and power within local areas to undertake developments and distribute funds). One such development within the youth work field was the setting up of the Youth Action Programme by the DfEE in 1992. This £10 million programme aimed to encourage youth workers to work at reducing young people being at risk of offending. Twenty-eight local authorities took part, setting up over sixty projects. Attached to the programme was a national evaluation that aimed to examine both how successful individual projects, and the overall programme, had been (France and Wiles 1996).

One final area where evaluation has grown is in the development of systematic inspections of programmes and practice. This is most evident in the work of OFSTED in education but can also be seen in other areas such as work being done by the Audit Commission (see, for example, their work on the Criminal Justice System – Audit Commission 1996). In youth work, OFSTED have slowly moved to a more systematic process of inspection. While it comes under the heading of inspection, it is in fact a form of evaluation. For example, in their document, *Inspecting Youth Work,* OFSTED state:

> Her Majesty's Chief Inspector of Schools has a duty to inspect and report upon the quality of education, the standards achieved and the efficient use of resources made available in LEA maintained or assisted institutions of further education. The purpose is to identify strengths and weaknesses so that the quality of education may be improved and the standards raised.
>
> (OFSTED 1996: 1)

The document follows on by showing how the inspection will achieve this and what its main evaluation criteria are. This includes a discussion about the indicators which are used to measure the quality of education provided by local youth services. In this sense, OFSTED inspections are evaluations.

Q5: Has your work been affected by any of these developments? What forms of external evaluation are now required of you and your agency?

It is more than likely that the majority of you have encountered evaluation through one or more of these developments. For example, within local authorities the recent developments discussed above have increased pressure on managers to explain the effectiveness of the service being provided (be it within the public or voluntary sector) and to provide justification to policy makers and politicians around 'cost effectiveness' and 'best value'. The result of this is that managers need to collect information about the service being provided. Some of this will come from management systems and data recording but there will be requirements for practitioners to collect more and varied information on their practice. Similar experiences will arise if you are involved in running projects funded by external bodies (such as SRB). What you will have discovered is that they require you to provide information about what you are doing and how you measure its success. This may well mean form-filling and answering questions about 'inputs', 'outputs', 'indicators' and 'outcomes'. For those of us who have trouble with the technical language and translating management or agency requests for information into practice, this can be very frustrating and confusing.

The language of evaluation

In the report to the Third Ministerial Conference for the Youth Service (1992), it was stated that there was a growing concern about the appropriateness of terms and practices such as 'learning outcomes', performance indicators, and many other such terms. Members of the Conference suggested that they did not always reflect the youth work context and process (1992: 14). Since that conference youth workers have found themselves having to respond to these terms more and more. For example, in the OFSTED Inspection Guidelines local services are asked to provide information about 'learning outcomes' and measures of performance (OFSTED 1996). But this language has also penetrated youth work from the recent developments discussed above. The reality is that youth work now finds itself in a position where, if it is to be an active partner in recent developments, it has to provide evidence of its success. This means it has to understand the professional language that is growing up around the development of evaluation, but also it needs to use this language to show the results of its own evaluation. At one level workers may feel this is a threat but it does not have to be. In Table 20.1 I have given a glossary of terms you may have encountered. I have added my own definitions of these terms.

At one level such language seems alienating but it does have an important contribution to make to the question of how we should evaluate. We should not be put off by this experience or our first encounter of the language. For example, what it suggests is that any evaluation needs to have three key steps:

1   As practitioners it is very important that we set down our broad aims – and that we ensure our objectives reflect these (the setting of aims and objectives).
2   It is also important that we are clear about what we are trying to achieve and how the work we design or plan will make this happen (the design of the programme/project or piece of work and its linkage to aims and objectives and intended outcomes).
3   It is also essential that we agree what our 'measures' should be so that when we monitor the work we can see the results (our outcomes) and then make decisions about whether it should continue or if we need to make changes (building in methods of measuring outputs and outcomes).

A model of this should look something like Figure 20.1 on page 279. I have added a fourth stage, communicating the results. As I discussed earlier (in the section on why we should evaluate) this is an important part of the process and one that we should build in from the beginning of our work.

As was suggested at the Ministerial Conference, good youth work needs to be planned, well structured and evaluated (1992: 14). The four stages above are central aspects of good 'reflective practice' and should provide us with a structure for planning our work. This is not to say that we should accept the 'top down' approach. As I mentioned earlier, what we need to do is take this structure and use it to construct our own methods. One result of using this model is that we can fit our results into management requirements and so reduce the amount of work we have to do.

It is usual that evaluation is 'imposed', designed and planned by 'experts'

Table 20.1 Evaluation terms

Aims	Objectives	Inputs	Outputs	Performance indicator	Monitoring	Process evaluation	Outcome evaluation
The ideal situation you would like to happen when the work is concluded. This might be the policy framework or the programme aims.	What each individual piece of work or initiative aims to achieve. Once they have been achieved they should contribute to the overall programme aims.	The resources that you bring together to carry out your planned work or initiatives. For example x amount of youth work hours and x amount of equipment.	These are the activities that arise as a result of your inputs and can (or should be) clearly defined as stages towards outcome evaluation. They should also be a part of your monitoring of the programme/ project or work. For example, outputs might include the setting up of a number of groups or the involvement of x number of young people in the programme.	This is what we agree should be measured as a way of making a judgement about the success of the programme/ project or piece of work. For example, if one of the objectives of the project is to increase the number of young people involved this can be measured using statistical data but it can include other forms of data.	At different stages of the programme/ project or piece of work we need to check that the objectives are being achieved. To do this we might check attendance records or do a 'mid stream questionnaire' or we might just observe some of the work to see that it is meeting its goals.	Process is given less attention in official approaches to evaluation yet it is essential as a method of identifying what caused the outcomes you are trying to measure. Process evaluation is a description of what actually happened.	Should be linked to your aims and objectives. These are the results of your inputs and show the success of outputs.

Stage One:	Setting aims and objectives
Stage Two:	Designing the planned work and ensuring it meets the aims and objectives.
Stage Three:	Deciding on measures for input, output and outcome.
Stage Four:	Report results.

Figure 20.1 The process of evaluation.

or 'managers'. But this does not have to be the case. As Everitt and Hardiker argue, 'evaluating for "good" practice places evaluation firmly within democratic processes involving practitioners and users' (1996: 1). It is this question I now want to turn our attention to.

Q6: Can you think of more 'bottom up' approaches that might be good practice for youth workers?

Towards a more participatory model of evaluation

An alternative approach to evaluation can be found in the literature on participation. This approach offers an opportunity for the development of methods which can offer young people active participation in defining the objectives, outcomes and even, in some cases, doing the evaluation themselves.

But what is a participatory approach to evaluation? In this section I want to outline some of the key issues surrounding this question and highlight some of the difficulties and problems such an approach may encounter. To conclude, I want to give a number of examples to show how a more participatory approach might work.

Feuerstein (1988), writing on how community evaluations can take place in developing countries, suggests that there are four methods of doing evaluation. First, there is the 'studying specimens' approach where people are only expected to play a very small part in the evaluation. Participants agree to be evaluated; then the evaluators ask questions, count numbers and examine processes. Once the evaluation is done there is no feedback of results. Second, there is the 'refusing to share results' approach. Some of the objectives of the evaluation are explained to participants. People might have a minor role to play in collecting and analysing the data but feedback of results is limited to what is seen as appropriate. Third, there is the 'locking up the expertise' approach. People take part in the decision to evaluate, selecting aims and objectives and carrying out the evaluation and analysis of the results. Participants also take part in feeding back and putting into practice changes and recommendations. But people are still very much dependent on external 'experts'. Monitoring is undertaken by others so that participants are unable to proceed on their own. Finally, there is the 'real partnership in development' approach. In this model people take part in deciding when and how to evaluate. They are involved in all aspects of the evaluation including the monitoring of progress. Participants are more than able to assess regularly their own development and carry out further periodic evaluations. The 'real partnership in development' approach is appealing. Not only does it encourage participants to be active in the evaluation process but it also creates the opportunity for groups to identify the objectives of the work they are getting involved in and decide how the results of the evaluation should be used.

A similar approach has been developed by Kuriel (1991). He divides the process of evaluation into nine stages, although these can be narrowed into four areas: establishing background information; setting evaluation objectives and indicators; data collection; and data compilation. At each stage participants should (and can) be involved in making decisions about the evaluation process. Many of the methods applied by Kuriel are practical, relatively quick and uncomplicated to implement. Methods such as 'write and draw', 'community mapping' and taking photographs, stimulate discussion and allow the least powerful community members opportunities to be involved in decision making (Kuriel 1991).

Underpinning participatory evaluation, therefore, is a belief that involving people in the process is an essential aspect of the work. (Feuerstein 1988). This should then be guided by five principles of 'good practice'. These are as follows:

1   In constructing the evaluation there needs to be an agreement about the 'participatory threshold' (Rebien 1996). The level and type of participation in the evaluation needs to be negotiated from the beginning. Participants should decide what is an 'acceptable' level of involvement. Key areas where participants should be included are: deciding the evaluation criteria/indicators, collecting and interpreting data and deciding how the information should be used. This needs to be agreed in the first stages with those who are willing to be involved.
2   It is important to be clear about what the evaluation is and why it is important to the work. Evaluation needs to be owned by the participants. But doing this requires a process which helps people understand what evaluation is. As Feuerstein (1988) suggests, the very idea of evaluation can be intimidating and needs to be de-mystified. Participants should then be encouraged to share responsibility and own the process (Tones and Tilford 1990).
3   The work needs someone within the process who will be trusted by the others to take responsibility for co-ordinating and linking with others. This can be a professional but it is better for it to be a 'participating member'. Watt and Purcell (1997) call these 'community development agents', Feurestein (1986) calls them 'community co-ordinators' and Penuel and Freeman (1997) call them 'participatory researchers'.
4   Groups need to be aware of the range of methods that can be used in evaluation and should be encouraged to draw upon different approaches. As Feuerstein argues, 'the real challenge lies not in getting the people to fit the method, but in getting the methods to fit the people' (1988: 24).
5   Finally and probably the most importantly, if young people and/or

community members are to be the central actors within the evaluation process then they need a support structure and training at different stages around issues that arise as the work progresses.

Actively involving participants in the process of evaluation offers new and exciting ways of working around the notion of evaluation. But it is not without its problems. First, much of the literature arises from work undertaken in the developing world. For example, Kuriel's account (1991) is developed from his work in India. This raises a question about the transferability of the approach to a different context. British society is more complex and stronger interconnections exist between community development programmes and the local and national state. Whether a similar approach can succeed here remains an unanswered question. Second, much of the work is focused on helping local people make changes to their lives; but realistically, not all members want to change or to participate. In terms of young people such a principle is driven by the belief that it is morally right for the young to be 'active citizens' because it offers them ways of learning about their responsibilities (France 1996). If participatory methods are forced upon participants they may then experience this as imposing and another form of social control. Third, principles that advocate a more 'equitable' relationship between workers and participants are commendable but how realistic are they? For example, Petersen and Lupton (1996) argue that in a society that is dominated by 'experts' and the belief in 'professional power' such objectives are unachievable. Senior decision makers look to the expert not the lay person for advice about how and what needs to change. Fauri (1975) suggests that this happens because policy making is made 'on the run' and lay perspectives are continually marginalised. Finally, there are a number of more pragmatic issues, around time and costs, that can be problematic in trying to implement the participatory approaches discussed above. Preparing and developing such methods can be very time-consuming and costly. It takes much effort and hard work from agencies involved to think through the implications and methods that need to be developed right from the beginning. Recent developments in evaluation have created an environment that demands results within limited time frames. Undertaking participatory evaluations, as advocated by writers such as Feuerstein (1988) and Kuriel (1991) may be difficult under such pressures.

But, although participatory evaluations may have a number of problems, this is not to say that we cannot learn from them, adapt them and mould them to our own circumstances and situations. As I discussed earlier, evaluation needs to be structured into four stages. If a total model of participatory evaluation is to be achieved, young people should be involved in all these stages (see Figure 20.2) but in reality achieving this level of participation will be very difficult. For example, as Hill (1997) suggests, the areas where young people are usually missing in participatory work is in the 'agenda setting' (Stage One of Figure 20.2) and the dissemination of results (Stage Four of Figure 20.2). This can happen for a number of reasons but is usually because workers have not been allowed the time to develop these approaches, agencies are not willing to fund such projects and lack understanding and commitment to the fully integrated model of participation (Hill 1997).

One response to this is not to try! But I am of the view that we need to move closer towards participatory approaches and this can only be done by

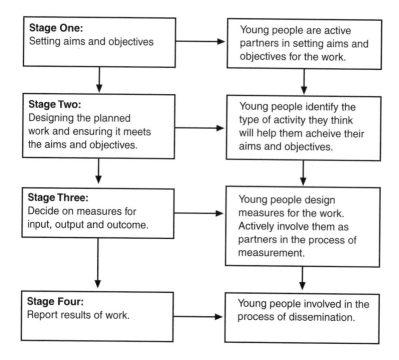

Figure 20.2 Involving young people in evaluation.

trying, at all stages of our work, to involve young people. In reality, we will not always be successful (France 1999) but success can be achieved in small ways. Let me give you two examples. One sits closer to the minimalist position of the model while the other is closer to total implementation (see if you can work out which is which).

Girls Against Violence project

This project was funded with Crime Prevention money provided by the police. It ran over twelve weeks for one session a week. It arose out of a growing concern by workers in the area about the increased levels of violence young women were both involved in and victims of. Working with a local young women's group, the workers got the women to discuss with them what their experience of violence was and what their needs were in relation to this experience. These findings were then used to form the central objectives of the project:

1   to increase young women's self-esteem and confidence in dealing with violence on the streets and in personal relationships.
2   to increase their understanding of the criminal justice system and how it responds to victims and perpetrators of violent crime.

From this, a programme was designed (again in consultation with the young women) which included self-defence sessions, advice and discussion sessions with the police, group discussion sessions on their experience of violence, etc.

As a part of the evaluation the workers designed a short questionnaire. The young women filled it in at the beginning of the programme and then at the end. Questions such as, 'Had they experienced violence (when, where and who from)?', 'Had they been violent to others?', 'When did it seem reasonable to use violence?' 'What were their attitudes to violence?', therefore focused on both experience and attitudes. By getting them to fill a second questionnaire in at the end, the workers were able to assess how these young women's experience had changed over the life of the project and whether they had gained in confidence and knowledge as a result of the project.

This information was then included in the final report to the funders.

Such an approach should not seem alien to youth work – in fact, it seems like an excellent piece of work that benefited young people and met their needs.

Children in care

Save the Children was concerned that young people in care were not being listened to. They therefore decided to commission an evaluation of local services in a local authority in the North of England (West 1995). They decided that young people should be the evaluators. This approach involved workers identifying a small group of young people in care who were interested in being active participants in such a project. The group identified what their own experience had been and what type of questions they might want to ask about the care system. From this the Children's Society trained young people to be researchers who then went out and investigated what other young people had to say about their experience. From the results of this work, recommendations were put forward that have not only been influential in changing the care system in the local authority under investigation but also influencing new national guidelines. The young people who undertook the work also became skilled researchers who gained in self-esteem and confidence – something that they had lost having been in the care system.

Neither of these two examples is a fully-implemented participatory approach to evaluation but both put young people at the centre of the process. One (the Children's Society evaluation) was able to be more thoroughly participatory because the funders committed the time and resources to support the work while the other was guided by the principles of involving young people but was only able to implement a limited version because of the time and funding constraints. The point I am making is that aiming for the ideal is important but also recognising the limits is a necessity. What is central is that we recognise that such an approach should not be rejected if we cannot implement it fully. The principles of participatory evaluations are not dissimilar to that of youth work itself, and therefore offer us the opportunity to develop new and exciting ways of working while being able to show funders and politicians the quality of our work.

Conclusion

Throughout this chapter I have tried to encourage you to take on evaluation and to see it as an opportunity. Hopefully, I have helped clarify what evaluation is while also showing you how it can be used in your everyday practice. Evaluation should not be feared (especially by the good practitioner) and I hope you will feel more confident about engaging with, and using evaluation methods.

Further reading

If you are interested in reading more about evaluation the following books might be of interest.

Cheetham, J., Fuller, R., McIvor, G. and Petch, A. (1992) *Evaluating Social Work Effectiveness*. Buckingham: Open University Press.
Feuerstein, M. (1986) *Partners in Evaluation*. London: Macmillan.
Weiss, C. (1998) *Evaluation*. New Jersey: Prentice-Hall.

References

Audit Commission (1996) *Mis-Spent Youth*. London.
Blackman, S. (1996) *Drugs Education and the National Curriculum*. London: Home Office.
Campbell, D. and Stanley, C. (1966) *Experimental and Quasi-experimental Designs for Research*. Chicago: Rand McNally and Co.
Central Research Unit (1999) *The Evaluation of the Hamilton Child Safety Initiative*. Glasgow: The Scottish Office.
Cheetham, J., Fuller, R., McIvor, G. and Petch, A. (1992) *Evaluating Social Work Effectiveness*. Buckingham: Open University Press.
Cook, T. and Reichardt, C. (1979) *Qualitative and Quantitative Methods in Evaluation Research*. London: Sage Publications.
Everitt, A. and Hardiker, P. (1996) *Evaluating for Good Practice*. Basingstoke: Macmillan.
Fauri, D. (1975) 'Constraints on consumer participation in social welfare administration and planning', *Journal of Social Welfare*, Spring, 23–33.
Feuerstein, M. (1986) *Partners in Evaluation*. London: Macmillan.
Feuerstein, M. (1988) 'Finding the methods to fit the people: training for participatory evaluation', *Community Development Journal* 23, 1, 16–25.
France, A. (1996) 'Youth and citizenship in the 1990s', *Youth and Policy* 53, Summer.
France, A. (1998) ' "Why should we care?" Youth, citizenship and questions of social responsibility', *Youth Studies Journal* 1, 1.
France, A. (1999) 'Exploitation or empowerment? Gaining access to young people's reflections on crime prevention strategies', in M. Barnes and L. Warren, (eds). *Paths to Empowerment*. London: Policy Press.
France, A. and Wiles, P. (1996) *The National Evaluation of the Youth Action Scheme*. London: DFEE.
France, A. and Wiles, P. (1997) 'The Youth Action Scheme and the future of youth work', *Youth and Policy* 57, Summer.
France, A. and Wiles, P. (1997a) 'Dangerous futures: social exclusion in late modernity and a role for youth work', *Social Policy and Administration*, Winter.
Hill, M. (1997) 'Participatory research with children', *Child and Family Social Work* 2, 171–83.
Kuriel, C.P. (1991) 'Participatory evaluation – methodological guidelines based on Indian experience', *Journal of Rural Development* 10, 225–30.

Love, J. and Hendry, L. (1994) 'Youth workers and young participants: two perspectives of youth work', *Youth and Policy* 46.

Maychell, P., Pathak, A. and Cato, J. (1996) *Providing for Young People.* Slough: NFER.

National Youth Agency (1992) *Third Ministerial Conference on the Youth Services.* Leicester: National Youth Agency.

OFSTED (1996) *Inspecting Youth Work.* London: HMSO.

Patton, M.Q. (1986) *Qualitative Evaluation Methods.* London: Sage Publications.

Penuel, W. and Freeman L.M. (1997) 'Participatory action research in youth programming: a theory in use', *Child and Youth Forum* 26, 3, 175–85.

Petersen, A. and Lupton, D. (1996) *The New Public Health – Health and Self in the Age of Risk.* London: Sage Publications.

Rebien, C. (1996) 'Participatory evaluation of development assistance: dealing with power and facilitative learning.' *Evaluation* vol. 2 no. 2, pp. 151–171.

Tones, K. and Tilford, S. (1990) *Health Education – Effectiveness, Efficiency and Equity,* 2nd edn. London: Chapman and Hall.

Watt, A. and Purcell, M. (1997) 'The new champions of sustainable community participation?' *Town and Country Planning* 66, 7/8, 210–13.

Weiss, C. (1998) *Evaluation.* New Jersey: Prentice-Hall.

West, A. (1995) *You're On Your Own: Young People's Research on Leaving Care.* London: Save the Children.

Index